Palgrave Studies in Green Criminology

Criminologists have increasingly become involved and interested in environmental issues to the extent that the term Green Criminology is now recognised as a distinct subgenre of criminology. Within this unique area of scholarly activity, researchers consider not just harms to the environment, but also the links between green crimes and other forms of crime, including organised crime's movement into the illegal trade in wildlife or the links between domestic animal abuse and spousal abuse and more serious forms of offending such as serial killing. This series will provide a forum for new works and new ideas in green criminology for both academics and practitioners working in the field, with two primary aims: to provide contemporary theoretical and practice-based analysis of green criminology and environmental issues relating to the development of and enforcement of environmental laws, environmental criminality, policy relating to environmental harms and harms committed against non-human animals and situating environmental harms within the context of wider social harms; and to explore and debate new contemporary issues in green criminology including ecological, environmental and species justice concerns and the better integration of a green criminological approach within mainstream criminal justice. The series will reflect the range and depth of high-quality research and scholarship in this burgeoning area, combining contributions from established scholars wishing to explore new topics and recent entrants who are breaking new ground.

More information about this series at
https://link.springer.com/bookseries/14622

James Gacek · Richard Jochelson
Editors

Green Criminology and the Law

palgrave
macmillan

Editors
James Gacek
Department of Justice Studies
University of Regina
Regina, SK, Canada

Richard Jochelson
Faculty of Law
University of Manitoba
Winnipeg, MB, Canada

Palgrave Studies in Green Criminology
ISBN 978-3-030-82411-2 ISBN 978-3-030-82412-9 (eBook)
https://doi.org/10.1007/978-3-030-82412-9

Cover illustration: Liyao Xie/Getty

This Palgrave Macmillan imprint is published by the registered company Springer Nature Switzerland AG
The registered company address is: Gewerbestrasse 11, 6330 Cham, Switzerland

Acknowledgments

We are sincerely grateful to a number of people for their advice, suggestions, and feedback in the preparation of this edited collection. To begin, we are thankful to the contributors themselves. Ranging from undergraduate to postgraduate students, and early career researchers to senior faculty members and luminaries in the field, from diverse backgrounds in law and criminology, we asked the contributors to think critically about the ways in which the green criminology-law nexus comes together, and we were pleasantly surprised with the high quality of the chapters received and the responses of the peer reviewers to those submissions. This edited collection could not have happened without your hard work, and we thank you immensely. A big thanks goes to Josie Taylor and her team at Palgrave Macmillan for their enthusiastic support for this project. The shortcomings of the edited collection are ours. Of course, the editors would like to thank their respective families and friends for putting up with them, even when deadlines were tight and patience wore thin—the joys of academic publishing!

James would like to thank Richard for his continued kindness, compassion, and support of the project, from the early thoughts to the final publication. Richard is a fantastic colleague, mentor, and friend; James appreciates his wisdom, thoughtfulness, and the ongoing pleasure of working with him over the years—especially when managing James' ramblings, rantings, and ruminations.

James would like to dedicate his work in the book in part to his new nephews, Elijah and Isaiah; every minute with them is an everlasting source of pleasure. Since you came into life you both have made it only better. James would also like to dedicate his work in the book in part to his sisters, Robin, Lauren, and Carly, and most importantly, Nancy and Rick, his parents; your immeasurable love serves as a constant reminder that when the family is together, he could stay forever.

Richard would like to thank James for being an ever-present and long-standing research collaborator. If not for James' leadership in this volume, the scope and success of this project would not have been possible. It is also exciting to see the stewardship over interdisciplinarity that James has developed in green criminology and its intersections with other disciplines, and his commitment to leading those endeavors.

Richard dedicates his efforts in this volume to his immediate family, furry ones included, and to his close academic collaborators in the Robsoncrim.com family who have helped support new and exciting projects like this one. Richard also remembers the support of his parents; were they here today, they would be surprised and delighted by this volume and the work contributed.

Praise for *Green Criminology and the Law*

"Throughout the past three decades Green Criminology has continued to expand and develop in ways that have captured the international scholastic imagination. The ongoing success of the green criminological enterprise is its ability to harness multi-disciplinary narratives and expertise to address the complex issues that threaten, compromise and eradicate the diverse ecosystems of the world's essential natural environments. This innovative text, draws on global socio-legal expertise to demonstrate how the discipline of law can and must contribute to ongoing environmental protection and preservation. This book is truly ground-breaking and its insightful and cutting-edge content is a must read for anyone and everyone concerned with redressing planetary demise and species existence - an outstanding achievement."

—Reece Walters, *Professor, Deakin University, Australia*

Contents

Notes on Contributors

Hadar Aviram is the Thomas Miller Professor at UC Hastings College of the Law, where she specializes in criminal justice and civil rights from a socio-legal perspective. She is the former President of the Western Society of Criminology and the author of three books, the last of which is *Yesterday's Monsters: The Manson Family Cases and the Illusion of Parole* (UC Press, 2020.) One of the leading voices in California and nationwide against mass incarceration, Professor Aviram is a frequent media commentator on politics, immigration, criminal justice policy, and social movements. A committed spokesperson for non-human animals and long-time vegan, in Fall 2019 Aviram was a Visiting Scholar at Harvard's Animal Law & Policy Program.

Rebekah Bowling tōku ingoa. Ko Tararua te maunga. Ko Ruamahanga te awa. Ko Ngāi Tahu te iwi. Nō Wairarapa ahau. *My name is Rebekah Bowling. Tararua is my mountain. Ruamahanga is my river. Ngāi Tahu is my iwi. I hail from the Wairarapa.* Rebekah is working toward her Master of Arts in Criminology at Te Herenga Waka—Victoria University of Wellington, examining the experiences of Māori correctional officers within the New Zealand prison system. Her other research interests focus on the intersection of colonization, Māori justice practices, and prison history, and she is set to publish her Honors thesis later this year with Professor John Pratt on Punishment in an *Early Colonial Society: The Inglorious History of Wellington Gaol, 1844–1931*. Rebekah is an avid reader, tutors multiple undergraduate criminology courses, and is the president of Victoria University of Wellington Korfball Club.

Avi Brisman is a Professor in the School of Justice Studies at Eastern Kentucky University, an Adjunct Professor in the School of Justice at Queensland University of Technology (Brisbane, Queensland, Australia), an Honorary Professor at Newcastle Law School at the University of Newcastle (Newcastle, New South Wales, Australia), and Editor-in-Chief of *Critical Criminology: An International Journal*.

Rebecca Jaremko Bromwich, Ph.D., LL.M., LL.B., is an Adjunct Professor at Carleton University in the Department of Law and Legal Studies. Dr. Jaremko Bromwich also teaches at Sprott School of Business in the M.B.A. program. She works as Manager, Diversity, and Inclusion for Gowling WLG across Canada and Russia. She has written many articles, book chapters and co-edited several anthologies on the subjects of feminism, equality, and law with a particular focus on criminal law and critical discourse analysis. Rebecca has also published a novel, and, last but certainly not least, she is a mother to four teenaged children.

Pierre Cloutier de Repentigny was appointed as Assistant Professor of Environment, Law, and Social Justice at Carleton University on 1 July 2021. They hold a Civil Law (LL.L.) and a Common Law Degree (LL.B.) from the University of Ottawa and a Master's Degree (LL.M.) from the University of British Columbia. Pierre is finishing their Ph.D. in law at the University of Ottawa. They are also a member of the Law Society of Ontario. Pierre's research focusses on marine biodiversity and the law, critical environmental law, critical legal theories, legal history, and trans justice. They are currently working on four projects: (1) the impact of growth discourse on the construction of international fisheries law; (2) the concept of anthropocenic responsibility; (3) a transformative approach to ecosystem management of whales in Canada; and (4) a community-based assessment of access to justice for trans people in Canada.

Sarah Monod de Froideville is a Lecturer at the Institute of Criminology at Te Herenga Waka—Victoria University of Wellington, New Zealand. Her current research is broadly centered on harms to the environment in the New Zealand context with a specific focus on (i) water-related harms and water security, (ii) historical pollution, and (iii) exploitative human-animal relations embedded into contemporary Aotearoa New Zealand culture. She also has ongoing interest in the intersections between media representations, crime, and youth justice, stemming from her past work on moral panics in relation to young people. Early papers and her monograph *Making Sense of Moral Panic: A Framework for Research* (Palgrave, 2017) paid close attention to the changing shape of panics in neoliberal societies focused on preventing risk.

Angela Fernandez is a Full Professor in the Faculty of Law and Department of History at the University of Toronto. Professor Fernandez is a member of the Brooks Animal Studies Academic Network (BASAN) with the Brooks Institute for Animal Law and Policy and a Fellow with the Oxford Center for Animal Ethics. She serves on the Board of Advisors and is one of the Directors of Animal Justice Canada. Her publications include a book on the first possession case that established the capture rule for wild animals in the United States, *Pierson v. Post* (1805), and she is working on a book about the Supreme Court of Canada's adoption of the capture rule for fish, *The Frederick Gerring* (1897). She grew up in St. John's Newfoundland, which seems significant to mention in the context of the contribution she makes to this collection on a mass die-off that happened at a fish farm in the province in 2019.

James Gacek is an Assistant Professor in the Department of Justice Studies at the University of Regina. Dr. Gacek holds his Ph.D. in Criminology from Edinburgh Law School at the University of Edinburgh, Scotland. He completed a Postdoctoral Fellowship in the Department of Sociology at the Memorial University of Newfoundland. He continues to extensively publish in reviews, journals, and international fora, particularly in areas of (1) corrections and community justice; (2) green criminology; and (3) the broader socio-politics of judicial reasoning. With Professor Richard Jochelson, he has co-authored Criminal Law and Precrime: Legal Studies in Canadian Punishment and Surveillance in Anticipation of Criminal Guilt (2018, Routledge), co-edited (with Richard Jochelson) Sexual Regulation and the Law: A Canadian Perspective (2019, Demeter Press), and is the sole author of the soon to be published *Portable Prisons: Electronic Monitoring and the Creation of Carceral Territory* (McGill-Queen's University Press, 2022). He can be found on Twitter (@JamesGacek).

Mark Hamilton is currently a teaching fellow in the Faculty of Law and Justice at the University of New South Wales, Australia, teaching in both Criminology and Law Programs. He was awarded his Doctor of Philosophy (Law) from the University of New South Wales in 2019. Mark has had considerable exposure to, and experience in, local government, planning, and environmental law, having worked at the Land and Environment Court of New South Wales before practicing law in a local government and planning practice in a national mid-tier law firm in its Sydney office. Mark has a strong interest in green criminology, environmental victims, and restorative justice, and is the author of *Environmental Crime and Restorative Justice: Justice as Meaningful Involvement*, which is part of the Palgrave Studies in Green Criminology series.

Olivia Hasler, Ph.D., holds a doctoral degree in Criminology from the University of Tasmania in Tasmania, Australia. Her thesis, entitled "State-Corporate Crime and Ecocide: A Critical Study of the Carmichael Coal Mine," innovates older criminological concepts, such as Sykes and Matza's techniques of neutralization, within a green criminological framework. Her work has conceptualized environmental harms, and the denial of those harms by state and corporate actors, as crimes. Dr. Hasler's main research interests include green white-collar crime, climate change activism, and ecocide.

Richard Jochelson is a Professor and Dean of Law at Robson Hall Law School, Faculty of Law at the University of Manitoba. He holds a Ph.D. in law from Osgoode Hall Law School at York University, a Masters in Law from University of Toronto Law School, and a Law Degree (LL.B.)

from University of Calgary Law School (Gold Medal). He is a former law clerk who served his articling year at the Alberta Court of Appeal and Court of Queen's Bench, before working at one of Canada's largest law firms. He worked for ten years teaching criminal and constitutional law at the University of Winnipeg prior to joining the law school at University of Manitoba. A principal investigator and co-investigator on several SSHRC awards, he has published peer-reviewed articles dealing with obscenity, indecency, sex work law, animal rights, judicial activism, police powers, criminal justice pedagogy and curriculum development, empiricism in criminal law, and conceptions of judicial and jury reasoning. He is a member of the Bar of Manitoba and has co-authored and co-edited several books with university, international and regional presses and published nearly 70 peer-reviewed and refereed articles, papers, and manuscripts. He can be found on Twitter (@robsoncrim).

Jack Lampkin is a former Police Constable and now leads the Degree Holder Entry Program at Leeds Trinity University. His teaching specialisms relate to response policing and the relationship between addictive behaviors and crime. Dr. Lampkin's research interests are primarily associated with green criminology and environmental harms. In particular, Jack has published work on Earth Jurisprudence and is currently developing ideas around astro-green criminology: the study of space-related environmental harms. Jack's Ph.D. thesis—conducted at the University of Lincoln, UK—explored the social and environmental harms associated with unconventional hydraulic fracturing (fracking).

Charles Louisson is a Postgraduate Researcher working for the University of Victoria Wellington New Zealand. He has recently received a Masters with Distinction for his research thesis, "Seeping Ugly" where he examined the experiences of environmental victims who live in close proximity to a legacy landfill located on Wellington's Southern coastline, New Zealand. Charles is an aspiring green criminologist who primarily contributes to the fields of historical pollution, environmental victimization, leachate contamination, agnotology, ainigmology in addition to numerous other related green criminological subjects. His research seeks to examine the many facets of being an environmental victim, how these experiences are accommodated by criminal justice systems, as well as the issues and complexities surrounding the establishment of culpability within the arena of environmental crimes and adverse phenomena.

Justin Marceau is the Brooks Institute Scholar and Professor of Law at the University of Denver, Sturm College of Law. He is the director of the law school's animal law program, and also an expert in criminal law and constitutional law. He is the author of *Beyond Cages* (Cambridge, 2019) and also the soon to be published *Carceral Logics* (Cambridge, 2022) co-edited with Lori Gruen. Justin's work focuses on how to improve the status of animals in law, and he is actively researching and writing about questions such as the role of victims' advocacy for animals, the relationship between the so-called "link" and superpredator discourse, and alternatives to policing and convictions when it comes to animal crimes.

Bill McClanahan is Associate Professor of Justice Studies in the College of Justice and Safety at Eastern Kentucky University, where he teaches courses on rural crime, criminological theory, environmental harm and crime, and music and justice. He earned a Ph.D. from the Department of Sociology at the University of Essex in the United Kingdom and a M.S. in criminology and criminal justice from Eastern Kentucky University. His research and writing at the intersection(s) of ecology, culture, police, and justice has appeared in academic journals and popular outlets including *Theoretical Criminology, The British Journal of Criminology, Commune Magazine, Deviant Behavior,* and *Crime, Media, Culture*. He is co-author, with Avi Brisman, Nigel South, and Reece Walters, of *Water, Crime, and Security in the Twenty-First Century: Too Dirty, Too Little, Too Much* (Palgrave, 2018) and author of the monograph *Visual Criminology* (Bristol University Press, 2021).

Angus Nurse is a Head of Criminology and Criminal Justice at Nottingham Trent University. He was previously Associate Professor, Environmental Justice at Middlesex University School of Law. Dr. Nurse has research interests in green criminology, criminality, critical criminal justice, animal rights, and human rights law. He is a member of the Wild Animal Welfare Committee (WAWC) and has previously worked in the environmental NGO field and as an Investigator for the Local

Government Ombudsman. His books include *Policing Wildlife* (Palgrave Macmillan, 2015), *Animal Harm: Perspectives on why People Harm and Kill Animals* (Ashgate, 2013), *Miscarriages of Justice: Causes, consequences and remedies* (Policy Press, 2018) co-authored with Sam Poyser and Rebecca Milne, *The Citizen and the State* (Emerald, 2020) and *Wildlife Criminology* (Bristol University Press, 2020) co-authored with Tanya Wyatt. He has edited special editions of *Crime, Law, and Social Change* and co-edited two special edited collections on green criminology.

Shawn Singh is a third-year law student at the University of Manitoba. He completed a Bachelor of Arts (Honours) degree in Criminology and has extensive experience in corporate management, public service, and community leadership. He often writes from a critical race perspective on a broad range of matters in Canadian criminal law, regulatory laws, and political governance. As a law student, Shawn enjoyed the opportunity of growing his researching and writing skills with nation-leading legal scholars at Robson Hall. As part of this experience, his work regarding the privacy implications of using algorithmic processing systems for law enforcement purposes was recently published by the Manitoba Law Journal. In addition to his academic work, Shawn engages regularly in the development of criminal justice policy and educating the public as an executive member of the Manitoba Criminal Justice Association and active participant with the Canadian Criminal Justice Association.

Krista Smithers is a Course Facilitator in the School of Justice Studies at Eastern Kentucky University in Richmond, Kentucky, where she recently completed her Masters of Science in Criminology and Criminal Justice.

Wesley Tourangeau is a Lecturer in Criminology in the School of Social and Political Sciences at the University of Lincoln in Lincoln, United Kingdom. Wesley's research takes a theoretically informed approach to exploring the complex systems of laws, policies, regulations, and discourses that influence interactions between humans, non-human animals, and the natural environment. Specific areas of research interest include green criminology, critical criminology, animal and environmental harms, food crimes, agricultural laws and regulations, socio-ecological sustainability, systems thinking, theories of power and influence, and qualitative research methods.

Brandon Trask is an Assistant Professor of Law at the University of Manitoba and an adjunct fellow at St. John's College. He holds a JD from the University of Manitoba and an LL.M. from the University of Toronto, where he is currently completing his SJD. Professor Trask's research focuses primarily on the areas of criminal law and evidence, constitutional law (with an emphasis on the *Charter*), and environmental law and policy, as well as areas related to progressive law and economics. Professor Trask previously worked as a Crown prosecutor in Nova Scotia (most recently with the Appeals and Special Prosecutions Section of the Nova Scotia Public Prosecution Service) and in Newfoundland and Labrador. He also previously taught through Memorial University of Newfoundland's Law and Society Program.

Rob White is a Distinguished Professor of Criminology at the University of Tasmania, Australia. He has written extensively in criminology, youth studies, and eco-justice. Among his recent publications are *Climate Change Criminology* (Bristol University Press, 2018), *Environmental Crime* (edited two volumes, Edward Elgar, 2020); *The Extinction Curve* (with John van der Velden, Emerald, 2021), *Critical Forensic Studies* (with Roberta Julian and Loene Howes, Routledge, 2021) and *Theorizing Green Criminology* (Routledge, 2021). He is Editor-in-Chief of *Forensic Science International—Animals and Environments*.

Tanya Wyatt is a Professor of Criminology at Northumbria University in Newcastle, UK. Dr. Wyatt's expertise is in green criminology, particularly the illegal wildlife trade, wildlife crime, non-human animal abuse and harm and the intersections with organized crime, corporate crime, and corruption. She has published dozens of journal articles and book chapters on these topics and has two books due out in 2021: *Is CITES Protecting Wildlife? Assessing Implementation and Compliance* and *Wildlife Trafficking: A Deconstruction of the Crime, the Victims, and the Offenders Second Edition.*

List of Figures

List of Tables

1

It Isn't Easy Being Green: The Triumphs and Trials of the Green Criminology-Law Nexus

James Gacek and Richard Jochelson

Introduction

A growing number of the world's seven billion inhabitants are realizing that their lives encounter nature in a plethora of ways. We see this happening as sea levels rise, forest fires burn, animal species[1] become

[1] Despite its problematic nature and a lack of good alternatives, while we refer to "animals" in this chapter, we are referring to nonhuman animals (see Beirne, 2011; Gacek & Jochelson, 2020).

J. Gacek (✉)
Department of Justice Studies, University of Regina, Regina, SK, Canada
e-mail: james.gacek@uregina.ca

R. Jochelson
Faculty of Law, University of Manitoba, Winnipeg, MB, Canada
e-mail: richard.jochelson@umanitoba.ca

J. Gacek and R. Jochelson (eds.), *Green Criminology and the Law*, Palgrave Studies in Green Criminology,
https://doi.org/10.1007/978-3-030-82412-9_1

endangered or extinct, and environmental protests continue to gain traction around the world. Increased use of social media now showcases, in almost real time, the devastating impacts and effects human actions are having upon our environments around the globe. Of course, we would be remiss if we did not mention that all of this is occurring while the COVID-19 pandemic continues to rage. At the time of writing, the pandemic reveals underlying and largely hidden harmful human activity as well as forms of negligence. Like an earthquake that shatters a city, filling the streets with debris and leaving only the bare infrastructure exposed, the pandemic illuminates the structural harm and violence informing our societies through its acceleration of death. Unlike an earthquake though, whose catastrophic eruption is triggered by geophysical processes, the transmission and transmutation of lethal viruses to the human species are being linked to unmediated destruction of natural environments and unchecked forms of urbanization. Also unsurprisingly, its victims are disproportionately vulnerable populations in lower socio-economic spheres, and in communities of color. We are living in a time of environmental and ecological reckoning. These calamities are not abstractions—they are real and in the here and now.

Given the disastrous consequences prolonged harmful human activity has upon nature, one could reasonably conclude that greater efforts to "go green" are a sensible resolution to the growing natural and human catastrophes witnessed perennially. Unfortunately, as a skeptical reader may believe, it is not easy being green. Certainly, individual responsibilities to recycle, shop ethically, consider veganism, reduce waste, and compost (to name a few) are important ways to be green—and in these pages we do not attempt to discount micro-efforts to preserve the planet. Yet too often it is the governments and corporations of the world that concerned environmental activists combat, attempting to rally the populace and these entities for greater social collective and environmental responsibility in equal measure. Public discourse on environmental responsibility and sustainability continues to put pressure on the public sectors of society and government apparati, especially as they have been portrayed as key causes of environmental problems (Walker & Wan, 2012). Unfortunately, certain entities, to save face with the public, adopt strategies to engage in symbolic communications with environmental issues, without substantially addressing them in action (Walker & Wan, 2012); in other words, these sectors of society talk the "green talk", but we constantly question whether they genuinely walk the "green walk" (Gacek, 2020).

Furthermore, let us not forget the denial, deception, and doubt which continues to plague conversations about ecological and environmental catastrophes (Brisman, 2014; McClanahan & Brisman, 2015). Certainly, one can be reminded of developed nations like the United States where, for example, the cultural spinning of "fake news" and doctoring (if not outright denial) of climate change facts swirled throughout the federal administration, under the helm and demagoguery of twice-impeached disgraced former President Trump. While climate change denial preceded his presidential legacy and is not new per se, such denial was only exacerbated further when he took office. Especially in the events during and the aftermath of the 2020 United States federal election, and the sociopolitical sentiment throughout, progressive thinking remains bombarded by denial, deception, and doubt in the "post-truth" era; indeed, it remains a turbulent if not tumultuous time to try to be greener, a matter that is not dispelled despite overwhelming scientific evidence about the need for green interventions. As Brisman (2018, p. 478) contends, our failure to see the signs that our climate is changing "is playing a part in political inaction on climate change, as well as our reluctance to curb our individual and collective consumptive practices contributing to it" (see also Brisman, 2014; McClanahan & Brisman, 2015). Yet, as van der Velden and White (2021, p. 6) remind us, the cost of doing nothing is becoming too great; over the next few decades our generation of Boomer elders will become extinct, and for the next generation, "everything we have taken for granted [will be] at stake. What we do, or fail to do, collectively will be decisive in shaping the roadmap for their lives." Fundamental change is desperately needed, but that fundamental change in course has yet to eventuate; "[o]minously, the climate and ecological *extinction curve* continues along its steep trajectory" (van der Velden & White, 2021, p. 2; emphasis in original).

Absence of strong political and cultural will, scholarly discussions continue to witness and speak to the harmful human activity impacting the earth. Specifically, criminology and law, in a multitude of ways, engage in these discussions of harm, and on earlier occasions we have examined how green criminology and law come together to produce and progress thought-provoking green deliverables to ameliorate further harm (Gacek & Jochelson, 2020). For example, we have suggested elsewhere that, when paired together, green criminology and law have the potential "to reconstitute the animal as something more than mere property within law, shed light on the anthropocentric logics at play within the criminal justice system, and promote positive changes to animal cruelty legislation" (Gacek & Jochelson, 2020, p. 1). Indeed, such scholarship could benefit greatly from moving into new lines of inquiry that emphasize "more-than-human legalities" (Gacek & Jochelson, 2020; see also Gacek, 2017) and this coupling of green criminology and law has the power to promote the advocacy-oriented scholarship of animal rights and species justice (for examples, see Gacek & Jochelson, 2017a, 2017b; Jochelson & Gacek, 2018; Gacek, 2019). Given the growing concerns and mounting prominence of animal rights and safeguards for animals, alongside the growing recognition that animals do lead emotionally rich and complex lives alongside humans (Gacek, 2019), "contemporary society's morality has shifted in favour of these issues" (Gacek et al., 2020, p. 3). Coupled with hospitable forms of rights protections (Regan, 1983; Singer, 1975), progressive legal reform, apprised of green criminology-law nexus logics, should demand a duty of care toward animals that "ought influence and be reflected back in constitutionalism, common law systems, and legislative reform" (Gacek et al., 2020, p. 4). Doing so represents a "fundamental socio-legal, and indeed, normative and ontological shift in animal recognition, moving us away from dogmatic teleology" (Gacek et al., 2020, p.4).

We remain excited to engage in discussions which highlight the significance of green criminology for law, and the ways in which law can provide distinct opportunities to further green criminological inquiry.[2] Since its initial proposal in the 1990s, green criminology has focused the criminological gaze on a wide array of harms and crimes affecting

[2] Of course, we remain mindful that the distinct legal systems operating in various international contexts might affect or complicate this analysis.

humans, animals other than humans, ecological systems, and the planet as a whole. As a continuously blossoming field of criminological inquiry, green criminology recognizes and examines behaviors that are both illegal and legal (yet detrimental), and in varying ways has made great efforts to provide insight into harms in a more fulsome manner. At the same time, there have been many significant legal instances, domestic, and international, including case law, legislation, regulation, treaties, agreements, and executive directives which have troubled the law's understanding of green harms, illegal and legal activity, pushing legal boundaries in the process.

Of course, our focus on the green criminology-law nexus is not immune to shortcomings, as we have indicated on a separate occasion (Gacek & Jochelson, 2020, p. 13):

> To be clear, we are not suggesting... that the marriage between green criminology and law is perfect; much like any marriage, such a coupling will have its moments of coalescence and conflict, of triumphs and trials. We recognize there are times where the intersection of green criminology and law will work in harmony for some researchers and provide tensions for others. Indeed, black letter law analyses have their place, as do complex theoretical interrogations of criminal law. As Jochelson, Khoday et al. (2017, p. vi) contend, speaking across disciplines between law and cognate disciplines like criminology "is an ever-present challenge." Nevertheless, "[w]e must never forget that good criminal law practice is informed well by social sciences and humanities. [Likewise], the cognate disciplines would also do well to take doctrinal analysis seriously and to include rigorous legal analyses in their own interpretations" (Jochelson, Khoday et al., 2017, pp. vi–vii).

Moreover, as educators in post-secondary educational institutions, we have raised green criminological and legal concerns with our students. Students form our first public, and an education apprised of green justice can foster empathy for environmental and ecological issues and movements for change (Gacek & McClanahan, 2021). In a similar vein to Greenberg (2014, p. 127), we believe that a meaningful post-secondary education:

> is an orchestra of instruments sometimes playing in harmony[,] at other times sounding disconnected. Our courses are the instruments at play: critical education, information, collaboration, communication, and integration on a stage of evidence-based research that will improve the quality of our communities, families and individuals by creating graduates and research that contribute to the promotion of civil society.

While we have proposed diverse discussions to consider the relationship between green criminology and law elsewhere (Gacek & Jochelson, 2020; Gacek et al., 2020), might there be others who wish to add their voices to this scholarly symphony?

Recognizing that humanity and nature are inextricably integrated (McClanahan & Brisman, 2015) we have assembled a collection from an international and critical pool of scholars who reflect on the green criminology-law nexus, broadly conceived. We asked the authors to consider how research and/or the teaching of law may give prominence to green criminological principles in order to foster reasoned and empathetic legal reforms and socio-legal transformation. We also asked prospective authors to consider analyzing how using the law in research and/or teaching green criminology expands the latitudes and longitudes of the discipline.

The contributors in this edited collection span many disciplinary fronts at the local, national, and international levels. In distinct ways, the contributors build upon and develop thought-provoking explorations of the green criminology-law nexus; several of them even reference one another in the process, indicating that a burgeoning intersection of green criminology and law may be developing! Together they provide a space for novel work and ideas in green criminology and law for both academics and practitioners working in the field. In doing so, this collection reflects the range and depth of high-quality research and scholarship, combining contributions from established scholars willing to explore new topics and recent entrants who are breaking new scholarly ground.

While it might not be easy to be green, we refuse to become a council of despair and our work a pejorative requiem for paradise lost; much like van der Velden and White (2021, p. 11), our book intends to "contest the imminent doom" we are witnessing by encouraging broader discussions with various publics about the significance of the green criminology-law nexus. In essence, this nexus believes in a paradigm shift toward *lex ferenda* (or the law as it ***ought to be***), a shift we assert is reasonable and achievable. What we know to be empathetically moral "must also be what we can prove in order to earn recognition, socially and legally" (Gacek et al., 2020, p. 19). The goal of migrating law to a higher moral ground combines the emotive and the empirical in equal measure; abject belief, or the mere desire for a better, greener world, is not enough; abject belief alone "brings us to spiritual straw person platitudes" (Gacek et al., 2020, p. 19). Compassion for green issues is not evangelical; belief "untethered to empirical reality diminishes dialogue, and fosters...proselytizing in place of reasoned debate. This is the sort of proselytizing that animates social media wars and denials of easily provable notions" (Gacek et al., 2020, p. 19). Compassion should be grounded in study, observation, and in values we can empirically validate, like dignity and equality (Gacek et al., 2020).

In short, the green criminology-law nexus strives for empathy apprised of knowledge. We vigorously believe there is a role for persistent rigorous intellectual inquiry explicating the nexus of and interstitial spaces between green criminology as an academic conception and the law as a normative and social construct (Gacek & Jochelson, 2020; Gacek et al., 2020). While publications focusing upon green criminology and its connections to harm and justice persist in the literature, our edited collection is grounded in a green criminological approach to understanding whether the law, both in effect and discursive implications (including pluralistic instantiations), reflects, refracts, or sublimates the social, political and ecological conditions of our times. As educators, the significance of these contact points between green criminology and law may have profound knowledge mobilization impacts that present an opportunity to laminate new ways of delivering education upon conventional pedagogical practices and methods of learning and knowing in higher educational settings. Given the multitudes of criminal and regulatory regimes including domestic and international implications, environmental crises, and the emerging field of socio-legal animal studies, this collection seeks to highlight the complex relationship between green criminology and law.

Of course, law is a human construct, and as a human construct, it has also historically regulated the interests of persons. Whether the subject has been humans themselves or human interests (for example, relationships to property), private or public, the law itself has typically not regulated nature so much as the ligature between the natural environment and humankind. Typically, one might see this sort of governance occur bluntly (through the criminal law) or through a web of interconnected regulatory laws (often referred to as administrative law). Green criminology ought to recognize that the iterative and reiterative nature of law, particularly (but not exclusively) in common law systems, provides an opportunity to shift the locus of law's attention from persons (or their relationships to each other, things or agencies) to the environment, animals, outer space or other nonhuman axes. There is a real opportunity for green criminology discourse to drive legal reform in this regard. Nonhuman animals and interests may need to be worthy of legal protections that are apposite to humanhood, even if those protections are connected to anthropomorphic concerns.

Law also is determined to redress harms. In the context of criminal law this redress might seek to deter offending, to punish an offender, to rehabilitate "bad" actors, to denounce or contain serial offenders and to keep society secure (see for example innumerable examples in the *Criminal Code of Canada*). Indeed, criminal law is, mainly, backward looking, seeking to solve the problems of past behaviors, while deterring future evils (Jochelson, Gacek et al., 2017). Criminal law is focused on guilty acts combined with guilty intentions. Sanctions can include liberty deprivations, like imprisonment. Regulatory law is less focused on intent and more focused on action (Jochelson, Gacek et al., 2017). It seeks to foster societal welfare, focusing on future harms, and its goals largely are preventative. Its deliverables result in regulatory sanction and very rarely would mete out liberty deprivations to actors that transgress regulation, although in some cases it may sanction property interests of criminal actors in the absence of a guilty intention, for example in peace bond contexts (Jochelson, Gacek et al., 2017).

Further, one can interrogate and be completely incapable of divining an answer to the question of, what ought to be the trigger for state action in responding to green crises, whether the law seeks to resolve conflict with government itself, individuals, agencies, or corporations? Should this trigger be harm (material, tangential or perceived), or precaution versus risk (actuarial or assumed)? For whose protection should state activity be unleashed—for humans, for nonhuman animals, for the environment, for the galaxy? Clearly, these are enormous philosophical questions that need to be engaged with in order to understand the green criminology-law tapestry. It is a braided analysis that is worthy of exploration in order to unpack further.

Already we have seen state action which interpolates and coalesces environmental concerns into human-generated law—whether it is broad regulatory schemes, or the designation of rivers as legal persons (a matter unpacked in one of the chapters outlined below). Yet we also recognize that something is lost in the immersion of green interests in law—law has a totalizing effect—it can never fully translate philosophy, science, Indigenousness, culture, or morality into ironclad rules without some coarseness or unexpected outcomes. The critical aspect of law that allows for the braided construct of green interests and law is the iterative and reiterative nature of law. In this regard, points of contact between law and the social remain critical as nodes of reform and reconstruction. It is at these nodes where this collection wages that material progress is possible.

Structure of the Book

In the coming chapters we showcase illuminating discussions exploring the complicated relationship between green criminology and law. These chapters analyze multiple layers of criminological and legal thought as they relate to each other and, together, account for the relationship between the pair. To that end, the interstitial spaces between green criminology as an academic conception and the law as a normative and social construct can be broadly understood and explored, enabling us to look at green justice issues holistically.

In Part I, the first set of contributors reconsider legal actors and institutional mechanisms as they relate to the green criminology-law nexus. Specifically, the contributors examine different aspects of the legal and court procedure, exploring how traditional modes of legal governance have adapted to include green justice issues. In Chapter 2 Brandon Trask critically examines the application of the public interest prong of the prosecutorial analysis in the context of environmental matters. To date in Canada, criminal prosecutions in the realm of environmental matters have often targeted supporters and protectors of the environment and of animals. Trask argues that Crown policy manuals must be reimagined and reinterpreted with respect to these types of prosecutions, given the public interest factors at play. In Chapter 3 Angus Nurse brings together several themes concerning policing, regulation, and prosecution of environmental harms. His chapter considers the work of regulators and quasi-judicial actors (e.g. environmental ombudsmen) to discuss how varied judicial and regulatory approaches can more effectively address environmental harms. Considering these issues, Nurse rightly identifies how green criminology's engagement with legal discourse examines complex issues in criminological enquiry that extend beyond the narrow confines of individualistic crime. In Chapter 4 Rob White argues in favor of the establishment and development of specialist environment courts as institutional mechanisms for responding effectively to environmental harm. Focusing upon the 40-year-old New South Wales Land and Environment Court (NSWLEC), White persuasively explores how ecocentrism is translated into judicial decision-making (particularly with respect to ascertaining the nature and quantum of environmental harm related to criminal offending), and how the legal frameworks underpinning this specialist court in Australia are fundamental to the possibility of good environmental outcomes (such as the institutional status of the court and its judges, and the penalties/sanctions available to it in sentencing offenders). In Chapter 5 Hadar Aviram provides an empirical study of activists from the animal liberation organization Direct Action Everywhere (DxE) to examine the place of criminal prosecutions in the activists' agenda for animal liberation. Relying upon the concept of "criminal legal consciousness", the final chapter in the section investigates the role of the criminal framework in shaping the perceptions and actions of the activists in planning an open rescue, engaging with law enforcement, preparing for trial, relying on the political necessity defense, and anticipating incarceration. Aviram suggests that nonviolent lawbreaking contributes unique features to the legal mobilization effort on behalf of animals and should be acknowledged by both scholars and activists as an integral tool for social change.

In Part II, the following set of contributors draw upon the green criminology-law nexus to challenge legislation and legal regulations. In Chapter 6 Angela Fernandez draws attention to the lack of any criminal law sanctions for mass fish farm escapes and die-off accidents in Canada. She contends the current regulation for such situations is inadequate. The well-being of farmed fishes (e.g. allowable densities) and how farmed fishes are slaughtered are issued the federal government of Canada should regulate, especially since provincial animal welfare laws do not even apply to fishes. Her chapter concludes with suggestions for legal change to the *Criminal Code of Canada* and offers recommendations for prosecutors interested in further considering animal welfare issues. We then move across the 49th parallel to the United States, where in Chapter 7 Krista Smithers, Bill McClanahan, and Avi Brisman offer a detailed discussion of the origins of plastic, including its discovery, initial applications, and growth in the United States (with relevant reference to other parts of the world). They examine how various nonhuman animal species and ecosystems have been negatively impacted by excessive human consumption and improper disposal of plastic. Given the ostensibly endless applications for plastic, this chapter suggests how one might discontinue its use at present levels, but acknowledges that such efforts have been frustrated by the power of the plastics industry during the coronavirus pandemic. Their ironic conclusion, then, is that we are bonded to plastic to the same extent that we are wedded to capitalism; the extent to which we are tied to the latter, we are betrothed to the former. The next chapter moves us back across the border into Canada, where Wesley Tourangeau, focusing on the Canadian context, examines in Chapter 8 the legal changes to industrial hemp production that accompanied the 2018 legalization of marijuana for recreational use. Prior to legalization, hemp cultivation was carefully managed under strict regulations within the Canadian *Controlled Drugs and Substances Act*, reflecting hemp's long-standing association with marijuana (both are cannabis, but only the latter has psychoactive properties). Canada's Industrial Hemp Regulations are now enabled through the new *Cannabis Act*, and the rules for growing hemp are less strict (e.g. less security requirements). While it remains unclear how this will impact Canada's hemp industry, he suggests it is essential to examine the continued legal entanglement of hemp and marijuana. Ultimately, Tourangeau contends this relationship continues to limit hemp's potential as a sustainable and ecologically beneficial food and fiber source. In order to grapple with this more nuanced form of criminalizing environmentally beneficial activities, he believes green criminology's approach to environmental harm needs redefining and reimagining. The last chapter of this section takes us across the Pacific Ocean to New Zealand, where Charles Louisson explores in Chapter 9 the paradoxical problem of governments implementing environmental legislation that can undermine its own efficacy. Drawing upon official documentation pertaining to landfill contamination in a coastal setting on the outskirts of New Zealand's capital city, as well as interview data with people living alongside the landfill, the chapter illustrates how, counterintuitively, environmental legislation pertaining to the contamination in the studied case of Houghton Bay effectively prioritized capital accumulation over ecological protection by devolving power to local authorities whose decision-making is dominated by resource austerity.

In Part III, the next set of contributors draw upon the green criminology-law nexus to retrace legal rights and individual and collective responsibilities toward nonhuman species and entities. We begin this discussion with Chapter 10, where Justin Marceau shines a spotlight on U.S. legislation alongside on-the-ground work of lawyers and advocacy groups at the intersection of animal law and criminal law. By examining two states, New York and Iowa, as case studies, his chapter demonstrates how criminalization does more to hinder than to advance animal protection efforts in law. While Marceau contends his chapter is not a blueprint for the next steps, he promotes a deliberate call for corporate or systemic accountability as it relates to animal protection in the United States. In Chapter 11 Pierre Cloutier de Repentigny explores, using critical environmental law methodology, the role of law regarding anthropocenic harm and responsibility. Cloutier de Repentigny contends Canadian environmental law has proven to be ineffective and incapable of capturing the hyperobject of anthropogenic biosphere degradation—in other words, anthropocenic harm. Using Canadian marine biodiversity degradation in Canada as an example, their chapter explores the disconnect between the methods of environmental law and the nature of and responsibility for the harm law should address. In doing so, they outline a way forward for a more anthropocenically responsible environmental law. In Chapter 12 Sarah Monod de Froidville and Rebekah Bowling trace the challenges and responsibilities of designating rivers as legal persons. Their chapter outlines how in 2017 the New Zealand government signed the Te Awa Tupua Act, giving the Whanganui River the same rights, powers, duties, and liabilities as a human citizen. However, Monod de Froidville and Bowling contend the legislation represents a compromise on behalf of Whanganui Iwi to reach an agreement with the Crown insofar as traditional practices of kaitiakitanga (guardianship) have not been fully restored. By reflecting upon the passage of the Te Awa Tupua Act, the authors set out to consider some of the complexities of recognizing environmental rights through legislation passed in redress of colonial harms. The final chapter of this section is authored by Rebecca Jaremko Bromwich, where she presents a critical discourse analysis of configurations of the environment as a maternal figure as they are deployed as discursive tools in governmentality. Looking through a feminist lens and working from a social constructivist theoretical framework, Chapter 13 critically assesses the uses, impact, and ideological content of the discursive figure "Mother Earth" as deployed in the Keystone XL Pipeline case. Jaremko Bromwich's study demonstrates that the figure of "Mother Earth" is consistently the dominant theme around which this activism is symbolically centered. Her chapter concludes that the figure of "Mother Earth" is being used by advocates in this case, self-identified as an Indigenous concept, fundamentally diverges from colonial, settler assumptions about gender and maternality and, rather than reinscribing patriarchal, capitalist logics, has revolutionary emancipatory potential to fundamentally undermine them.

In Part IV the final set of contributors assess and explore future directions for the intersections between green criminology and law; given the goal of empathy apprised of knowledge, where might this nexus take us? The discussion begins by blasting us off into outer space, thanks to Lampkin and Wyatt in Chapter 14. Although over half a century has passed since the first humans stepped foot on another celestial body, Lampkin and Wyatt contend that green criminology has remained virtually silent on issues pertaining to human uses of, and interactions with, the extraterrestrial world. Furthermore, there are no binding international agreements regarding the ownership of space objects and, as a result, the United States recently attempted to preserve the Apollo landing site through enacting domestic legislation. This chapter attempts to advance the conceptual boundaries of both disciplines by analyzing how earth jurisprudence could act as a mechanism for protecting extraterrestrial environments and highlighting why green criminologists should be concerned with the extraterrestrial world. The authors achieve this by underlining the cosmic dimensions of Earth jurisprudence and the significance of the universe as an object of study. In Chapter 15 Shawn Singh brings us back down to Earth to promote public calls for action toward Indigenous reconciliation by exploring how the Canadian federal government's business consortium model influences Indigenous leaders to reconsider energy production management. While the approach appears to meet the objectives of reconciliation and contemporary climate activists, the authors contend it can alternatively mitigate Canada's responsibility for climate change and create new criminal outcomes for fossil fuel-based energy producers, including Indigenous leaders themselves. While the author acknowledges the risk of criminalization is high, he outlines how Indigenous leadership in energy production can create community prosperity that will meaningfully support the objective of reconciliation. In Chapter 16, Mark Hamilton examines how restorative justice benefits the green criminology-law nexus. Over the past two decades there has been increasing use of restorative justice conferencing to repair the harm occasioned by environmental offending. Recognizing that harm to the environment can come from both legal and illegal activities, Hamilton explores whether restorative justice conferencing has potential application for repairing environmental harm emanating from legal activities. Restorative justice conferencing can take many forms but the form proposed for this chapter is face-to-face conferencing which is essential to a facilitated dialog between stakeholders to a crime or conflict. As Hamilton demonstrates, the challenge for the use of conferencing for legal activity is enticing those harming the environment to come to conferencing to gain an appreciation of the impact of their activities and devising ways to minimize or eliminate such harm. The final chapter in this section is authored by Olivia Hasler, who argues in Chapter 17 that the intersections of green criminology and law can be applied to formulate a crime against "ecocide". In her view, A law of ecocide at the international level (modelled after Higgins' Ecocide Act 2010) would incorporate two legal concepts—superior responsibility and strict liability—in order to eliminate the denial narratives used by powerful actors to rationalize environmentally harmful activities. Such a law would also integrate green criminological principles to impose a pre-emptive legal duty of care to prevent the risk of damage to or loss of any ecosystem. This chapter demonstrates how an international law of ecocide would (1) prevent the risk of destruction of ecosystems; (2) prohibit government decisions that would result in the destruction of ecosystems; and (3) pre-empt decision-making that may lead to significant environmental harm, using the Australian Government's controversial approval of the Carmichael Coal Mine as a case study.

References

Beirne, P. (2011). Animal abuse and criminology: Introduction to a special issue. *Crime, Law, and Social Change, 55*, 349–357.

Brisman, A. (2014). The visual acuity of climate change. In P. Davies, P. Francis, & T. Wyatt (Eds.), *Invisible crimes and social harms* (pp. 61–80). Palgrave Macmillan.

Brisman, A. (2018). Representing the 'invisible crime' of climate change in an age of post-truth. *Theoretical Criminology, 22*(3), 468–491.

Gacek, J. (2017). Species justice for police eagles: Critiquing the Dutch 'Flying Squad' and animal–human relations. *Contemporary Justice Review: Issues in Criminal, Social, and Restorative Justice, 21*(1), 2–15.

Gacek, J. (2019). Confronting animal cruelty: Understanding evidence of harm towards animals. *Manitoba Law Journal, 42*(4), 315–342.

Gacek, J. (2020). Corporate greenwashing and Canada goose: Exploring the legitimacy-aesthetic nexus. *International Journal of Crime, Justice and Social Democracy, OnlineFirst, 9*, 1–15.

Gacek, J., & Jochelson, R. (2017). Placing 'Bestial' acts in Canada: Legal meanings of 'Bestiality' and judicial engagements with sociality. *Annual Review of Interdisciplinary Justice Research, 6*, 236–261.
Gacek, J., & Jochelson, R. (2017). 'Animal Justice' and sexual (ab)use: Consideration of legal recognition of sentience for animals in Canada. *Manitoba Law Journal, 40*(3), 335–362.
Gacek, J., & Jochelson, R. (2020). Animals as something more than mere property: Interweaving green criminology and law. *Social Sciences, 9*(122), 1–16.
Gacek, J., Jochelson, R., & Dueck-Read, A. (2020). Critiquing the conception of 'Crimes against Nature': The necessity for a new 'Natural' law. *International Journal of Offender Rehabilitation and Comparative Criminology, OnlineFirst*, 1–24.
Gacek, J., & McClanahan, B. (2021). Learning about the illegal and the 'Lawful yet Awful': Progressing public criminology in the university classroom. *Journal of Criminal Justice Education, OnlineFirst*, 1–19.
Greenberg, H. (2014). A justice experience at the University of Regina: A history of an interdisciplinary, academic, liberal arts program. *The Annual Review of Interdisciplinary Justice Research, 4*, 120–134.
Jochelson, R., & Gacek, J. (2018). 'Ruff' justice: Canine cases and judicial law making as an instrument of change. *Animal Law Review, 24*(1), 171–195.
Jochelson, R., Gacek, J., Menzie, L., Kramar, K., & Doerksen, M. (2017). *Criminal Law and precrime: Legal studies in Canadian punishment and surveillance in anticipation of criminal guilt*. Routledge.
Jochelson, R., Khoday, A., & Ireland, D. (2017). Robson Crim: A vision for multivalent interrogations of criminal law. *Manitoba Law Journal, 40*, i–vii.
McClanahan, B., & Brisman, A. (2015). Climate change and peacemaking criminology: Ecophilosophy, peace and security in the 'War on Climate Change.' *Critical Criminology, 23*, 417–431.
Regan, T. (1983). *The case for animal rights*. University of California Press.
Singer, P. (1975). *Animal liberation: The definitive classic of the animal movement*. Harper Collins Publishers.
Van der Velden, J., & White, R. (2021). *The extinction curve: Growth and globalization in the climate endgame*. Emerald Publishing Limited.
Walker, K., & Wan, F. (2012). The harm of symbolic actions and greenwashing: Corporate actions and communications on environmental performance and their financial implications. *Journal of Business Ethics, 109*(2), 227–242.

Part I

Reconsidering Legal Actors and Institutional Mechanisms

2

Standard Concerns: An Examination of Public Interest Considerations with Respect to Prosecutions of Environmental Advocates and Indigenous Land Defenders

Brandon Trask

"Everyone is aware that individually and collectively, we are responsible for preserving the natural environment."—Supreme Court of Canada Justice Charles Gonthier (*R v Canadian Pacific Ltd*, 1995, p. 1075)

"[W]e are political prisoners[…] We are not criminals. We violated the injunction because we are so terribly aware that emissions from fossil fuels are destroying our climate, our planet, and our children's future. The impacts of this pipeline are more criminal than anything we've done."—Jean Swanson, CM (Lukacs, 2019, p. 100)

B. Trask (✉)
University of Manitoba, Winnipeg, Canada
e-mail: brandon.trask@umanitoba.ca

J. Gacek and R. Jochelson (eds.), *Green Criminology and the Law*, Palgrave Studies in Green Criminology,
https://doi.org/10.1007/978-3-030-82412-9_2

"There have indeed been instances in human history—not many but enough to be significant—in which disobedience to law has proved of benefit to law and to society. Is that a paradox? Perhaps so. But it's true."—Manitoba Chief Justice Samuel Freedman (Clarke, 2014, p. 204)

Prologue

Prior to beginning my academic career as an assistant professor of law at the University of Manitoba, I worked as a Crown prosecutor in both Nova Scotia (most recently with the Appeals and Special Prosecutions Section of the Nova Scotia Public Prosecution Service) and Newfoundland and Labrador. My time as a Crown prosecutor gave me a very important opportunity to see "where the rubber meets the road"—specifically, it allowed me to make observations about the importance of properly utilizing prosecutorial discretion to ensure the criminal justice system works toward benefitting society on the net rather than focusing on the prosecution of marginalized people in relation to relatively trivial offenses. After all, green criminology implores scholars, policymakers, and decision-makers to focus on "actions that are socially harmful" (Linden, 2009, p. 22) *rather than merely those that are technically illegal. Green criminology has much to offer those interested in crafting and enforcing laws with a view to the betterment of society. The law should work for people pursuing societally beneficial aims rather than against them.*

Introduction

Most Canadians now say that they support the development of initiatives and provisions that protect the environment (MacNeil, 2019, p. 35). However, strong economic interests within Canada support the continued exploitation of the land in the form of the environmentally harmful extraction of oil, gas, and minerals (MacNeil, 2019, pp. 79–83). There is therefore significant tension between the stated views and desires of most Canadians and the economic interests of powerful corporations and influential individuals associated with them (MacNeil, 2019, pp. 115–116).

A discussion of this dissonance necessarily has power-discrepancy and political-economy implications. A significant demonstration of power in society is the ability to enact and enforce laws that protect individual or group interests. For instance, the ability to label particular actions as "criminal" is a reflection of power. Crimes are legal constructions, which vary substantially over time and by location. Importantly, it is vital to appreciate that "there is nothing inherent in any act that makes it unlawful" (Linden, 2009, p. 18).

There are times at which civil disobedience will be justified as being in the pursuit of the broader public interest. Where individuals acting on behalf of the interests of society as a whole—particularly with a view to protecting the environment—face charges stemming from their peaceful actions, prosecutors should give careful consideration to terminating the prosecution due to public interest concerns. Crown attorneys in Canada should therefore be empowered and encouraged to undertake a fully informed, contextualized decision with regard to the public interest—beyond simply a devotion to the status quo (in the form of respect for law and order) that trumps all other concerns. There must be recognition of the fact that some civil disobedience (especially protest-focused actions related to the protection of the environment and of Indigenous lands) should be tolerated and may in fact be essential to the functioning of democracy.

Overview of the Prosecution Standard in Canadian Jurisdictions

Although there are minor variations among the different public prosecution services across the country, the core test applied to each prosecution (whether public or private) in Canada involves a two-step analysis: (1) an assessment of whether sufficient evidence exists upon which a prosecution may continue; and (2) a determination of whether a prosecution in the case at bar would serve the public interest (Benidickson, 2019, pp. 178–179). The two prongs of this core test are discussed below.

First Prong: *Is There Sufficient Evidence Upon Which to Base a Prosecution?*

The first prong of the test, which focuses on assessing the sufficiency of available evidence in relation to a potential prosecution, varies somewhat across jurisdictions within Canada. Overall, this is intended to be an objective assessment (Ontario, n.d.). Specifically, the most onerous version of this test stipulates that a Crown attorney may only proceed with a prosecution if a review of the available evidence results in a determination that there is a "substantial likelihood of conviction" (British Columbia Prosecution Service, 2021, p. 2). According to the British Columbia *Crown Counsel Policy Manual*, this means "at a minimum, that a conviction according to law is more likely than an acquittal" (British Columbia Prosecution Service, 2021, p. 2). Alberta Crown prosecutors employ a "reasonable likelihood of conviction" test, which permits the continuation of a prosecution where a review of the case reveals that there is "sufficient evidence [for the Crown prosecutor] to believe that a reasonable jury, properly instructed, is more likely than not to convict the accused of the charge(s) alleged" (Alberta Justice, 2006, p. 5).

A slightly less onerous sufficiency of evidence test exists in Nova Scotia, where Crown attorneys may proceed where they determine that there is a "realistic prospect of conviction" in a given case, meaning that "the prospect of displacing the presumption of innocence must be real" as opposed to merely "technically or theoretically available" (Nova Scotia Public Prosecution Service, 2015, p. 3).

Arguably the least onerous test for Crown attorneys in Canada in relation to the sufficiency of evidence stage of the analysis permits prosecutions to continue where it is determined that there exists a "reasonable prospect of conviction" (Ontario, n.d.), although it should be noted that this test has different meanings in different jurisdictions, despite utilizing the same terminology. For instance, in Ontario, the *Crown Prosecution Manual* clarifies that this standard "does not require 'a probability of conviction'" (Ontario, n.d.), whereas in New Brunswick, this standard means that a Crown can proceed with a prosecution only where it is determined that "an impartial trier of fact properly directed in accordance with the law[...] is more likely than not to convict the accused on the offence charged based on the evidence available" (New Brunswick, 2017, p. 1).

If the first prong of the test is not met, in most jurisdictions, the prosecution must be terminated—without progressing to weigh public interest considerations. However, in British Columbia, the *Crown Counsel Policy Manual* outlines that "[i]n exceptional circumstances, where the relevant public interest factors weigh so heavily in favour of a prosecution that it is necessary to resort to a lower charge assessment standard in order to maintain public confidence in the administration of criminal justice, a charge may still be approved even though the usual evidentiary test is not met" (British Columbia Prosecution Service, 2021, p. 6). Under this exception, prosecutors in British Columbia may be able to proceed with matters where there is merely a "reasonable prospect of conviction," using the Ontario-informed interpretation that this phrase "does not require that a conviction be more likely than an acquittal" (British Columbia Prosecution Service, 2021, p. 6).

Regardless of the differences with respect to the jurisdiction-specific requirements for the first prong of the prosecution standard test, if it is determined that there is "sufficient" evidence upon which to continue with a prosecution, in all Canadian jurisdictions, the Crown attorney then moves on to the second prong of the test—assessing whether a prosecution would be in the public interest.

Second Prong: *Is It in the Public Interest to Continue with a Prosecution?*

There is great similarity among all Canadian jurisdictions with regard to the second prong of the prosecution standard test, which asks the Crown attorney to determine whether it is in the public interest to continue with a prosecution (Benidickson, 2019, pp. 178–179). A common recognition across jurisdictions is that this analysis must consider case-specific factors in reaching a determination with regard to the public interest (Nova Scotia Public Prosecution Service, 2015; Ontario, n.d.). The *Guide Book of Policies and Procedures for the Conduct of Criminal Prosecutions in Prince Edward Island* includes a phrase that seems to capture the sentiment of every province's approach to the public interest aspect of the prosecution standard analysis: "prosecution decisions may take into account the public interest, but must not include any consideration of the political implications of the decision" (Prince Edward Island Justice and Public Safety, 2009, pp. 3–1).

The basis of the second prong of the prosecution standard is encapsulated by comments made in 1951 by Sir Hartley Shawcross, then Attorney-General of England:

> The truth is that the exercise of a discretion in a quasi-judicial way as to whether or when I must take steps to enforce the criminal law is exactly one of the duties of the office of the Attorney-General, as it is of the office of the Director of Public Prosecutions. It has never been the rule in this country—I hope it never will be—that suspected criminal offences must automatically be the subject of prosecution. The public interest ... is the dominant consideration. (*R v Faber*, 1987, p. 61)

The *Guide Book of Policies and Procedures for the Conduct of Criminal Prosecutions in Prince Edward Island* clarifies that "[p]ublic interest is not the same as public opinion. Public interest imports the notion of enduring public good and order. It also concerns the effect of a decision on other important public policies and institutions. Public opinion connotes a more temporary mood or collective feeling influenced by current events or circumstances" (Prince Edward Island Justice and Public Safety, 2009, pp. 5–7). While most Crown policy manuals list some potential public interest factors to consider, it is clear that this second prong is intended to be a subjective assessment and that the particular factors vary from case to case. Conditional upon the facts of each case, a Crown attorney must consider the applicable factors to consider and must also decide upon the weight to be given to each factor in making an ultimate determination as to whether it is in the public interest to proceed with a prosecution. Typically, these determinations will turn on factors relating to "the nature of the offence or on the circumstances of the offender or the victim" (New Brunswick, 2017, p. 2).

Although many Crown policy manuals simply provide prosecutors with a list of possible factors to consider in assessing the public interest prong of the test while stating that these factors must be contextualized and weighed appropriately for any given case (demonstrating the latitude granted to Crown attorneys in this subjective aspect of the decision-making process), the detailed *Guide Book of Policies and Procedures for the Conduct of Criminal Prosecutions in Prince Edward Island* seems to imply that the default approach should be for Crown attorneys to continue with a prosecution if the first prong of the prosecution standard is satisfied: "The proper decision in many cases will be to proceed with a prosecution if there is sufficient evidence available to justify a prosecution. Mitigating factors present in a particular case can then be taken into account by the court in the event of a conviction" (Prince Edward Island Justice and Public Safety, 2009, pp. 5–7).

However, the Nova Scotia Crown policy manual stipulates that "[t]he responsible, dispassionate application of the stated tests [...] is the best way to minimize the risk of prosecuting innocent persons and to effectively utilize finite justice resources. Declining to exercise this important discretion is likely to be just as destructive to the administration of justice as making inappropriate decisions" (Nova Scotia Public Prosecution Service, 2015, p. 10).

Perhaps the strongest statement in a provincial Crown policy manual with regard to the need to exercise proper discretion in the context of making a public interest determination comes from British Columbia: "Justice does not require that every provable offence must be prosecuted. The resources of the criminal justice system are not unlimited. If reasonable alternatives are available, they should be pursued. Prosecution should be reserved for cases requiring the full force of the criminal justice system, with all its available sanctions" (British Columbia Prosecution Service, 2021, p. 3).

Of note, none of the Crown policy manuals make overt reference to how Crown attorneys should assess and weigh public interest factors in the context of charges relating to environmental advocacy and Indigenous land protection, though Prince Edward Island clarifies that a prosecutor

> should consider as irrelevant [...] the race, national or ethnic origin, colour, religion, gender, sexual orientation, political associations, activities or beliefs of the accused or any other person involved in the investigation [...]; the Crown Attorney's personal feelings about the accused or the victim [...]; possible political advantage or disadvantage to the government or any political group or party; or [...] the possible effect of the decision on the personal or professional circumstances of those responsible for the prosecution decision. (Prince Edward Island Justice and Public Safety, 2009, pp. 5–8)

Moreover, the Ontario Crown policy manual stipulates that "[t]here is no class of cases that are of necessity outside the public interest to prosecute" (Ontario, n.d.).

The Unique Character of Prosecutions of Environmental Advocates and Indigenous Land Defenders

The (Contextualized) Role of the Crown Attorney

While Crown policy manuals typically attempt to imbue readers with the impression that Crown attorneys are apolitical actors making apolitical decisions, this view is not reflective of reality. Though generally not motivated by direct partisan political considerations, the decision of whether to prosecute someone is an inherently political decision, as it involves the use of the criminal law power of the state *vis-à-vis* an individual, after making a determination as to public interest considerations. Recognizing this function of a Crown attorney in deciding whether to continue with a prosecution—in particular by focusing on the subjective second prong of the test—is vital to the critical examination of cases involving charges against people whose actions are themselves driven by public interest concerns (for instance, environmental advocates and Indigenous land defenders). Despite political leaders not typically directing prosecutorial decision-making (however, there are exceptions—see: Lukacs, 2019, p. 12), all of the components of the criminal justice system were developed by political leaders with particular aims and concerns in mind. (In fact, Adam Smith went so far as to remark that "[c]ivil government is in reality instituted for the defense of the rich against the poor, or of those who have some property against those who have none at all" [Bowles et al., 2005, p. 501].)

Generally speaking, government is a very unique entity; it acts as the maker of the rules, enforcer of the rules, and also as an important economic actor (Bowles et al., 2005, p. 501). Government leaders—those entrusted with making and changing laws and designing, funding, and overseeing public institutions—"have their own objectives and face their own constraints" (Bowles et al., 2005, p. 516). Above all, politicians are concerned with ensuring that they are able to stay in power by being re-elected (Bowles et al., 2005, p. 516). These concerns are not as simplistic as they may initially seem. For instance, for a government hoping to be re-elected, it is vital to ensure that businesses and investors operating within a particular jurisdiction do not engage in what is termed a "capital strike," which is the business-side equivalent to a labor strike (Bowles et al., 2005, p. 521). During a labor strike, workers refuse to fulfill their ordinary role in the economy by not working (Bowles et al., 2005, p. 521). Similarly, during a capital strike, business leaders refuse to fulfill their typical function in the economy, meaning that they refuse to invest (Bowles et al., 2005, p. 521). Capital strikes can have devastating impacts on governments; if business leaders refuse to invest in a particular jurisdiction,

> [T]he result will be unemployment, economic stagnation, and probably a decline in living standards. This explains why political leaders in particular areas are apt to be easily influenced by the demands of business leaders. If the former do not go along with the wishes of the latter, the population of the area will suffer economic hardships and, placing at least part of the blame for their difficulties on their political leaders, will vote the incumbents out in the next election. (Bowles et al., 2005, p. 520)

In a country as large and diverse as Canada, the concerns of certain jurisdictions will sometimes significantly contrast with the concerns of other jurisdictions. For instance, while Alberta's economy is heavily dependent on the development of the fossil fuels sector (MacNeil, 2019, pp. 88–89), Prince Edward Island is extremely susceptible to the effects of climate change, especially with regard to rising sea levels (MacNeil, 2019, p. 107).

The federal government, which oversees the environmental impact assessment and approval process with regard to significant developments like oil and gas pipelines, is often pressured by the provinces and territories with regard to issues of importance to voters in particular regions (Froschauer, 1999, pp. 1–54). These pressures explain why, despite signing on to the 2016 Paris Agreement on climate change, Prime Minister Justin Trudeau's government approved (and later purchased from Kinder Morgan for $4.5 billion [Lukacs, 2019, p. 95]) the Trans Mountain Pipeline carrying oil from Alberta to the coast of British Columbia, along with allowing further seismic testing in the Arctic and oil and gas exploration in the Gulf of Saint Lawrence, among other environmentally harmful developments (Lukacs, 2019, pp. 49 & 95). Trudeau has publicly celebrated these developments; in an interview with *The Guardian*, he said, "We're actually able to approve pipelines at a time when everyone wants protection of the environment. We're able to show that we get people's fears and there are constructive ways of allaying them—and not just ways to lash out and give a big kick to the system" (Lukacs, 2019, p. 12).

When people do "lash out and give a big kick to the system" (Lukacs, 2019, p. 12), they tend to draw the ire of the criminal justice system. This is because, as Justice William Orville Douglas of the Supreme Court of the United States observed, the government's "eternal temptation… has been to arrest the speaker rather than to correct the conditions about which he complains" (Kaplan, 2017, p. 309). Police officers (those employed by municipal, provincial, and federal police forces, as well as corporate police forces, such as the Canadian National Railway Police and the Canadian Pacific Railway Police), prosecutors, jail guards, and others within the criminal justice system focused on the maintenance of law and order are categorized as "guard labour," which refers to the fact that these individuals generally work "to maintain the existing structure of power and ownership" (Bowles et al., 2005, p. 501) rather than to create goods or materials. Although the enforcement of laws is generally regarded as beneficial for society, it is important to recognize that, in some cases, enforcement works to serve the interests of only particular people (Bowles et al., 2005, p. 501). Given the important role Crown attorneys play in determining, through the application of the two-prong prosecution standard, whether to proceed with a prosecution, they are uniquely positioned to genuinely act in the public interest rather than merely operating to "perpetuate the structure of the society including the power and economic advantages of the dominant class" (Bowles et al., 2005, p. 501), as is typically the function of guard labor.

How Advocates Working in the Public Interest Are Unique

Environmental advocates and Indigenous land defenders sometimes engage in civil disobedience after failing to make sufficient progress through more traditional routes of engagement with public institutions. After all, environmental groups and Indigenous communities struggle to compete with the monetary might of the affluent oil-industry companies and other corporations that effectively lobby government and seek injunctions through the courts. Given that, at present, "the social function of lobbying is to take money and turn it into political power" (Kollmar & Koen, 2017, p. 11), and given that there are well-documented and wide-ranging access to justice issues in the Canadian legal system (Semple, 2015), those working within the criminal justice system (including police, Crown attorneys, and judges) should be receptive to considering whether environmental advocates and Indigenous land defenders truly have meaningful alternatives to civil disobedience at their disposal in their pursuit of the public good, in the form of environmental and social justice. There must be awareness and acknowledgment of the fact that marginalized people are often effectively excluded from the democratic decision-making process (Hurlbert, 2018, p. 254).

As Arthur Manuel, co-chair of the Global Indigenous Peoples' Caucus at the United Nations' Permanent Forum on Indigenous Issues, states,

"When we try to assert our rights to our land, Canada uses the courts and the police to oppress us" (Manuel, 2015, p. 249). He further explains:

> If we try to stop industrial resource extractors from moving onto our lands, injunctions against us are quickly awarded and the police swoop in for mass arrests. Canadian jails are full of our young men and women. Many of our community members, my own daughters and our Elders among them, have spent time in jail for trying to resist the assault on our Aboriginal land. (Manuel, 2015, p. 250)

Indigenous legal principles, which are often improperly overlooked in the current iteration of the Canadian legal system (Robinson, 2015, p. 90), are imbued with, among other things, a profound connection to the land (Manuel, 2015, pp. 257–258). As Manuel states, "Indigenous peoples' duty to protect our lands is primordial, and the assault on our lands and resources today is unprecedented" (Manuel, 2015, p. 255). While "a legal war of attrition to contain, minimize, or dismiss Indigenous rights" (Lukacs, 2019, p. 148) has been waged through the courts, many Indigenous land defenders are taking more significant measures, which many advocates see as the "only realistic path to safety and survival" (Lukacs, 2019, p. 130). The result of this shift toward civil disobedience in the face of urgent environmental concerns and a lack of accessible or effective options through tradition avenues means that many environmental advocates and Indigenous land defenders are "being treated like [criminals] for doing a job that serve[s] the needs of everyone in the country: protecting the forests, valleys, waters, and climate that all life depends on" (Lukacs, 2019, p. 174).

During 2018, hundreds of protestors were arrested and charged with criminal contempt in relation to breaching a court-ordered injunction against blocking access to worksites related to the development of the Trans Mountain Pipeline in British Columbia (*Trans Mountain Pipeline ULC v Mivasair*, 2019 [BCCA], paras. 3–13). (To underscore the point about the mixing of government interests and roles, it is worth reiteration that this pipeline is now owned by the Canadian government, after it was purchased from Kinder Morgan.) By May 2019, a total of 196 individuals were ultimately convicted of criminal contempt of court as a result of their participation in protests against the Trans Mountain Pipeline project between March 2018 and August 2018 (*Trans Mountain Pipeline ULC v Mivasair*, 2019 [BCCA], para. 3). In one particularly concerning sentencing hearing stemming from criminal contempt rulings flowing from these protests, Justice Fitzpatrick of the Supreme Court of British Columbia sentenced three Indigenous men—James Leyden, Justin Bige, and Stacy Gallagher, referred to in the court decision collectively as "the Contemnors"—to 28 days' incarceration each for their roles in these "peaceful protests" (*Trans Mountain Pipeline ULC v Mivasair*, 2020 [BCSC], para. 130). Of note, none of the men had any prior criminal records (*Trans Mountain Pipeline ULC v Mivasair*, 2020 [BCSC], para. 34). Moreover, this sentencing decision was issued during the midst of the COVID-19 pandemic (*Trans Mountain Pipeline ULC v Mivasair*, 2020 [BCSC], paras. 163–166). In her sentencing decision, Justice Fitzpatrick vehemently rejected the submission that these Indigenous land defenders were not violating any laws because of the existence of Indigenous legal principles requiring protection of the land (*Trans Mountain Pipeline ULC v Mivasair*, 2020 [BCSC], para. 117). Justice Fitzpatrick ruled:

> [117] [...] this Court must continue to signal to the community at large, including the Aboriginal community and its leaders, that disrespect of the court's order will not be tolerated and that consequences will follow if that occurs[...].
> [118] Mr. Leyden's counsel also argues that, while not an excuse, Mr. Leyden "reasonable beliefs" as to the validity of the Injunction in the face of what he understood as a higher imperative, stands as a mitigating factor.
> [119] I strongly disagree.
> [120] Firstly, there is no higher imperative in respect of the Injunction, save as might have been imposed by the Court of Appeal. None of the Contemnors sought to overturn the Injunction if they considered that it did not apply to them. They did nothing in that respect. They have disobeyed a court order that applies to them and for that, they must face the consequences[...].
> [121] Secondly, the protests were fundamentally directed at the environmental issues raised in the community about Trans Mountain's proposed

pipeline expansion project. Certainly, some people in the Aboriginal community viewed that issue through the lens of their right to object and oppose the project, at least in part based on their right to be consulted by the government. However, the Aboriginal voices against the pipeline were only one of many; some in the Aboriginal community support the project, even to the point of indicating a desire to buy Trans Mountain from the federal government.

[122] To allow a lesser sentence here because of the Contemnors' beliefs in their cause through the Aboriginal lens would be to draw a distinction from the hundreds of other protestors who were arrested and faced charges. In my view, such a distinction does not exist.

[123] I would venture to say that all of the protestors who the police arrested were fervent in their passion toward protecting the environment and their view that Trans Mountain was acting in a fashion that threatened the environment. Passion for a cause does not justify giving an offender a pass from the consequences of their illegal conduct.

[124] In *Peter Kiewit Sons Co.* [et al v Perry et al, 2007 BCSC 305], Justice B. Brown stated:

[16] I have no doubt that the individuals before me sincerely believe that their cause was just. However, we have many individuals and groups in society who are passionately committed to what they view as just causes. Poverty, homelessness, health care immediately come to mind. If each individual or group chose to break the law and breach court orders to enforce their view of a correct response to a just cause, our democratic society would quickly fail. This is not a frivolous or theoretical concern. As the Newfoundland Supreme Court said in the *Health Care* case which I have quoted, our courts deal every day with parties who lose; who feel passionately that they should not have to obey the orders of the courts. When a group of citizens chooses to publicly defy the order of the court, they encourage each individual to disobey court orders which they do not like. It is this defiance which undermines the rule of law and brings the administration of justice into disrepute.

[125] Indigenous issues in our society have clearly gained some prominence in the public discourse. However, that does not mean that Aboriginal citizens of Canada have some elevated ability to disregard court orders when they feel like it, or by asserting that they had "no choice" but to act otherwise under Aboriginal laws or traditions. Clearly, Aboriginal people, including the Contemnors, have choice in that respect.

> Nor does it mean that they have some greater ability to escape the consequences of illegal behavior. (*Trans Mountain Pipeline ULC v Mivasair*, 2020 [BCSC], paras. 117–125)

The sentiments expressed in this sentencing decision seem to be reflective of the judicial approach to the Trans Mountain Pipeline protestors more generally—essentially, that participation in these peaceful protests, in violation of an injunction obtained by the corporation, constituted an offense against society due to the disregard for the rule of law.

Martin Lukacs, an investigative journalist and author, relays relevant quotes relating to the rule of law in this context. Stuart McCarthy, senior vice-president of BlueSky Strategy Group, a firm that "lobbied the [Trudeau] Liberal government on behalf of the Canadian Association of Petroleum Producers" (Lukacs, 2019, p. 95), said to Lukacs during a conversation about opposition to the Trans Mountain Pipeline in British Columbia that "[y]ou have to impose the rule of law[...] otherwise the country will simply descend into anarchy" (Lukacs, 2019, p. 95). McCarthy further stated, "You don't need the military, just use the police. And send in some fire trucks. [...] It's not going to be pretty. But we have to draw the line. [...] The protestors are a noisy minority. [...] There's maybe 300 hardcore activists. Most of the Indigenous ones are imports. And declaring the project part of the 'national interest' means you could deal with them as a terrorist threat" (Lukacs, 2019, p. 96). Some of McCarthy's comments are troublingly similar to those of then-Natural Resources Minister Jim Carr, who said:

> If people choose for their own reasons not to be peaceful, then the government of Canada, through its defence forces, through its police forces, will ensure that people will be kept safe.[...] We have a history of peaceful dialogue and dissent in Canada. I'm certainly hopeful that the tradition will continue. If people determine for their own reasons that that's not the path they want to follow, then we live under the rule of law. (Lukacs, 2019, pp. 96–97)

It is difficult to reconcile these comments from Carr, which seem to contemplate the protestors' ability to mount peaceful opposition to the pipeline project, with Justice Fitzpatrick's comments that participation in peaceful protests, which violated a court-ordered injunction, necessitated the imposition of custodial sentences against Indigenous land defenders, unless of course one is of the view that any violation of a court order constitutes "violence" against society.

Interestingly, an examination of an earlier pipeline project in British Columbia, the Enbridge Northern Gateway Pipelines, reveals that "[w]hile security state agencies such as the [Royal Canadian Mounted Police] never hesitate to publicly declare their neutrality or impartiality, internal files show the extent to which the RCMP consider their role as a cheerleader of industry and an active enforcement arm supporting Enbridge's efforts" (Crosby & Monaghan, 2018, p. 71). For instance, during one meeting of national security stakeholders, which discussed, among other things, the advantages and disadvantages of the pipeline development, it was stated by one official that "we all have a vested interest in the Enbridge Northern Gateway Pipeline Project" (Crosby & Monaghan, 2018, p. 71). In discussions among police agencies and other stakeholders, it was clarified that "potential criminal threats to the [Northern Gateway] Project [are] those associated to Aboriginal sovereignty concerns, environmental extremists and lone wolves; each having the potential and capability of conducting acts of unlawful civil disobedience, sabotage, vandalism, thefts and other criminal actions" (Crosby & Monaghan, 2018, p. 70). The police response to pipeline protests, culminating in large numbers of arrests and charges, "reveals the ability of corporate power to command policing resources in the objective of advancing extractive capitalism" (Crosby & Monaghan, 2018, p. 71).

It is within this context that Crown attorneys with carriage of cases involving environmental advocates and Indigenous land defenders must make their informed decisions with regard to the second prong of the prosecution standard. Is it indeed in the public interest to prosecute protestors, if there is sufficient evidence upon which a prosecution may be based?

How Should Crown Attorneys Assess Whether it is in the Public Interest to Prosecute Environmental Advocates and Indigenous Land Defenders?

Given the complex, politically charged background leading to virtually any charge against environmental advocates and Indigenous land defenders engaged in peaceful protests and civil disobedience more generally, Crown policy manuals should make it clear that Crown attorneys have the ability to critically engage in an analysis of the relevant public interest factors. It is far too simplistic to take the approach that any violation of the letter of the law (in the Trans Mountain case, this was a court order in the form of a civil injunction) warrants criminal prosecution because of a belief that the public interest demands respect for law and order. It is time to recognize that, in certain situations, acts of civil disobedience may in fact help to advance the public interest. Human history is replete with examples showing that not all laws deserve blind adherence.

Given the hurdles to bringing challenges to policies, rulings, and provisions through traditional avenues by marginalized groups and those attempting to act in the public interest, it is understandable—and sometimes necessary—for these groups to occasionally resort to protests and acts of civil disobedience. As Sachiko Charlotte Gyoba, a retired schoolteacher jailed in August 2018 for protesting the development of the Trans Mountain Pipeline in British Columbia, articulated, "People have to stand up when they see an injustice. If they don't, then democracy doesn't work for anybody" (Lukacs, 2019, p. 99). (It should be noted that Gyoba was born in 1943 in an internment camp in British Columbia for individuals of Japanese descent [Lukacs, 2019, p. 99].)

While there likely should not be a conclusive categorical determination made with regard to the public interest analysis where protesters face charges, Crown policy manuals should underscore the importance of Shawcross's guidance with regard to the second prong of the prosecution standard: "It has never been the rule in this country—I hope it never will be—that suspected criminal offenses must automatically be the subject of prosecution. The public interest … is the dominant consideration" (*R v Faber*, 1987, p. 61). While this analysis needs to continue to be done on a case-by-case basis for practical reasons, it must be clarified that Crown attorneys have an opportunity—and a responsibility—to act as an "emergency escape ramp" within the criminal justice system; applying the vast criminal prosecution resources of the state against individuals engaged in public-interest-serving advocacy—in a peaceful form—is the equivalent of an out-of-control transport truck heading down a winding mountain road, and Crown attorneys must step in to avert disaster. This role of assessing the public interest cannot be passed along to the judiciary; in the Canadian criminal justice system, it is up to the Crown to decide which cases are worthy of prosecution. Due to the unique factors discussed, Crown attorneys must be granted the ability to undertake an expansive analysis of the relevant public interest factors in cases involving environmental advocates and Indigenous land defenders. In the absence of a clear determination that the broader public interest necessitates a prosecution, cases should not proceed.

Conclusion

The ability to define what is criminal behavior is a unique power—and it is legitimate to question whether, in prosecuting those trying to protect the environment, the state is properly using the criminal law and prosecutions function. Crown attorneys must recognize their unique position within the criminal justice system and act at all times in the public interest. Green criminology concepts are helpful to ensure that the bigger picture is kept in view; the focus of the criminal justice system must be to work toward the improvement of society and the reduction of truly socially harmful actions (Linden, 2009, p. 22). In some cases, that will surely mean the termination of prosecutions involving those attempting to utilize—in a peaceful manner—the tools that are meaningfully at their disposal to protect the land, water, and air for the benefit of everyone. The law should not be used as a tool to harm society by perpetuating the marginalization and prosecution of environmental advocates and Indigenous land defenders when these individuals are acting to benefit society on net.

References

Cases

R v Canadian Pacific Ltd. (1995). 2 SCR 1028.
R v Faber. (1987). 38 CCC (3d) 49.
Trans Mountain Pipeline ULC v Mivasair. (2019). BCCA 156.
Trans Mountain Pipeline ULC v Mivasair. (2020). BCSC 1512.

Articles and Manuscripts

Benidickson, J. (2019). *Environmental law* (5th ed.). Irwin Law.

Bowles, S., Edwards, R., & Roosevelt, F. (2005). *Understanding capitalism: Competition, command, and change* (3rd ed.). Oxford University Press.

Clarke, R. G. (2014). The 1970s: War measures and the chief justice. *Manitoba Law Journal, 37*, 201–220, Special issue: A judge of valour: Chief Justice Samuel Freedman—In his own words.

Crosby, A., & Monaghan, J. (2018). *Policing indigenous movements: Dissent and the security state*. Fernwood Publishing.

Froschauer, K. (1999). *White gold: Hydroelectric power in Canada*. UBC Press.

Hurlbert, M. A. (2018). Energy, climate, the earth and justice. In M. A. Hurlbert (Ed.), *Pursuing justice: An introduction to justice studies* (2nd ed., pp. 237–259). Fernwood Publishing.

Kaplan, W. (2017). *Why dissent matters: Because some people see things the rest of us miss*. McGill-Queen's University Press.

Kollmar, L., & Koen, R. (2017). Lobbying against democracy. *Journal of Anti-Corruption Law, 1*(1), 9–45.

Linden, R. (2009). Crime, criminals, and criminology. In R. Linden (Ed.), *Criminology: A Canadian perspective* (6th ed., pp. 3–28). Nelson.

Lukacs, M. (2019). *The Trudeau formula: Seduction and betrayal in an age of discontent*. Black Rose Books.
MacNeil, R. (2019). *Thirty years of failure: Understanding Canadian climate policy*. Fernwood Publishing.
Manuel, A. (2015). Indigenous rights and anti-colonial struggle. In E. Finn (Ed.), *Canada after Harper: His ideology-fuelled attack on Canadian society and values, and how we can resist and create the country we want* (pp. 246–259). James Lorimer & Company.
Robinson, P. (2015). The environment: Good stories, bad policies, and what to do. In E. Finn (Ed.), *Canada after Harper: His ideology-fuelled attack on Canadian society and values, and how we can resist and create the country we want* (pp. 85–91). James Lorimer & Company.
Semple, N. (2015). The cost of seeking civil justice in Canada. *The Canadian Bar Review, 93*(3), 639–673.

Online Documents

Alberta Justice. (2006, November 28). *The decision to prosecute*. https://open.alberta.ca/dataset/8fa0bd3b-2bbe-400d-85d2-3ba8101d83e2/resource/70bbab1d-9c31-4649-8b9a-dc9d2c3f73b8/download/guid-decision-to-prosecute-2006-11-28.pdf.
British Columbia Prosecution Service. (2021, January 15). *Crown counsel policy manual: Charge assessment guidelines*. https://www2.gov.bc.ca/assets/gov/law-crime-and-justice/criminal-justice/prosecution-service/crown-counsel-policy-manual/cha-1.pdf.
New Brunswick. (2017, November 21). *Public prosecutions operation manual: Pre-charge screening*. https://www2.gnb.ca/content/dam/gnb/Departments/ag-pg/PDF/en/PublicProsecutionOperationalManual/Policies/Pre-chargeScreening.pdf.
Nova Scotia Public Prosecution Service. (2015, November 23). *The decision to prosecute (charge screening)*. https://novascotia.ca/pps/publications/ca_manual/ProsecutionPolicies/DecisionToProsecute.pdf.
Ontario. (n.d.). *Crown prosecution manual: Charge screening*. https://www.ontario.ca/document/crown-prosecution-manual/d-3-charge-screening.
Prince Edward Island Justice and Public Safety. (2009, November). *Guide book of policies and procedures for the conduct of criminal prosecutions in Prince Edward Island*. https://www.princeedwardisland.ca/sites/default/files/publications/guide_book_of_policies_and_procedures_for_the_conduct_of_criminal_prosecutions.pdf.

3

Green Criminology, Policing and Protecting the Environment

Angus Nurse

Introduction

Environmental harms and crimes that affect non-human nature (including animals) have the potential for greater societal impact than the 'everyday' crimes that are the subject of mainstream criminal justice and much criminological study. Yet such crimes are often dealt with outside of the mainstream of criminal law and criminal justice. Instead of falling within the remit of the criminal law, some environmental harms are engaged with specifically through the prism of environmental law and within a civil and administrative framework rather than a distinctly criminal justice one. The 'policing' of environmental harms is also often dealt with by environmental regulators and other enforcers rather than by mainstream policing agents (Nurse, 2013a, 2016). Arguably this sets

A. Nurse (✉)
Department of Criminology and Criminal Justice, Nottingham Trent University, Nottingham, UK
e-mail: angus.nurse@ntu.ac.uk

J. Gacek and R. Jochelson (eds.), *Green Criminology and the Law*, Palgrave Studies in Green Criminology,
https://doi.org/10.1007/978-3-030-82412-9_3

such harms apart from mainstream crime and justice issues and denotes them as somehow 'other' within contemporary conceptions on crime and justice. Green criminology considers these issues through a critical criminological lens incorporating a wide range of mechanisms for achieving environmental protection outside of standard justice tools. In this context, the green criminological approach provides a means for considering the effectiveness of legal and justice approaches to harms of global significance, those that impact on non-human nature and have specific negative impacts on the environment in the anthropocene (Holley & Shearing, 2018). Green criminology provides a mechanism for rethinking the study of criminal laws, ethics, crime and criminal behaviour and how best to provide for a holistic justice approach. The green criminological framework also provides potential for rethinking how best to police and protect the environment from harm. As White (2007, 2012) observes, given the potential for environmental harms to extend far beyond the impact on individual victims that are the norm with 'traditional' crimes of interpersonal violence and property crime, green crimes should be given importance if not priority within justice systems. Our conception of the type of crimes and harm under consideration also needs to expand in order to consider global threats such as climate change that are arguably ignored by mainstream criminology and criminal justice discourse (White, 2018).

This chapter brings together several themes concerning policing, regulation and prosecution of environmental harms. The chapter considers the work of regulators and quasi-judicial actors (e.g. environmental ombudsmen) to discuss how varied judicial and regulatory approaches can more effectively address environmental harms. In doing so, it considers themes discussed elsewhere in some of this book concerning the purpose and intent of law, the nature of law enforcement and the application of a green criminological approach to understanding and implementation of law and how justice should or could work in respect of green crimes and harms. The chapter discusses the ineffectiveness of criminal law approaches, particularly against major corporations whose operations need to continue irrespective of any criminal sanctions imposed on individual corporate actors. Even where sanctions may be imposed at a corporate level, the economic power of corporations is such that sometimes even large fines, can be easily absorbed by some corporations (Greife & Maume, 2020). Thus, the effectiveness of a predominantly criminal prosecution approach as having a deterrent effect is questionable. Accordingly, green criminology has identified the benefits of civil and administrative mechanisms that focus more on repairing harm and changing behaviour and that can work alongside other sanctions or enforcement approaches. Mechanisms such as environmental ombudsmen whose remit is to remedy injustice rather than to punish can also be effective (Edge, 1971; Nurse, 2016). Considering these issues, this chapter identifies how green criminology's engagement with legal discourse examines complex issues in criminological enquiry that extend beyond the narrow confines of individualistic crime.

Green Criminology and the Framework of Environmental Harms

A core concern of green criminology is how best to address environmental harms through justice systems and the application of environmental laws. Stallworthy (2008, p. 4) identifies environmental law as being a 'conceptual hybrid' a form of law that borrows from lots of other areas such as the criminal law, tort (civil wrong and implementing principles of rights and obligations) and even the law of contract. From a green criminological harm-based perspective (Lynch & Stretesky, 2014) this may seem unnecessarily complex and lack a straightforward approach for engaging with deviance and non-compliant behaviour that causes environmental damage. However, Stallworthy's analysis is useful in identifying that environmental law is concerned with the idea of rights, responsibilities and obligations. Thus, when environmental damage occurs the public policy and law enforcement response is arguably concerned with who is responsible for that damage, whose rights may have been infringed and which obligations have been breached. Unlike traditional street and property crimes, environmental crimes (and environmental harms) frequently have long-lasting and irreversible effects and 'the harms associated with green crimes *far exceed* those associated with ordinary street crimes (Lynch & Stretesky, 2014, p. 8 emphasis in the original). It has also been identified that 'the systemic causal chains that underpin much environmental harm are located at the level of the global political economy—within which the transnational corporation stands as the central social force' (White, 2012, p. 15). Much environmental harm is linked with ostensibly legal activity and a considerable amount of environmental crime is transnational in nature. This raises questions about the effectiveness of justice systems in dealing with environmental offenders and the damage they cause. Effective environmental enforcement mechanisms arguably need to address not just the punishment of offenders but also remediation of the environmental harms. Without doing so, arguably such systems fail to achieve the objectives of green criminology's ecological justice approach centred on protection and redress for non-human nature (Benton, 1998). Arguably this also requires a more expansive notion of eco-justice that 'do[es] away with the anthropogenic concept of ecological rights promoted by legal and criminological approaches to the concept of rights' (Lynch et al., 2019, p. 14). This chapter explores the extent to which contemporary eco-justice systems are equipped to deal with corporate environmental offending which in many cases is a consequence of the operation of neoliberal markets. The drive for profits and anthropocentric attitudes towards the environment and exploitation of natural resources arguably create a situation where corporate environmental crime is a foreseeable and even natural/inevitable consequence. Where that is the case and where corporations have the resources to continue paying fines and the expertise to navigate regulatory justice systems, an alternative to the law enforcement 'detection apprehension and punishment' approach of mainstream criminal justice might be required.

From a green criminological perspective, there have been some important developments in creating the legal framework for protecting the environment. The 1972 UN Stockholm Conference that resulted in the UN Declaration on the environment was arguably ground-breaking in expressing the idea of environmental protection in terms of rights and responsibilities. The key concept of a right to a healthy environment and the need to protect the environment for future generations is contained within its core principles:

> Man has the fundamental right to freedom, equality and adequate conditions of life, in an environment of a quality that permits a life of dignity and well-being, and he bears a solemn responsibility to protect and improve the environment for present and future generations.
>
> (Principle 1, UN Declaration on the Environment)

The Declaration contains a set of principles that arguably provided a guide to the preservation and enhancement of the environment (Sohn, 1973, p. 423). Its principles were built upon in the UN General Assembly's World Charter for Nature, adopted in 1982 which contains the following five principles of conservation:

1. Nature shall be respected and its essential processes should be unimpaired.
2. Population levels of wild and domesticated species should be at least sufficient for their survival and habitats should be safeguarded to ensure this.
3. Special protection should be given to the habitats of rare and endangered species and the five principles of conservation should apply to all areas of land and sea.
4. Man's utilization of land and marine resources should be sustainable and should not endanger the integrity or survival of other species.
5. Nature shall be secured against degradation caused by warfare or other hostile activities.

In principle, the UN's World Charter for Nature provides a mechanism for protecting non-human nature from harm by providing a conservation framework that should implement species and habitat protection measures. In practice implementation of the Charter relies on national environmental protection legislation to achieve this although Sections 21–24 of the Charter provide authority for individuals to enforce international conservation laws and these provisions has been used by NGOs as a basis on which to conduct direct action to prevent animal harm (Roeschke, 2009).

Since the 1972 Stockholm conference a series of both broad and species and ecosystem specific nature and wildlife conventions have been adopted that provide the basis for national environmental protection law. The Convention on Biological Diversity was signed by 150 world leaders at the 1992 Rio Earth Summit (at time of writing more than 187 countries have ratified the convention). The convention is an international agreement aimed at promoting sustainable use of biological diversity and protecting ecosystems. The convention has three main goals:

- The conservation of biodiversity,
- Sustainable use of the components of biodiversity, and
- Sharing the benefits arising from the commercial and other utilization of genetic resources in a fair and equitable way.

The Convention as part of international environmental law provides official recognition of biological diversity as 'a common concern of humankind' requiring protection through international law. The agreement between countries enshrined in the convention covers all ecosystems, species and genetic resources. Legal instruments such as treaties are rarely sufficient on their own (Pirjatanniemi, 2009) and international law instruments often require implementation through national legislation before they become effective. The convention sets principles for the sharing of benefits arising from genetic resources and links conservation efforts with sustainable use of biological resources and is legally binding on countries that join it. However, the principle of state sovereignty means that countries may take their own view on what amounts to sustainable use of 'their' national resources commensurate with the convention's underlying ethos that ecosystems, species and genes must be used for the benefit of humans. The convention, as international law that protects ecosystems, identifies that use of resources (including wildlife) should not be done in any manner that leads to the long-term decline of biological diversity. It does so on the basis of the precautionary principle, i.e. where there is a threat of significant reduction or loss of biological diversity, lack of full scientific certainty should not be used as a reason for postponing measures to avoid or minimize such a threat. Cameron and Abouchar describe the precautionary principle as a guiding principle which aims 'to encourage-perhaps even oblige-decision makers to consider the likely harmful effects of their activities on the environment before they pursue those activities' (1991, p. 2). While man's harmful impact on the environment may be inevitable, the precautionary principle within international environmental law aims to manage that harm in a way that brings environmental, economic and social benefits.

The Convention's provisions also include: measures and incentives for the conservation and sustainable use of biological diversity; regulated access to genetic resources; access to and transfer of technology, including biotechnology; measures for environmental impact assessment; education and public awareness and a requirement for national reporting on efforts to implement treaty commitments (Convention on Biological Diversity, 2014). While this list is not exhaustive, it illustrates the legal framework for environmental protection that the Convention seeks to achieve. Stallworthy notes that the Convention retains an emphasis on national sovereignty arguing that 'many aspects regarding conservation are premised upon what amounts to encouragement of appropriate protection measures' (2008, p. 11). National Biodiversity Strategies and Action Plans (NBSAPs) are the principal instruments for implementing the Convention (Article 6) requiring countries to prepare a national biodiversity strategy (or equivalent instrument) and to ensure that this strategy is properly integrated into the planning and activities of agencies whose activities can have an impact (positive and negative) on biodiversity. Arguably this requires state bodies to be aware of and monitor and report on actions carried out in respect of a state's biodiversity obligations. Article 26 of the Convention states that the objective of national reporting is to provide information on measures taken for the implementation of the Convention and the effectiveness of these measures and state reporting takes place against the background of a (regularly updated) strategic plan agreed on by states at regular meetings known as the Conference of the Parties (COP).

Measures such as the biodiversity Convention place environmental protection firmly within international law which is broadly a product of cooperation and collective agreement between states and codifies state obligations in respect of legal standards. Schaffner (2011) identifies treaties and conventions as the primary international law mechanisms. Such signed agreements arguably reflect areas considered to be of such importance that only a consensus between states can deal with the subject matter. However, in practice international law is a combination of 'hard' law in the form of such written agreements or principles which are directly enforceable by national or international bodies; and 'soft' law which incorporates a range of different measures including codes of conduct, resolutions, agreements commitments and joint statements. There is no 'world court' able to enforce international law (albeit some court mechanisms exist) and it largely remains for states to choose whether or not to agree with the relevant provisions of international law as the International Court of Justice (ICJ) states 'in international law there are no rules, other than such rules as may be accepted by the State concerned, by treaty or otherwise' (Military and Paramilitary Activities in and Against Nicaragua [Nicaragua v United States of America] ICJ Rep 1986, 269) (the Nicaragua Case). Arguably states comply with international law only where doing so serves national interests, accordingly flexibility exists in states' compliance with international law obligations. This is especially true of 'soft' international law which sets out shared standards or aspirations for states, but which is not directly enforceable and subject to varied interpretations commensurate with state interests. From a green criminological perspective, international environmental law arguably fails to provide ecological justice because it is primarily concerned with 'managing' rather than entirely preventing negative human impact on the environment. For example, White and Heckenberg (2014) identify that in relation to wildlife trade the function of law is to define legal notions of harm and criminality and not to provide for the health and well-being of animals. In this regard, the logic of international wildlife law 'is not simply to protect endangered species because they are endangered; it is to manage these 'natural resources' for human use in the most equitable and least damaging manner' (White & Heckenberg, 2014, p. 133). The principle of 'sustainable use' permeates environmental and wildlife law even at the international level thus, for example, international wildlife law's aim is often to regulate the use of wildlife rather than to criminalize it (Nurse, 2015; Wyatt, 2013). Ruhl (1997) suggests that environmental law discourse is dominated by six principles:

- libertarianism (freedom of contract and markets)
- limited acceptance of regulatory restraint
- a regulatory approach which balances (market) interests with minimizing environmental harm
- substantive environmental law through the use of sustainability and precautionary principles
- environmental justice and the sharing of costs and benefits among citizens
- a deep green perspective prioritizing ecological over human interests.

Thus, while the ideal may be for ecological justice and species justice from a 'deep green' perspective that places an absolute prohibition on environmental and wildlife exploitation, Ruhl's principles indicate the conflict between market interests (i.e. economically based exploitation) and conservation and protectionist principles. Thus, the reality is that environmental and wildlife laws primarily operate from a sustainable use perspective implementing a light touch regulatory approach that arguably fails to achieve the full level of protection advocated by green criminology.

Policing the Environment

Enforcement of green laws requires considering more than just who should be punished when environmental offences occur. Effective environmental justice needs to provide a framework for environmental protection, a mechanism for enforcing that framework and effective tools for dealing with environmental wrongdoing including a means of resolving environmental harms when they occur. As indicated earlier in this chapter, the broad international law framework exists but the detail of environmental justice systems frequently places responsibility at state level and in the hands of a range of environmental regulators, enforcers, investigators and prosecutors given the dictates of state sovereignty (Megret, 2011). Mitchell (1996) identifies compliance as predicated on: primary rules; information structures and data monitoring; and non-compliance response mechanisms which can result in either formal or informal sanctions. But given the retention and primacy of state sovereignty, breaches of international environmental and wildlife protection obligations at a state level require international action to resolve. Stallworthy describes this as 'adjudicative international dispute settlement' (2008, p. 13) which at best provides for a formal sanction but more frequently can be seen as advisory. Bodies such as the ICJ, the UN's primary court, can adjudicate on international wildlife law matters and there are also some international arbitration panels which may deal with environmental law issues. However, one difficulty with such measures is the need for states to voluntarily submit to their jurisdiction and to co-operate in the enforcement of judgments. There are examples of where this has worked such as the 2010 case lodged by Australia against Japan in which the ICJ was asked to consider whether scientific whaling carried out by Japan was in fact commercial whaling being carried out in breach of a moratorium on this activity under the International Whaling Convention. The ICJ ruled in Australia's favour and Japan agreed to suspend the whaling activities complained of in compliance with the ICJ's ruling (Nurse, 2014). But such cooperation can in principle be withheld and where this happens the lack of an effective international policing mechanism to uphold such court judgments is problematic.

The reality is that many practices that cause environmental harm are ostensibly legal and there is an argument that only those things defined by criminal law as offences can really be classed as green crimes. Situ and Emmons (2000, p. 2) define this as follows:

> The strict legalist perspective emphasizes that crime is whatever the criminal code says it is. Many works in criminology define crime as behaviour that is prohibited by the criminal code and criminals as persons who have behaved in some way prohibited by the law.

In short, the strict legalist view determines that crime only exists where the criminal law defines it as such. An alternative approach to environmental legislation sometimes advocated by activists is the social legal perspective which argues that some acts, especially by corporations, 'may not violate the criminal law yet are so violent in their expression or harmful in their effects to merit definition as crimes' (Situ & Emmons, 2000, p. 3). This approach 'focuses on the construction of crime definitions by various segments of society and the political process by which some gain ascendancy, becoming embodied in the law' (Situ & Emmons, 2000, p. 3). Successive green criminologists (Beirne, 2009; Lynch & Stretesky, 2014; Nurse, 2013b, 2015; Wellsmith, 2011; White & Heckenberg, 2014) have identified that mainstream criminology routinely ignores or marginalizes environmental and wildlife crimes, particularly where these fall outside the remit of criminal justice systems and are dealt with by regulatory, administrative or civil justice systems (Nurse, 2014; Stallworthy, 2008).

Thus, state environmental law protection might be criticized as follows:

> The modern environmental administrative state is geared almost entirely to the legalization of natural resource damage. In nearly every statutory scheme, the implementing agency has the authority—or discretion—to permit the very pollution or land destruction that the statutes were designed to prevent. Rather than using their delegated authority to protect crucial resources, nearly all agencies use their statutes as tools to affirmatively sanction destruction of resources by private interests.
>
> (Wood, 2009, p. 55)

Wood's central point, that natural resource management can be characterized as an 'ongoing' experiment, is a sound one. A central problem of natural resource law is its implementation as management rather than protective law and it is often characterized by an overly complex layered system which is based on permitting natural resource exploitation in a manner which Wood describes as being 'a colossal failure, despite the good intentions and the hard work of many citizens, lawyers, and government officials' (2009, p. 43). Green criminology, for example, identifies that the transnational nature of wildlife trafficking requires a coordinated approach across borders (Wyatt, 2013, p. 143). Accordingly, several agencies may be involved in enforcement including customs, border and immigration agencies, police, environmental protection agencies and conservation monitoring agencies. The international law mechanisms discussed above are usually not applicable to individual and corporate wildlife crimes and so this form of wildlife offending becomes an international crime problem, predominantly dealt with via cooperation between countries. This raises jurisdictional problems related to which law applies to the offence (and the difficulty of determining where the offence was committed and precisely defining it for purposes of charging), compatibility between legal systems and police cooperation.

Given the much wider and more serious harms that green criminology deals with, arguably a wider conception of how law and regulatory systems should deal with crime and harm is required. In particular, considerations of how regulators and other quasi-judicial actors may be more effective in addressing widespread environmental harms, especially where they are able to use restorative approaches that directly address environmental harms.

Regulation and Legal Alternatives

Various scholars have observed the potential for alternate approaches to environmental justice particularly the use of environmental regulators, often employing a mixture of civil and criminal law to achieve their goals (Nurse, 2015; Stallworthy, 2008; White & Heckenberg, 2014). Situ and Emmons (2000) identify the Environmental Protection Agency (EPA) and Department of Justice (DoJ) as the main enforcers of environmental law in the US. Specialist environmental agencies such as the US Fish and Wildlife Service, the EPA (US) and English Nature (UK) can provide both regulatory and criminal enforcement options. However, limitations are often placed on these agencies by virtue of their enacting legislation and tightly defined jurisdiction (Stallworthy, 2008), determined by both political and practical considerations. Across jurisdictions, a range of problems have been identified within environmental law enforcement as follows:

1. Lack of resources
2. Inconsistency of legislation
3. Inconsistency in sentencing
4. Lack of police priority and inconsistency in policing approaches.

Investigatory and prosecution philosophy is also a significant factor. White and Heckenberg (2014, p. 218) identify that environmental protection agencies generally have a role to deal with pollution and waste offences, parks and fisheries departments deal with 'green' issues such as conservation, animal welfare and land use, whereas specialist animal welfare or animal control agencies may deal with animal abuse and domestic animal issues. How offences are dealt with and which enforcement priorities are determined and implemented is largely a matter of law, policy, resources and priorities. Situ and Emmons (2000) identify that investigations and enforcement action is either proactive or reactive although the reality of environmental crime enforcement activity is that reactive enforcement approaches dominate. White and Heckenberg (2014, pp. 200–202) identify environmental regulation as broadly operating along a continuum from direct command and control from the state through to voluntary regulation by business. However, the basics of environmental governance frameworks are summed up by Potoski and Prakash (2004, p. 152) as follows:

> Across the United States and around the world, businesses have joined voluntary governmental and nongovernmental environmental regulations. Such codes often require firms to establish internal environmental management systems to improve their environmental performance and regulatory compliance. Meanwhile, governments have been offering incentives to businesses that self-police their regulatory compliance and promptly report and correct violations.

As this indicates, the central issue of environmental governance is state regulatory (rather than criminal justice) control, allied to a self-policing structure intended to promote and encourage voluntary corporate environmental responsibility rather than to directly compel it. However, the largely voluntary nature of Corporate Social Responsibility (CSR) frameworks means corporations have considerable discretion in how they implement environmental responsibilities that are not strictly dictated by law as well as which methods to adopt and the manner in which the information is made publicly available (Spence, 2011). Effective environmental enforcement should arguably be based on the use of the 'polluter pays' principle for environmental damage which was adopted by the OECD in 1972 as a background economic principle for environmental policy (Turner, 1992). As an economic mechanism, making goods and services reflect their total cost including the cost of all the resources used, would require polluters to integrate (or internalise) the cost of use or degradation of environmental resources. As a legal mechanism, increasingly legislators, regulators and the courts should apply the basic principles of restorative justice and incorporate the 'repair of harm' principle and mediation or contact between victim and offender as tools to remedy or mitigate corporate environmental damage. However, this raises questions concerning the extent to which 'standard' courts and mainstream justice are equipped to address the specific (and specialised) nature of environmental harms.

Environmental Courts and Quasi-Judicial Bodies

The nature of environmental crimes and harms are such that mainstream legal systems are arguably ill-equipped to deal with them, in part because they fall outside of the normative business of the courts and legal profession. In the UK at least, environmental law is not considered to be one of the seven foundations of legal knowledge taught as a compulsory subject in law degrees (Bar Standards Board, 2021). Thus, environmental law is arguably classified as a specialized subject, taken as an elective and frequently ending up as the domain of specialized practitioners. In a 1992 article and lecture entitled Are the Judiciary Environmentally Myopic? Lord Woolf, at the time one of the most senior UK judges questioned whether the judiciary was equipped to deal with environmental cases. Lord Woolf noted that a single environmental incident, for example pollution, could comprise of multiple offences under various different pieces of legislation. An incident which killed wildlife and resulted in human harm while also constituting regulatory breach by exceeding emission limits and other pollution controls could engage with criminal, civil and administrative laws and the need for punishment, remediation and civil damages. Such incidents could also engage with analysis and development of policy which Lord Woolf contended the judiciary lacked competence to deal with and which were better dealt with by professional policymakers (Woolf, 1992).

The need to consider consequences beyond the initial direct impact requires consideration of a 'therapeutic jurisprudence approach' that incorporates focus on the therapeutic and anti-therapeutic benefits of consequences of the court process; the perception that court processes can go beyond pure punishment to incorporate reform and rehabilitation (Hoyle, 2012). The notion of specialist green courts reflects the perceived benefits of specialism versus generalism (Stempel, 1995; Woolf, 1992). Lord Woolf's contention was that the lack of specialist knowledge of environmental matters risked judicial scrutiny through criminal law processes being inadequate. Similarly, White (2013, p. 269) identifies that empirical evidence shows that when specialist courts are in place or when judicial officers with specialist environmental knowledge are placed within generalist systems, there is a greater likelihood of both offender prosecution and use of appropriate sanctions. Accordingly, Lord Woolf's conclusion that a case exists for a special environmental tribunal with general responsibility for overseeing and enforcing environmental law which would be a 'multi-faceted, multi-skilled body which would combine the services provided by existing courts, tribunals and inspectors in the environmental field' has merit (1992, p. 14). Part of Lord Woolf's analysis related to the distinctive aspects of environmental crimes such as 'the possibility of a single pollution incident giving rise to many different types of legal actions in different forums—a coroner's inquest if deaths are involved; criminal prosecution, civil actions, and judicial review if public authorities are involved' (Macrory, 2010, p. 64). The implication of Lord Woolf's analysis was that a single specialized environmental forum with expertise to deal with all matters relating to the environmental incident would be better than generalized consideration of environmental cases through the standard court system.

Preston (2014) identified 12 characteristics necessary for the success of environmental courts. Broadly speaking these relate to:

1. The status and authority of the court
2. Independence from Government and with a high level of impartiality
3. A comprehensive and centralized jurisdiction
4. Judges and members are knowledgeable and competent
5. The court operates as a multi-door courthouse
6. The court providing access to scientific and technical expertise
7. The court facilitates access to justice
8. Achieves just, quick and cheap resolution of disputes
9. Responsive to environmental problems and is relevance
10. Develops environmental jurisprudence
11. Underlying ethos and mission
12. Flexible, innovative and provides value-adding function.

Preston's analysis identifies the importance of a specialized court as a tool to address some of the perceived problems of poor implementation of environmental law (Amirante, 2012). The ideal is that rather than environmental matters being dealt with as a general enforcement issue, the status and authority of the court as a specialised forum signals the importance of environmental issues and its role is one of developing jurisprudence in environmental cases that might influence the decisions of other courts and practitioners. In this regard, a specialized environmental court can also play an important role in situating the intrinsic value of the environment as a key factor in judicial decisions. Incorporating Preston's principles, such courts can provide specialist expertise in judicial consideration and administration of cases. But they can also apply specialist knowledge to 'valuation of the harm, degrees of seriousness, extent and nature of victimization, and remedies suited to the nature of the crime' (White & Heckenberg, 2014, p. 262). Thus, specialist green courts offer the potential for consistency in sentencing, identified as a special concern of the New South Wales Land and Environment Court (White, 2013, p. 270). Arguably such courts also 'offer the benefit of evolving procedural norms suited to their jurisdiction and secure more effective jurisprudence through the development of judicial and prosecutorial expertise' (Nurse, 2016, p. 170). This arguably provides the value-added function alluded to in Preston's principles that in theory allows for uniformity, consistency and predictability in the consideration of specialist evidence and legal argument concerning environmental harms. Specialist environmental courts arguably also allow for a tailored judicial approach that incorporates the use of restorative justice and mediation with a focus on repairing environmental damage at the centre of the court's consideration.

Environmental Ombudsmen

Separate from the consideration of specialist courts, Environmental Ombudsmen have also emerged as a way of resolving citizens' environmental complaints through independent investigation and adjudication. For example, Hungary's Environmental Ombudsman. The Commissioner for Future Generations was operational from May 2008 to January 2012 and acted as one of the country's four Parliamentary Ombudsmen before his functions were assigned to his legal successor, the Office of the Commissioner for Fundamental Rights. The Environmental Ombudsman had a remit to safeguard citizens' constitutional right to a healthy environment, providing for a mechanism through which citizens' complaints of environmental wrongdoing could be investigated. The Environmental Ombudsman's jurisdiction was to investigate a broad range of Hungarian environmental issues such as: the degradation of urban green areas; noise pollution by aviation; and licencing of individual industrial installations that might result in pollution and environmental harm. The Environmental Ombudsman also acted as a policy advocate for sustainability issues across all relevant fields of national or local legislation and public policy thus acting as an advocate for future generations and investigating the extent to which sustainability principles operated in practice. The Ombudsman also had a role to develop a strategic scientific research network through undertaking or promoting projects targeting the long-term sustainability of human societies. Other jurisdictions have also employed Environmental Ombudsmen in various forms. The Environmental Ombudsman Team was reactivated in May 2012 as part of the Office of the Public Ombudsman in the Philippines with a remit to handle cases filed with the office against government officials and individuals accused of violating environmental laws. Public sector Environmental Ombudsmen's jurisdiction varies according to their enacting legislation and the civil code in which they operate but is generally concerned with some variation on decision-making fault. The mandate of the Philippines Environmental Ombudsman is to:

> take cognizance of any act or omission committed by any public official, employee, office or agency mandated to protect the environment and conserve natural resources that appears to be illegal, unjust, improper or inefficient, or any malfeasance, misfeasance or nonfeasance committed by any public officer or employee, including co-conspirator private individuals, if said act or omission involves any violation of environmental laws or concerns or relates to environmental protection or conservation considerations.
>
> (Office of the Ombudsman, 2014, p. 2)

The Philippines Environmental Ombudsman's jurisdiction codifies some of these activities by specifically referring to action concerning natural resources that is 'illegal, unjust, improper or inefficient' (Office of the Ombudsman, 2014, p. 2). Thus, a failure to take action to protect the environment, taking incorrect action or unreasonable delay in taking action (inefficiency) would all fall within the Environmental Ombudsman's jurisdiction.

Ideally an Environmental Ombudsman's investigation identifies fault and recommends a remedy for the harm caused. Where the nature of the events makes it impossible to put the complainant back in the position that they would have been in had the 'maladministration' (fault) not occurred, ombudsmen are often empowered to recommend financial compensation and other remedies to address the harm caused. In environmental cases, this likely involves some action which mitigates the environmental damage or otherwise provides for positive environmental action. Thus in a pollution event where the fault has been a factor in the nature and scale of the pollution a suitable remedy might be compensation for the affected community as well as meeting the costs of clean-up or mitigation work. A potential criticism of ombudsmen is that in some jurisdictions their decisions on complaints are recommendations only, thus a public authority may not be required to accept the decision or take the action identified by an Ombudsman as necessary to remedy a complaint. As a result, a complaint can be upheld and tangible proposals for remedying the injustice made, yet the complainant still does not receive an effective remedy. However, Owen (1999) argues that the Ombudsman's ability to only recommend but not enforce is a central strength of the Ombudsman model rather than a weakness as it 'requires that recommendations must be based on a thorough investigation of all facts, scrupulous consideration of all perspectives and vigorous analysis of all issues'. His contention is that complaint outcomes and remedy recommendations based on reasoned analysis rather than coercive power are more powerful, as a coercive process is more likely to create a 'loser' who is less likely to embrace change and carry out remedies. Studies of 'negotiated compliance' (Hawkins, 2002; Hutter, 1997) also demonstrate how the informal mediated practice can sometimes achieve better settlements and resolution than might have been achieved had an issue been pursued to enforcement (or court action).

Ombudsmen are primarily a civil or administrative law option, whose purpose is not to punish offenders but instead to resolve complaints and hopefully bring about some form of behavioural change. In doing so they embody green criminology's ecological and species justice notions of providing justice for the environment as a victim (Benton, 1998; Lynch & Stretesky, 2014). They also demonstrate practical implementation of the 'polluter pays' principle and the need for public authorities to consider environmental concerns in their decision-making and to be accountable for resulting environmental harm when they fail to do so.

Conclusions

As the discussion in this chapter identifies, environmental crimes and harms require a rethinking of some approaches to policing, regulation and prosecution. Arguably criminology is primarily concerned with the classification of deviance via the criminal law and the prosecution of offences classed as crimes according to a strict socio-legal definition. Green criminology, however, is concerned with some wider notions of environmental harm irrespective of the legal classification afforded to the activity. This is consistent with an environmental law approach that deals with many green harms outside of the strictly criminal law approach and that also places responsibility for some enforcement and addressing deviance in the hands of regulators who have discretion to use a mixture of administrative, civil, criminal and restorative tools to address environmental harm.

Thus, a green criminological approach argues for a holistic and harm-based approach to the application of environmental laws that facilitates the use of a range of judicial and restorative approaches to address environmental harm.

References

Amirante, D. (2012). Environmental courts in comparative perspective: Preliminary reflections on the National Green Tribunal of India. *Pace Environmental Law Review, 29*(2), 441–469.

Bar Standards Board. (2021). *Bar Qualification Manual—Part 2 Academic Component of Bar Training*. Bar Standards Board. The Bar Qualification Manual (barstandardsboard.org.uk). Accessed 10 Mar 2021.

Benton, T. (1998). Rights and Justice on a shared planet: More rights or new relations? *Theoretical Criminology, 2*(2), 149–175.

Cameron, J., & Abouchar, J. (1991). The precautionary principle: A fundamental principle of law and policy for the protection of the global environment. *Boston College International and Comparative Law Review, 14*(1), 1–28.

Edge, K. (1971). Enforcing environmental policy the environmental ombudsman. *Cornell Law Review, 56*(5), 847–863.

Greife, M. J., & Maume, M. O. (2020). Do companies pay the price for environmental crimes? Consequences of criminal penalties on corporate offenders. *Crime Law and Social Change, 73*, 337–356. https://doi.org/10.1007/s10611-019-09863-4.

Hawkins, K. (2002). *Law as last resort*. Oxford University Press.

Hutter, B. (1997). *Compliance: Regulation and environment*. Clarendon Press.

Lynch, M., & Stretesky, P. (2014). *Exploring green criminology: Toward a green criminological revolution*. Ashgate.

Lynch, M., Long, M., & Stretesky, P. (2019). *Green criminology and green theories of justice*. Palgrave Macmillan.

Macrory, R., & Woods, M. (2003). *Modernizing environmental justice: Regulation and the role of an environmental tribunal*. University College, London.

Megret, F. (2011). The problem of an international criminal law of the environment. *Columbia Journal of Environmental Law, 66*(2), 195–254.

Mitchell, R. B. (1996). Compliance theory: An overview. In L. Werksman, J. Cameron & P. Roderick (Eds.), *Improving compliance with international environmental law*. Earthscan.

Nurse, A. (2013). *Animal harm*. Ashgate.

Nurse, A. (2013). Privatising the green police: The role of NGOs in wildlife law enforcement. *Crime, Law and Social Change, 559*(3), 305–318.

Nurse, A. (2015). *Policing Wildlife: Perspectives on the Enforcement of Wildlife Legislation*. Palgrave Macmillan.

Nurse, A. (2016). *An introduction to green criminology and environmental justice*. Sage.

Nurse, A. (2014). The beginning of the end? The International Court of Justice's decision on Japanese Antarctic Whaling. *Journal of Animal Welfare Law*, Spring: 14–17.

Owen, S. (1999). The ombudsman: Essential elements and common challenges. In L. C. Reif (Ed.), *The international ombudsman anthology: Selected writings from the international ombudsman institute* (pp. 51–72). Kluwer Law International.

Pirjatanniemi, E. (2009). Desperately seeking reason—New directions for european environmental criminal law. *Scandinavian Studies in Law, 54*, 410–430.

Potoski, P., & Prakash, M. (2004). The regulation dilemma: Cooperation and conflict in environmental governance. *Public Administration Review, 64*(2), 152–163.

Preston, B. J. (2014). Characteristics of successful environmental courts and tribunals. *Journal of Environmental Law, 26*, 365–393. https://doi.org/10.1093/jel/equ019.

Pring, G., & Pring, C. (2009). Specialized environmental courts and tribunals at the confluence of human rights and the environment. *Oregon Review of International Law, 11*(2), 301–330.

Roeschke, J. E. (2009). Eco-terrorism and piracy on the high seas: Japanese whaling and the rights of private groups to enforce international conservation law in neutral waters. *The Villanova Environmental Law Journal*, *XX*(1): 99–136.

Ruhl, J. D. (1997). The case of the Speluncean polluters: Six themes of environmental law, policy, and ethics. *Environmental Law, 27*, 343–373.

Schaffner, J. (2011). *An introduction to animals and the law.* Palgrave Macmillan.

Sohn, L. B. (1973). The Stockholm declaration on the human environment. *Harvard International Law Journal, 14*(3), 423–515.

Spence, D. B. (2011). Corporate social responsibility in the oil and gas industry: The importance of reputational risk. *Chicago-Kent Law Review, 86*(1), 59–85.

Stallworthy, M. (2008). *Understanding environmental law.* Sweet and Maxwell.

Stempel, J. W. (1995). Two cheers for specialisation. *Brook Law Review, 67*, 88–89.

Turner, R. K. (1992). *Environmental policy: An economic approach to the polluter pays principle.* University of East Anglia.

White, R. (2013). Environmental crime and problem-solving courts. *Crime Law and Social Change, 59*, 267–278.

White, R. (2018). *Climate change criminology*. Bristol University Press.

White, R., & Heckenberg, D. (2014). *Green criminology: An introduction to the study of environmental harm.* Routledge.

White, R. (2007). Green Criminology and the pursuit of social and ecological justice. In P. Beirne & N. South (Eds.), *Issues in green criminology: Confronting harms against environments, humanity and other animals.* Willan.

White, R. (2012). The foundations of eco-global criminology. In R. Ellefsen, R. Sollund, & G. Larsen (Eds.), *Eco-global crimes: Contemporary problems and future challenges.* Ashgate.

Wood, M. (2009). Advancing the sovereign trust of government to safeguard the environment for present and future generations (Part 1): Ecological realism and the need for a paradigm shift. *Environmental Law, 39*, 43–89.

Woolf, H. (1992). Are the judiciary environmentally myopic? *Journal of Environmental Law, 4*(1), 1–14. https://doi.org/10.1093/jel/4.1.1.

Wyatt, T. (2013). *Wildlife trafficking: A deconstruction of the crime, the victims and the offenders.* Palgrave Macmillan.

4

Environmental Crime, Ecological Expertise and Specialist Environment Courts

Rob White

Introduction

This chapter provides an overview of issues surrounding the prosecution and sentencing of environmental crimes. It demonstrates the value of the establishment and development of specialist environment courts as institutional mechanisms for responding effectively to environmental harm. The chapter begins by discussing the perceived limitations of non-specialist courts in dealing with environmental offences. The chapter then draws upon the experiences of the New South Wales Land and Environment Court in order to reiterate the fundamentals of criminal law (such as mitigating and aggravating factors in sentencing), explore how ecocentrism is translated into judicial decision-making (particularly with respect to ascertaining the nature and quantum of environmental harm related to criminal offending), and how the legal frameworks

R. White (✉)
School of Social Sciences, University of Tasmania, Hobart, TAS, Australia
e-mail: r.d.white@utas.edu.au

J. Gacek and R. Jochelson (eds.), *Green Criminology and the Law*,
Palgrave Studies in Green Criminology,
https://doi.org/10.1007/978-3-030-82412-9_4

underpinning this specialist court are fundamental to the possibility of good environmental outcomes (such as the institutional status of the court and its judges, and the penalties/sanctions available to it in sentencing offenders). Specific legislation and cases will be referenced to illustrate general observations.

The perspectives underpinning this chapter include critical green criminology (White, 2018a) and Earth Jurisprudence (Koons, 2009). These incorporate different topical interests, but the connection lies in the adoption of an ecocentric approach to the study of criminal justice and/or environmental law. Ecocentrism refers to an approach to law and crime that is environment-centred rather than solely human-centred. Put simply, ecocentrism views the environment as having value for its own sake apart from any instrumental or utilitarian value to humans (White, 2017a, 2018b). Protection of the environment may be based on conceptions of the rights of nature and/or duties to nature. Various legislative and regulatory mechanisms may thus be invoked in promoting an ecocentric approach, ranging from laws granting legal personhood of rivers through to laws that entrench a general environmental duty of care (Freiberg, 2019; Pecharroman, 2018).

A central concern of criminology is the notion of harm, including how it is conceptualised and responded to within particular social and legal contexts. In this chapter, the harm referred to has been legally determined to be serious enough to be considered criminal in nature. Courts are obliged to deal with criminal matters as mandated by relevant legislation, yet, as discussed below, how they do so does vary in practice. The chapter illustrates approaches to environmental harm based on ecocentrism and how this, in turn, is facilitated and developed in the context of specialist environment courts.

Limitations of Courts in Dealing with Environmental Offences

The more serious the offence, the harsher the response or sentencing tariff. Seriousness of offence is indicated in the application of the principle of proportionality, which refers to the idea that the severity of punishment should be commensurate with the seriousness of the criminal conduct. Ordinal proportionality concerns the relative seriousness of offences compared to other offences (for example, murder versus burglary). Cardinal proportionality relates to the notion that the penalty (within a scale of punishments) should not be out of proportion to the gravity of the crime involved (Preston, 2007).

An overarching question for this chapter is whether, both legislatively and judicially, the level of seriousness of environmental harm is sufficiently acknowledged. At an empirical level, for example, environmental offences can be compared with other offences such as homicide or burglary, and the severity of penalty that accompanies conviction for particular acts and omissions can be assessed in order to gauge ordinal proportionality. Most offences involving the environment are prosecuted in lower courts (or dealt with by civil and administrative penalties), and most penalties are on the lower rather than higher end of the scale. For instance, the majority of all environmental crimes in the United Kingdom are dealt with in the Magistrate's Court and the most common sanction is fines, and these are low level (Bell et al., 2013). In Canada, analysis has also confirmed the ambiguities in law and leniency in punishment when it comes to environmental offences (Fogel & Lipovsek, 2013). Generally, environmental crime tends to be seen only as an infraction or misdemeanour—that is, less serious—than felony or indictable offences.

Across jurisdictions, prison time has remained the exception not the norm. In jurisdictions such as Flanders, Belgium even when prison sentences are imposed, they are not always executed but are often used as a suspended or probationary sentence (Billiet & Rousseau, 2014). In the United States, where incarceration for federal environmental offences occurs, the mean sentence lengths are small and occur when the defendant is an individual rather than a corporation (Lynch, 2017). Imprisonment tends to be given to offenders who have violated non-environmental laws as part of their offence (such as conspiracy, tax fraud, drug or firearm offences) (Lynch, 2017).

Thus, there are consistent claims that courts (in a generic sense, but generally referring to magistrate-level [or lower level] courts) deal with environmental issues in a trivialising and/or uninformed way, and that the penalties imposed by courts tend to be lenient and thereby inconsequential in terms of deterrence or reprobation. These issues have been acknowledged in jurisdictions such as Sweden, Canada, the United States, and the United Kingdom, and Europe more generally (Chin, Veening, & Gerstetter, 2014; Cochran et al., 2016; Du Rees, 2001; EFFACE, 2016; Lynch et al., 2016). They have also been noted in Australia (Bates, 2013), where research on sentencing has also examined questions of consistency and proportionality (that is, how consistent the court has been in applying additional maximum penalties in cases where they appear to be warranted). While not focussed on the issue of leniency per se, one study demonstrated that a substantial number of cases involved sentences that were well below the expected threshold (Burke, 2016).

From the point of view of green criminology, the apparent low level of penalty, generally, appears to indicate that such harms are philosophically not considered particularly serious compared to others (and especially those involving human subjects). The implication is that courts are not adopting an ecocentric approach in decision-making, including cases that involve harm to non-human environmental entities, since the penalties appear lenient. While the evidence for this remains thin given the dearth of relevant substantive studies in this area, this perception seems to be confirmed in other ways as well. For instance, even where there are severe penalties available, these may not be applied by the judiciary, especially if they are not familiar with environmental crime and its consequences. This then relates to cardinal proportionality. The experience in the United Kingdom, for example, has been that the trivialisation of environmental offences in the courtroom serves to impede enforcement as a whole and to diminish the threats posed by prosecution (Bell et al., 2013). Specifically, the level of sentences given in courts, principally magistrate's courts, for environmental crimes has been seen to be too low for them to be effective either as punishment or a deterrent. This is not necessarily due to the legislative regime within which magistrates work but includes factors such as perceptions by magistrates regarding the seriousness of environmental crime and their relative inexperience in dealing with such crimes.

However, the sentencing process and outcomes change remarkably when the court has specialist expertise in dealing with environmental crime. An indication of this is provided by the New South Wales Land and Environment Court [NSWLEC] which has been in operation for over 40 years. In this instance, the administration of justice has occurred primarily from the point of view of ecocentric considerations. The difference between the NSWLEC and other courts in criminal proceedings is significant and striking.

A Specialist Environment Court: The NSWLEC

The NSWLEC is the oldest specialist court of its kind in Australia. It has criminal jurisdiction and thus deals directly with environmental crimes. It has superior status to magistrate courts and therefore can provide an indication of how courts operate when environmental harm is deemed serious enough to warrant higher court attention. Whereas much of the extant literature on environmental crime and courts is critical of lower court activity in this domain, little has been written on either specialist environmental courts, or on courts that have higher court status (Voigt & Makuch, 2018). From this vantage point, it may well be that the issues of leniency, ignorance and inappropriateness either melt away or manifest in quite different ways. This is indicated, for example, in a study which demonstrated that additional maximum penalties for harming threatened species have failed in practice due to various factors, including the mulching of the evidence needed to ascertain the number of threatened plants destroyed, the numbers of which determine the quantum of possible additional penalty (Burke, 2016).

The NSWLEC was created by the *Land and Environment Court Act* in 1979. The *Environmental Planning and Assessment Act 1979* (NSW) which forms the basis for most of the decisions of the Court, includes among its objects, the encouragement of the protection of the environment and the encouragement of ecologically sustainable development. The Court has three principal functions that span administrative, civil and criminal domains. First, it acts as an administrative tribunal, determining planning and building appeals on their merits. Second, it also acts in a supervisory role in regards cases of civil enforcement of planning and administrative law and judicial review of administrative decisions in those fields. Third, it has a summary criminal jurisdiction that involves prosecution and punishment for environmental offences (Preston, 2014).

The NSWLEC is part of the New South Wales court system and is equivalent to the Supreme Court in the hierarchy of courts in New South Wales. The judges of the Court have the same rank, title, and status as judges of the Supreme Court of New South Wales, as set out in the *Land and Environment Court Act 1979* (NSW) s 9(2). The NSWLEC has a wide jurisdiction to hear and determine many different types of cases. These are grouped by the relevant class of the Court's jurisdiction, and include Class 5 cases, namely, criminal proceedings for offences against planning or environmental laws.

The general tasks of the Court are broadly guided by the principles of 'ecologically sustainable development' as outlined in the *Protection of the Environment Administration Act 1991 (*NSW), where it is noted in Pt 3, 6, (2) that ecologically sustainable development can be achieved through the implementation of the following principles and programmes:

(a) the precautionary principle—namely, that if there are threats of serious or irreversible environmental damage, lack of full scientific certainty should not be used as a reason for postponing measures to prevent environmental degradation.

 In the application of the precautionary principle, public and private decisions should be guided by:

 (i) careful evaluation to avoid, wherever practicable, serious or irreversible damage to the environment, and
 (ii) an assessment of the risk-weighted consequences of various options,

(b) inter-generational equity—namely, that the present generation should ensure that the health, diversity and productivity of the environment are maintained or enhanced for the benefit of future generations,

(c) conservation of biological diversity and ecological integrity—namely, that conversation of biological diversity and ecological integrity should be a fundamental consideration,
(d) improved valuation, pricing and incentive mechanisms—namely, that environmental factors should be included in the valuation of assets and services, such as:

 (i) polluter pays—that is, those who generate pollution and waste should bear the cost of containment, avoidance or abatement,
 (ii) the users of goods and services should pay prices based on the full life cycle of goods and services, including the use of natural resources and assets and the ultimate disposal of any waste,
 (iii) environmental goals, having been established, should be pursued in the most cost effective way, by establishing incentive structures, including market mechanisms, that enable those best placed to maximise benefits or minimise costs to develop their own solutions and responses to environmental problems.

The notion of 'ecologically sustainable development' does not in and of itself privilege environmental considerations over economic considerations insofar as both considerations are meant to be integrated in decision-making processes. Nonetheless, p3,6(c) of the *PEA Act* states that conservation of biological diversity and ecological integrity should be a fundamental consideration in decision-making.

Sentencing Principles and Practices

The sentencing decisions exercised by judicial officers involve the assessment of a range of factors, including mitigating and aggravating factors, as set out in Section 21A of the *Crimes (Sentencing Procedure) Act 1999*. Under the Act, the NSWLEC also has to take into account other relevant matters in passing sentence such as, for example, when and if there is a guilty plea, the degree to which the administration of justice has been facilitated by the defence, and the degree to which the offender has assisted law enforcement authorities in relation to the offence.

General Sentencing Principles

Sentencing is a core function of those courts invested with responsibility for adjudicating criminal cases. In deciding sentence, the court typically weighs up a range of matters, including sentencing aims, sentencing principles, offender-specific factors, offence-specific factors, legislative intent, and the specific facts of the case. Case law as well as statutory obligation provide the general framework within which an 'intuitive synthesis' is made, and this in itself provides a concrete indication of the seriousness of the harm and the gravity of the offence.

The sentencing of adult offenders in New South Wales is governed by the *Crimes (Sentencing Procedure) Act 1999* (NSW) which sets out the purposes of sentencing in s 3A. These aims include punishment, deterrence, rehabilitation, denunciation, and community protection. Although not explicitly included in sentencing purposes, increasingly the aim of restorative justice is being incorporated into sentencing provisions, including in the specific area of environmental offences. Within the context of the criminal law and particular mandate of the NSWLEC, there is no specific or explicit reference to 'restorative justice' per se as a method or remedy. The *Protection of the Environmental Operations Act 1997—S 250* does make reference to an additional order (c) the offender to carry out a specified project for the restoration or enhancement of the environment in a public place or for the public benefit; and subsection (1A) allows that without limiting subsection (1)(c), the court may order the offender to carry out any social or community activity for the benefit of the community or persons that are adversely affected by the offence (a 'restorative justice activity') that the offender has agreed to carry out. While clearly oriented towards 'repairing the harm', this does not necessarily include victim-offender interactions and exchanges characteristic of the restorative justice *process* more generally, where the emphasis is on repairing the relationship between offender and victim (White, 2017b). In the history of the NSWLEC there have in fact only been two instances in which restorative justice, involving processes of mediation and community conferencing, has been used, although opportunities to do so have occurred over time (see Hamilton, 2021).

Various options that are available in sentencing for environmental offences reflect purposes of sentencing such as general deterrence, restoration and reparation. Additional orders in the *Protection of the Environment Operations Act 1997 (NSW)*, for example, include orders for restoration and prevention; orders for payment of costs, expenses and compensation; orders to pay investigation costs; monetary benefit orders; publication orders; environmental service orders; environmental audit orders; payment into an environmental trust; order to attend a training course; order to establish a training course; and order to provide financial assistance.

Specific penalty provisions and provisions setting out factors which are relevant to the sentencing exercise are also contained in specific legislation. In addition, particular categories of defendant may require special sensitivity by the judiciary to social and cultural circumstances (MacKenzie et al., 2010). Maximum penalties for criminal offences are specified in the offence provisions themselves, and may involve a wide range of sentencing orders, from dismiss the charge without conviction through to imprisonment.

In determining sentence, the sentencing judge considers the details of the offending conduct (the circumstances in which it occurred and the objective seriousness of the harm) and the subjective characteristics of the offender which might be considered as either aggravating or mitigating the seriousness of the particular instance of the offence (their general reputation and good character, prior criminal history, expressions of remorse and so on). Criminal punishment combines consequentialist aims (such as deterrence, rehabilitation and community protection) and expressive aims (such as denunciation and retribution) (White et al., 2019). The intent is to deter others from engaging in similar acts or omissions, and to send a message to the community that such offences are indeed wrong and harmful. The degree of penalty indicates the extent to which the court ascertains seriousness of harm (that is, the objective damage caused by the specific action) and the gravity or seriousness of offence (that also incorporates the culpability of the offender).

Criminal law frequently rests upon the premise that two elements must be present to constitute a crime—the act (and, less commonly, an omission), and the intent. That is, there is a conduct element (*actus reus*) comprising wrongful acts, omissions or a state of affairs that constitute a violation of the law, and there is also a mental element (*mens rea*) where the focus is on criminal intent and the awareness that actions were wilful and wrongful. The mental element may take several forms such as intention, recklessness or knowledge in relation to the prohibited conduct, but there are many crimes known as offences of *strict liability* (and of absolute liability), which do not require any such awareness at all. The latter offences are particularly relevant to environmental crimes insofar as the public interest is favoured over traditional approaches to subjective elements such as intent (Bates, 2013). The mental element is nonetheless relevant at sentencing, as discussed below.

Strict liability means that regardless of intent or fault, if someone commits an act (or omission) that is strictly prohibited by law then they must be held to account. Strict liability laws thus punish people regardless of their state of mind, although the defendant may in defence plead 'honest and reasonable mistake of fact' and if this is supported by some *prima facie* evidence the prosecution will have to rebut this defence beyond reasonable doubt (Bates, 2013). For offences classified as 'absolute liability' offences, there is no defence that can be pleaded, although it has rarely been interpreted in Australia that environmental offences are of absolute liability (Bates, 2013). Strict liability offences are regarded as so undesirable as to merit the imposition of criminal punishment; yet, maximum penalties for strict liability offences are generally lower than for crimes committed with intent (Bates, 2013).

While guilty in the eyes of the law regardless of intent, recklessness or negligence, subjective factors do nonetheless come into play at the sentencing stage, where judges weigh up such factors as part of sentencing determinations. It has been observed that 'A strict liability offence that is committed intentionally or negligently will be objectively more serious than one which is committed unintentionally or non-negligently' (Preston, 2007, p. 147). Intent is thus still important in environmental crime cases. But consideration of intent is not relevant to the assessment of guilt or innocence as, depending on the legislation, the act in and of itself may be considered worthy of penalty.

System Filters

Many instances of environmental harm do not make it to court in the first place due to the implementation of regulatory regimes that place emphasis on the use of administrative measures such as 'penalty infringement notices'. Verbal communication and written warning letters may also be used to encourage compliance. Agencies such as the NSW Environmental Protection Authority [EPA], for example, generally place emphasis on regulatory compliance and enforcement rather than criminal prosecution as such. Through audits and inspections, the EPA ensures that licencing agreements are monitored and where possible encouragement is provided to licensees to take fewer environmental risks with the assistance of the Authority. The net result of this approach is that only where there is sufficient evidence to establish a serious criminal case for prosecution will the case proceed to court. These alternative enforcement strategies ensure that only the most serious of matters reach court, and only the most serious of these come to the NSWLEC rather than being referred to local and district courts.

There is thus already a degree of seriousness attached to cases dealt with by the NSWLEC given the prior filtering of offences that has occurred. Entry into the courts tends to be at the lower end—magistrate's courts or equivalent—since more infractions and offences are similarly pitched at the lower end of the harm spectrum (see also European Union Action to Fight Environmental Crime [EFFACE], 2016; Bricknell, 2010). In some jurisdictions, the reason why magistrate's courts predominate as the key forum for dealing with environmental crimes is because such crimes are 'strict liability' offences. That is, while all criminal cases start in a magistrate's court, cases will only go to trial and may transfer to the Crown Court if a defendant pleads not guilty—and most in fact plead guilty. This, too, is part of the filtering process (Chin, Veening, & Gerstetter, 2014).

Gravity of Offence

The basis for sentencing is the gravity or seriousness of the offence. This is comprised of different elements, of which seriousness of harm is but one. Seriousness of harm is largely determined by the NSWLEC on the basis of *ecological* indicia. The gravity of offence, as distinct from the seriousness of harm, takes into account subjective factors pertaining to the offender as well as objective factors pertaining to the offence. In this sense, sentencing is an inherently anthropocentric activity—it is the human perpetrator who is at the centre of the punishment process. An ecocentric approach, therefore, is more limited, nuanced and complicated when it comes to determinations that involve human-related factors (such as the state of mind of the perpetrator of harm). For example, disregard of the wellbeing and integrity of the local environment on the part of the offender forms part of the sentencing rationale, as it is indicative of propensities towards environmentally harmful behaviour. The question is to what degree or in what ways ecocentric considerations feature in the final sentencing decision.

In determining an appropriate sanction, the NSWLEC thus considers both objective circumstances and subjective factors in determining a suitable penalty. While *mens rea* is not pertinent in determining guilt, since these are strict liability cases, the mental element (including for example, expressions of remorse and the prior record of the defendant) is nonetheless relevant in determining the gravity of the offence overall. Overall, the NSWLEC bundles together a range of indicia in ascertaining the seriousness of the offence. These are illustrated in Table 4.1.

These various indicia interrelate in unique ways in each case. In the course of its deliberations, the Court ultimately makes judgement as to which indicia are most important in any given situation and bases its final sentencing decision on this assessment.

Table 4.1 Case-based indicia of gravity/seriousness of offence

Level of gravity/seriousness	Examples of key indicia
Low	• deemed to not constitute significant environmental harm • there is absence of actual harm to the animal • the harm is of low impact • the total area is not significant • the actions involved protected fauna only • there is low culpability • remediation is possible
Moderate	• there is more significant environmental harm • threatened species are affected • there is significant damage to habitat • the offender ignores and/or undermines regulatory and statutory obligations • there are uneven or limited amounts of damage there is limited possibility for remediation
High	• significant and serious environmental harm larger scale and extent of damage • endangered species • profit and commercial gain from the illegal activity premeditated and intentional action • no or little remediation possible

Source Drawing from White (2017a)

Expertise and Determining the Quantum of Harm

Expertise

Detailed investigation, analysis and expert perusal are exercised and drawn upon by the NSWLEC in determining the specific degree and type of environmental harm in each instance. This requires the Court to carefully consider the evidence and expert opinion from varying sources to categorise the specific harm in question. This process of assessment demands of the NSWLEC prerequisite knowledge of basic ecological processes and contexts.

For example, the NSWLEC actively filters out 'bad' science and 'poor' expertise. Where warranted, expert testimony has been rejected by the Court, and persons who are not qualified to give specific expert opinion have been dismissed (White, 2017c).

In a similar vein, disputes involving expert witnesses include cases where the conflict is not over the basic facts (such as causing damage to habitat of a threatened species, knowing that the land concerned was habitat of that kind) but over the *amount* of vegetation that was cleared, and its *impact* on the threatened species. This means making decisions regarding which expert testimony is most reliable and in relation to the estimates or opinions being made. Poor methods and methodologies, particularly where there is conflicting expert evidence, provides occasion for the NSWLEC to disregard certain evidence, especially when countered by expert opinion given by scientists of known repute (White, 2017c).

A wide range of experts is called upon and many different disciplines and scientific techniques are utilised in attempts to ascertain the nature, extent and dynamics of environmental harm. As with any court, the NSWLEC has to appraise who is an expert for what, and to what extent. Determining the precise nature of environmental harm, including its seriousness, is subject to distinct categorisation based upon the establishment, over time, of clusters of indicia (White, 2017a). These categorisations assist in helping to define the parameters of harm within which environmental harm is perpetrated. Each case is unique in some respects, given variable circumstances and a diversity of objective and subjective factors at play in any given situation. Categorisations of harm based upon prior decisions and knowledge built up by the Court over time, as well as critical scrutiny of expert opinion (which likewise indirectly builds expertise), enable the NSWLEC to continue to develop specific indicia for evaluating environmental harm to non-human environmental entities. The success of the Court depends upon judges being knowledgeable and competent—they need to be environmentally literate (Preston, 2014).

Ecological Sustainability

The specific indicators of the ecocentric approach demonstrated by the NSWLEC have been described elsewhere (White, 2017a, 2018b). These include, for example, the extent to which the intrinsic worth of the non-human environmental entity is taken into consideration, the use of ecological perspectives to estimate the degree of harm to non-human environmental entities, and the kinds of expertise mobilised by the Court to adequately capture the nature and complexities of the environmental harm. These indicators of ecocentrism are, however, open to various interpretations. For instance, an ecocentric approach includes support for the regulation of human behaviour in ways that reflect notions of ecological sustainability.

Indeed, the principles of Ecologically Sustainable Development (ESD) provide a guiding framework for deliberations about natural resource use and environmental protection. How ESD principles are applied, however, is contentious in that they can be used to support anthropocentric instrumentalism that is exploitative of nature as well as an ecocentric approach that is protective of the integrity of the natural world (Bosselmann, 2010; De Lucia, 2015). ESD can be interpreted as 'sustainable management' or a form of 'socio-ecological integrity' or 'sustainable use' (Bosselmann, 2010). Unless ESD principles are embedded as an environmental bottom-line in legislation, they tend to be weakened in overall judgement approaches that weigh up the economic, the social and the environmental as if they were equal. A significant practical issue in regards sustainability is whether the procedural use of ESD principles is obligatory (that is, required) or advisory (simply encouraged). Duties and obligations will vary depending upon whether ESD is an object of legislation, a relevant consideration, or a strategic concept applied by administrators (Dwyer & Taylor, 2013).

From an ecocentric perspective, sustainability is linked to ecological integrity. To maintain the integrity of an ecosystem means taking into account a number of characteristics of ecosystems. This requires sensitivity towards and knowledge of how ecosystems operate and their intrinsic complexity (Bosselmann, 2010). Whether they are applied and how ESD principles are applied is concretely manifest in the indicia utilised by a court in determining matters such as environmental harm (White, 2017a, 2018b). An ecocentric approach would consider such principles in the light of non-human interests and through reference to ecological concepts such as interconnectedness, totality, community, diversity, relationships and scale (Koons, 2009; Maloney & Burdon, 2014). Moreover, the dynamic nature of ecosystems places considerable pressure on administrators and the judiciary insofar as there frequently is a degree of uncertainty involved (Preston & Adam, 2004a, 2004b). The ever-changing nature of 'nature' reinforces the importance of a case-by-case analysis and a general openness to the idea that legal remedies will always be crude approximations of natural developments. From the point of view of addressing harm to non-human environmental entities, much depends upon the level of expert knowledge in regards ecological integrity, health and sustainability.

Sanctioning Offenders

A range of penalty types, approaches and mechanisms have emerged in Australia in recent years in regards environmental sentencing options indicating a shift upwards in ordinal rankings of seriousness (that is, these sorts of crimes compared to other crime types) and/or attempts to fashion responses that better match the nature and dynamics of environmental harm. Altogether such measures appear to denote a change in the seriousness with which the community regards environmental offences, as reflected in legislative changes to offence classifications and sentence regimes (White, 2017a). How this burgeoning range of sentencing options translates into sentencing outcomes warrants ongoing scrutiny and is of particular interest to the present chapter. This is because the quantum of penalty and the judicial rationales for these provide an indication of ecocentrism insofar they demonstrate the level of severity of offences involving non-human environmental entities. The type of penalty given can also provide insight into the value placed on addressing environmental harm.

Sentencing options available to the NSWLEC for enforcement and compliance purposes are provided under the *Protection of the Environment Operations Act 1997 (NSW)*. Options include terms of imprisonment, fines, clean-up or preventative action orders, and orders for compensation to those who suffered damage to property as a result of the offence or who incurred costs in taking steps to clean up the harm caused by the offence. The *National Parks and Wildlife Amendment Act 2010 (NSW)* expanded the range of measures a court may impose. These include additional orders that provide the court may do any one or more of the following:

(a) Order the offender to take specified action to publicise the offence (including the circumstances of the offence) and its environmental and other consequences and any other orders made against the person,
(b) Order the offender to take specified action to notify specified persons or classes of persons of the offence (including the circumstances of the offence) and its consequences and of any orders made against the person (including, for example, the publication in an annual report or any other notice to shareholders or a company or the notification of persons aggrieved or affected by the offender's conduct),
(c) Order the offender to carry out a specified project for the restoration or enhancement of the environment in a public place or for the public benefit,
(d) Order the offender to pay a specified amount to the Environmental Trust established under the Environmental Trust Act 1998, or a specified organisation, for the purposes of a specified project for the restoration or enhancement of the environment or for general environmental purposes,
(e) Order the offender to attend, or to cause an employee or employees or a contractor or contractors of the offender to attend, a training or other course specified by the court,
(f) Order the offender to establish, for employees or contractors of the offender, a training course of a kind specified by the court.

Section 194(2) extended the purview of the Court beyond the specific factors laid out in s 194(1) by permitting the Court to 'take into consideration other matters that it considers relevant'. This gives the NSWLEC wide discretion in determining what factors to take into account in sentencing offenders. This includes consideration of factors beyond that of solely expressing the seriousness of the offence per se. For example, especially in the context of harm to non-human environmental entities, judicial balancing of sentencing purposes in the NSWLEC generally reflects a concern with remediation as well as punishment of the offender.

Use of Sentencing Options

Legislation now allows for considerable flexibility in sentencing environmental offenders and this, in turn, has enabled the NSWLEC to better tailor sentencing to fit the crime and the offender. As part of this trend, the interests of the non-human environmental entities that have been harmed are also being directly addressed. The NSWLEC uses a full repertoire of sentencing options as part of criminal proceedings for offences against environmental laws (White, 2017b). Given the lack of such options in other jurisdictions, for example, in the European Union, this provides an exemplar of practice that could well provide direction for potential legal reforms elsewhere (Chin et al., 2014). It also provides an illustration of how an ecocentric orientation is translated into sentencing outcomes.

The flexible use of sentencing options was enhanced when a wider range was made available to the Court, especially under the expanded suite of penalties post-2010. Thus, while community service was used solely for deterrent purposes prior to 2010 (since it was imposed as a general criminal justice sanction and implemented through that system), after the legislative changes of 2010, community service has been re-directed to specific environmental purposes and thus has become reparative as well as deterrent.

A fine is the most common penalty for environmental offences in places such as the USA, the UK, Belgium and Australia (Bates, 2013; Billiet & Rousseau, 2014; Stretesky et al., 2013). This implies that both ordinal proportionality (the seriousness of environmental offences compared to other criminal offences) and cardinal proportionality (the penalty levels within the overall scale of punishments) do not fully reflect the seriousness of the offence as construed by those arguing that offenders who transgress against ecosystems, non-human animals and plants should be more fully held to account. Yet, the nature of the 'intuitive synthesis'—which encapsulates consideration of objective harm and subjective circumstance—means that factors such as capacity to pay have a bearing on sentencing determinations as well as indicia pertaining to environmental harm. The Court weighs up a wide range of factors and does so in accordance with sentencing principles such as consistency and proportionality. A serious offence, therefore, does not always result in a high range penalty outcome, depending upon circumstances.

If the purpose of the NSWLEC is seen to reside primarily in terms of reparation of harm and deterrence of future offending, then what counts is how sentencing can best contribute to these purposes. Fines, in this instance, are not simply a 'cost of business' (Bricknell, 2010). They are intended to be large enough to have deterrent effect but, just as importantly, they are translated into meaningful projects and programmes that attempt to concretely remediate the damage and repair the harm. The linking of fines to specific environmental purposes thereby marks it off from more generic fine schemes in which the money is channelled into consolidated revenue.

The tailoring of sanctions and remedies by the court, over time, particularly in the direction of reparation is significant. When specific remedies are examined, they seem to indicate evidence of specialist knowledge and expertise by the judiciary about the nature of environmental harm and sustained efforts to ensure that the sentence fits the crime (White, 2017b). This requires sensitivity to the importance of ecological principles, including regeneration and reparation, as well as knowledge of what might be most suitable in given circumstances. The content of extended environmental service orders also indicates reliance upon and/or awareness of scientific knowledge and methodological *nous*, as well as reflecting experience of likely offender behaviour post-hearing. With respect to this, the fact that the NSWLEC is a specialist court also seems to be particularly important.

The NSWLEC draws upon a wide range of sentencing options in response to specific offences and offenders. It is not only this range that is significant, however. What also appears to make a difference is the *combination of sanctions*. It is the combining of different sanctions to match circumstances (and specific offenders and offending) that allows the Court to provide tailor-made solutions to the problem of environmental harm before it. From the point of view of ecocentrism, this also provides for more supportive and nuanced responses to the harms against non-human environmental entities than the application of fines as a punitive measure in its own right. In other words, the non-human environmental entity is treated as 'victim' insofar as it is deemed worthy and of value enough to warrant specific treatment intended to repair the harm. While violation of environmental law is a crime against the state, victim needs can nonetheless be acknowledged through such sentencing strategies. The effectiveness of combining different types of orders is that they put a spotlight on the fact that a crime has been committed, while simultaneously producing an environmental good (Bricknell, 2010). Not only does the NSWLEC determine the nature of the harm to non-human environmental entities by reference to ecological criteria, it imposes penalties that include measures designed to ensure the maintenance, restoration or preservation of the harmed plant and animal species, ecological community and ecosystem.

Conclusion

Specialist expertise is vital to an ecocentric approach because assessing harm in instances involving non-human environmental entities demands an appreciation of and reliance upon ecological and other associated types of specialist knowledge (such as botany and zoology).

Specialist environment courts provide an ideal forum for the development and deployment of such expertise and accordingly they have greater insight into the nature of environmental offences (Preston, 2014; Voigt & Makuch, 2018). There need not be a separate court, as such, as long as specialist expertise can be acquired by judiciary within the particular court that hears environmental crime cases. By contrast, the lack of expertise on the part of the judiciary has been shown to present as an added difficulty in even establishing proof of the perpetration of an environmental offence (Fogel & Lipovsek, 2013).

The substantive work of the NSWLEC has resulted in the development of detailed frameworks within which specific types of environmental harm can be categorised. This manifests in the use of particular indicia as benchmarks for assessing harm (White, 2017a, 2017b, 2018a). These methods of categorisation are variously applied insofar as they are suited to the assessment of specific offences and have developed organically over time as the Court has developed its specific expertise. The principle of consistency has ensured that this process of assessment and development of indicia is intentional and structured rather than random, ad hoc and arbitrary. Like cases are examined in relation to like cases, and prior judgements are drawn upon to provide relevant sentencing templates.

Adoption of an ecocentric approach is enhanced by the intersection of legislative frameworks supportive of ecological sustainability, the employment of assessment methods that categorise harm and facilitate determination of its seriousness according to ecological criteria, and the developing ecological expertise of the judiciary that is in part fostered by regular exposure to relevant experts (such as botanists, arborists, and ecologists) in the course of Court proceedings. The NSWLEC operates in statutory context that provides for substantial penalties for environmental offences, and that provides a broad spectrum of sanctions that can be drawn upon in sentencing offenders. The cost to offenders therefore can be substantial and involve financial, reputational, and resource implications. Many of the penalties imposed by the NSWLEC also include requirements that the defendant *do* something. That is, they are not simply passive recipients of penalties such as fines (or, indeed, of imprisonment). Rather, punishment is something which must also be accomplished *by* the offender. This is time, energy and resource consuming, especially if it involves relatively substantial remediation or rehabilitation works. Combining financial sanctions such as fines with activity-based sanctions such as remediation means that compared to many other jurisdictions, the NSWLEC imposes sentences of greater burden to the offender than otherwise has been the case. This, too, is one of the strengths of a specialist environment court.

References

Bagaric, M., & Edney, R. (2014). *Sentencing in Australia.* Lawbook Company.

Bates, G. (2013). *Environmental law in Australia.* LexisNexis Butterworths.

Bell, S., McGillivray, D., Pedersen, O., Lees, E., & Stokes, E. (2013). *Environmental law* (9th ed.). Oxford University Press.

Billiet, C., & Rousseau, S. (2014). How real is the threat of imprisonment for environmental crime? *European Journal of Law Economics, 37*(2), 183–198.

Bosselmann, K. (2010). Losing the forest for the trees: Environmental reductionism in the law. *Sustainability, 2*, 2424–2448.

Bricknell, S. (2010). *Environmental crime in Australia. AIC reports research and public policy series 109.* Australian Institute of Criminology.

Burke, A. (2016). Threatened species, endangered justice: How additional maximum penalties for harming threatened species have failed in practice. *Environmental Planning and Law Journal, 33*, 451–466.

Chin, S., Veening, W. & Gerstetter, C. (2014). *European Union Action to Fight Environmental Crime [EFFACE], Policy Brief 1: Limitations and challenges of the criminal justice system in addressing environmental crime.* http://www.efface.eu. Accessed Feb 2016.

Cochran, J., Lynch, M., Toman, E., & Shields, R. (2016). Court sentencing patterns for environmental crimes: Is there a 'Green Gap' in punishment? *Journal of Quantitative Criminology*. https://doi.org/10.1007/s10940-016-9322-9.

De Lucia, V. (2015). Competing narratives and complex genealogies: The ecosystem approach in international environmental law. *Journal of Environmental Law, 27*(1), 91–117.

Du Rees, H. (2001). Can criminal law protect the environment? *Journal of Scandinavian Studies, 2*(1), 109–126.

Dwyer, G., & Taylor, M. (2013). Moving from consideration to application: The uptake of principles of ecologically sustainable development in environment decision-making in New South Wales. *Environmental Planning and Law Journal, 30*, 185–219.

European Union Action to Fight Environmental Crime [EFFACE]. (2016). *Environmental crime and the EU: Synthesis of the research project*. Ecologic Institute.

Fogel, C., & Lipovsek, J. (2013). Green crime in the Canadian courts. *Journal of Politics and Law, 6*(2), 48–52.

Freiberg, A. (2019). General duties as regulatory tools in environmental protection: Principles, practice, problems. *Environmental and Planning Law Journal, 36*(1), 40–56.

Hamilton, M. (2021). *Environmental crime and restorative justice: Justice as meaningful involvement*. Palgrave Macmillan.

Koons, J. (2009). What is Earth Jurisprudence? Key principles to transform law for the health of the planet. *Penn State Environmental Law Review, 18*, 47–68.

Lynch, M. (2017). The sentencing/punishment of federal environmental/green criminal offenders 2000–2013. *Deviant Behavior, 38*(9), 991–1008.

Lynch, M., Barrett, K., Stretesky, P., & Long, M. (2016). The weak probability of punishment for environmental offences and deterrence of environmental offenders: A discussion based on USEPA criminal cases, 1983–2013. *Deviant Behavior, 37*(10), 1095–1109.

MacKenzie, G., Stobbs, N., & O'Leary, J. (2010). *Principles of sentencing*. Federation Press.

Maloney, M., & Burdon, P. (Eds.). (2014). *Wild law: In practice*. Routledge.

Pecharroman. L. (2018). Rights of nature: Rivers that can stand in court. *Resources, 7*(13). https://doi.org/10.3390/resources7010013.

Preston, B. (2007). Principled sentencing for environmental offences—Part 2: Sentencing considerations and options. *Criminal Law Journal, 31*, 142–164.

Preston, B. (2014). Characteristics of successful environmental courts and tribunals. *Journal of Environmental Law, 26*(3), 365–393.

Preston, B., & Adam, P. (2004a). Describing and listing threatened ecological communities under the threatened species conservation act 1995 (NSW): Part 1—The assemblage of species and the particular area. *Environmental Planning and Law Journal, 21*(4), 250–263.

Preston, B., & Adam, P. (2004b). Describing and listing threatened ecological communities under the threatened species conservation act 1995 (NSW): Part 2—The role of supplementary descriptors and the listing process. *Environmental Planning and Law Journal, 21*(5), 372–390.

Stretesky, P., Long, M., & Lynch, M. (2013). Does environmental enforcement slow the treadmill of production? The relationship between large monetary penalties, ecological disorganization and toxic releases within offending corporations. *Journal of Crime and Justice, 36*(2), 233–247.
Voigt, C., & Makuch, Z. (Eds.). (2018). *Courts and the environment*. Edward Elgar Publishing.
White, R. (2017a). *The sentencing of environmental offences involving non-human environmental entities in the NSW land and environment court*. Master of Laws (LLM) thesis, University of Tasmania.
White, R. (2017b). Reparative justice, environmental crime and penalties for the powerful. *Crime, Law and Social Change, 67*(2), 117–132.
White, R. (2017c). Experts and expertise in the land and environment court. *Australian Journal of Forensic Sciences, 49*(4), 392–402.
White, R. (2018a). Critical green criminology. In W. DeKeseredy & M. Dragiewicz (Eds.), *Routledge handbook of critical criminology*. Routledge.
White, R. (2018b). Ecocentrism and criminal justice. *Theoretical Criminology, 22*(3), 342–362.
White, R., Perrone, S., & Howes, L. (2019). *Crime, criminality and criminal justice*. Oxford University Press.

5

Standing Trial for Lily: How Open Rescue Activists Mobilize Their Criminal Prosecutions for Animal Liberation

Hadar Aviram

Introduction

A moving YouTube video depicts the rescue of Lily, a delightful piglet, from a factory farm (Direct Action Everywhere, 2017). A man wearing a flashlight on his forehead is seen entering a dark, cramped, filthy facility, taking Lily in his arms and gently removing her from the premises. He is later depicted caring for her, offering her medication as he hugs her in a pink blanket, and escorting her into the sunshine. The text reads:

> This is the story of a piglet who was saved, and of a man who found her in a cage. Lily's mom gave birth at a "crate-free" farm, but the bars stopped her from caring for her babies. The ground was so hard that she couldn't sleep. The air was so dirty that she couldn't breathe. One day, Lily's foot got caught and injured. Her mom tried to break her out, but

H. Aviram (✉)
UC Hastings College of the Law, San Francisco, CA, USA
e-mail: aviramh@uchastings.edu

J. Gacek and R. Jochelson (eds.), *Green Criminology and the Law*, Palgrave Studies in Green Criminology,
https://doi.org/10.1007/978-3-030-82412-9_5

> she couldn't escape. Then, a strange man arrived. He heard Lily's mom crying. He saw Lily couldn't walk, and he knew she had to be saved. He said goodbye to Lily's mom. He promised to give Lily a better life. And Lily came back to life. She learned to play; she stepped into the sun. She had the life her mom dreamed.

The "strange man" is Wayne Hsiung, co-founder of Direct Action Everywhere (DxE), an animal liberation organization. The video tells a moving story of rescue, redemption, and a new start to life. It exemplifies the twofold purpose of open rescue: to save lives while documenting the animal suffering inherent in large-scale industrialized food production. Open rescue is unique for its "openness" and "semi-respectability" (Milligan, 2017): by videotaping themselves without concealment, the rescuers "take full responsibility for the fact that you did it and you openly publicize the fact that you did it" (Bryant, 2004). A corollary of the overt nature of the action is that open rescuers face the risk of criminal charges, convictions, and incarceration. From the perspective of a factory farmer or a county prosecutor, Wayne is (allegedly) a criminal, having broken into a private facility, documented it, and removed the owner's property without permission and with the intent to permanently deprive. Lily is property. And we are watching incontrovertible proof of criminal trespass and larceny.

Green criminology joins a family of critical and radical theories in its three-decade mission to challenge and expand the boundaries of criminal categories (Lynch, 2020). Like other works on crimes of the powerful (Barak, 2005), the study of "green crimes," whose definition is still debated in the field, transcends the boundaries of formal criminal law (Lynch et al., 2017) and expands its concerns to many forms of harm that are not formally criminalized (Potter, 2010) or that are inadequately vindicated by law enforcement (Nurse, 2017; White, 2013). Accordingly, a key mission of green criminology is to draw attention to structures of power and inequality that hinder criminalization and enforcement, and particularly to parties harmed by "green crimes" who have no voice or adequate representation, such as underserved, disenfranchised human communities (Brisman, 2009; Johnson et al., 2016; Ruggiero & South, 2013) and nonhuman entities (Spapens et al., 2016) such as nonhuman animals (Beirne, 1999, 2018; Eliason, 2012; McMullan & Perrier, 2002), plants (Kishor & Damania, 2007), and the ecosystem (Brisman, 2018; Kramer, 2013). These works generally find that these types of harms are undercriminalized; while many of them call for further involvement of formal law in vindicating environmental harms (Favre, 2005), others doubt the efficacy and desirability of criminalization and punitiveness (Marceau, 2019).

Where formal law is already deeply involved (arguably overinvolved!) is on the other side of the coin: the overcriminalization of behavior that *protects* nonhuman victims and *upholds* environmental values. Some works have tackled the overbroad and oppressive definitions of ecoterrorism (Buell, 2009; Long, 2004; Hirsch-Hoefler & Mudde, 2014); others provided ethnographical understandings of so-called "ecoterrorists" (Pike, 2017). In the specific context of pro-animal action, several works critiqued the framework of ag-gag laws (Wilson, 2014; Marceau, 2015; Sanders, 2019), and have offered defenses of legal violations consisting of direct action and open rescue (James, 2014; Tremblay, 2012). These works join long traditions in legal and socio-legal civil rights scholarships, which vindicate protest and civil disobedience (e.g., Barkan, 1979; Bayles, 1970; Hall, 1971; Macfarlane, 1968; Morawetz, 1986; Munk, 1971).

This chapter's contribution to the latter "wing" of environmental criminology ties these works to the socio-legal concept of legal consciousness. Focusing on social movements (Cramer, 2021; Kirkland, 2008; Kostiner, 2003) as well as on everyday life (Ewick & Silbey, 1998; Merry, 1990; Sarat & Kearns, 1995), legal consciousness literature examines the role of law in people's worldviews (how individuals understand society, their place in it, and their position relative to others), perceptions (how individuals make sense of specific events), and decisions (how individuals decide when and how to act, including both deliberate choices to use the law and choices to leave it dormant: Chua & Engel, 2019).

In the context of social movements for animals, legal consciousness interrogates the shift from animal ethics and philosophies (Regan, 2005; Singer, 1975) toward a legal and political turn manifested in the increased deployment of "rights language" (Francione, 2015; Milligan, 2015). In *Unleashing Rights*, Helena Silverstein (1996) found that, despite its limitations, the concept of rights was widely deployed in the animal rights movements, complete with legal mobilization through legislation and litigation. She also found an important distinction in the use of "rights": when rights were deployed in official legal contexts, such as in litigation, they were used in their formal, limiting meaning—not in the context of animals' rights, but in the context of the activists' First Amendment rights to free speech and protest. However, in movement advocacy outside the courtroom, the animal advocacy community freely used rights language to frame the debate and galvanize activists, expanding the narrow definition of "rights" to action on behalf of animals beyond formal legal institutions.

"Rights talk" is debated and criticized in animal ethics scholarship, which raises concerns that it frames the debate in terms of utilitarianism (Garner, 2008) and perpetuates either an anthropocentric and anthropomorphizing perspective (Carbone, 2004; O'Neill, 1997) or mechanical quests for animal equality (Milligan, 2015); other concerns are that movements, especially in the U.S. context, tend to recur to "rights talk" in "an extremely confused and contradictory way," which "erodes the distinction between 'animal rights' and 'animal welfare'" with "significant implications for the movement's law reform goals" (Bourke, 2009). Yet others worry that prosecuting and punishing animal cruelty in the name of "animal rights" is not only ineffective, but a misrepresentation of the interests of animals (Marceau, 2019). Despite these critiques, animal rights are rhetorically persuasive; as Sunstein and Nussbaum (2004) argue, "every reasonable person believes in animal rights," a position supported by Gallup polls in which a third of Americans believe animals should be given the same rights as people, while 62% say they deserve some protection but can still be used for the benefit of humans (Rifkin, 2015).

The utility of the legal rights framework to the pro-animal movement is obvious when applied to the quest for protective laws or for convictions and punishment for animal cruelty; what is less obvious is how useful this concept is in the context of open rescue, when the activists themselves are on the receiving end of the criminal justice system. This tension between operating against the law and seeking to create legal change animates this project, which examines the legal consciousness of DxE activists facing prosecutions for open rescue from factory farms. Using ethnographic methods and legal analysis, I address the following research questions: How do open rescuers of animals from factory farms perceive and conceptualize their own actions with reference to the law? How do their open rescue plans and legal strategy—especially their plans to rely on the necessity defense at their criminal trials—reflect their perception and serve their animal liberation mission? And, normatively, should their framework be embraced by the animal liberation community?

To answer these questions, I analyzed primary and secondary sources to gauge the theoretical underpinnings of open rescue and the extent to which existing theories of animal welfare, rights, and liberation are helpful for crafting and assessing the necessity of defense. I also turned to ethnographic tools: between 2016 and 2019, I conducted interviews with activists and lawyers, participated in animal rights events, lobbying, and protests, and conducted social media analysis to learn how the activists themselves locate their actions with respect to the existing and desirable legal structure. To protect my interlocutors from the possibility that I would be required to provide incriminating information, I refrained from directly participating in illegal activities and from learning about such plans *ex ante*; my knowledge of open rescue comes from interviews recounting past actions, and my first-hand observations were limited to purely legal activities such as meetings with lawmakers, bill drafting, protests protected by the First Amendment, conversations about trial strategies, and attendance at public talks and events. Given my personal sympathies with the animal liberation movement (I am vegan and participated in animal advocacy prior to the inception of this project), I tried to balance my "native" sympathies toward my research subjects (Kanuha, 2000; O'Reilly, 2009) with briefs and materials by farmer organizations, as well as blog posts and other materials by animal rights activists who, for various reasons, were critical of DxE as an organization and of its open rescue actions. I also exercised special caution regarding my involvement in crafting legal strategy for the activists' trials: even though much of my fieldwork involved conversation with activists and their lawyers about trial strategy, I opted for caution whenever situations I witnessed could be interpreted as raising attorney–client privilege and am reporting only on situations in which my status as a researcher was clear, lawyers and clients were not discussing tactics in my presence, and no risk was forthcoming to my subjects.

Doing Crime, Courting Legality: The Place of Lawbreaking in the DxE Activist Space

DxE's founding mission is to "achieve revolutionary social and political change for animals in one generation." An abolitionist, animal liberationist organization, DxE seeks to bring an end to "the mass torture and killing of nonhuman animals and the blatant disregard for their home - our planet - as well as the unjust and oppressive institutions and ideologies that harm all animals" (DxE website, 2013). The movement's reading materials, as well as my observation, indicate that the activists' commitment to lawbreaking is part and parcel of their mission, which is legal in nature and involved a variety of lawful strategies and actions. Indeed, the lawbreaking itself is designed to bring about legal change, which poses challenges of legitimacy and credibility for the movement.

DxE's "forty-year roadmap to animal liberation" (2016) envisions two simultaneous, parallel processes: the gradual delegitimization and outlawing of the consumption and exploitation of animals, and the gradual legitimization of open rescue. For example, by 2030, the roadmap envisions a normalization of animal rights within the progressive, activism-saturated city, cultural stigma on eating animals, and support from national political figures as well as mainstream civil rights organizations. Year 2035 would see a state-level referendum banning the production and sale of animal flesh, as well as support for open rescue becoming a common position among progressive politicians. By 2040, the roadmap envisions animal liberation statutes passing at the state level, anti-animal rights thinking perceived as "oppressive," and support for open rescue becoming the default position among progressive politicians and the media. In 2045, DxE hopes to see at least one national government fund a network of sanctuaries as reparations and support for open rescue crossing party lines; in 2050, animal rights would reach a point of national consensus, sanctuaries would become prominent, and lawsuits to recognize animal personhood would become common. Finally, by 2055, the roadmap predicts a Constitutional Bill of Animal Rights passing in one or more states or countries, a "Marshall Plan" for animals devoting a small percentage of the GDP to resettle animals in lifetime sanctuary, and significant gains in addressing wild animal suffering.

DxE's activities include theatrical protests which, while controversial, enjoy First Amendment protections. The activists have staged funerals for turkeys at Whole Foods (Moyer, 2015), and some of them created controversy and experienced blowback (Folley, 2019) when they created disturbances in baseball games (Mahbubani, 2016) and political events (Piper & Matthews, 2020). But the group also engages in traditional legislative lobbying efforts. In March 2018, I joined DxE activists at San Francisco City Hall; after a protest outside, the activists testified about the fur industry at an open meeting. A small delegation of activists, including two lawyers (and myself), visited one of the City Supervisors, where they suggested legislative action the city could take for animals, including a detailed draft of a "right to know" law; this law would require the food retailers to clearly display adverts about the conditions in which animals used for food were raised.

This was not the only positive, collaborative encounter of DxE with the legislature. They met CA Assemblymember Ash Kalra to discuss statewide initiatives and pro-animal legislation, as well as convinced the Berkeley City Council to pass a resolution which supported them in their upcoming open rescue trials and called for an investigation of factory farms in Sonoma County, where said the open rescue took place (King, 2020). This resolution was framed using rights language, as a "rights to rescue" resolution.

These and other efforts on DxE's part demonstrate the complicated entanglement of the legal and the illegal in the organization's efforts. "The law" comes off not as a monolith of injustice to animals, but as a tool to violate and court, to challenge and to use, depending on context. But perceiving and addressing legality through these multiple perspectives is challenging because engaging in radical activism, which involves lawbreaking (albeit nonviolent), can hurt the organization's legitimacy, an essential social currency for a healthy partnership with the law.

When courting lawmakers, drafting bills, or testifying, DxE activists rely on several techniques to garner legitimacy. They rely on the legal expertise and resume of members with one foot in the legal community; they foster partnerships with supporters who are not vegan or not as committed to the vision of absolute animal liberation, who advance their goals in the short term; they do their homework, in terms of carefully drafting and vetting their bill proposals and resolutions before presenting them to legislators; and they downplay their involvement in lawbreaking activities, while highlighting the importance of legal developments for furthering the pro-animal cause.

Planning Lawbreaking, Courting Law Enforcement

Open rescue operations are designed to accomplish two things. First, the activists document farm conditions using 3D technology; the footage, which acts as "moral journalism" (Wiesslitz & Ashuri, 2011) by "bearing witness" (Tait, 2011) to the horrors of factory farming, is later used with VR equipment from a tech company partner when tabling at vegan festivals or guest speaking on campuses. Second, upon entering the factory farm, the activists identify animals that might imminently die or suffer irreparable harm unless removed from the facility, rescue them, and procure veterinary care for them. Beyond the value of the animals' lives, this boosts activist morale by inserting some optimism into emotionally devastating activist work; also, storytelling about individual animals, such as the aforementioned video and many others, serves as powerful public messaging.

Successfully conducting open rescue requires walking a legal tightrope between avoiding and courting law enforcement. A considerable degree of subterfuge is needed, not only because the activists seek to complete their mission (getting the animals and footage out of the facility) before getting caught, but also out of concern for the veterinarians and sanctuary owners who help care for the animals later, to whom the activists tell as little as possible about the provenance of the animals. This is necessary because the recent FBI search for the two piglets taken from Smithfield Farms involved a campaign of intimidation against the sanctuaries (Greenwald, 2017). The efforts to avoid detection are evident in this activist narrative of an open rescue:

> I joined a team of activists in walking onto a fur farm in the dead of night. Right as we approached the barn, a car pulled up. Someone flashed a flashlight right at us and we dropped to the ground. I thought, this is it, we're not getting inside now, but after a while he went into another building and we were so close, so we kept going. Inside, we found rotting corpses, and terrified babies rattling their tiny metal cages. One little girl calmed down immediately in our arms. She had no reason to trust humans, but she trusted us. And I just couldn't let her go, so I kept her in my arms when we left and carried her through the night, knowing that we could be caught at any moment if that worker just turned on a light, or if this baby got scared and jumped out of my arms. But she stayed calm with every fence we crossed. And all the way home. And now, Mabel is part of my family, and she is [my rabbit] Jonah's best friend. (DxE, 2019a)

At the same time, the activists anticipate, and welcome, engagement with law enforcement officials before and after the operation. In May 2018, the activists provided me with video clips from their documentation at chicken farms and asked me to provide them with a legal opinion on the application of the common law necessity defense, as well as a specific California Penal Code provision, to open rescue. This preemptive step indicated that they expected engagement with law enforcement; indeed, sometimes they actively seek it by calling the local sheriff and complaining about inhumane conditions (including violations of California's Agricultural Code) at the factory farm. The calls are invariably fruitless, as Jackie explained: "We call. We call all the time. Do you know how often we've called the D.A.? They do nothing. Then when the farm owner calls them, the sheriff shows up right away." The activists know this and make the calls anyway because, in their subsequent trials, they plan to rely on the necessity defense, one of whose conditions is the exhaustion of legal alternatives prior to the commission of the crime.

The activists expect to get arrested and are quite stoic—even humorous—about the eventual outcome of engagement with law enforcement (Sarah: "[The sheriff] looked for a moment like he was gonna let us go, but then sometime happened and he took us in." Wayne: "Did you know I'm banned from [walking into] Whole Foods?... It was a condition for dismissing the charges."). The prospect of arrest in itself is not perceived as a hardship. The hard-core activists that are involved in open rescue operations live in crowded activist houses, are indigent or close to indigent, and don't expect to spend longer behind bars. They seek and receive legal advice, but most of the know-how comes from activists within the movement with legal knowledge.

Courting Support: Criminal Prosecution as Landmark Litigation

DxE's public appeals for help and support with the upcoming criminal trials reflects a multifaceted construction of their lawbreaking: on one hand, portraying their criminality status as absurd and, on the other, presenting the criminal trials as landmark litigation for the animals ("a powerful case in support of the Right to Rescue"). By doing so, the activists blur the line between legality and illegality, exercising the freedom to frame and interpret their own trials outside the criminal context. This construction is evident in DxE's invitation to the 2019 Animal Rights California Convergence, a statewide gathering for activists:

> Animal rights activists are facing felony charges for rescuing animals from industrial farms in Sonoma County. Yet, in the face of this legal repression, the movement is growing. And this fall, we are uniting to make a powerful case in support of the Right to Rescue. We will take action to protect Rose, the chicken we rescued from a factory farm last September, and we will demand that our government respond to the public's concern for animals by protecting them under the law. This will be a global effort with people around the world asking for an Animal Bill of Rights!

> The California Convergence will include trainings to empower and educate yourself as an activist, community events to build connections in the animal rights movement, and a coordinated action with cities around the world asking legislators to support an Animal Bill of Rights. Let's change the world for animals. Are you ready? (DxE, 2019b)

Or the language in this donation pitch:

> In 2020, we are putting Big Ag on trial. I am facing 16 felony charges in 3 states for exposing criminal animal abuse at some of the most violent places on this planet. This year for the first time ever, DxE will have the opportunity to challenge animal abusing companies like Smithfield and Petaluma Poultry in front of a Judge, jury, and the entire world. What's our goal? To enshrine groundbreaking Right to Rescue legislation in the letter of the law. And you can help us make that dream a reality. (DxE, 2019c)

This approach confounds the nature of the cases, and the role of the defendants, with civil lawsuits pursued by DxE as plaintiffs, and is remarkably similar to their description of *DxE v. Diestel Turkey Ranch*, a lawsuit based on evidence from an open rescue operation (Moyer, 2015):

> In November 2015, Direct Action Everywhere released an investigation and open rescue of Diestel Turkey Ranch, the defendant in the lawsuit and a Whole Foods supplier. DxE found turkeys who had been mutilated by debeaking, who were diseased and struggling to breathe, and who had weakened and died.

> The activists openly rescued two birds in need of immediate medical care, rushed them to a veterinarian, and nursed them back to health. Meanwhile, Diestel continues to lie to the public by advertising its turkeys with misleading terms such as "thoughtfully raised". (DxE, 2019d)

This characterization of the cases as virtuous action against the real criminals—factory farms—is, of course, hotly contested by their mainstream adversaries; Diestel farmers and Whole Foods executives cast them as radicals, whose goal "isn't farm animal welfare but rather a total end to animal agriculture and meat consumption... Everything they say, do and show is produced with that specific goal in-mind" (Moyer, 2015). Humane Watch, a website opposing the animal rights movements, refers to the activists as criminals and terrorists, and even condemns more moderate organizations, such as the Humane Society of the United States, for associating with DxE activists (Humane Watch, 2018). These moderate organizations, in turn, are hostile toward DxE's lawbreaking tactics (Marceau, 2019).

The reservedness, and sometimes downright hostility, of the animal rights movement toward DxE might explain why they have been unable to secure movement lawyers for legal representation (Bryant, 2011; Marceau, 2019) and instead are represented by generalist criminal lawyers. When I asked animal rights lawyers, including instructors in law school animal rights clinics, whether they would represent people such as the DxE defendants, the answer was a resounding "no," and the universal explanation was, "because it's a criminal case." Astonished that the distinction between animal rights and criminal cases was not as clear to me as it was to them, the lawyers explained that most of their movement litigation expertise was done in the civil context. Criminal practice, by contrast, was perceived as a distinctive field, in which they "wouldn't know what they were doing." The concern was twofold: one, that it would be unethical to expose the defendants to the real consequences of criminal convictions and punishment without the appropriate expertise, and that criminal cases were not a suitable forum for the landmark-litigation ideological theater sought by the activists, because any run-of-the-mill criminal judge would find effrontery in a defendant's attempt to turn their "criminal case" into a "soapbox."

"Compassion Should Never Be Illegal": The Necessity Defense as a Vehicle for Ideological Litigation

At their trials, the DxE defendants plan to rely on the necessity defense—a criminal justification (Greenawalt, 1984) for situations in which a person violates the law in order to prevent or mitigate a greater harm that would occur save for the legal violation (Christie, 1999). Most U.S. states have not codified the necessity defense; it is, however, available through case law, and sometimes explicitly articulated only in jury instructions (e.g., Judicial Council of California, 2020). Prevailing in a necessity defense requires proof that the offender acted in an emergency to which they did not contribute, under circumstances that would lead a reasonable person to believe the action was necessary to prevent significant bodily harm to themselves or someone else, with no adequate legal recourse, and did not create a greater danger than the one avoided (Model Penal Code 3.02; *Regina v. Dudley and Stephens*; Fuller, 1949). Because a successful necessity defense affirms a person's moral code above written law, it "provides a practical means of radical change; moreover, it does so within the confines of existing political institutions" (Martin, 2005).

Between the 1960s and 1980s, political activists successfully argued necessity in lower courts (Aldridge & Stark, 1986; Climate Defense Project, 2017; NLG, 1985; Pearson, 1992; Quigley, 2003), but courts became more hostile to "political necessity" defenses following Ninth Circuit decision in *U.S. v. Schoon* (1993). *Schoon* distinguished between "direct" civil disobedients—that is, to people who violated the very law against which they were protesting and were thus eligible to raise the necessity defense—and "indirect" protests, in which the defense was unavailable (Cavallaro, 1993; Schopp, 1996). Open rescuers arguably commit both direct and indirect civil disobedience: they challenge both the exploitation and cruelty of the animal industry (indirectly, through a trespass onto the factory farms' premises), and ag-gag laws (directly, through the documentation). As James (2014) explains, activists could convincingly satisfy the elements of the defense: imminent harm to the animals could be proven by their condition at the factory farm. Intent to prevent harm (rather than to steal a thing of value) could be proven through the negligible financial value of a sick and dying animal. Causality between the action and the harm prevention would be proven through the exigency of saving sick animals; significance of the prevented harm would be shown via proof of legal violations of animal cruelty laws by the factory farms.

But the activists face an uphill battle bringing this argument to court, not only because of judges' hesitance to introduce ideological defenses and turn the trial into political theater, but also because the success of the defense hinges upon introduction of horrifying 3D footage as evidence, which factory farms are likely to argue is more prejudicial than probative (Douglas et al., 1997). Even if allowed to present the evidence at trial, the activists still need to persuade juries in farming communities, where the trials are scheduled take place, that the balance of evils favored the open rescue—a tall order anywhere given the low value of animal lives in mainstream society (for these and other reasons, some scholars argue that in the anti-nuclear activism context—which bears some important similarities to direct action for animals—defendants should not settle for the traditional necessity arguments and should instead embrace a full-fledged political argument "legitimate civil resistance" [Khoday, 2018]).

These hurdles do not deter the activists who, in the tradition of civil disobedience movements that preceded them, "[do] not define winning as getting a not guilty verdict" (NLG, 1985); indeed, for the activists, having the opportunity to show the footage to rural jurors is in itself the point of the trial. My interviewees repeatedly mentioned the Gallup poll in which most people reported support for animal rights, expressing confidence that, when given the chance, juries would broadly interpret "significant harm to someone" to include animals. But to them, this was less an instrumental path toward a legal victory, and more an opportunity for public education; for this reason, they declined plea offers that would carry no prison time, pushing toward trials and risking conviction and incarceration. On the eve of the COVID-19 pandemic, before the trials were postponed, the activists were organizing a strong courtroom presence in DxE t-shirts:

> Repeated evidence of criminal animal cruelty has been exposed at factory farms in Sonoma County. Legislators and government officials have been contacted dozens of times with this footage and have taken no action. Instead, Sonoma County officials have arrested the nonviolent activists who exposed this cruelty and enacted their right to rescue suffering animals.
>
> Jon Frohnmayer and Rachel Zeigler are going to court for their preliminary hearing on eight felonies they're facing for trying to rescue dying animals. Evidence will be presented on both sides and the judge may make a decision.
>
> We need YOU to come to court *in your blue DxE shirt* and show your support for these activists. We must demonstrate that the public cares about animals and supports activists who make sacrifices to save them. Take off work or school if you can!
>
> Post if you need us to coordinate rides.
>
> WHERE: Meet us inside the courthouse at 600 Administration Drive in Santa Rosa. Come through the metal detectors and up the stairs.
>
> WHAT TO EXPECT: We will need to be quiet and respectful in the courtroom and all phones will have to be turned off. We may have to wait patiently for the case to be called. There is no talking or whispering allowed while the judge is present. We will be representing our movement as respectable, nonviolent, and kind throughout the event.
>
> WEAR/BRING: Wear a blue DxE shirt. We'll bring extras for people who don't have one. Bring as little stuff with you as possible because we will have to go through metal detectors to enter. Do not bring signs or other protest materials. Do not wear shorts, tank tops, or open toed shoes. (DxE, 2020)

If mainstream animal rights activists were concerned about the perverse effects of ideological displays in court, the activists were welcoming them, and this attitude also characterized their reactions to the prospect of incarceration.

Doing Time for the Animals: The Prospect of Incarceration as Martyrdom, Kinship, and Retreat

Because the DxE activist trials have not yet come to a conclusion, the activists' constructions of the possibility of incarceration do not reflect actual experience behind bars, and my conversations with the activists belied considerable naivete about the conditions in California's prisons and jails. Some activists saw prison as an opportunity to "meditate a lot" and some said that, because their current living situations were already communal and nonmaterialistic, incarceration would not overwhelmingly impact their quality of life. The activists romanticized the prospect of incarceration in other ways.

First, publicly and in private conversations, activists mentioned the long legacy of dissenters and civil disobedients who served time behind bars in the furtherance of racial, gender, and class equality; Martin Luther King, Jr. and Emmaline Pankhurst were the two names I heard mentioned most often.

Second, my study was conducted against the backdrop of internal conflict and a change of leadership within DxE. Some activists—primarily people active in other social justice scenes—experienced the leaders' emphasis on "calling in" as opposed to "calling out" an anathema, and interpreted them as a cultish strategy to quell and silence opposition (Adams, 2018; Gethen, 2018). The movement was also dealing with the public and internal fallout from several controversial incidents, one of which saw a young White male activist jumping on stage and snatching the microphone from Kamala Harris at a political event and speaking about cruelty to animals; there were understandable concerns that this incident, which many read as an example of White patriarchy. Ruminating on the prospect of incarceration, one leader constructed it as a retreat experience, saying, "frankly, jail seems like it would be a nice break from the stress I'm experiencing now."

Finally, incarceration offered the prospect of transcending the human–nonhuman animal divide. In *For the Wild*, Sarah Pike (2013) identifies the roots of committed activism in youth or adolescence; her interviewees often express a sense of wonder about nature and animals from childhood. intermingled with deep grief about the destruction of the Earth and the suffering of animals. Many activists tell "stories of co-becoming with nonhuman others and experiencing the pain and suffering of those others" (Pike, 2013, p. 72).

This sense of "co-becoming," combined with DxE's advocacy perspective comparing animals to humans, imbues the prospect of incarceration with a sense of solidarity between them and the animals. In a Facebook post from September 12, an activist reported that "[a]ctivists [were] ASSAULTED while exposing animal cruelty at the largest pig farm in France. Imagine the violence these pigs face on a daily basis...." In my years of studying and advocating about prison conditions, I've often heard references to inmates being treated "like animals." For DxE activists, who document the horrors experienced by farm animals, these analogies seem more like euphemisms, as the realities faced by the animals are far worse. Incarceration is therefore perceived as the minimal amount of sacrifice owed to the cause, incomparable to what the animals are suffering. An activist facing felony charges for open rescues in Utah reflected on the consequences of his possible conviction for rescuing turkeys:

> A google news search for "Utah prison" shows weekly incidents of inmates catching new murder charges for killing each other, illustrating just how horrific, unjust, unsafe and corrupt our prison systems are, but even if I end up there, I'll be infinitely more lucky than any of the 46 million turkeys who are being killed for this week's "holiday". (Picklesimer, 2019)

Conclusion

My findings underscore the importance of incorporating direct action and pro-animal lawbreaking into green criminology inquiries. The discipline's focus on harms that should be crimes (but are not) would benefit from a counterpart interest in actions that are crimes (but, according to the activists, should not be). Legal consciousness, in particular, offers a window into the potential usefulness of criminal law as a "green" vehicle for change—not merely (or even primarily) through criminal prosecutions, but also through affirmative defenses.

The importance of lawbreaking as a green transformation tool evokes the social movement concept of the "radical flank effect" (Robnett et al., 2015). Under certain conditions, radical flanks such as DxE confer advantages upon the larger social movements to which they belong. First, radical actions make moderates within the movement appear more reasonable to outside actors by shifting the boundaries of discourse; second, and relatedly, radical actions sometimes create crises that lead government actors to collaborate with moderates. In that sense, more radicalism yields more offers to work with moderates (Baron et al., 2016), particularly when the distinction between the "unreasonable" radicals and the "plausibly cooperative" moderates are salient to outsiders, when moderates themselves publicly reject radical action and capitalize on their perception as the "reasonable" flank (Freeman, 1975), and when the timing radical actions coincide with a tide of social change that tips the balance in favor of cooperation with the larger cause.

This project's takeaways are, therefore, fourfold. For green criminologists, it affirms the important role of law in general, and activists' engagement with legal doctrine, to comprehend criminologically relevant behavior that is not always the focus of the discipline. For social movement scholarship, this project highlights the importance of taking criminal law into account as a form of "political case." Legal consciousness scholars in particular would do well to pay attention not only to when and how the law manifests in the plans and strategies of activists, but also *what kind of law* is at play, and how said law is framed to achieve political goals. For activists, the study highlights the importance of a broad definition of what is useful for the movement; the versatility of tactics within DxE shows the convergence of legality and illegality in a struggle toward profound social change. And most importantly, for factory-farmed animals, this project highlights the commitment and versatility of tactics that can be employed in their defense; not all of these tactics operate in exactly the way the activists hope, but in the broader context of the animal liberation movement, each shade of activism contributes to the overall goal.

References

Adams, C. (2018). Why I am boycotting events if DxE is also an invited speaker. *Carol Adams blog*, April 21, 2018. https://caroljadams.com/carol-adams-blog/why-i-am-boycotting-events-if-dxe-is-also-an-invited-speaker.

Aldridge, R., & Stark, V. (1986). Nuclear war, citizen intervention, and the necessity defense. *Santa Clara Law Review, 26*(2), 299–353.

Barak, G. (2005). The crimes of the powerful and the globalization of crime. *Revista Brasiliera De Direito, 11*(2), 104–114.

Barkan, S. E. (1979). Strategic, tactical and organizational dilemmas of the protest movement against nuclear power. *Social Problems, 27,* 19–37.

Baron, D. P., Neale, M., & Rao, H. (2016). Extending nonmarket strategy: Political economy and the radical flank effect in private politics. *Strategy Science, 1*(2), 105–126.

Bayles, M. (1970). The justifiability of civil disobedience. *The Review of Metaphysics, 24*, 3–20.

Beirne, P. (1999). For a nonspeciest criminology: Animal abuse as an object of study. *Criminology, 37*(1), 117–148.

Beirne, P. (2018). *Murdering animals: Writings on theriocide, homicide and nonspeciesist criminology*. Palgrave.

Bourke, D. (2009). The use and misuse of "rights talk" by the animal rights movement. In P. Sankoff & S. White (Eds.), *Animal law in Australasia: A new dialogue* (pp. 128–150). The Federation Press.

Brisman, A. (2009). It takes green to be green: Environmental elitism, "ritual displays," and conspicuous non-consumption. *North Dakota Law Review, 85*(2), 327–370.

Brisman, A. (2018). Representing the "invisible crime" of climate change in an age of post-truth. *Theoretical Criminology, 22*(3), 468–491.

Bryant, T. (2004). Trauma, law, and advocacy for animals. *Journal of Animal Law and Ethics, 1*(6).

Bryant, T. (2011). Trauma, law, and advocacy for animals. *Journal of Animal Law and Ethics, 1,* 63–138.

Buell, L. (2009). What is called ecoterrorism. *Gramma: Journal of Theory and Criticism, 16,* 153–166.

Carbone, L. (2004). *What animals want: Expertise and advocacy in laboratory animal welfare*. Oxford University Press.

Cavallaro, Jr., J. L. (1993). The demise of the political necessity defense: Indirect civil disobedience and United States v. Schoon. *California Law Review, 81,* 367–368.

Christie, G. C. (1999). The defense of necessity considered from the legal and moral points of view. *Duke Law Journal, 48,* 975–1042.

Climate Defense Project, Political Necessity Defense Jurisdiction Guide, February 27, 2017. https://drive.google.com/file/d/1mMSZyX_EaU-I_j97lH1jOWINlGTvkXXR/view.

Cramer, R. (2021). *Birthing a movement: Midwives, law, and the politics of reproductive care*. Stanford University Press.

Chua, L. M., & Engel, D. (2019). Legal consciousness reconsidered. *Annual Review of Law and Social Science, 15,* 336–353.

Dass, R. (2010 [1971]). *Be here now*. HarperONE.

Direct Action Everywhere. "Bunny Saved From Becoming A Fur Coat", You Tube, June 20, 2019. https://www.youtube.com/watch?v=1noHWuSUISE&t=1s.

Direct Action Everywhere v. Diestel Turkey Ranch (2017). https://www.berkeleyside.com/wp-content/uploads/2019/12/2017.01.30-Direct-Action-Everywhere-v.-Diestel-Turkey-Ranch-Complaint-filed.pdf.

Direct Action Everywhere, "Piglet Refuses to Give Up", YouTube, July 5, 2017. https://www.youtube.com/watch?v=jGb2y8kLms4.

Direct Action Everywhere Facebook Page, "DxE Vs. Big Ag: Help us win the Right to Rescue in 2020!" November 4, 2019. https://www.facebook.com/donate/2537356073158817/2537356106492147/.

Direct Action Everywhere Facebook Page, "Support the Right to Rescue Resolution at Berkeley City Council!" November 12, 2019. https://www.facebook.com/events/1231-addison-st-berkeley-ca-94702-united-states/support-the-right-to-rescue-resolution-at-berkeley-city-council/2354335144880811/.

Direct Action Everywhere Facebook Page, "Pack the Courtroom for Open Rescue Activists!" February 20, 2020. https://www.facebook.com/events/376672216575126/.

Direct Action Everywhere, Forty-Year Roadmap to Animal Liberation, Google Docs, published September 2016. https://docs.google.com/document/d/1YN7KpuShiZItqVuQtWv6ykrjrNv6rAnmjVOcsofRj0I/edit.

Direct Action Everywhere, New Activist Handbook, February 2018. https://static1.squarespace.com/static/515cca87e4b0bca14d767b61/t/5a7a8423e4966bd8be1f7ccb/1517978698932/Activist+Handbook+v4.pdf.

Douglas, K., Lyon, D., & Ogloff, J. (1997). The impact of graphic photographic evidence on Mock Jurors' decisions in a murder trial: Probative or prejudicial? *Law & Human Behavior, 21*, 485–501.

DxE. (2016). The Strategic Roadmap to Animal Liberation. DxE. https://docs.google.com/document/d/e/2PACX-1vRsSeDBvp0Q00kRuXXXBdoMprEe6vTOitveFYosZrbR21vSKRu79SexI5-l3Qe3r_n_sxE-hzrHPMIQ/pub.

DxE. (2019a). DxE, "Bunny Saved from Being a Fur Coat", YouTube. June20, 2019. https://www.youtube.com/watch?v=1noHWuSUISE.

DxE. (2019b). DxE Facebook Page, Animal Rights Convergence Event Page. https://www.facebook.com/events/2705734512821134/?active_tab=about.

DxE. (2019c). DxE donation pitch, Facebook. https://www.facebook.com/donate/2537356073158817/2537356106492147/.

DxE. (2019d). DxE Press Release, Animal Advocacy Network Sues Whole Foods Turkey Farm for "Humane" Fraud. https://www.legacy.directactioneverywhere.com/press-release-diestel-lawsuit.

DxE. (2020). DxE, Pack the Court Facebook Event. https://www.facebook.com/events/376672216575126/.

DxE website. (2013). DxE Core Values. DxE. https://www.directactioneverywhere.com/core-values.

Eliason, S. (2012). From the king's deer to a capitalist commodity: A social historical analysis of the poaching law. *International Journal of Comparative and Applied Criminal Justice, 36*(2), 133–148.

Ewick, P., & Silbey, S. (1998). *The common place of law: Stories from everyday life*. University of Chicago Press.

Favre, D. (2005). Judicial recognition of the rights of animals—A new tort. *Michigan State Law Review, 2005*, 333–366.

Folley, A. (2019). DxE Protester Takes Mic from Kamala Harris While Onstage at Event. *The Hill*, June 1. https://thehill.com/homenews/house/446498-protester-takes-mic-from-kamala-harris-while-on-stage-at-event.

Francione, G. (2015). *Animal rights: The abolitionist approach*. Exempla Press.

Freeman, J. (1975). *The politics of women's liberation: A case study of an emerging social movement and its relation to the policy process*. Addison-Wesley Longman Limited.

Fuller, L. L. (1949). The case of the speluncean explorers. *Harvard Law Review, 62*(4), 616–645.

Garner, R. (2008). The politics of animal rights. *British Politics, 3*(1), 110–119.

Gethen, P. A. (2018). My adventures in animal rights activism. *Medium*, April 23. https://funcrunch.medium.com/my-adventures-in-animal-rights-activism-9715e26db222.

Greenawalt, K. (1984). The perplexing borders of justification and excuse. *Columbia Law Review, 84*(8), 1897–1927.
Greenwald, G. (2017). The FBI's Hunt for two missing piglets reveals the Federal Cover-Up of Barbaric factory farms. *The Intercept*, October 5. https://theintercept.com/2017/10/05/factory-farms-fbi-missing-piglets-animal-rights-glenn-greenwald/.
Hall, R. T. (1971). Legal toleration of civil disobedience. *Ethics, 81,* 128–142.
Hirsch-Hoefler, S., & Mudde, C. (2014). "Ecoterrorism": Terrorist threat or political ploy? *Studies in Conflict & Terrorism, 37*(7), 586–603.
Humane Watch. (2018). PETA Defendes Extremist Group's Illegal Activity. *Humane Watch Website*, July 3, 2018. https://humanewatch.org/peta-defends-extremist-groups-illegal-activity/.
James, J. (2014). When is rescue necessary? Applying the necessity defense to the rescue of animals. *Stanford Journal of Animal Law and Policy, 7*(1), 1–51.
Johnson, H., South, N., & Walters, R. (2016). The commodification and exploitation of fresh water: Property, human rights and green criminology. *International Journal of Law, Crime and Justice, 44,* 146–162.
Judicial Council of California Criminal Jury Instructions 2020. https://www.courts.ca.gov/partners/documents/CALCRIM_2020.pdf.
Kanuha, V. K. (2000). 'Being' Native versus 'Going Native': Conducting social work research as an insider. *Social Work, 45*(6), 439–447.
Kirkland, A. (2008). *Fat rights: Dilemmas of difference and personhood*. New York University Press.
Kostiner, I. (2003). Evaluating legality: Toward a cultural approach to the study of law and social change. *Law & Society Review, 37*(2), 323–368.
Khoday, A. (2018). 'We have to give up business as usual': Anti-nuclear protests and the construction of a defence of 'legitimate civil resistance'. In J. Black-Branch & D. Fleck (Eds.), *Nuclear non-proliferation in international law—Volume IV*. T.M.C. Asser Press.
King, C. (2020). As Berkeley residents face felony trial, Berkeley city council affirms its 'right to rescue' animals from abuse. *The Daily Californian,* January 28, 2020. https://www.dailycal.org/2020/01/28/animals-rights/.
Kishor, N., & Damania, R. (2007). Crime and justice in the Garden of Eden: Improving governance and reducing corruption in the forestry sector. In J. E. Campos & S. Pradhan (Eds.), *The many faces of corruption: Tracking vulnerabilities at the sector level*. World Bank Publications.
Kramer, R. (2013). Carbon in the atmosphere and power in America: Climate change as state-corporate crime. *Journal of Crime and Justice, 36*(2), 153–170.

Long, D. (2004). *Ecoterrorism.* Facts on File.

Lynch, M. J. (2020). Green criminology and environmental crime: Criminology that matters in the age of global ecological collapse. *Journal of White Collar and Corporate Crime, 1,* 50–61.

Lynch, M. J., Long, M. A., Stretesky, P. B., & Barrett, K. L. (2017). *Green criminology: Crime, justice, and the environment.* University of California Press.

Macfarlane, L. J. (1968). Justifying political disobedience. *Ethics, 79,* 24–55.

Mahbubani, R. (2016). Animal rights activist speaks out after being Tackled by San Francisco Giants Left Fielder Angel Pagan. *NBC Bay Area,* October 2. https://www.nbcbayarea.com/news/sports/animal-rights-activist-speaks-out-after-being-tackled-by-san-francisco-giants-left-fielder-angel-pagan/126478/.

Marceau, J. F. (2015). Ag gag past, present, and future. *Seattle University Law Review, 38,* 1317–1344.

Marceau, J. F. (2019). *Beyond cages: Animal law and criminal punishment.* Cambridge University Press.

Martin, S. P. (2005). The radical necessity defense. *University of Cincinnati Law Review, 73*(4), 1527–1607.

McMullan, J., & Perrier, D. (2002). Lobster poaching and the ironies of law enforcement. *Law & Society Review, 36*(4), 679.

Merry, S. E. (1990). *Getting justice and getting even: Legal consciousness among working-class Americans.* University of Chicago Press.

Milligan, T. (2015). The political turn in animal ethics. *Politics and Animals, 1,* 6–15.

Milligan, T. (2017). Animal rescue as civil disobedience. *Res Publica, 23,* 281–298.

Morawetz, T. (1986). Reconstructing the criminal defenses: The significance of justification. *The Journal of Criminal Law and Criminology, 77,* 277–307.

Moyer, J. (2015). Whole foods thanksgiving turkeys endure 'horrific conditions' at Calif. farm, activists say. *Washington Post*, November 4. https://www.washingtonpost.com/news/morning-mix/wp/2015/11/24/whole-foods-thanksgiving-turkeys-endure-horrific-conditions-at-calif-farm-animal-rights-activists-say/.

Munk, A. W. (1971). Civil disobedience: Conscience, tactics, and the law. *Annals of the American Academy of Political and Social Science, 397,* 211–212.

NLG. (1985). Creative Defenses in Civil Disobedience Cases. *Guild Prac. 42*(1).

Nurse, A. (2017). Green criminology: Shining a critical lens on environmental harm. *Palgrave Communications, 3*(1), 1–4.
O'Neill, O. (1997). Environmental values, anthropocentrism, and specieism. *Environmental Values, 6*(2), 127–142.
O'Reilly, K. (2009). *Key concepts in ethnography*. Sage.
Pearson, Jr. James O., Annotation. (1992). "Choice of Evils," Necessity, Duress, or Similar Defense to State or Local Criminal Charges Based on Acts of Public Protest. 3 A.L.R.5th, 521, 533–537.
Picklesimer, P. (2019). Facebook post, November 25.
Pike, S. (2013). *For the wild: Ritual and commitment in radical eco-activism*. University of California Press.
Pike, S. (2017). *For the wild: Ritual and commitment in radical eco-activism*. University of California Press.
Piper, K., & Matthews, D. (2020). The animal rights protesters disrupting Joe Biden and Bernie Sanders Rallies, explained. *Vox*, March 3. https://www.vox.com/future-perfect/2020/2/19/21142969/bernie-sanders-joe-biden-protesters-vegan-activists.
Potter, G. (2010). What is green criminology? *Sociology Review*, 8–12. http://www.greencriminology.org/monthly/WhatIsGreenCriminology.pdf.
Quigley, W. P. (2003). The necessity defense in civil disobedience cases: Bring it to the Jury. *New England Law Review, 38*, 24–26.
Regan, T. (2005). *Empty cages: Facing the challenge of animal rights*. Rowman & Littlefield.
Regina v. Dudley and Stephens, 14 QBD 273 DC (1884).
Rifkin, R. (2015). In U.S., more say animals should have same rights as people, Gallup social and policy issues, May 18. https://news.gallup.com/poll/183275/say-animals-rights-people.aspx#:~:text=Gallup%20first%20asked%20Americans%20about,all%20major%20U.S.%20demographic%20groups.
Robnett, B., Glasser, C., & Trammell, R. (2015). Waves of contention: Relations among radical, moderate, and conservative movement organizations. *Research in Social Movements, Conflicts and Change, 38*, 69–101.
Ruggiero, V., & South, N. (2013). Green criminology and crimes of the economy: Theory, research and praxis. *Critical Criminology, 21*, 359–373.
Sanders, S. (2019). Ag-gag free nation. *Wake Forest Law Review, 54*(4), 91–131.
Sarat, A., & Kearns, T. (1995). *Law in everyday life*. University of Michigan Press.

Schopp, R. F. (1996). Verdicts of conscience: Nullification and necessity as jury responses to crimes of conscience. *Southern California Law Review, 69,* 2040–2120.
Silverstein, S. (1996). *Unleashing rights: Law, meaning, and the animal rights movement*. University of Michigan Press.
Singer, P. (2015 [1975]). *Animal liberation: The definitive classic of the animal movement*. Open Road Media.
Spapens, T., White, R., & Huisman, W. (Eds.). (2016). *Environmental crime in transnational context global issues in green enforcement and criminology.* Routledge.
Sunstein, C., & Nussbaum, M. (2004). *Animal rights: Current debates and new directions*. Oxford Scholarship Online.
Tait, S. (2011). Bearing witness, journalism and moral responsibility. *Media, Culture & Society, 33*(8), 1220–1235.
Tremblay, H. (2012). Eco-terrorists facing Armageddon: The defence of necessity and legal normativity in the context of environmental crisis. *McGill Law Journal, 58*(2), 321–364.
United States v. Schoon, 939 F.2d 826. (1991).
White, R. (2013). *Environmental harm: An eco-justice perspective*. University of Bristol Press.
Wiesslitz, C., & Ashuri, T. (2011). 'Moral journalists': The emergence of new intermediaries of news in an age of digital media. *Journalism, 12*(8), 1035–1051.
Wilson, L. (2014). Ag-gag laws: A shift in the wrong direction for animal welfare on farms. *Golden Gate University Law Review, 44*(3), 311–335.

Part II

Challenging Legislation and Legal Regulations

6

Fish Farms in Canada: Where Is the Law?

Angela Fernandez

Introduction

An estimated 2.6 million salmon died in a massive die-off incident off the Southern coast of Newfoundland and Labrador at the end of August and beginning of September 2019 at ten fish farms operated by the Norwegian company Northern Harvest Sea Farms, owned by the international company MOWI.[1] A March 16, 2020 report on the incident conducted by the Fisheries and Marine Institute of Memorial University of Newfoundland concluded that this "mass mortality event," spread

[1] Holly McKenzie-Sutter, "Mass salmon die-off in Newfoundland," *Canada's National Observer*, October 13, 2019, https://www.nationalobserver.com/2019/10/13/news/mass-salmon-die-newfoundland.

A. Fernandez (✉)
Faculty of Law, University of Toronto, Toronto, Canada
e-mail: angela.fernandez@utoronto.ca

J. Gacek and R. Jochelson (eds.), *Green Criminology and the Law*, Palgrave Studies in Green Criminology,
https://doi.org/10.1007/978-3-030-82412-9_6

over ten of the company's sites in Fortune and Harbour Breton Bays, an area of sixty kilometers (or thirty-three nautical miles), was "most likely" caused by "prolonged increase in water temperatures," which "reduced dissolved oxygen levels" and this led to "asphyxiation (hypoxia) as the final cause of death."[2] This Report was issued approximately six months after the event, just as Canada was going into its first Covid-19 lockdown. The conclusion of the Report was clear that high temperature waters were not solely to blame for the die-offs: "The unprecedently high water temperatures were certainly a major contributing factor to the ME [Mortality Event] but Atlantic salmon can endure temperatures between 15–18 °C without other contributing factors."[3] It did not address the question many were wondering about, namely, whether overstocking of the fish in the pens was also a contributing factor.

There was a lot of media surrounding this event. However, there was little or no coverage of what happened to these fish, specifically how they died. The MUN Report gives the following (chilling) description:

> Salmon, by avoiding the warm surface temperatures, became crowded at the bottom of net pens and depleted oxygen from the water faster than it could be replenished, creating a hypoxic and stressful environment which caused the salmon to die. Dead fish lying on the bottom of the net pen then tightened up the net pen, worsening the hypoxic environment. Also fish handling during therapeutic treatments for sea lice stressed the salmon and increased their oxygen needs, worsening conditions further. An algal bloom in the area, as suggested by satellite imagery, would exacerbate the poor environmental conditions because algae remove oxygen from the water at night. A toxic algal bloom would make matters even worse.[4]

Fish need oxygen in the water in order to breathe. If they are unable to move and pass oxygenated water over their gills, they drown (Foer, 2009,

---

[2] Fisheries and Marine Institute, Memorial University of Newfoundland, *A Review of the 2019 Newfoundland and Labrador South Coast Cultured Atlantic Salmon Mortality Event*, March 16, 2020, Executive Summary, 3, https://www.gov.nl.ca/ffa/files/publications-pdf-2019-salmon-review-final-report.pdf [MUN Report].

[3] Ibid., Conclusion #1, 19.

[4] Ibid., Executive Summary, 3.

p. 30). If the water does not have enough oxygen in it for the fish's needs or if a fish does not have enough room to swim, they will suffer a slow death by asphyxiation, feeling distress and pain in the process (Balcombe, 2016; Braithwaite, 2010; Cassuto & O'Brien, 2019; Vettese et al., 2020; Wadiwel, 2016).

The Report explains that once dead fish started to accumulate at the bottom of the net pens (sometimes in the hundreds), the unsupported walls of the nylon net pens collapsed, "greatly restricting the available water inside, and consequently restricting the much needed water exchange across the bottom of the net pen."[5] This was a "mass asphyxiation" event, with 100% mortality at six of the ten sites.[6] Where is the animal welfare law that would incentivize salmon farm companies to take better care of their fish or visit serious consequences upon them in the wake of a mass die-off event that caused so much suffering and such slow and awful deaths, 2.6 million of them?

The Newfoundland *Animal Health and Protection Act* provides a broad definition of "animal" as "a non-human vertebrate." Finfish like salmon have a spine or backbone, i.e., are vertebrates under the scientific meaning of the term, and would therefore count as an "animal" under the Act.[7] However, Part II, the part of the act that includes the prohibition against causing an animal to be in distress, does not apply to fish as defined in the *Wild Life Act*.[8] The *Wild Life Act*, in turn, defines fish as either "fresh water" or those "which run up from the sea into inland

[5] Ibid., 20, point #6. If you are trying to imagine what kind of space we are talking about, each net pen is 100 m in circumference and is fifteen meters (i.e., about 50 feet) deep. See ibid., 11.

[6] Ibid., 19. This was the "hypoxic squeeze hypothesis," which the report adopted over the "temperature hypothesis" and the "disease hypothesis," and was described in the following way: "an unusual set of natural environmental conditions triggered a series of events that lead to mass asphyxiation of salmon, with up to 100% mortality at some sites." The three hypotheses are laid out at p. 8. The Terms of Reference on p. 6 set out that six of the sites had 100% mortality rate, with most fish dead by Monday September 2 (mortality for the first site was reported to the provincial government on August 28). The remaining four sites were added to the official mortality event on October 11 and they had partial mortality by that time, 30–50%.

[7] S. 2 (1)(a), *An Act Respecting the Health and Protection of Animals*, SNL2010 Chapter A-9.1, amended 2013 cl, https://www.assembly.nl.ca/legislation/sr/statutes/a09-1.htm#9.

[8] See ibid., ss. 2(4) and 18.

water."[9] The definition would seem then to apply to anadromous fish such as salmon. Arguably, however, *farmed* salmon do not meet the definition because they are (apart from escapees) prevented from actually engaging in this migration from the sea back up inland rivers. Either way, the protection from distress provision states that the prohibition does not apply "in respect of a class of animals prescribed by regulation, or animals living in circumstances or conditions prescribed by regulation, or where the distress is a result of a treatment, process, or condition that occurs in the course of an accepted activity."[10]

Fish are regulated in Newfoundland under the provincial *Wild Life Act*, the *Fish Inspection Act*, and the *Aquaculture Act*. This is Newfoundland after all and fishing, at least of wild fish, would certainly qualify as an "accepted activity." However, this was not always true of fish farming, as "aquaculture" was barely a known word as recently as the 1980s and the province of Newfoundland and Labrador was taking little interest in it at that time (Wildsmith, 1982a, 1, p. 185). The provincial *Aquaculture Act* was first passed in 1990 and, as its long title's inclusion of the word "encouragement" suggested, one of its stated purposes was to "promote, in consultation with the private sector, the prudent and orderly development of an aquaculture industry."[11]

When the North Atlantic cod populations collapsed in the mid-1990s, aquaculture was billed as one of the saviors of an economically and socially disastrous situation. The editors of a special issue in the *Dalhousie Law Journal* on the catastrophic collapse wrote: "The fishery crisis haunts lawyers as it is evidence of the abysmal failure of law to deal with world problems at all levels. Will the future be much different? Will aquaculture arrive?" (Russell & McConnell, 1995, p. 10). This question carried with it the hope that cultured or farmed fish could replace the gaping economic and social hole left in the lives of many Atlantic Canadians (Bavington, 2010).

---

[9] S. 2(b), *Wild Life Act*, RSNL 1990, Chapter W-8, https://www.assembly.nl.ca/legislation/sr/statutes/w08.htm.

[10] S. 18(3), *An Act Respecting the Health and Protection of Animals*.

[11] S. 3(a), *An Act Respecting the Encouragement and Regulation of an Aquaculture Industry in the Province*, RSNL 1990 Chapter A-13, https://www.assembly.nl.ca/Legislation/sr/statutes/a13.htm#4.

In her recently published indictment of the role government and industry have played in the devastation of wild salmon on the west coast of Canada, *Not on My Watch* (2021), fish scientist and activist Alexandra Morton writes that although "salmon farms were considered the next great generator of employment [in British Columbia] … the jobs math never did add up. It did not take many people to run the increasingly mechanized farms and the jobs paid far less than loggers were making" (2021, p. 62; "industry was on a trajectory to minimize employment through mechanization," p. 65). The empty nature of the promise was appreciated in the 1980s. For example, one study to test the viability of salmon farming in British Columbia created a "model fish farm scenario," forecasting the employment of just three full-time employees and one seasonal assistant, consistent with how salmon farming was done at the time in the United States and elsewhere (Wildsmith, 1982a, p. 162). The lawyer and legal scholar from Nova Scotia who reported this, Bruce Wildsmith, wrote in his book proposing a legal framework for aquaculture in the province: "It would appear to be a positive factor in the economics of salmon farming that operations may be organized so as not to be labor intensive. This may be seen as a negative factor with respect to employment levels within a province" (Wildsmith, 1982a, p. 162). Wildsmith's book *Aquaculture: The Legal Framework* (1982a) also noted the risks of disease spread, parasite transmission, and pollution effects (discussed in more detail below).

Wildsmith explained that he had obtained a mandate to draft a model piece of aquaculture legislation for the provincial government in Nova Scotia (see Preface, Wildsmith, 1982a). He argued in favor of finding provincial jurisdiction over the industry and creating private property rights in the fish on a farm (see Chapters 3 and 4). Characterizing his constitutional argument as "a reasonably good but not unequivocal case … for the validity of provincial legislation dealing with aquaculture" (p. 81), Wildsmith also called it an attempt at "an intelligent guess" at what a court would say about the matter (p. 225). One book review at the time noted the "surprising" nature of this argument given the fact that "[t]he issue of constitutional jurisdiction over offshore areas has raged across the globe in the last twenty years, sparking political and judicial controversy in nearly every coastal federation; in nearly every case the federal government has been found to be the owner and legislator of offshore resources" (Penick, 1984, p. 73). In 1967, the Supreme Court of Canada held that marine waters and the seabed were not the property of British Columbia.[12] Given the similarity in the boundary descriptions of British Columbia and Nova Scotia, the reviewer wrote, it was "a bit surprising" to see Wildsmith fall on the provincial side of the question. The federal jurisdiction was confirmed in the case of Newfoundland's offshore resources.[13]

However, the federal government has never passed an aquaculture act, choosing instead to regulate the industry through Regulations under the *Fisheries Act* and Memoranda of Understanding (MOU) worked out with each of the provinces (see VanderZaag et al., 2006, pp. 50–60). In 2009, Morton sued the provincial government and the Supreme Court of British Columbia held that it was not permissible for the province and the federal government to agree that their MOU from 1988 formalized the federal government's withdrawal from aquaculture regulation and licensing in the province.[14] Hinkson J. wrote that "the Province does not have jurisdiction to license private fisheries" because "[t]he management of fisheries … is a matter of exclusive federal jurisdiction."[15] "[O]nly the federal government had the jurisdiction to grant private fishery rights in tidal waters," unless it "validly delegates that power to the provincial

---

[12] *Reference re Offshore Mineral Rights*, [1967] S.C.R. 792. The United States, motivated by the desire to protect its offshore oil production, declared in 1945 that the country had the right to control mineral sources on its continental shelf. "No one had ever owned a continental shelf" before and given that "cod and most other commercial fish are mostly found on continental shelves, the implications for fishing were enormous" (Kurlansky, 1997, p. 160). Other countries, including Canada, followed the US lead, which eventually led to the United Nations *Law of the Sea* to set out a twelve-mile territorial sea and 200-mile "exclusive economic zones" which Canada started patrolling in 1977 (Wildsmith, 1982a, p. 17).

[13] See *Reference re Newfoundland Continental Shelf*, [1984] 1 S.C.R. 86, https://decisions.scc-csc.ca/scc-csc/scc-csc/en/item/5159/index.do.

[14] The judge ordered a temporary suspension of invalidity of most of the provincial legislation in order to give the federal and provincial government time to fix the problem. See *Morton v. British Columbia (Agriculture and Lands)* 2009 BC SC 136, https://www.canlii.org/en/bc/bcsc/doc/2009/2009bcsc136/2009bcsc136.html (*Morton v. B.C.* [S.C. 2009]). The 1988 agreement is available here: https://www.gov.nl.ca/ffa/files/department-pdf-canada-nl-memorandum-understanding-aquaculture-dev-1988.pdf.

[15] *Morton v. B.C.* (S.C. 2009), paras. 172, 173.

government."[16] The new MOU entered into in 2010 gave the Federal government "the primary management and regulation of aquaculture in B.C.," specifically the role and responsibility for issuing licenses and the province was assigned the role and responsibility for issuing tenures.[17] Morton wrote that "[i]n the end, the federal government hasn't done any better than the province, but at least the salmon of the Broughton survived another decade" (2021, p. 113).

Industry has advocated for private property rights in the fish in their farms, arguing that they are analogous to farmed land animals. The Supreme Court of Canada held in 1897 that fish in the sea are not owned until they are reduced to a possession from which they cannot escape.[18] This is the capture rule of *Pierson v. Post*.[19] Fish in nets in the ocean do not pass the test.[20] Wildsmith saw a legislative override of this uncertain ownership at common law as essential to the aquaculture industry, calling the nature and extent of an aquaculturist's property rights their "single most important legal issue" (Wildsmith, 1982a, p. 93). The Model Act he proposed gave full property rights to the aquaculturist but allowed anyone to take with impunity any fish who traveled outside a protected area of 100 m from the leased area (p. 236). This approach was adopted in Newfoundland, New Brunswick, and Nova Scotia.[21] It

[16] Ibid., paras. 159, 160. The example given was an agreement similar to the 1912 *Oyster Fisheries Agreement* under the authority of an Order in Council delegating authority from Parliament to the province to grant farm licenses. See para. 186.

[17] See Government of Canada, "Aquaculture in British Columbia," https://www.dfo-mpo.gc.ca/aquaculture/pacific-pacifique/index-eng.html. See also the *Pacific Aquaculture Regulations*, SOR/2010-270, https://laws-lois.justice.gc.ca/eng/regulations/SOR-2010-270/.

[18] See *Frederick Gerring Jr. (The) v. R.* (1897) 27 SCR 271. In the *Gerring* case, the Supreme Court of Canada upheld the seizure of an American ship caught "fishing" within the three-mile limit of Nova Scotia despite the fact that the fish were netted outside the limit and the crew were only bailing the fish in impermissible waters. Key to the three-judge majority ruling was the fact that the fish were not yet reduced to capture and many did and would escape in the bailing process. I am working on a co-authored book-length study of this case.

[19] *Pierson v. Post*, 3 *Caines Reports* 175 (1805) (NY SC). See Fernandez (2018, pp. 264–268) (discussing the *Gerring* case and its adoption of the capture rule).

[20] See *Young v. Hitchens*, (1844) 6 Q.B. 606, 115 E.R. 228.

[21] See s. 5(1) of the Newfoundland *Aquaculture Act* declaring that all aquatic plants or animals specified in the aquaculture license, while contained within the boundaries of the site, are "the exclusive personal property of, and belong to, the licensee"; s. 5(2) specifies that if any of these aquatic animals escape, they "shall remain the exclusive personal property of the licensee while within 100 m of the boundary of the site." Wildsmith's s. 28 used the language "the exclusive

was not adopted in British Columbia, Prince Edward Island, and Quebec (Clarkson, 2014, p. 23). And, indeed, there was a dramatic moment in Morton's case in which Hinkson J. declined to give Marine Harvest the answer it wanted to the question whether they had property rights in the fish when the case was sent back to him by the British Columbia Court of Appeal.[22]

The problem with the industry/government argument of exclusive ownership and property rights is that it flies in the face of animal welfare, which is notoriously compromised in the case of land animals, especially those raised for food. Like most intensively farmed food animals, the conditions in which farmed fish live are not well known. Here scale matters, as keeping a few fish in a private pond with adequate space might not look particularly cruel but when the practice is adopted on a large scale many serious problems develop for both the animals (wild

---

property of the lessee" (see Wildsmith, 1982a, p. 257). In 1996, s. 61 of the Nova Scotia statute used the "exclusive property" language, extending it also to escapes within 100 m. See *Fisheries and Coastal Resources Act*, RNS 1996, c. 25, https://www.canlii.org/en/ns/laws/stat/sns-1996-c-25/latest/sns-1996-c-25.html. This structure was carried over from the 1983 statute, which tracked Wildsmith's proposal carefully, including his language of "aquatic flora and fauna." It did not, however, specify, as he recommended in his s. 30, that "any person may, beyond one hundred metres" of release or escape "capture and appropriate for his own use" any fish released into or escaping to the natural environment, with two more provisions relating to interfering with fish on a farm (taking, appropriating, converting, or otherwise destroying or injuring, removing or mutilating) without the consent of the owner. See Wildsmith, 1982a, p. 258; ss. 17 & 18, An Act Respecting the Encouragement and Regulation of Aquaculture, 32 Eliz. II, SNS 12 1983, c. 2, The New Brunswick Act in 1988 used the "exclusive property" language but only while the animal is "contained within the boundaries of the aquaculture site." See s. 16(5), *Aquaculture Act* SNB 1988, c A-9.2, https://www.canlii.org/en/nb/laws/stat/snb-1988-c-a-9.2/latest/snb-1988-c-a-9.2.html. This act was repealed in 2011. However, this provision was kept the same. See s. 22, *Aquaculture Act*, RSNB 2011, c. 112, https://www.canlii.org/en/nb/laws/stat/rsnb-2011-c-112/latest/rsnb-2011-c-112.html.

22 See *Morton v. Marine Harvest Canada Inc.*, 2009 BCCA 481, https://www.canlii.org/en/bc/bcca/doc/2009/2009bcca481/2009bcca481.html?autocompleteStr=Morton%20v.marine%20harvest&autocompletePos=1. Hinkson J. held the line, stating that he "made no finding … as to the ownership of the fish. I do not consider it necessary to resolve the matter in order to rule on the petition" (para. 38). A decision of "the extent and nature of the property rights in the fish … should be left for another day when it can be reached on a complete evidentiary record and a full argument on the issue" (para. 46). See *Morton v. B.C. (Agriculture and Lands)*, 2010 BSC 100, https://www.canlii.org/en/bc/bcsc/doc/2010/2010bcsc100/2010bcsc100.html?resultIndex=3T. The east coast laws that restrict the public right to fish by giving "exclusive" property rights to escaped salmon within a 100 m of the net pens are likely unconstitutional because "[o]nly Parliament can enact competent legislation to create an exclusive fishery in tidal waters" (see Clarkson, 2014, pp. 126, 133).

and farmed), as well as their environment. While there are many of these problems to choose from (including the development of infectious diseases that can pass from farmed to wild fish), let us next examine just one set of issues relating to sea lice and how that arose and was dealt with in the context of the 2019 Newfoundland mass mortality event.[23]

Sea Lice

"[A] generic term for many species of parasitic copepods that latch onto the bodies of fish and other marine creatures and feed off their living tissues," sea lice are not a major threat ordinarily to wild fish (Balcombe, 2016, p. 216). However, as Morton has spent decades explaining, wild fish that must pass by fish farms are put at extreme risk of being exposed to these lice, literally spilling out in clouds into the waters around the open-net farms. She further explains:

> In the natural world … so few salmon stay in the [Broughton] archipelago [the area in British Columbia between the northern portion of Vancouver Island and the mainland where Morton lives] over the winter that there are not enough to host large sea louse populations. So come springtime, when young wild salmon leave the rivers and enter the ocean for the first time, there are not enough sea lice to harm them. However, in this new unnatural world [of fish farms], where schools of 600,000 to a million Atlantic salmon are swimming in circles in farms along the coast, sea lice

[23] Infectious salmon anemia virus (ISAv) was found at two of the ten sites, one before and one six weeks after the mortality event (MUN Report, 16). I am not going to deal with this disease, however, as the controversies surrounding it could fill a book (and do fill much of Morton's). Chile had a serious problem with ISAv in 2011 when it killed millions of fish and cost the industry $2 billion. See Alexei Barrionuevo, "Norwegians concede a role in Chilean salmon virus," *New York Times*, July 27, 2011, https://www.nytimes.com/2011/07/28/world/americas/28chile.html. Those interested in "ag gag" legislation might take note of Bill 37, a 2012 attempt by the British Columbia government to criminalize the reporting of animal diseases, including a reportable fish disease such as ISAv, punishable by two years in jail and a fine of $75,000. It did not pass. See ss. 17 and s. 90(1)(b) of the proposed *Bill 37-2012 Animal Health Act*, https://www.bclaws.gov.bc.ca/civix/document/id/lc/billsprevious/4th39th:gov37-1. On this bill and the controversy around the lengths, the Department of Fisheries and Oceans (DFO) and the Canadian Food Inspection Agency went to *not* confirm there was ISAv in British Columbia, see *Salmon Confidential*, dir. Twyla Roscovich, October 2, 2013, https://topdocumentaryfilms.com/salmon-confidential/.

> breed on the crowded fish like never before and release billions of larval lice every spring into the young salmon migration routes. (p. 71)

In other words, the wild salmon are exposed to unnatural concentrations of lice as they swim past the farms. Usually, in the wild, sea lice do not pose a major threat because the wild fish with sea lice will be weaker and will die, picked off by predators. However, in the fish farm pens where there are no predators, the lice on the weaker farmed fish proliferate and there is no way for any of the rest of the confined population to escape. "[I]n the artificial conditions of intensive confinement, where the next host fish is just inches away, sea lice thrive. As they chew through the mucus, flesh and eyes of fishes helpless to escape them," creating what ethologist and behavioural biologist Jonathan Balcombe has called "farmed fish hell" (Balcombe, 2016, p. 216). Morton, who has spent countless hours trying to save young wild salmon from these parasites, calls their suffering "incalculable" and likens it to "having a parasite the size of a rat attached to you, gnawing away, and having no hands to remove it" (Morton, 2021, p. 72).

The media reported that workers present during the Newfoundland die-off, specifically at the Harbour Breton location, thought that sea lice were responsible for the mass die-off that was unfolding. One Union representative and longtime plant work reported that just two salmon carried as many as 385 sea lice.[24] The MUN Report did not find evidence to conclude that there were high levels of sea lice, relying on admittedly limited data of *average* counts and at only eight of the ten sites.[25] It did find, however, that handling already hypoxic fish, specifically giving bath treatments for sea lice and the stress this placed on the fish, were "a significant contributing factor to elevated mortality."[26]

---

24 "Warm water, not sea lice, caused massive salmon die-off, says chief vet," *CBC News*, October 1, 2019, https://www.cbc.ca/news/canada/newfoundland-labrador/warm-water-salmon-die-off-1.5302950.

25 See MUN Report, 15 (explaining that the Aquatic Health Division veterinary report provided to them on February 7, 2020 "included limited information about sea lice infestations, other than noting that average sea lice counts were below 6 adult females per salmon per site"; the company's data "showed that average counts were below 2 on all but two of the sites in late July/early August").

26 Ibid., 19.

Their increased oxygen needs could not be met in the deoxygenated environment.

The antibiotic used to treat farmed fish to try and keep sea lice populations under control is called SLICE.[27] Morton's view is that this drug can only be "a temporary fix" due to drug-resistance that develops in the lice (see Morton, 2021, pp. 85, 95). She figures its use, along with her efforts to effectively medivac young wild salmon past the farms, bought the wild population in the Broughton "a fifteen-year life extension" (p. 86). Yet, when used, SLICE creates other problems. As Morton explains, "[s]ea lice, lobster, and prawns are all crustaceans; what kills one of them is likely to kill all of them" (p. 170). "The cheapest, least stressful, delousing treatment is soaking the feed with Slice," writes Morton. However, small fish, what the industry calls "nonperformers," do not eat the pellets soaked in the delousing drugs (p. 215). When the feed method ceases to be effective, due to the numbers of these smaller fish or when the lice develop resistance, "the wellboats show up":

> They suck the farm salmon up out of the pens, bathe them in delousing drugs and pump them back into the pens. That chemical bath is dumped in the ocean. The fish farmers say the drug is all used up when the bath is dumped, but the fishermen [on the east coast] said that whenever the wellboats show up the lobster vanish. (p. 174)

Lobster fishing on the east coast erupted in violence between Mi'kmaq and non-Indigenous commercial fishermen in Nova Scotia in the fall of 2020 when the Sipekne'katik First Nation launched its own off-season fishery.[28] Is this fighting over this increasingly scarce wild resource yet another problem created by the fish farms?

---

[27] The chemical name is Emamectin Benzoate. See *Morton v. B.C.* (S.C. 2009), para. 54.

[28] See Robin Levinson-King, "Inside Canada's decades-long lobster feud," *BBC News*, October 19, 2020, https://www.bbc.com/news/world-us-canada-54472604.

Not on My Watch

An American, Alexandra Morton came to the Broughton in 1979 searching for the family of the two whales she worked with at a Marineland of the Pacific outside Los Angeles, a female orca named Corky and a male named Orky, who were both captured off the coast of British Columbia when they were five years old in 1968 and 1969 (Morton, 2021, pp. 5–6). Watching Corky lose one baby after another (one still born and six live) and the suffering she endured, moved Morton to want to find and study Corky's family (pp. 9–10). Photographic evidence of Corky's mother from the day of her capture identified her as a member of what is known as the A5 pod of the northern resident orca (p. 10). Fish farms arrived in the Broughton in 1988 (p. 24). In the 1990s, "the resident fish-eating orca families left the area and never came back" (p. 31). Morton shifted her attention to the fish that any remaining whales would need in order to survive (e.g., the southern resident orca, which will only eat Chinook salmon, are an endangered species in both Canada and the United States).[29]

Morton figures that the serendipity of her presence in the Broughton and the fishermen coming to her with concerns about the farms is the only reason that the sea louse epidemics became public knowledge. She writes in *Not on My Watch*:

> Had these outbreaks remained hidden, the industry would have known what was happening and maybe some in DFO [the Federal Department of Fisheries and Oceans] would have been made aware, but neither of them would have done anything to save the Broughton salmon. The salmon would have died off in the early 2000s. The rights of the public and the First Nations to wild salmon were nowhere on the radar of DFO, the provincial Ministry of Agriculture [who were given jurisdiction for the "farms" by DFO] or the industry. (p. 120)

[29] See World Wildlife Fund, "Southern Resident Killer Whale," https://wwf.ca/species/southern-resident-killer-whales/. For a short moving documentary on the plight of this species of whale, see "Coextinction," dirs. Gloria Pancrazi and Elena Routledge, https://www.storyhive.com/projects/3820#project_video.

This is a sobering thought, that without the action of one private individual, who just happened to be there and who happened to care, the wild fish would already be gone. Morton sees her science and activism, in allied partnership with the Musgamagw in whose territory the farms are located, as having slowed down the extinction; however, "with rising drug resistance and disease outbreaks, the wild salmon were going to be just as dead in the near future" (p. 120). So where is law? Where is government?

The Environment

When Wildsmith wrote *Aquaculture: The Legal Framework*, he recognized that "[a]quacultural operations could be sources, as well as recipients of pollution," such as fertilizers and other chemicals, as well as feces from the fish (Wildsmith, 1982a, p. 123). However, most of his discussion of pollution had to do with *protecting* aquacultural operators from the pollution of others given how "very sensitive" aquaculture is to "changes in natural conditions, such as quantity and quality of water" (p. 229). He noted that fish farmers in the United States were exempt from United States federal water quality regulations and the source providing that information stated that "pollution caused by aquaculture is normally miniscule" (p. 133, n. 16, quoting from G. Bowden, *Coastal Aquaculture Law and Policy*, p. 86).[30]

"Miniscule" would hardly characterize the large amounts of waste that fish farms produce in their day-to-day operations (see Clarkson, 2014, pp. 86–88, 91).[31] It certainly would not apply to what inhabitants on the Southern coast of Newfoundland were dealing with in terms

[30] This appears to be a typo for Gerald Bowen (no d), *Coastal Aquaculture Law and Policy: A Case Study of California* (Boulder, CO.: Westview Press, 1981), a book Wildsmith reviewed favorably in the journal *Marine Policy* (Wildsmith, 1982b).

[31] Giving estimates of uneaten food and waste and explaining that they cause "hypernutrification" on the seabed floor and "[t]he constant loading of feed and waste on the seabed can result in high levels of sulfur, creating a desert where a benthic community previously existed" (Clarkson, 2014, p. 88). Sulfur overload will lead to increased mortality for surrounding animals, as the bacteria that cause the decomposition of the feed and waste consume oxygen, which is depleted when the sea bed is overloaded with nutrients. This is known as "anoxic" condition (p. 91).

of the stench caused by the rotting bodies of the at least 2.6 million dead salmon. In early October 2019, a member of the Atlantic Salmon Federation on a boat touring the cleanup site was quoted in the *Globe and Mail* saying that "[i]t was an absolutely awful smell."[32] The fish sludge, pink from the colorant in feed used to dye farmed salmon flesh, was reported here as being "more than 15-m thick in some areas" of Fortune Bay. The "mort removal," i.e., process of cleaning up the dead and decomposing fish, estimate was that there was 5000 tons of material.[33] The Information and Privacy Commissioner of Newfoundland and Labrador found that "[d]eceased fish were not disposed of in the ocean. Images of pink slurry being pumped from vessels merely represented excess water (which contained some organic material but not all remains) after fish had been removed from pens" (Harvey, 2020, pp. 6–7, para. 14). He wrote that "aside from some organic material contained in water pumped from seiner vessels, the majority of the deceased salmon biomass was not disposed of in the marine environment" (p. 9, para. 22). The "mort removal" renderings were sent to land-based disposal sites in Stephenville (a dairy company) and Burgeo (a fish meal plant).[34] It is unclear why a more precise number of how much was dumped could not be arrived at if those facilities know how much of the estimated 5000 tons they each received. The environmental report produced by the Mi'kmaq Alsumk Mowimsikik Koqoey Association (MAMKA), a group chosen by Northern Harvest to do on-site monitoring, found that only 2% of adjacent shores were affected by the fat deposits in the sludge, with most impact having dissipated by April 2020.[35] It did not discuss what negative environmental effects those fat deposits would have, including the effect of the sludge on algal growth creating the anaerobic conditions

---

32 See Greg Mercer, "Newfoundlanders raise a stink after as many as 1.8 million dead farmed salmon are dumped on south shore," *The Globe and Mail*, October 8, 2019, updated October 9, 2019, https://www.theglobeandmail.com/canada/article-newfoundlanders-raise-a-stink-after-18-million-dead-farmed-salmon-are/.

33 MUN Report, 22. A low estimate given the numbers of fish involved.

34 Ibid., 24–25.

35 Mi'kmaq Alsumk Mowimsikik Koqoey Association (MAMKA), *Post Event Environmental Monitoring of the High Temperature Mortality Event in Fortune Bay: Final Report*, April 24, 2020, ii, http://mamka.ca/wp-content/uploads/2020/04/04_24_20-MAMKA-Northern-Harvest-Mortality-Event-2019-Final-Report.pdf.

that would negatively affect wild populations (lobster and wild fish like cod).

Algal blooms are caused by pollution (Morton, 2021, p. 51), specifically, in the vicinity of fish farms, uneaten food pellets, and fish feces. In November 2019, a farm owned by Cermaq located in a part of the UNESCO Clayoquot Sound Biosphere Reserve in British Columbia had an estimated 200,000 fish die due to algal blooms.[36]

S. 36(3) of the federal *Fisheries Act* prohibits anyone from depositing "a deleterious substance of any type in water frequented by fish."[37] It is a wide definition that would seem to apply to the pink sludge, even if it contained mostly water.[38] However, the federal government, which has jurisdiction over the management and protection of wild fishes under s. 91(12) of the *Constitution* had nothing to say about the mass die-off event in Newfoundland. The MUN Report tells us that the federal Department of Fisheries and Oceans (DFO) was notified on September 4, 2019, not by the province or the company but "by DFO fishery officers who had become aware of the situation through fish harvesters in the area."[39] Once it was determined by speaking to the Province and the Newfoundland Aquaculture Industry Association that this was not "a fish health/disease issue," DFO reviewed the *Aquaculture Activities Regulations* of the *Fisheries Act* and concluded that a non-infectious mortality

---

[36] See Simon Little and Paul Johnson, "Environmentalists, fish farm spare over mass fish die-off at Vancouver Island facility," *Global News*, November 25, 2019, https://globalnews.ca/news/6217229/environmentalists-fish-farm-die-off-vancouver-island/. An astonishing number of penned salmon, thirty-nine million, are reported as having died from a toxic algal bloom they could not swim away from in Chile. See Andrew Nikiforuk, "Harmful Algal Blooms Kill Farmed Salmon Near Tofino," *The Tyee*, November 20, 2019, https://thetyee.ca/News/2019/11/20/Algal-Blooms-Tofino/ (surveying massive algal bloom suffocations in Norway, Scotland, and Chile, in addition to the events in Clayoquot Sound and Newfoundland).

[37] *An Act Respecting Fisheries*, R.S.C., 1985, c. F-14, https://laws.justice.gc.ca/eng/acts/F-14/page-8.html#docCont.

[38] See ibid., s. 34(1)(a) and (b) ("any substance that, if added to water, would degrade or alter [...] the quality of that water so that it is rendered or is likely to be rendered deleterious to fish or fish habitat" or "any water that contains a substance in such quantity or concentration [...] that it would if added to any other water, degrade or alter [...] the quality of that water so that it is rendered or is likely to be rendered deleterious to any fish or fish habitat").

[39] MUN Report, 30.

event *inside* the boundaries of the facility was not covered by the Regulations.[40] It is unclear, however, how DFO approved the dumping of the pink sludge if they took the position that the Regulations authorizing that dumping (see below) did not apply.

Like British Columbia, the other provinces with coastal fisheries have Memoranda of Understanding with the federal government. Newfoundland, Nova Scotia, and New Brunswick have a predominantly provincially controlled regulation relating to aquaculture, whereas British Columbia (since the *Morton* case in 2009) and Prince Edward Island are federally controlled (Mitchell, 2014, p. 7). Environmental protection, along with fish health, are shared responsibilities under the Memorandum of Understanding signed by DFO and the Newfoundland and Labrador provincial Department of Fisheries and Aquaculture in 1988 (p. 17). The provincial *Environmental Protection Act* prohibits the unauthorized release of a substance into the environment that might cause an adverse effect (p. 17).[41]

Here were two pieces of legislation, the Federal *Fisheries Act* and the provincial *Environmental Protection Act*, that would seem on their face to prohibit the dumping of the pink sludge into Fortune Bay, whatever the percentage of the 5000 tons it was. The MUN Report noted that the *Aquaculture Activities Regulations* made pursuant to the *Fisheries Act* permit aquaculture facilities with an active license to deposit "deleterious substances" into the marine environment.[42] The definition of

---

[40] Ibid. The interpretation was based on s. 13(1) of the *Aquaculture Activities Regulations*, SOR/2015-177, https://laws.justice.gc.ca/eng/regulations/SOR-2015-177/page-1.html#docCont setting out that "fish morbidity or mortality" triggered a reporting requirement for the facility owner only for deaths "outside the aquaculture facility" observed from any part of the facility. However, this provision only applies to the situations of deposits of drugs or pesticides in s. 2(a) and (b), not (c) the "biochemical oxygen demanding matter" (BODM).

[41] See s. 7, *An Act Respecting Environmental Protection*, SNL 2002 Chapter E-14.2, https://www.assembly.nl.ca/legislation/sr/statutes/e14-2.htm. However, s. 12(a) allows the Minister to "classify or allow the releases of substances." S. 4(2) permits an approval "under another enactment" if it is stated in the regulations. The regulations may cover releases of substances. See s. 111(1)(b). According to the Office of the Information and Privacy Commissioner, the Department of Municipal Affairs and Environment played a limited role in the mass mortality event, specifically, confirming through its Pollution Prevention Division with the Department of Fisheries and Land Resources that mortalities would be disposed of at approved facilities (Harvey, 2020, p. 4, para. 5).

[42] MUN Report, 30.

"deleterious substance" in these *Regulations* relate to drugs, pest control products, or "biochemical oxygen demanding matter" (defined as "any organic matter that contributes to the consumption of oxygen that is dissolved in water or sediment" (BODM)).[43] DFO decided that the release of organic waste (i.e., dead fish material) was a permitted activity for licensed aquaculture facilities.[44] The sludge must have been characterized by them as BODM, since it was not a drug or pesticide. This decision would seem to be in conflict with their interpretation (see above) that the Regulations did not apply. Moreover, there is a 300-day lead time for making a deposit under these Regulations, specifically requiring the facility to submit details on "the predicted contours of the footprint of the biochemical oxygen demanding matter that will be deposited," an exemption from which depends how large the site is.[45]

The provincial Fisheries and Land Resources Minister Gerry Byrne suspended Northern Harvest's license from October 11, 2019 to May 6, 2020 due to the Company's "failure to disclose to the department in a timely manner, all information regarding" the mass mortality event.[46] "Mort removal" went on until October 25.[47] The *Aquaculture Activities Regulations* only apply to valid license holders and they did not apply "in the absence of an active license," i.e., after October 11.[48] Was the deposit of waste from the incident dumped in the harbor after this date and therefore in violation of the *Fisheries Act*? Was all of the dumping in violation of the *Fisheries Act*, given the DFO interpretation that the *Aquaculture Activities Regulations* did not apply?

---

43 See *Aquaculture Activities Regulations*, s. 2.

44 MUN Report, 30.

45 See ibid., s. 8(1)(a). The provision does not apply if the facility's license "permits a maximum standing biomass of 2.5 t or less or a maximum annual production of 5 t or less." See s. 9(2). The licenses in question likely do not meet this exception, as these numbers indicate very small operations.

46 Fisheries and Land Resources, "Public Advisory: Provincial Government Reinstates Northern Harvest Sea Farms Aquaculture Licenses," May 6, 2020, https://www.gov.nl.ca/releases/2020/flr/0506n02/.

47 MUN Report, 22.

48 Ibid., 30. See *Aquaculture Activities Regulations*, s. 4.

So many questions and so many issues still not addressed after no less than three publicly available reports, specifically about DFO's interpretation of the Regulations. At least two other significant issues have not been addressed. First, were these net pens overstocked? If they were, surely they would have contributed to the paucity of oxygen leading to the mass asphyxiation. Secondly, just how many fish escaped?

Densities

One of the MUN Report final recommendations for Northern Harvest is that they use deeper net pens "to provide appreciable deep-water cold refuge for salmon should surface water become unusually warm as it did in August 2019."[49] This recommendation states that its calculations to use a 20-m deep net rather than a 15-m deep one (with an additional 6-m cone at the bottom) and the benefit this would bring "assume that stocking density remains unchanged, at around 3.6 kg/m^3."[50] What does that stocking density look like? And, more importantly, was Northern Harvest exceeding it at the time of the mass mortality event?

Provincial Minister Byrne was on record in an industry publication the day before he suspended the Northern Harvest license claiming that the numbers of dead fish could not exceed two million, as the cages could only hold two million fish.[51] The discrepancy between this and the number that was settled on, 2.6 million rather than the earlier 1.8 million that appeared in many media reports, would seem to suggest that the cages were indeed overstocked by at least 600,000 fish plus, given that not all of the sites had a 100% mortality rate. Overstocking would have been highly relevant to understanding why the environment the fish were in became so deoxygenated. An Access to Information request asking for the maximum stocked population numbers for 2019 and 2020 was rejected on privacy grounds, specifically that the government could not

[49] MUN Report, Final Recommendations 1(b), 33.

[50] Ibid.

[51] See Owen Evans, "NL's fisheries minister says Northern Harvest lost 'no more than 2 million fish' and 'would caution before anyone draws a conclusion on photos,'" *Salmon Business*, October 10, 2019, https://salmonbusiness.com/nls-fisheries-minister-says-northern-harvest-lost-no-more-than-2-million-fish-and-would-caution-before-anyone-draws-a-conclusion-on-photos/.

disclose information "harmful to the business interests of a third party."[52] This is a response that would suggest that there was indeed a problem.

Animal food industries are notoriously bad self-regulators. The image that is often used is "the fox guarding the henhouse" (Wolfson & Sullivan, 2004). Hence the questionable futility of advising the offending company to adopt deeper nets or use net pens with stiffer wall structures that cannot collapse in on the fish and collectively smother them.[53] Would it not be better to recommend that *government* require the company to take on those measures as part of the licensing conditions? Like all factory farmers, fish farmers "calculate how close to death they can keep animals without killing them. That is the business model. How quickly can they be made to grow, how tightly can they be packed, how much or little can they eat, how sick can they get without dying" (Foer, 2009, pp. 92–93). Mortality rates of 10–30% are considered acceptable in the fish farming industry (Balcombe, 2016, p. 216). Given the "extreme and unprecedented" nature of this mass mortality event, there is little incentive for the company to not simply resume business as usual.[54]

Consider the following description provided by Morton of her experience finally looking down into the water of one of the pens:

> After decades of circling the farms in my speedboat, trying to understand what was going on inside, I found it shocking to look straight down into the water of the pen. As a farmer stood right beside me, I parted the bird net slightly and slipped the camera on the pole into the water among the fish drifting near the surface. The fish were barely alive, emaciated and sculling in random directions; many of their eyeballs were white, which indicated that the fish were blind. I turned the camera towards their tumors and open sores. Salmon were stacked like firewood right up against the nets, accessing the clean oxygen-rich water. The water was laced with stringy, mustard coloured strands, fish diarrhea, I realized when one fish let loose a stream of it in front of the camera. (Morton, 2021, pp. 218–219)

[52] The request was made on March 16, 2021 (amended March 17) and denied on April 13, 2021. See https://atipp-search.gov.nl.ca/public/atipp/requestdownload?id=15005.

[53] MUN Report, Final Recommendations 1(a), 33.

[54] Ibid., Executive Summary, 3.

If this situation was hidden from someone with such a long-standing interest in fish and fish farms, how is the average person consuming one of these fish expected to know about the kinds of conditions they are reared in? Where is the law and government?

Escapes

Escapes from fish farms have attracted significant attention in recent years. For instance, an estimated 20,000 farmed salmon escaped from a farm in Hermitage Bay, Newfoundland in 2013 prompting a high-profile scientific study of the hybridization and population genetic changes in wild populations of salmon (see Wringe et al., 2018). In addition to interbreeding resulting in less suitability to a wild environment, escaped fish will compete for space and resources with the native fishes, significant in the case of a carnivorous fish like salmon who eat a lot of other fishes in order to survive, including baby salmon. There is also the significant risk of the transmission of diseases like ISAv and parasites such as sea lice.

On August 21, 2018, fish farm structures near Puget Sound in Washington State collapsed, resulting in the escape of an estimated 250,000 Atlantic salmon from a fish farm owned by Cook Aquaculture (Morton, 2021, p. 229). The State departments of Ecology, Fisheries and Wildlife, and Natural Resources identified the cause of the collapse as failure to clean the nets containing the fish.[55] Was this also a factor in the Newfoundland mass mortality event?

The MUN Report does not focus on failure to clean the nets nor does it name the issue as a contributing factor. However, two of its recommendations do speak to the matter noting, for example, that "[w]hile recognizing that August is a vacation month for Canadians," the company had to do better than it did in its diver response to "a spike in mortality in early to mid-August," noting that although the frequency of dives to remove dead fish from the pens did increase, it was a delayed

[55] See Lynda V. Mapes, "Fish farm caused Atlantic salmon spill near San Juans," *The Seattle Times*, January 30, 2018, https://www.seattletimes.com/seattle-news/fish-farm-caused-atlantic-salmon-spill-state-says-then-tried-to-hide-how-bad-it-was/.

response.[56] The Report also recommended that a more accurate record of deaths be kept, which would in the hot month of August increase the diving frequency from twice a week to daily.[57] Hence, it would seem that failing to adequately clean the nets and "timely mort removal" was a problem.[58]

Northern Harvest was very aware that escapes would make this very bad situation worse, as their mort removal plan prioritized decreasing "the weight in the net pen to prevent collapse and avoid fish escapes."[59] The provincial Minister has the authority under the *Aquaculture Act* to deploy an inspector to investigate "the adequacy of measures being taken to ensure … animals being cultured do not escape."[60] Was that done here? If not, why not?

Was Northern Harvest overstocking its pens? How many fish escaped? The MUN Report does not ask or answer these questions. The public attention to the escapes in Washington State led to in a bill passed in March 2018 to end open-water salmon aquaculture operations in the state by 2025.[61] It is significant that like Northern Harvest in Newfoundland, Cooke also tried to blame an environmental cause like water temperature for the collapse of the nets, specifically, strong tides associated with the solar eclipse, and they lowballed the number of escapes, just as Northern Harvest did with the number of deaths. However, the Washington State Departments called the company out on their false reporting (the state commissioner of public lands stating in the media, "[w]e all know how to count fish, Dr. Seuss made it easy: One Fish, Two Fish") as well as its negligent operations.[62] Yet despite the fact that the Newfoundland disaster occurred just six months later, neither issue, the

---

[56] MUN Report, Recommendation #4, 34.

[57] Ibid., Recommendation #5, 34.

[58] Ibid., 36.

[59] Ibid., 22.

[60] *Aquaculture Act*, s. 6(3)(b).

[61] See Lynda V. Mapes, "State kills Atlantic salmon farming in Washington," *The Seattle Times*, March 2, 2018), https://www.seattletimes.com/seattle-news/politics/bill-to-phase-out-atlantic-salmon-farming-in-washington-state-nears-deadline/. It must be noted that the bill only applies to non-native fish. See Wash. Rev. Code, Title 79, Ch. 79.105, s. 79.105.170, https://app.leg.wa.gov/RCW/default.aspx?cite=79.105.170.

[62] Mapes, "Fish farm caused Atlantic salmon spill near San Juans".

false reporting to the provincial ministry (the basis for the license suspension) or falling below a standard of care in its operations, was raised in the Report.

Given the proximity of the Washington and Newfoundland incidents, it is surprising that the MUN Report did not ask squarely whether similar factors were at play regarding false reporting and negligence on the company's part. The 2018/2019 license for one of the ten sites involved in this incident includes the standard clause that its operations "shall be conducted with due diligence, in a reasonable manner and in accordance with good husbandry practices" and its license conditions require cleaning and disinfection of equipment in accordance with "disinfection protocols as outlined and specified by the AAHD."[63]

The licenses obtained through another Access to Information Request reveal a lot of discrepancies between where the sites are supposed to be located and where Google Earth shows them to actually be, as well as problems with sites being larger than their licensed size.[64] Hence, even if the Minister were to put stricter conditions in the licenses relating to stocking densities or impose "limits on the intensity with which aquaculture is conducted and organisms are concentrated at a site," as he or she is empowered to do under the *Aquaculture Act*, or to "specify measures to be taken to prevent the escape of aquatic animals," to mitigate risks associated with the development or spread of pathogenic agents, or to "minimize the risk of damage to the environment," it seems that in practice much of what is in the licenses may be flouted with impunity, including very basic information about the operation.[65]

---

[63] License # AQ15-LIC-0885, for a twenty-hectare farm in McGrath Cove South, Belle Bay, Lease # C-119897, https://atipp-search.gov.nl.ca/public/atipp/requestdownload?id=8845 (see pp. 18–19 of the 241 page PDF obtained via an October 31, 2018 Access to Information request). Licenses are not made publicly available, except in Quebec (see https://www.mapaq.gouv.qc.ca/Fr/Peche/md/Services/Pages/etablissementspermis.aspx). Lack of transparency is a serious problem at the present time when a public access request can take months and changes in licensing conditions can be made without notice. See Clarkson (2014, p. 168). See also s. 4(3)(f) of the *Aquaculture Act*, which requires the licensing application to state that the operation will be conducted "with diligence, in a reasonable manner and in accordance with standards, practices, and procedures set by the Minister." The AAHD is the Aquatic Animal Health Division of the provincial Department of Fisheries and Land Resources.

[64] Information obtained by Research Assistant River Sommerhalder.

[65] See ss. 4(6)(b), (f) and (g) of the *Aquaculture Act*.

Conclusion

Morton describes the "Salmon are Sacred" activism that she has been involved in, from the "Get out Migration" rally in 2010 (walking the 300-km length of Vancouver Island) (see Morton, 2021, pp. 104–115, which was "the biggest environmental rally in the history of British Columbia"), to the remarkable 280 days of occupation of a fish farm by Indigenous protestor Ernest Alfred starting on August 24, 2017 (pp. 230–289).[66] Morton singles out the win in Washington State as highly motivating during the occupation, as it showed it was politically possible to push out the farms (p. 279; see also p. 229, highlighting the role that Indigenous fishermen from the Lummi Nation played in the wake of finding 20,000 of the escaped Atlantic salmon in Washington State rivers). Salmon are more than food to Indigenous people; they are linked to culture, identity, and sovereignty (p. 214). They are teachers.[67] They are also relatives or kin.[68] As Sea Shepherd's founder Paul Watson has put it: "When I see a salmon farm, I see slavery and the debasement of the spirit of the fish that West Coast First Nations viewed as the buffalo of the sea" (quoted in Balcombe, 2016, p. 236). Sea Sheppard sent their ship the *Martin Sheen* to British Columbia in 2016 and 2017 (see Morton, 2021, pp. 206–232). Discussions about death of wild salmon on these tours invoked comparisons to European viruses like smallpox killing so many Indigenous people and the elimination of the buffalo (p. 134). Morton recalls a local Namgis event in which the screening of footage from inside a salmon pen had to be turned off partway through due to the number of people who were in tears, connecting the suffering of farmed fish to the suffering they experienced in residential schools (p. 228).

---

66 See interview "Alexandra Morton: Why Salmon are Sacred," *The Green Interview*, October 2011, https://thegreeninterview.com/interview/morton-alexandra/.

67 For one such Tlingit teaching, see *Shanyaak'utlaax: Salmon Boy* (February 6, 2019), https://www.youtube.com/watch?v=iGH8cmKKZ78.

68 See McGregor (2018, p. 282), explaining how lands and waters are relatives or teachers in Anishinaabe knowledge systems. See also Salmón (2000, p. 1327) on "kincentric ecology" understood in part as the insight from Indigenous people in North America "that life in any environment is viable only when humans view the life surrounding them as kin".

Events like "Get Out Migration" and Alfred's occupation sought to increase awareness about the role salmon play in the lives of Indigenous people, feeding upstream life from bears to trees. The "[t]rickle down effects" of losing wild salmon "impact [all] salmon-dependent wildlife: bears, eagles, and orcas" (Balcombe, 2016, p. 216). Morton explains: "When wild salmon enter the rivers to spawn, bears, eagles, wolves and other predators catch them and carry them into the forest to feed on. As these fish remains decompose, nutrients are released into the soil," specifically Nitrogen-15, which is only found in the ocean and helps support tree growth (Morton, 2021, p. 35). As a keystone species, the wild salmon are "a power cord between the open ocean and the forests, collecting the energy of sunlight hitting the open ocean and carrying it up the mountains" (p. 105). We need them.

Shortly after the mass mortality event in Newfoundland, the provincial government brought in a new Policies and Procedures Manual adopting new twenty-four hour public reporting requirements in the event of escape or "any abnormal mortality event" taking place on a licensed aquaculture site.[69] Specifics of mortality events must also be reported to the provincial ministry within twenty-four hours, setting out, for instance, the estimated number of fish involved.[70] This Minister was motivated to do something about the difficult situation he had been put in in terms of fearing he was in violation of the company's privacy for speaking out (he would now have a twenty-four hour public reporting requirement, as would they) and if they were required to report their mortality numbers (to him and to the public) within twenty-four hours, he would not find himself giving wrong numbers to the public

[69] Newfoundland and Labrador, Fisheries and Land Resources, *Aquaculture Policy and Procedures Manual* September 2019, "AP-17—Public Reporting," ss. 4 and 8, pp. 61–62 (revised October 10, 2019 and November 4, 2019), https://www.gov.nl.ca/ffa/files/licensing-pdf-aquaculture-policy-procedures-manual.pdf. The licenses already required reporting to the Aquatic Animal Health Division "[m]ortality and morbidity events greater than 0.05% per day for three consecutive days or greater than 400 kg of 2% of the inventory over a 24-h period or greater than 10,000 kg or 5% of the inventory over a 5-day period." See Condition #6, License # AQ15-LIC-0885.

[70] See *Aquaculture Policy and Procedures Manual*, s. 11(f), p. 62. The MUN Report is critical of the policies in this manual for being too vague (see pp. 31–32).

(that would turn out to be embarrassing).[71] Hence, the statement by the MUN Report that the new reporting requirements "would not have helped in a major way with the recent ME [mortality event]" is not quite accurate.[72] They would have helped the Minister.

The manual also set out that starting in January 2021, sea lice "abundance numbers" must also be reported to the department and to the public on a monthly basis.[73] An "Integrated Pest Management Plan—Including Sea Lice Management Plans" sets out that these numbers (where applicable) are to be sent to a third-party database such as Fishitrends.[74] This is a plan to *manage* sea lice not to institute penalties for exceeding limits. Morton characterizes such management as a "regulatory loophole," pointing out that as long as companies keep their lice numbers under the government limits and execute the plan, it is irrelevant if the plan works (2021, p. 319). Everyone at the Fish Health Committee meetings she attended in British Columbia knew that "the solution to sea lice was to institute fines for exceeding the limits" (p. 320).

Hence, it is more or less business as usual for the farms. They are free to take as much risk with the lives of the fishes as their insurance will permit.[75] The conditions for rampant sea lice transmission will continue with dense (and likely over) stocked pens. The inevitable waste created by the operation (excess feed and feces) will continue to create toxic algal blooms. More fish die and more divers must put themselves at risk

---

[71] Minister Byrne said, at least initially he did not make a public disclosure regarding the incident, as he understood (incorrectly it turned out) that he would be in violation of the *Access to Information and Protection of Privacy Act*, S.N.L. 2015, c. A-1.2. See Harvey (2020, 10, para. 26). This is the same legislation relied on to deny the Access to Information request as to maximum stocked populations. Hence, despite the Privacy Commissioner's decision, the Department appears to be continuing to rely on a capacious understanding of what it would mean to release information that would harm the business interests of MOWI.

[72] MUN Report, 31.

[73] *Aquaculture Policy and Procedures Manual*, s. 7, pp. 61–62.

[74] Ibid., "AP-40—Integrated Pest Management Plans—Including Sea Lice Management Plans," s. 7, pp. 118–119.

[75] Wildsmith speaks about the important role that insurance will need to play in the industry. See Wildsmith (1982a, pp. 128–130). At the time of writing, there was only one insurance company in Halifax that would provide aquaculture insurance. See 134, n. 47. It is almost quaint.

in order to clean the pens more frequently.[76] It would be difficult to conclude from the Newfoundland 2019 mass mortality event that the industry is being properly regulated or that the existing law (federal and provincial) is strong enough to protect the interests of the animals and the environment. The province's decision to temporarily suspend the company's license hardly constitutes appropriate punishment.[77] There were no fines or other penalties imposed.[78] There was literally no public action or even a statement by DFO, which twisted itself into a pretzel shape to both stay as far away from this event as possible, while at the same time issuing the permission to dispose of the pink sludge (see above). DFO says nothing about the impact on the wild populations of fish for which they are responsible. This is quite incredible when wild Atlantic salmon on Newfoundland's southern shore have been designated as threatened by the Committee on the Status of Endangered Wildlife in Canada and are being considered for inclusion on the Federal endangered species statute.[79] The only environmental assessment was done by a group collaborating under the protocols of a DFO-sponsored program

[76] A diver was injured in the 2019 Newfoundland event. See "Diver Airlifted from Salmon Clean-Up in Fortune Bay, Work-Stop Order Issued," *CBC News*, October 7, 2019, https://www.cbc.ca/news/canada/newfoundland-labrador/stop-work-order-fortune-bay-1.5311394. There was quite a lot of attention to this aspect of the event. See e.g., "As Diving Resumes at Salmon Die-Off Site, Doctor Wants More Action to Avoid Decompression Sickness," *CBC News*, October 10, 2019, available at https://www.cbc.ca/news/canada/newfoundland-labrador/diving-compression-sickness-treatment-improvements-1.5315927. Most of the twenty divers brought in to help the usual two company divers had never dived in a fish pen (MUN Marine Institute Report, p. 24). The Report noted that "diver safety was a major concern" but did not mention the injury or the work stop-order and its impact on the company's response time in terms of mort removal.

[77] S. 4(15) of the *Aquaculture Act* allows the Minister to cancel the license but only where directives relating to the maintenance of the site have not been followed, there are repeated breaches for which there have been suspensions under s. 4(10), or if the licensee stops owning or holding a lease or right of occupancy for the site, perhaps if they were to sell or transfer it.

[78] There are provisions for penalties in ss. 15 and 16 of the *Aquaculture Act* (fines not exceeding $5000 and/or imprisonment of not more than six months, as well as administrative penalties). These can apply in situations in which a person knowingly provides false or misleading information. However, there must be a duty to provide the information in the act or under the regulations, which were not there before the new Policy Manual was adopted. See s. 14(e).

[79] See *Salmonid Association of Eastern Newfoundland v. Her Majesty the Queen in Right of Newfoundland and Labrador*, 2020 NLSC 34, para. 109, https://www.canlii.org/en/nl/nlsc/doc/2020/2020nlsc34/2020nlsc34.html?resultIndex=1 (the statute is the *Species at Risk Act*, S.C. 2002, c. 29). This case, brought by the group Ecojustice just one month after the mass mortality event resulted in another Northern Harvest (MOWI) fish farm in Newfoundland

and chosen by the company.[80] Nothing was said or done relating to animal welfare, not at the time and not since the conclusion was released that the fish died by "hypoxic squeeze."[81]

There is now a provision in the provincial government's Policy Manual enacted pursuant to the *Aquaculture Act* to "ensure optimal animal welfare." However, it was not in place at the time of the event. The obligation is set out for "transport, sampling, fish handling, depopulation, and normal operations."[82] It must be asked, are responses to a mass mortality event of such proportions part of normal operations? The Information and Privacy Commissioner seemed to think so. He wrote "[t]he event was not unusual, as similar mass mortality events—though perhaps not on the same scale—have occurred in the Newfoundland and Labrador aquaculture industry in the past" (Harvey, 2020, p. 7, para. 17). Global warming will likely make such incidents involving spiraling deoxygenated environments inside pens more common. The MUN Report recommended a review of "salmon handling practices and policies in the context of fish welfare and health under extreme conditions which are likely to become the new norm."[83] If these mass mortalities become an insurable risk in "normal operations," then the policy manual's animal welfare provision would apply, as would the "humane euthanizing" requirement it includes.[84]

"Humane euthanizing" is not defined in the Policy Manual. The standard method for slaughtering Atlantic salmon in Canada is percussion with a stunner followed by bleeding-out performed in an ice

---

being ordered to conduct an environmental assessment of the impact of expanding its operations in Stephenville.

80 The program is called "Aboriginal Aquatic Resource & Oceans Management." See MAMKA Report, Executive Summary, p. i.

81 MUN Report, p. 8.

82 *Aquaculture Policy and Procedures Manual*, "AP 42—Animal Welfare," s. 1, p. 122.

83 See MUN Report, Recommendation 6, 34. The Report refers to "the next ME [mortality event]," "future ME [mortality events]," and "similar future events" (27, 27 and 28, 28).

84 See *Aquaculture Policy and Procedures Manual*, "AP 42—Animal Welfare," ss. 2 and 3, p. 122. These provisions require the facility's designated veterinarian perform the euthanasia or employees overseen and instructed by that veterinarian using the "[p]roper tools necessary for humanely euthanizing animals".

slurry.[85] This meets the World Organization for Animal Health (OIE) standards.[86] There are lots of methods used to slaughter fish that do not meet the OIE standard, including asphyxia in ice.[87] Asphyxia in slowly deoxygenating water would meet no standard. Both drowning and smothering are forbidden methods of euthanasia under the Regulations made pursuant to the *Animal Health Protection Act*, although it is unclear if the Regulations apply to farmed salmon.[88] Leaving so many of the fish to die over the Labor Day weekend would certainly be out of step with the obligation to provide them with a humane death. "Optimal animal welfare" must mean more than mere avoidance of an inhumane death or pain and suffering; it should include positive goals and conditions.[89]

Justin Trudeau, the Prime Minister of Canada, when he was running for re-election in the Fall of 2019, promised to phase out open-net farming in British Columbia by 2025 and to move the industry to land-based operations, a position advocated for by Morton and other environmental groups (Morton, 2021, p. 310).[90] However, fish farms

---

[85] See the Final Report of the European Commission, *Welfare of Farmed Fish: Common Practices During Transport and at Slaughter*, September 2017, s. 9.2 "Canada," http://publications.europa.eu/resource/cellar/facddd32-cda6-11e7-a5d5-01aa75ed71a1.0001.01/DOC_1.

[86] See ibid., Executive Summary, 6.

[87] Ibid.

[88] The *Animal Protection Regulations* are made pursuant to ss. 29 and 66 of the *Animal Health and Protection Act*. See ss. 11(e) and 11(j), *Newfoundland and Labrador Regulation 2012*, https://www.assembly.nl.ca/legislation/sr/annualregs/2012/nr120035.htm. However, s. 29 is in Part II, which does not apply if farmed salmon are considered (anadromous) fish under the *Wildlife Act* (as explained at the outset of the chapter) and s. 66 is in Part VI, which does include fish as a protected animal.

[89] "Positive animal welfare" focuses on an animal's individual experience without respect to their human-centered utility. The idea is that animals need positive experiences to have a normal life and appreciate what they lose when confined and manipulated in terms of culture, sense of self, personality, social bonds, cognitive potential, autonomy, play, and curiosity. Becca Franks, "Positive Animal Welfare for Aquatic Animals," Canadian Animal Law Conference, September 13, 2020.

[90] See Paul Withers, "Liberal promise to end open-pen salmon farms in B.C. making waves on east coast," *CBC News*, October 1, 2019, https://www.cbc.ca/news/canada/nova-scotia/liberal-promise-open-pen-salmon-farms-bc-canada-1.5303565. The promise has been scaled back to a commitment to develop a plan to transition away from the open net but they will not be removed by that date. See Sarah Cox, "Trudeau government backpedals on election promise to phase out B.C. open net salmon farms by 2025," *The Narwhal*, February 13, 2020, https://thenarwhal.ca/trudeau-government-backpedals-on-election-promise-to-phase-out-b-c-open-net-salmon-farms-by-2025/.

in containment tanks on land are still bad for wild fish because most farmed aquatic species (e.g., salmon, trout, and shrimp) are carnivorous and feeding them "puts additional pressure on wild fish and invertebrates for fishmeal" (Jacquet et al., 2019, p. 40). As Jonathan Balcombe explains, "[p]aradoxically, the production of factory-farmed fish does not relieve the pressure on wild fish populations. The primary food fed to farmed fishes is, well, fish" (Balcombe, 2016, p. 214). He estimates that two to five pounds of "reduction" or "feed fishes" such as mackerel and herrings are eaten for every one pound of the larger carnivorous fish like salmon, sea bass, and blue fin tuna that diners prefer (p. 215). "Scientists estimate that one-third of the global fish catch is turned into feed for other animals, roughly half of which goes to aquaculture" (Jacquet et al., 2019, p. 40). Like the raising of other animals for food, "[t]here is nothing sustainable about feeding fish to fish, to produce fewer fish" (Morton, 2021, p. 317).[91]

Land containment systems also require a lot of fresh water and energy to remove waste and control things like oxygen, salinity, and temperature (Clarkson, 2014, p. 147). Moving the "production" of seafood to this kind of system might feel like a step in the right direction; however, as with ordinary aquaculture, it "arguably merely shifts the cause of environmental damages" (Lee & Cloutier de Repentigny, 2019, p. 35). As these authors put it, "[a]n overreliance on the treadmill of technology fails to engage with the underlying social, political, and economic problems with the way natural resources are conceptualized and managed, and simply delays or displaces the issues" (p. 56), "replac[ing] one set of problems with another" (p. 59). Generally speaking "solutions to ecological concerns likely do not lie within the current productionist frame of

[91] Wildsmith noted that "one of the biggest expenses in many aquaculture operations is feeding the aquatic stock being cultivated," citing from a *Report of the FOA Technical Conference on Aquaculture, Kyoto, Japan, 26 May–2 June 1976*, estimating that 40% to 70% of the operating cost of most aquaculture operations is for food (Wildsmith, 1982b, pp. 126, 134, n. 33). Morton thinks that bright lights are used on farms to attract herring and other marine life in order to help feed the salmon stock (Morton, 2021, pp. 258, 260). The industry claims that the salmon are too domesticated to hunt wild fish. However, how are they able to survive and be found upriver if they cannot do this? Morton's footage from inside a pen showed them doing just this (p. 219). She also thinks herring are being caught and rendered into feed, which is illegal because the stocks are in a collapse and other herring fisheries are prohibited (p. 245).

mind that created the environmental crisis we seek to solve in the first place" (p. 63).

Land containment systems are not a solution for animal advocates either, as the industry will still be poorly regulated, the fish will be densely packed and still subject to all manner of risks. In a country quickly adopting one provincial "ag gag" law after another, and a national law looming on the horizon, Morton's solution—fish farmers should "move into tanks on land, erect tall fences around them and post *Keep Out* signs—even get some guard dogs" (Morton, 2021, p. 210)—is chilling.[92] Putting operations behind high walls with that kind of legal protection will interfere with the ability to do undercover investigations to expose how the animals are being treated. Fishes are particularly vulnerable to abuse in this environment as many people view them as insentient and not capable of feeling pain and there is a lot of temptation to cut corners when it comes to procedures that call for the use of anesthesia, for example. We typically do not register fish vocalizations and so do not hear a significant reaction to *anything* that is done to them. Workers dealing with enormous numbers of individuals will handle them roughly and leave them to die in cruel ways, throwing them into barrels where they suffocate slowly or are crushed by the weight of other fish. All of this (and worse) are shown in the Compassion Over Killing undercover investigation conducted on a fish farm in Bingham Maine.[93]

To someone on the West coast with a keystone species to protect, Atlantic salmon are the invaders. However, farmed Atlantic salmon also deserve our empathy. Morton writes, gazing down on the little salmon in a pen next to her: "As eggs they were released from their mothers with a knife. Hatched in trays, reared in steel tanks … they migrated to sea in the belly of a Norwegian registered ship. Now they were going in circles in a pen seven thousand kilometres from the ocean they belonged to" (p. 257). This is a sad plight indeed. Atlantic salmon on the East coast

---

[92] Alberta, Ontario, and Prince Edward Island all passed ag gag statutes in 2019 and 2020. Manitoba passed one in 2021. And there is a national bill in the works. See Animal Justice, "Fighting Canada's dangerous 'Ag Gag' laws," September 10, 2020 (updated April 2021), https://animaljustice.ca/blog/fighting-canadas-dangerous-ag-gag-laws. See also Lazare, 2020.

[93] See their video "Aquaculture: A Sea of Suffering". https://animaloutlook.org/investigations/.

might be closer to the waters they evolved in; however, their lives on the farms are no different, swimming in circles in concrete pens with not enough space, just like Orky and Corky. Little will improve for farmed fishes in a land-based containment system. All fish on the East coast of Canada swim with the ghosts of the cod fishes. Fish, all fish, deserve better than this. There is law relating to fish farms in Canada; the problem is that little of it is doing anything to protect the fishes, the ones that are left in the wild or the ones in the pens. As tends to be the case with all farmed animals, government is virtually indistinguishable from the industry it is supposed to be regulating. And industry is being reckless with the lives of the fishes and their surrounding environment.

Acknowledgement The author wishes to thank the members of the Brooks Institute for Animal Rights, Law and Policy 2021 Summer Academic Workshop, especially Jennifer Jacquet and Becca Franks. Thanks also to Angela Lee. The author also gratefully acknowledges the able research assistance of Clara Pencer, John River Sommerhalder, and Deniz Yilmaz. Sooin Kim of the Bora Laskin Law Library provided heroic reference support during the first and second Covid-19 lockdowns when this chapter was written. The editors were especially patient in waiting for the piece to be completed despite delays caused by that challenging time.

References

Balcombe, J. (2016). *What a fish knows: The inner lives of our underwater cousins*. Scientific American; Farrar, Straus and Giroux.

Bavington, D. (2010). *Managed annihilation: An unnatural history of the Newfoundland cod collapse*. University of British Columbia Press.

Braithwaite, V. (2010). *Do fish feel pain?* Oxford University Press.

Cassuto, D. N., & O'Brien, A. M. (2019). You don't need lungs to suffer: Fish suffering in the age of climate change with a call for regulatory reform. *Canadian Journal of Comparative and Contemporary Law, 5*, 31–75.

Clarkson, A. R. (2014). *The jurisdiction to regulate aquaculture in Canada.* LL.M. thesis, University of British Columbia. https://open.library.ubc.ca/media/download/pdf/24/1.0103615/3.

Fernandez, A. (2018). *Pierson v. Post, the hunt for the fox: Law and professionalization in American legal culture*. Cambridge University Press.

Foer, J. S. (2009). *Eating animals.* Back Bay Books; Little Brown.

Harvey, M. (2020, April 17). *Office of the information and privacy commissioner, Newfoundland and labrador. A-2020-005*. Department of Fisheries and Land Resources. https://www.oipc.nl.ca/pdfs/A-2020-005.pdf.

Jacquet, J., Franks, B., Godfrey-Smith, P., & Sánchez-Suárez, W. (2019, Winter). The case against octopus farming. *Issues in Science and Technology, 44*, 37–44.

Kurlansky, M. (1997). *Cod: A biography of the fish that changed the world.* Vintage Canada.

Lazare, J. (2020). Ag-gag laws, animal rights activism, and the constitution: What is protected speech? *Alberta Law Review, 58*(1), 83–105.

Lee, A. & Cloutier de Repentigny, P. (2019). Farming the sea, a false solution to a real problem: Critical reflections on Canada's aquaculture regulations. *Ottawa Law Review, 50*, 29–63.

McGregor, D. (2018). Indigenous environmental justice, knowledge, and law. *Kalfou, 5*(2), 279–296.

Mitchell, L. J. (2014, April 15). *East coast environmental law. Comparative analysis of five aquaculture regulatory frameworks in Canada.* https://www.ecelaw.ca/images/PDFs/Aquaculture_Regulation_Comparative_Analysis_for_Website.pdf.

Morton, A. (2021). *Not on My Watch: How a renegade whale biologist took on governments and industry to save wild salmon.* Random House Canada.

Penick, F. V. W. (1984). Legal regime for aquaculture. Review of aquaculture: The legal framework. *Marine Policy, 8*, 72–73.

Russell, D. A., & McConnell, M. L. (1995). Preface to "After the collapse: Being a collection of studies on the experience of the 'collapse' of Atlantic Canada's fishery in the years 1994 and 1995 and the phenomenon of change." *Dalhousie Law Journal, 18*(1), 5–11.

Salmón, E. (2000). Kincentric ecology: Indigenous perceptions of the human-nature relationship. *Ecological Applications, 10*(5), 1327–1332.

VanderZaag, D. L., Chao, G., & Covan, M. (2006). Canadian aquaculture and the principles of sustainable development: Gauging the law and policy tides and charting a course. In D. L. VanderZaag & G. Chao (Eds.), *Aquaculture law and policy: Towards principled access and operations* (pp. 49–114). Routledge.

Vettese, T., Franks, B., & Jacquet, J. (2020, Summer). The great fish pain debate. *Issues in Science and Technology, 36*(4), 49–53. https://issues.org/the-great-fish-pain-debate/.

Wadiwel, D. J. (2016). Do fish resist? *Cultural Studies Review, 22*(1), 196–242.

Wildsmith, B. H. (1982a). *Aquaculture: The legal framework*. Emond-Montgomery.

Wildsmith, B. H. (1982b). Aquaculture—Down to specifics. Review of Gerald Bowen, Coastal aquaculture law and policy: A case study of California (Boulder, CO: Westview Press, 1981). *Marine Policy, 6*(4), 339–340.

Wolfson, D. J., & Sullivan, M. (2004). Foxes in the hen house: Animals, agribusiness, and the law: A modern American fable. In C. R. Sunstein & M. C. Nussbaum (Eds.), *Animal rights: Current debates and new directions* (pp. 205–233). Oxford University Press.

Wringe, B. F., Jeffrey, N. W., Stanley, R. R. E., Hamilton, L. C., Anderson, E. C., Fleming, I. A., Grant, C., Dempson, J. B., Veinott, G., Duffy, S. J., & Bradbury, I. R. (2018). Extensive hybridization following a large escape of domesticated Atlantic salmon in the Northwest Atlantic. *Communications Biology, 1*(108), 1–9. https://www.nature.com/articles/s42003-018-0112-9.pdf.

7

Plastic: From Miracle Material to Detritus and Disaster: A History of Benefits, Harms, Pandemics, and the Limitations of Regulation

Krista Smithers, Bill McClanahan, and Avi Brisman

Introduction

In 2009, marine research scientists aboard the New Horizon laboratory vessel departed San Diego, California, to embark on the Scripps Environmental Accumulation of Plastic Expedition. Prior to this voyage, little was known about what would come to be called the "Great Pacific Garbage Patch," other than that it was an area in which oceanic currents converged in such a way that particles of plastics and other nonbiodegradable waste accumulated in a gyre. Upon the vessel's arrival to the gyre, some 1000 miles off of the coast of California, researchers

K. Smithers · B. McClanahan (✉) · A. Brisman
School of Justice Studies, Eastern Kentucky University, Richmond, KY, USA
e-mail: Bill.Mcclanahan@eku.edu

A. Brisman
e-mail: Avi.Brisman@eku.edu

J. Gacek and R. Jochelson (eds.), *Green Criminology and the Law*, Palgrave Studies in Green Criminology,
https://doi.org/10.1007/978-3-030-82412-9_7

were stunned at the results of their analyses of samples of water collected at various depths, finding it to contain large quantities of "microplastics"—a term coined five years earlier by Professor Richard Thompson of the University of Plymouth to refer to small particles of plastic under 5 mm in length. Researchers aboard the New Horizon laboratory vessel also observed several species of marine wildlife, such as small crabs and other "biological inhabitants," residing in plastic bottles and other pieces of plastic refuse. Over the next decade, the "Great Pacific Garbage Patch" and its cruelly unlucky inhabitants would capture the attention of an increasingly wide audience, with moments of media interest from a host of outlets, including CNN, *Nature*, *National Geographic*, and *The New York Times*. This mainstream media attention was buttressed by viral videos like one uploaded to YouTube in 2015 in which researchers in Costa Rica discovered a plastic drinking straw embedded in the nostril of an Olive Ridley sea turtle (Pacific Ridley sea turtle) and removed it with pliers before releasing the suffering turtle. (At the time of this writing, the video[1] has been viewed just under 80 million times.) Public revulsion and subsequent calls for action followed each moment of mediated attention to the problem of marine plastic pollution, culminating in efforts to ban plastic bags, cups, drinking straws, and other single-use items, as well as campaigns to diminish waste at the individual level with reusable aluminum drinking straws and water bottles.

Indeed, within the past several years, attempts in the United States (US) to reduce single-use plastics—largely through regulatory measures such as plastic bag and straw bans—have garnered substantial media attention. Most notable among these efforts has been a California municipality's rule aimed at decreasing the consumption of plastic straws by proposing fines up to US$1000 and six months in jail for restaurant workers who distribute plastic straws absent a consumer's request (Hafner, 2018). Other states and municipalities have also attempted to cut plastic waste, such as by charging consumers fees for plastic bags or banning them outright, in addition to advertising and encouraging the use of personal reusable bags (Gibbens, 2019)—although, as we will

[1] The video is available here: https://youtu.be/d2J2qdOrW44.

explain later, many such measures have been placed on hold due to the COVID-19 pandemic.

Green criminology, meanwhile, which emerged from critical criminology in the 1990s (Lynch, 1990; South, 1998) and has since gone on to apply a "green" criminological perspective to a diverse cast of issues and problems affecting the given natural environment, has often taken up several central dimensions of the problems associated with plastic pollution, including harms to animals (e.g., Beirne, 1999; Sollund, 2011; Wyatt, 2013), harms to hydroecology and global water systems (e.g., Brisman et al., 2018; McClanahan, 2014), issues of consumption (especially patterns of consumption in capitalist societies) (e.g., Ferrell, 2013; Ruggiero & South, 2013), harmful and exploitative global systems of waste exchange (Bisschop & Walle, 2013), climate change (Kramer & Bradshaw, 2020; White, 2018) and more. It seems to us, then, that there is ample opportunity to consider the interconnected ecological issues of plastic pollution in future green criminological research agendas, and that in order for law to more fully keep abreast of trends in ecology and human behavior alike, there is ample need for law to be informed by the insights offered by green criminology.

In this chapter, we describe the problem of plastic pollution from a green criminological perspective, beginning by exploring the history of plastic and the role it plays in today's world. From here, we turn to some of the ways in which plastic production and pollution is implicated in harms to atmospheric, hydrological, and terrestrial ecologies and wildlife (marine or otherwise). Next, we offer a brief sketch of the dominant approaches to plastics regulation, noting the ways in which regulatory schemes have reconfigured causal chains of production, consumption, and pollution in order to place responsibility on the shoulders of consumers. We conclude by returning to the critical roots of green criminology with some thoughts on consumption itself.

A Brief History of Plastic

Plastic, once defined simply as an object or material which was "pliable and easily shaped," now refers to the vastly developed body of polymer materials utilized in a multitude of products and applications in almost all aspects of human life. Indeed, despite its contemporary ubiquity—we would wager, for example, that no one reading this chapter is less than a few centimeters from a staggering amount of plastics—plastic has not always comprised such a seemingly outsized proportion of the material objects we bring into being.

Prior to World War II (WWII), cork (much of it shipped from Europe) was used in great quantities in the United States because, at the time, it was the most flexible material (Ewing & Belile, 2019). While the plastic industry had already become established prior to the start of the war for the production of novelty goods for the upper classes, cork was the ideal material for insulation in various items, including gaskets and other plane parts and metal bottle caps and lids used in new methods of food storage (Ewing & Belile, 2019). When the war started, the United States feared that it would be unable to import cork from Europe due to German blockades of shipping routes in the Atlantic Ocean. As a result, the United States restricted the use of cork for defense and endorsed a research and development program, which led to the beginning of a nascent plastic industry (Ewing & Belile, 2019). Throughout the war, plastic came to play an integral role in the industrial mass production of instruments used in battle (e.g., body armor, helmet liners, parachutes, plane cockpits, plexiglass plane cockpits, ropes), providing stronger and (seemingly) sustainable alternatives to cork, as well as rubber (Young America Films, 1944). Because of its utility in the war effort, plastic was heralded as a miracle material and a lifesaver.

After the war, plastic initially appeared to serve little purpose, leaving workers without jobs and the plastic industry scrambling to find its niche during times of peace (Ewing & Belile, 2019). The industry responded, however: nylon, for example, used in part in automobile wheels and parachute production, was repurposed for toothbrushes and women's pantyhose. Plexiglass, utilized in place of glass in airplanes, became the replacement for automobile windshields (Ewing & Belile, 2019; Young America Films, 1944). Soon, plastic began to be produced for everyday domestic items marketed primarily toward housewives, a miracle material that revolutionized industrial and domestic practices alike. Indeed, within a short period of time, plastic appeared to be everywhere—from Tupperware food receptacles and plastic food wrap to containers for cleaners, soaps, and various other liquids to Lycra in clothing (e.g., spandex). Of the most contemporarily ubiquitous and visible examples were plastic bags, which were introduced in 1977 as an alternative to paper bags and, by 1979, more plastic was being produced than steel in the United States (Ewing & Belile, 2019).

Meanwhile, the amount of waste (including, of course, newly pervasive plastic waste) produced by Americans' rate of consumption increased steadily and, by 1986, there was so much waste in New York City that local landfills were struggling with a lack of space (Hanbury et al., 2019). In 1987, the people of Islip, Long Island, were faced with landfill capacity issues because the amount of waste exceeded regional landfills' capacity. Lowell Harrelson, a businessman, proposed to load the excess waste onto a barge and ship it south along the coast (Hanbury et al., 2019). Soon after his proposal, Harrelson leased a barge named the Mobro 4000, loaded it with waste, and departed for North Carolina to deliver it to a landfill willing to accept the load. Unloading was denied by the landfill, however, because of fear of biohazardous waste from medical facilities after a hospital bedpan was found on the barge. This led to the barge being denied entry at subsequent landfills, leaving the loaded container ship floating along the coast for about five months before a solution was reached (Hanbury et al., 2019). Eventually, the garbage was incinerated where it had originated, and the residue was sent to the original destination in North Carolina. The Mobro 4000 became a symbol of the growing waste problem in the United States, sparking a sense of individual responsibility for household waste and marking a substantial increase in recycling rates in the 1980s (Hanbury et al., 2019).

Today, plastic permeates all aspects of life and ecology, including air, food, land, and water. Unfortunately, and as noted at the outset, plastic particles appear in the middle of the world's oceans, including those furthest from human civilization. According to data from the United Nations Environment Programme (UNEP, 2018), 300 million tons of plastic waste enters the ecosystem every year. Researchers estimate that since the early 1950s, when plastic production skyrocketed, the industry has produced more than 8.3 billion tons of plastic, 60% of which has ended up in a landfill or the natural environment (UNEP, 2018). The annual estimates of plastic waste and the lack of recycling demand attention, especially as consumption rates are projected to continue to increase.

In fact, plastic waste results from the indiscriminate consumption of single-use plastics and a culture of consumption fostered by the convenient availability of material goods through superstores and online shopping. As Sinha and Plamondon (2017) claim, six of the "absolute worst plastic pollution culprits" include: plastic bags, plastic water bottles, plastic coffee and tea cups and lids (or plastic lined cups), plastic food containers, plastic utensils, and plastic straws. These are consumed in vast quantities on a daily basis, generally without concern for where they will end up after being discarded. Thus, while plastic is now used for countless purposes in nearly all facets of our daily existence, its over-utilization is threatening the integrity of our oceans, endangering wildlife, and causing harm to human health.

Plastic and Environmental Harm

The production, use, and improper disposal of plastic presents various harms to the ecosystem and its inhabitants. "Marine plastic pollution"—probably the most contemporarily visible form of plastic pollution, due to the sorts of headline-grabbing moments described at the outset of this chapter—refers the disposal or abandonment of any persistent, manufactured, or processed solid plastic polymer material in the marine and coastal environment (Le Guern, 2018; UNEP, 2018). In addition to the dumping of waste materials along beaches and at sea, littering inland can impact marine and coastal areas because of the movement of water toward the oceans. The detrimental impacts of plastic on the oceans stem from the very same qualities that heralded it a "miracle material" during and after WWII, including its buoyancy, durability, heat resistance, and light weight (Le Guern, 2018).

During its emergence as a miracle material, one of the qualities most admired by consumers was its sturdiness and resilience. Unfortunately, this means that plastic will not biodegrade. When other materials in the ecosystem break down, they return to base elements that may reenter the natural cycle. A simple example would be an animal dying, decomposing, and becoming fertilizer for the plant life in the immediate area. In contrast, plastic is incapable of returning to the base components used to create it (Le Guern, 2018). When plastic degrades through a process called "photodegradation," the result is microplastics, the small particles described in the introduction of this chapter.

Plastic is light weight means it is buoyant, resulting in widespread dispersal (regardless of where the plastic enters the ecosystem) and in concentrations of microplastics like the "Great Pacific Garbage Patch," mentioned above. Many in the media claimed these "islands of garbage" were the size of Texas and visible from space in order to sensationalize the issue of plastic litter for readers.[2] In truth, much of the accumulation of plastic in the oceans' gyres are soupy collections of microplastics, as well as raft-like agglomerations of bags, bottles, fishing nets, and other large plastics that can nevertheless *not* be seen from space (Le Guern, 2009/2018; Parker, 2018; Rochman & Browne, 2013). This truth, though, stands next to another, more important truth: these collections are vast, shameful, threats to oceanic life. Just as the content of these "islands" and "patches" are varied, so, too are the origins of marine plastics, although there are some familiar culprits: approximately 10% of overall microplastic waste in the oceans comes from tires, according to a 2017 study, while a 2017 report by International Union for Conservation of Nature put the figure at 28%. Research from *National Geographic* submits that fishing gear comprises 76% of the "Great Pacific Garbage Patch" (Parker, 2018; Root, 2019) and, of course, there are also the infamous single-use plastic items, such as the straw in the turtle's nose or the plastic six-pack ring around the seabird's neck.

The long life and mobility of plastic accumulating in the oceans, combined with plastic's porous nature, which allows it to absorb toxic substances, render it a serious threat to ecosystems around the world (Le Guern, 2018). Indeed, plastic debris has the potential to collect or absorb toxic substances from the water in which it is floating (Le Guern,

[2] For a detailed description of the ways in which media conditions social attitudes toward the environment and ecological harm and crime, see, e.g., Brisman and South (2014, 2016).

2018). As plastic moves in the ocean currents, it can act as a carrier, contaminating receiving waters or marine life that mistakenly ingest it as food. This pollution is not only harmful, but widespread; as reported by the US Environmental Protection Agency (EPA, 2019a), plastic in its various forms and sizes can be found in most habitats, both marine and terrestrial.

Plastic and Threats to Marine Life and Wildlife

The sizes and forms of plastic pose various threats to the health of marine life. Birds, dolphins, fish, seals, turtles, and other animals have accidentally ingested plastic or have become entangled in and suffocated by shaped plastic materials (Gourmelon, 2015; Le Guern, 2018). Consumption can cause nonhuman animals to choke or can impede digestion of food, and various plastics are also known to leak toxic chemicals into their immediate environment, as well as any animals that ingest them (Le Guern, 2009/2018).

Extensive research into consumption habits of seabirds provides insight into viable explanations for why seabirds consume plastic materials, as well as potential health risks associated with ingestion. Phillips and Waluda (2020) published an analysis of a time-series study spanning twenty-six years, wherein they documented plastic consumption by seabirds in southern Georgia. Not only did the time-series reveal the forms and sizes of ingested plastic, but also the ingested plastics' point of origin and potential source of pollution.

Seabirds and other marine life which consume plastic mistakenly identify it as food due to similarities in color, shape, and size (Wehle & Coleman, 1983; Phillips & Waluda, 2020). Whereas the marine turtle selects plastic bags, mistaking them as their preferred snack—jellyfish—seabirds may consume a variety of different plastics that it confuses for food (Wehle & Coleman, 1983). Direct physical effects of plastic consumption contributing to poor health and potential death in individual seabirds of various species include blockage of enzyme secretion, partial gut obstruction, suppressed appetite, ulcerations in stomach and intestinal linings, and weight loss (Phillips & Waluda, 2020; Wehle & Coleman, 1983).

In addition to the direct physical threats, plastic poses a potential biological–chemical danger upon ingestion. As mentioned above, plastics release toxic chemicals as they photodegrade and can adsorb toxic substances from polluted waters like a sponge. Once in the stomach of an organism, the absorbed toxins can then be transferred from the plastic to the tissues of that organism. Wehle and Coleman (1983) found that plasticizers and other harmful additives may concentrate in the fatty tissues of seabirds, resulting in aberrant behavior, eggshell thinning, or tissue damage. They surmised that as tissues were mobilized for energy, the toxins may be released in lethal doses.

Public Health and Economy

The aforementioned detrimental impact of plastic litter upon marine life causes a chain reaction of effects that extend to humans. When humans consume fish, they are ingesting what the fish ate, including any plastic toxins residing within tissues. Research has also demonstrated that microplastics can be found in drinking water from around the world, and even in beer (Kosuth et al., 2018), while other recent research has found that nearly all major brands of bottled water contain microplastics (Mason et al., 2018), with an average of 325 microplastic particles per liter of bottled water. The most common polymer found in bottled water has been polypropylene (PP), and often, the plastic particle fragments are visible to the naked eye. These data suggest that most of the contamination comes from packaging or the bottling process itself.

Significant economic impacts also occur when marine debris affects tourism, the fishing industry, and navigation (EPA, 2019b). The areas experiencing the adverse effects of marine plastic pollution must divert resources and money into resolving the issues. When plastic litter is accumulating in tourist and high foot-traffic locations, such as beaches and parks, local and regional economies suffer. Vacationers may look for other places to visit if they perceive a place as visually unappealing or unsanitary, thus decreasing the amount of potential capital entering the area. Further consequences include the undue investment of resources to cleaning, maintaining, and advertising the beach to better appeal to tourists.

Plastics Regulation in the United States

The life cycle of plastic is comprised of three stages: *production*, *consumption*, and *disposal*. For the purposes of this chapter, our discussion of the production stage focuses on the production of plastic materials purchased or utilized by *individual* consumers as opposed to businesses or corporations.[3] The production stage of plastic is where plastic is developed and formed into a marketable product, such as microbeads, packaging, plastic bags, plastic straws, single-use bottles, and Tupperware. For the consumption stage, we center our discussion on the consumption of plastic products by individuals. Finally, for the disposal phase, we examine regulations surrounding the disposal of plastic materials.

Production

The US Congress passed the Microbead-Free Waters Act of 2015 over concerns surrounding the effects of cosmetic-utility microbeads that were being washed down the drain and impacting small fish and other wildlife, who were mistaking the microbeads for food (EPA, 2019b). As of today, this is the only US federal law restricting the production of a *specific* plastic product. Much regulation in the plastic production/manufacturing sector concerns reduction of hazardous air pollutants emitted as a by-product of manufacturing plastics. The Clean Air Act (CAA) of 1970[4] authorizes the EPA to establish air quality standards

[3] Our aim here, of course, is not to claim that it is individual-level consumers who bear the burden of responsibility for plastic pollution in comparison to much more powerful corporate-industrial actors. Instead, we focus on the individual consumer *precisely because* that is the source of marine plastic pollution which has been responsibilized by those same powerful corporate-industrial actors.

[4] 42 U.S.C. §§ 7401 et seq.

in the interest of public health and welfare, and to regulate the emissions of hazardous air pollutants from multiple sources. Under the CAA, states were directed to develop state implementation plans (SIPs), which would apply to industrial sources in their state, making the industries accountable to the state in which they were located (EPA, 2019c). The Clean Water Act (CWA) of 1972,[5] seeks to regulate pollutants released into US waters. A number of programs have been established under the CWA, including the requirement of a permit to discharge any pollutant from a point source in navigable waters. Thus, the plastic industry is regulated insofar as the manufacturing of plastic must comply with the provisions of the CAA and CWA.

Consumption

There are currently no federal laws in the United States restricting the use or purchase of plastics—single-use or otherwise. There are, however, a few states making progress in the movement to restrict and ban single-use plastic items, namely, plastic bags, straws and, in some places, foamed plastics. *National Geographic* publishes a special series called "Planet or Plastic?"—a multi-year effort to raise awareness by providing various information and resources regarding bans on plastic. One such piece in the series described the "complicated landscape" in plastic legislation (Gibbens, 2019). The map from Gibbens' article, reproduced in Fig. 7.1, categorizes states according to the stage of state legislation regarding preemptions and bans on plastic—current as of August 2019.

California was the first state to take the initiative to ban plastic bags, and more than 250 local jurisdictions in the state have additional plastic restrictions on items, such as straws and foamed plastics (Gibbens, 2019). While California lawmakers are discussing the phasing out of all plastic products that are not 100% recyclable in the state, the recyclability of plastic according to the resin identification coding (RIC) system (Table 7.1), and the process of recycling it, are completely different matters.

[5] 33 U.S.C §§ 1251 et seq.

Fig. 7.1 *National Geographic*; Planet or plastic? See the complicated landscape of plastic bans in the United States (*Source* Sarah Gibbens. August 15, 2019)

At the state level, Hawaii does not ban single-use plastics, but each of its four counties do, making it a de facto state-wide ban if not a *de jure* one. Connecticut implemented a state ban on the use of plastic bags, causing retailers to switch to paper bags and to promote reusable bags. While not all regulations start in small government, much US legislation has roots in local ordinances and municipal regions, moving from cities and towns to the county and state level and sometimes resulting in federal adoption of similar regulations. Many of the campaigns against plastic consumption make pleas to the morals and conscience of consumers. Such appeals serve as a way of assigning responsibility for environmental health to the individual.

Table 7.1 System of coding plastic resins

Resin code	Description	Packaging applications
1 PET	Polyethylene (PET, PETE) Aka. Polyester	Beverage bottles, food jars (e.g., jams, jellies, peanut butter), microwaveable trays, ovenable films **Non-packaging applications**: carpet, engineering moldings films, monofilament, strapping, and textiles
2 HDPE	High-density polyethylene (HDPE)	Bags for cereal box liners, grocery, and retail. Bottles for cosmetics, dish and laundry detergents, household cleaners, juice, milk, and shampoo **Non-packaging applications**: Injection molding, reusable shipping containers
3 PVC	Polyvinyl chloride (PVC, Vinyl)	Flexible packaging (bags for bedding and medical, deli and meat wrap, shrink wrap, and tamper resistance). Rigid packaging (blister packs, clamshells) **Non-packaging applications**: Flexible applications (medical blood bags, medical tubing, and wire insulation). Major uses are rigid applications (decking, fencing, pipe, railing, siding, window frames)
4 LDPE	Low-density polyethylene (LDPE)	Bags for bread, dry cleaning, newspapers, fresh produce, frozen foods, and household garbage; shrink wrap and stretch film; coatings for paper milk cartons and hot and cold beverage cups; container lids, squeezable bottles (e.g., honey, mustard), toys **Non-packaging applications**: Major uses are in injection molding applications, adhesives and sealants, and wire and cable coverings

(continued)

Table 7.1 (continued)

Resin code	Description	Packaging applications
5 PP	Polypropylene (PP)	Containers for deli foods, margarine, takeout meals, and yogurt; medicine bottles; bottle caps and closures; bottles for catsup (Ketchup) and syrup **Non-packaging applications**: Major uses are in fibers, appliances, and consumer products, including durable applications such as automotive and carpeting
6 PS	Polystyrene (PS)	Food service items (cups, cutlery, bowls, hinged takeout containers, meat and poultry trays, plates, and rigid food containers such as yogurt). These items may be made with foamed or non-foamed PS Protective foam packaging for electronics, furniture, and other delicate items; packing peanuts, known as "loose fill"; compact disc cases and aspirin bottles **Non-packaging applications**: Major uses in agriculture trays, building insulation, cable spools, coat hangers electronic housings, video cassette cartridges, and medical products and toys
7 Other	Other	Three- and five-gallon reusable water bottles, some citrus juice and catsup bottles; oven-baking bags, barrier layers, and custom packaging

Source Sinha and Plamondon (2017)

Plastics regulations have also, like so many other things, become occasional planks in the platforms of the sorts of culture wars that configure American politics, with conservative and right-wing politicians and commentators raising the specter of plastic bag and straw bans as evidence of a nefarious leftist regulatory agenda. As such, bans more or less predictably reflect the geographies of American electoral politics. State-wide bans on the consumption of plastic material(s) are present in eight states; six states of these states' legislatures have Democratic control, and two are divided between Democrats and Republicans (NCSL, 2019). The eighteen states with preemption laws preventing municipalities from passing legislature banning plastic materials are held primarily by the Republican Party (Legis. Control 14/18; Gov. Party 11/18; State Control 11/18). Meanwhile, those states that have passed some form of plastic regulation or ban are primarily Democratic (Legis. Control 7/7; Gov. Party 6/7; State Control 6/7).

Disposal

As noted above, plastic does not biodegrade and presents various harms for the nonhuman inhabitants of ecosystems, as well as the economy and human health. Thus, there is a debate as to how to manage the plastic waste properly, effectively, and ethically. While we tend to imagine that the plastics we purchase are ultimately recycled, whether dropped in curbside recycling bins or in public municipal waste containers, most of the time, plastic is sent to landfills or discarded (littered); recycling rates tend to be low—8.4% (3.0 million tons) in 2017 (EPA, 2019d). Why is this the case and how did this come to be? One possible answer—and one that we find significant support for in the critical foundations of green criminology—is that public opinion on plastic was largely constructed under the silent influence of the plastics industry itself. As investigative reporting by National Public Radio and PBS's *Frontline* has demonstrated (Sullivan, 2020), the plastics industry—through lobbying and other legal and legislative efforts as well as through public relations campaigns and more subtle forms of public messaging—has promoted the notion that a significant amount of used plastics are ultimately recycled, despite industry knowledge that the vast majority of used plastics (including those sold to developing economies in the Global South by the comparatively wealthy nations of the North) ultimately winds up buried in landfills, not recycled. Among the mechanisms through which the plastics industry has constructed and promulgated this image of widespread recycling (and, of course, the individual-level responsibilization it has fostered), perhaps none is as powerfully ubiquitous as the familiar system, described below, by which plastics are labeled and numbered to indicate their recyclability.

In 1988, the Society of Plastics Industry (SPI) developed the voluntary plastic RIC system, noted above, to address an increasing need of recycling programs in communities due to rising rates in waste. In 2008, SPI began working with ASTM International, an international standards organization formerly known as American Society for Testing and Materials, to ensure that progressive developments in the plastic industry were updated in the RIC system. While the RIC system was developed to identify resin content rather than recyclability, today the system is utilized by municipalities and various entities managing the end-of-life of plastics (ASTM, 2018). The RIC system consists of six categories of plastic resins, and a seventh category to include outliers as shown in Table 7.1.

The most commonly accepted RIC designations are one, three, and seven (Sinha & Plamondon, 2017), and as part of ongoing efforts by ASTM International, assigned task groups are striving to expand identification of materials currently designated as "other" in the RIC system. This can further assist consumers, manufacturers, and recycling programs in increasing the amount of plastic recycled properly. Rochman and Browne (2013) present an argument for classifying plastic waste as hazardous, which would allow the EPA to act through the Comprehensive Environmental Response, Compensation, and Liability Act (known as "CERCLA" or the "Superfund"). Under CERCLA (42 U.S.C. §9601 et seq. [1980]), the government funds the cleanup of orphaned hazardous waste sites when liability cannot be determined. When liability of the hazardous waste site is identifiable, the EPA is granted power to seek responsible parties and assure cooperation in cleanup (EPA, 2019a).

If classified as "hazardous," the plastic debris/waste already filling the oceans and other sites of accumulation within US jurisdiction would be susceptible to action by the EPA through CERCLA (Rochman & Browne, 2013). While Rochman and Browne's argument is appealing and compelling, it has not been embraced by the plastics industry.

In early 2020, the EPA prepared a draft proposal of federal regulations that extend producer responsibility when it comes to the recycling of its own products. While one may wonder why such measures have not been undertaken already, it is important to remember that the United States lacks an efficient recycling program at the national level. Recycling occurs at the local or municipal level and there is no federal oversight. Recycling is thus highly dependent upon the availability and convenience of recycling programs within municipalities, as well as individual consumer recycling habits and knowledge. Many plastic materials/products could be recycled; local recycling programs may not have the means (equipment or finances) to recycle specific items. Common recycling policies for residential properties include curbside recycling of glass, metals, and plastics, drop-off recycling, deposit-refund systems (bottle bills), and marginal pricing for household waste. Again, however, recycling methods and acceptable materials are dependent on the local recycling center's capabilities, contributing to a complex and inconsistent landscape of disposal options and experiences.

While a municipality's ability to collect and recycle plastics is key, the process is heavily dependent on individual households' and consumers' willingness to accept responsibility. According to Nixon and Saphores (2014), the most important determinants of household recycling are an individual's attitude toward recycling. If individuals view recycling as inconvenient or that the added effort bears little impact, recycling habits are likely to decrease. Thus, omitting perceived recycling obstacles and benefits as well as moral considerations may positively affect household recycling (Nixon & Saphores, 2014). Of course, the economics of household recycling—and recycling in general—are also a determinant force in household recycling; as Koford et al. describe, "ethical duty" accounts for roughly 63% of household willingness to recycle, while economic motivations compel the remaining 37% of participation in household plastic recycling (Koford et al., 2012, p. 750).

There are two main collection methods employed by municipalities for recyclable materials: curbside pick-up and drop-off locations. The increased convenience of curbside pick-up is more likely to encourage individuals and households to recycle, as there is less hassle involved (Nixon & Saphores, 2014). Interestingly, drop-off locations are more common in rural areas and, according to the data from Nixon and Saphores (2014) study, rural residents are more likely to recycle than their urban and suburban counterparts. But Nixon and Saphores (2014) do not explain *why* rural residents are more likely to recycle, having collected only quantitative data that they recycle at higher rates. The increased likelihood of rural residents to recycle over their urban counterparts may be a product of the intimacy many rural residents have with the environment which may encourage increased feelings of responsibility or action to keep the environment clean and healthy. Future work in green criminology might build on existing work connecting green and "rural" criminologies (Brisman et al., 2014) in order to investigate the effects of place on attitudes toward the environment and the adoption of pro-ecological habits.

Aside from municipal recycling programs, some environmentally conscious businesses and organizations provide alternative recycling locations and services that can accept recyclable materials that the municipality may not be able to accept or process. Additional approaches to encouraging and facilitating recycling, as well as waste reduction, include market-based instruments, such as deposit-refund programs (mentioned above) and unit-based pricing. Deposit-refund programs require consumers to pay a deposit that can be returned when the recyclable product is recycled appropriately. Unit-based pricing programs charge individuals for the disposal of their trash, but these programs can lead to illegal dumping of waste, thus causing more harm than good (Nixon & Saphores, 2014; Viscusi et al., 2013).

Recycling at the level of the individual consumer must be learned and become habit in order for the process to be effective. The attitudes, beliefs, knowledge, and norms of individuals are of importance when considering the likelihood of individuals to commit to recycle regularly. The first step toward consumer responsibility in the purchase and management of plastics is a thorough consumer education regarding the items and materials (Dauvergne, 2018; Fisk, 1973).

If people do not know about or believe the extent of harm propagated by plastic, or understand how to recycle, or care about the effects of plastic, or assert that changing their current practices would be inconvenient, they are less likely to recycle. Knowledge of recycling programs (e.g., what materials are accepted, where to recycle) and environmental concerns surrounding plastic have a positive correlation with the inclination to recycle in the United States (Nixon & Saphores, 2014). The most effective factor to encourage recycling of any materials is to make the act more convenient. The more convenient and less complicated the act of recycling is for the consumer, the more willing the individual will be to partake in it. If the individual does not have to separate plastic from other recyclables (e.g., paper, glass) or separate plastic by RIC codes, recycling is likely to increase. Unfortunately, the less effort exerted by the individual, the more work for recycling facilities—and the more costly it will be for municipalities.

Discussion and Conclusion

As stressed throughout this chapter, plastic takes many forms and there are seemingly endless applications and areas where it is used. Consider the difference between "extended-use" and "single-use." These identifications refer to the manufacturer's intended use of products by consumers. Single-use plastic is meant to serve one function for a discrete, limited time and is then to be recycled or discarded as waste. Extended-use plastic is supposed to be used for longer periods of time, requiring replacement only when broken or worn beyond use. Examples of extended-use plastics could include car parts, reusable plastic bottles, toothbrushes, and various appliances. Once a reusable plastic needs replacement, the material may be discarded, recycled, or, in some instances, returned to the manufacturer.

Knowing the present extent of harm caused by plastics in ecosystems and the adverse effects on wildlife begs the question: Why is plastic available for mass consumption in the form of single-use plastics in the first place? One of the greatest hurdles for reducing plastic pollution is the deeply ingrained *plastic culture* wherein plastic use and consumption is part of the daily lives of the average person in the United States. The plastic industry turned plastic from a novelty to a perceived necessity for consumers—all at the expense of planetary health (see generally: Sullivan, 2020). Furthermore, items that were once passed down as heirlooms, such as fountain pens and precious China sets, were replaced with plastics that are now thrown away. The utility, price, and accepted risks of plastic are often provided as reasons for continued use, while the perceived recyclability of plastics provides consumers with the impression that the plastics they consume will not cause any of the known harms associated with plastic waste.

The health of the planet is critical to the existence of every human and nonhuman animal. Arguably, humans hold more responsibility for maintaining the health of the planet than other forms of life due simply to the collective negative impact by humans in the last century alone. Unofficially, the Anthropocene is the current geological age in which human activity has greatly altered the environment and climate. It is within the power of governments to affect the practices of many individuals under their authority. If governments were to limit the production of plastic to essential products, such as those in the medical field, or to those products that are not so easily replaced or discontinued, plastic pollution and its adverse impacts would be reduced.

The use of plastic by individuals increases during times of crisis, as the COVID-19 pandemic has demonstrated (Smith & Brisman, 2021). The consumption of items such as masks, plastic gloves, small bottles of hand sanitizer, sanitary wipes, household cleaning supplies, and toilet paper—each of these products, of course, making use of plastic in one way or another—was so high that retail supply chains were (and in some cases still are) disrupted. Consumption of these items, which are either plastic (gloves, masks) or have plastic packaging (cleaning supplies, hand sanitizers, toilet paper), was essential to the continued health and well-being of individuals. There are, though, viable alternatives to these seemingly necessary plastics that are considered less preferable as they require more effort on part of the consumer. Alternatives include metal or glass beverage bottles and food containers, metal straws, and hygiene products (e.g., body wash, conditioners, oils, shampoo made without microplastics); paper, metal, and glass can often be used for wrapping or as containers. These plastic alternatives, though, require individual consumers to be mindful, for businesses to be proactive, and for public health officials to make clear that reusable items will *not* cause the spread of COVID-19, despite the plastics industry's comments to the contrary (see generally: Smith & Brisman, 2021).

As noted at the outset, the majority of plastic exists in a linear economy, wherein it is produced with raw materials (nonrenewable resources/fossil fuels), used, and then thrown away, ending up in landfills and the oceans. Comparably, in a circular economy, the materials would continuously reenter the cycle or be reused, with little or no waste. While there are various recycling programs across the United States, run primarily by local governments, current levels of recycling are anemic and ineffective. Even so, many applications for plastic are unparalleled by alternative materials, making it unreasonable to strive for complete removal of plastics from society. While eliminating plastic in/from society is currently beyond the realm of possibility, the control over *what forms* plastic takes, *where it is distributed*, and *how it is consumed* is a significantly more attainable goal for the United States.

A relatively short-term goal the US government could adopt in order to begin to address the issues of marine plastic pollution would be the elimination of single-use plastics, which appears to already have significant public support and are increasingly popular legislatively (Wagner, 2017). Cloth bags provide an excellent alternative to the plastic bags, which are used to bag fresh vegetables, fruits, and the like. There is an adjustment period where consumers must train themselves to bring their reusable bags along for grocery or market trips. The United States could take the next step and end production of the following single-use plastics: foamed plastics, plastic bags, packaging, straws, and beverage bottles. Otherwise, we might see the end not just of the oceans as we know them, but also the end of the countless aquatic and terrestrial species which rely on our planetary oceanic ecology.

References

Beirne, P. (1999). For a nonspeciesist criminology: Animal abuse as an object of study. *Criminology, 37*(1), 117–148.

Bisschop, L., & Walle, G. V. (2013). Environmental victimisation and conflict resolution: A case study of e-waste. In R. Walters, D. S. Westerhuis, & T. Wyatt (Eds.), *Emerging issues in green criminology* (pp. 34–54). Palgrave Macmillan.

Brisman, A., McClanahan, B., & South, N. (2014). Toward a green-cultural criminology of "the rural." *Critical Criminology, 22*(4), 479–494.

Brisman, A., McClanahan, B., South, N., & Walters, R. (2018). *Water, crime and security in the twenty-first century: Too dirty, too little, too much*. Springer.

Brisman, A., & South, N. (2014). *Green cultural criminology: Constructions of environmental harm, consumerism, and resistance to ecocide*. Abingdon: Routledge.

Brisman, A., & South, N. (2016). Green cultural criminology, intergenerational (in) equity and 'life stage dissolution'. In *Greening criminology in the 21st century* (pp. 233–246). Abingdon: Routledge.

Dauvergne, P. (2018). Why is the global governance of plastic failing the oceans? *Global Environmental Change, 51*, 22–31.

Environmental Protection Agency [EPA]. (2019a). Plastic and rubber products manufacturing (NAICS 326). Retrieved from https://www.epa.gov/regulatory-information-sector/plastics-and-rubber-products-manufacturingnaics-326.

Environmental Protection Agency [EPA]. (2019b). Trash-free waters. Retrieved from https://www.epa.gov/trashfree-waters.

Environmental Protection Agency [EPA]. (2019c). Summary of the clean air act. Retrieved from https://www.epa.gov/laws-regulations/summary-clean-air-act.

Environmental Protection Agency [EPA]. (2019d). Facts and figures about materials, waste and recycling. Retrieved from https://www.epa.gov/facts-and-figures-about-materials-waste-and-recycling/plastics-material-specific-data.

Ewing, G. (Producer/Writer), & Belile, C. T. (Ed.). (2019). *Planet or plastic? A brief history of how plastic has changed our world* [Video file]. National Geographic.

Ferrell, J. (2013). *Cultural criminology and green criminology* (pp. 349–364). Routledge.

Fisk, G. (1973). Criteria for a theory of responsible consumption. *Journal of Marketing, 37*(2), 24–31.
Gibbens, S. (2019). See the complicated landscape of plastic bans in the US. *National Geographic*. Retrieved from https://www.nationalgeographic.com/environment/2019/08/map-shows-the-complicated-landscape-of-plastic-bans/#close.
Gourmelon, G. (2015). *Global plastic production rises, recycling lags* (pp. 1–7). Worldwatch Institute, Vital Signs.
Hafner, J. (2018). Plastic Straws illegal unless requested under California bill—With up to a $1,000 fine attached. *USA Today*.
Hanbury, H. W. (Producer), Weiser, S. (Reporter), & Howard, B. (Ed.). (2019). *The garbage barge that helped fuel a movement* [Digital Documentary]. Retrieved from https://www.retroreport.org/video/voyage-of-the-mobro-4000/. Accessed January 27, 2020.
Koford, B. C., Blomquist, G. C., Hardesty, D. M., & Troske, K. R. (2012). Estimating consumer willingness to supply and willingness to pay for curbside recycling. *Land Economics, 88*(4), 745–763.
Kosuth, M., Mason, S. A., & Wattenberg, E. V. (2018). Anthropogenic contamination of tap water, beer, and sea salt. Retrieved from https://journals.plos.org/plosone/article?id=10.1371/journal.pone.0194970.
Kramer, R. C., & Bradshaw, E. A. (2020). Green criminology and climate change. In A. Brisman, & N. South (Eds.), *Routledge International Handbook of Green Criminology* (2nd ed.). Abingdon: Routledge.
Le Guern, C. (2009; updated 2018). When the mermaids cry: The great plastic tide. Retrieved from https://plasticpollution.org.
Lynch, M. (1990). The greening of criminology. *The Critical Criminologist, 2*, 3, 4, 11, 12; reprinted in South, N., & Beirne, P. (Eds.). (2006). *Green criminology* (pp. 165–170). Ashgate.
Mason, S. A., Welch, V. G., & Neratko, J. (2018). Synthetic polymer contamination in bottled water. *Frontiers in Chemistry, 6*, 407.
McClanahan, B. (2014). Green and grey: Water justice, criminalization, and resistance. *Critical Criminology, 22*(3), 403–418.
National Conference of State Legislatures (NCSL). (2019, August). 2019 State & legislative partisan composition. Retrieved from https://www.ncsl.org/Portals/1/Documents/Elections/Legis_Control_2019_Post-Election%20Nov%2022nd.pdf.
Nixon, H., & Saphores, J. D. M. (2014). How effective are current household recycling policies? Results from a national survey of US households. *Resources Conservation and Recycling, 92*, 1–10.

Parker, L. (2018). The Great Pacific garbage patch isn't what you think it is. *National Geographic*. Retrieved from https://www.nationalgeographic.com/news/2018/03/great-pacific-garbage-patch-plastics-environment/.

Phillips, R. A., & Waluda, C. M. (2020). Albatrosses and petrels at South Georgia as sentinels of marine debris input from vessels in the southwest Atlantic Ocean. *Environment International, 136*(105443), 1–10.

Rochman, C. M., & Browne, M. A. (2013). Classify plastic waste as hazardous. *Nature, 494*, 169–171.

Root, T. (2019). Tires: The plastic polluter you never thought about. *National Geographic*. Retrieved from https://www.nationalgeographic.com/environment/2019/09/tires-unseen-plastic-polluter/.

Ruggiero, V., & South, N. (2013). Green criminology and crimes of the economy: Theory, research and praxis. *Critical Criminology, 21*(3), 359–373.

Sinha, J., & Plamondon, C. (2017). *Life without plastic: the practical step-by-step guide to avoiding plastic to keep your family and the planet healthy*. Page Street Publishing.

Smith, O., & Brisman, A. (2021). Plastic Waste and the Environmental Crisis Industry. *Critical Criminology, 29*, 289–309.

Sollund, R. (2011). Expressions of speciesism: The effects of keeping companion animals on animal abuse, animal trafficking and species decline. *Crime, Law and Social Change, 55*(5), 437–451.

South, N. (1998). A green field for criminology? A proposal for a perspective. *Theoretical Criminology, 2*(2), 211–233.

Sullivan, L. (2020, September 11). How big oil misled the public into believing that plastic would be recycled. NPR Morning Edition. https://www.npr.org/2020/09/11/897692090/how-big-oil-misled-the-public-into-believingplastic-would-be-recycled.

United Nations Environmental Program (UNEP). (2018). *Single-use plastics: A roadmap for sustainability*. UNEP.

Viscusi, W. K., Huber, J., Bell, J., & Cecot, C. (2013). Discontinuous behavioral responses to recycling laws and plastic water bottle deposits. *American Law and Economics Review, 15*(1), 110–155.

Wagner, T. P. (2017). Reducing single-use plastic shopping bags in the USA. *Waste Management, 70*, 3–12.

Wehle, D. H. S., & Coleman, F. (1983). Plastics at sea. *Natural History, 92*(2), 20–26.

White, R. (2018). *Climate change criminology*. Policy Press.

Wyatt, T. (2013). *Wildlife trafficking: A deconstruction of the crime, the victims, and the offenders*. Springer.

Young America Films. (1944). *Plastics: A supplementary film* [Video file]. Retrieved from https://archive.org/details/Plastics_2.

8

Criminalizing Environmentally Beneficial Activities: Hemp and Canada's *Cannabis Act*

Wesley Tourangeau

Introduction

The focus of green criminology scholarship has been the human actions (or inactions) that result in environmental harm. As a result, considerable attention is paid to the legality of these actions—some environmentally harmful activities are proscribed by law, but some of the most significantly impactful activities (e.g., burning fossil fuels, producing and consuming single-use plastics, and adopting high-meat diets) are not regulated or criminalized. By contrast, insufficient focus has been placed on the environmental harms that result from the prohibition, over-regulation, and overall hampering of actions that benefit, or have the potential to benefit, the environment. That is, limited attention has been paid to the criminalization of environmentally beneficial activities—much of which is likely attributable to the rarity (actual or perceived) of

W. Tourangeau (✉)
School of Social and Political Sciences, University of Lincoln, Lincoln, United Kingdom

J. Gacek and R. Jochelson (eds.), *Green Criminology and the Law*, Palgrave Studies in Green Criminology,
https://doi.org/10.1007/978-3-030-82412-9_8

such instances, as well as their perceived relevance to the scope of green criminology, and criminology more broadly. Nevertheless, there are key lessons to be uncovered through the ongoing study of such practices. Brisman's (2011) book chapter, titled *The indiscriminate criminalisation of environmentally beneficial activities*, is perhaps the clearest presentation of the different ways in which certain activities that benefit the environment can be proscribed by law. The criminalization of pedicab drivers and illegal forms of garbage collection (e.g., dumpster diving) are the two main examples outlined, though Brisman (2011) also discusses the environmental benefits of hemp and its complex history of prohibition. Due to this history, and its immense potential in terms of sustainable farming and sustainable product manufacturing and consumption, hemp offers a unique and useful example of the myriad ways in which environmentally beneficial activities are criminalized, over-regulated, or otherwise hampered through various policies, practices, and discourses.

Hemp, also referred to as industrial hemp, is the name given to the non-psychoactive varieties of *Cannabis sativa* that are grown for food, fiber, and other industrial uses. As such, hemp is distinguished from psychoactive varieties of *Cannabis sativa* that are grown for medical, recreational, or other uses—these varieties are commonly referred to as marijuana, or simply cannabis. Predating the medicinal use of cannabis by millennia, the history of hemp as a source of fiber, fabric, and paper goes back an estimated 10,000 years (Earleywine, 2002). For example, hemp fiber was used for centuries to make strong and durable ropes, and offers a sustainable resource for making various products like paper and textiles (Earleywine, 2002; Gibson, 2006). Russia played a major role in growing hemp and manufacturing sails and ropes, which were commonly used on American, Canadian, and European ships (Campos, 2012; Earleywine, 2002; Roulac, 1995). Italian ships outfitted with fibers and ropes made by Venetian hemp spinners were particularly famous for their quality (Earleywine, 2002).

Although hemp was once described as essential to world commerce, the prohibition of marijuana in the twentieth century (in the USA, Canada, and elsewhere) created a legal context that made it nearly impossible to continue cultivating hemp (Roulac, 1995). Moreover, hemp and marijuana share a complex history that has been, at times, further obfuscated by conspiracies and sensationalized news stories (Campos, 2012). By Campos' (2012) account, when Spanish conquistador Pedro Quadrado began cultivating cannabis in Mexico around 1530, this was the plant's first introduction to North America—though already common in Spain as a fiber source for sailing. It took hundreds of years for the term "marijuana" and discourses connecting its use to "madness" to develop, evolve through news media, and result in a continental prohibition of the plant that started in Mexico and quickly moved north (Campos, 2012). Over the last couple of decades there has been widespread decriminalization of marijuana and a small resurgence of hemp farming in Canada and other parts of the world, largely for seed and oil. It is now commonplace to see hemp seeds, hemp granola, and hemp-based milk on grocery store shelves. However, this resurgence is overshadowed by the ongoing legacy of marijuana prohibition and associated stigmas, making it a critical topic for criminology—especially green criminology, which is well suited for engaging with the nexus of law, harm, and environmental sustainability.

The criminological discussion of hemp began in 1997 (if not before), with Halsey's (1997) analysis of pulp and paper production in Australia. The prohibition of hemp cultivation is contrasted with the legal destruction of old-growth forests for paper production, as the former is decidedly more renewable than the latter (Halsey, 1997), providing an archetypal example of criminalizing environmentally beneficial activities. Many years later, I examined the (over-)regulation of hemp in Canada; while not prohibited in Canada since 1998, the regulatory structures controlling the production of hemp resulted in clear challenges and limitations for this industry (Tourangeau, 2015). This is a more nuanced view of criminalizing environmentally beneficial activities wherein the regulations that permit the growth of hemp also outline what is *not* permitted, including who can grow hemp and where it can be planted (Tourangeau, 2015). With the passing of Canada's *Cannabis Act*, the rules for cultivating and processing hemp have become less strict (e.g., less security requirements) and new opportunities to expand this industry are being pursued. While it remains unclear how this new regulatory climate will impact Canada's hemp industry, it is necessary to examine the continued legal entanglement of hemp and marijuana, and the ways in which this entanglement creates lingering impacts on hemp farmers and the industry more broadly. The present chapter seeks to further expand how we understand the criminalization of environmentally beneficial activities by considering the more favorable socio-legal context that accompanied Canada's 2018 legalization of marijuana for recreational use. After detailing the environmental benefits of hemp and outlining the new regulatory context of hemp since the passing of the *Cannabis Act*, this chapter will present a typology for the criminalization of environmentally beneficial activities. The aim of this typology is to further our understandings of the complex and nuanced circumstances under which environmental harms are a consequence of laws, regulations, and policies that proscribe, control, and otherwise hamper activities that can benefit the environment and aid transformations to a more sustainable world.

The Environmental Benefits of Hemp

Arguments against environmental harms rely on clear indications of preventable, human-caused ecological damage. By contrast, arguments against the criminalization of environmentally beneficial activities rely on evidence of the benefits, or potential benefits, of a given action—particularly in comparison to alternative actions. The environmental benefits of hemp can be divided into two categories: (1) the (potential) ecological benefits of hemp farming, and (2) the production and consumption of various hemp-based products in comparison to less sustainable alternatives.

While it is important to recognize that the environmental benefits of growing hemp risk being exaggerated (Cherney & Small, 2016), there are key characteristics that showcase hemp's potential contributions to sustainable farming. Growing hemp offers the benefits of relatively low-input requirements as well as improving soil health, including soil remediation (Adesina et al., 2020; Smith-Heisters, 2008). Hemp is a low-input, low-impact crop, particularly in comparison to crops like potato and sugar beet (van der Werf, 2004), and requires less water than other crops, like maize and alfalfa (Ranalli & Venturi, 2004). Further, hemp can be grown in many different types of soil (though ideal conditions increase fiber quality) and requires little to no pesticides (Ehrensing, 1998; Schumacher et al., 2020; Smith-Heisters, 2008). Its ability to outcompete weeds both eliminates the need for herbicides and also creates a nearly weed-free field for the next crop (Roulac, 1995), making it suitable in a crop rotation (van der Werf, 1994). But perhaps the most interesting benefit of farming hemp is its tap root. In some soils the main root of a hemp plant can reach over two meters deep (Ehrensing, 1998). The decay of this deep root system provides soil aeration and fertilization (Cherney & Small, 2016), and the deep roots are also suitable for soil remediation (Rheay et al., 2020). According to Rheay et al. (2020), hemp can be used in phytoremediation of heavy metals, radionuclides, and organic contaminants, which can even be coupled with growing hemp for bioenergy production.

In addition to the ecological benefits of hemp farming, the production and consumption of hemp-based products offers environmental benefits when specific comparisons to less sustainable alternatives are considered. Halsey's (1997) arguments on the environmental harms of paper production rely upon a comparison between hemp and a less sustainable alternative—wood pulp from the clear-felling (near-complete removal of trees from an area) of old-growth eucalypt forests. Hemp is well suited for paper production, particularly due to its long and strong fibers, high-cellulose content (related to yield), and low-lignin content (a component that must be removed using chemicals) (Roulac, 1995; Smith-Heisters, 2008). Though, when not compared to paper production from the clear-felling of old-growth forests, which has significant impacts on ecosystem health and biodiversity (Halsey, 1997), the advantages of hemp over wood pulp are less clear. That is, using hemp may not be more sustainable than tree plantations for paper production (Smith-Heisters, 2008), as revealed in a life cycle assessment comparing industrial hemp and eucalyptus paper (da Silva Vieira et al., 2010). Beyond paper production, there are a wide range of hemp-based products being developed that may benefit from further study in terms of overall sustainability, including plastics (Pappu et al., 2019), insulations (Kymäläinen & Sjöberg, 2008), and reinforced concrete (Awwad et al., 2012).

It is clear that hemp has significant potential for offering environmental benefits through the production and consumption of sustainable products. However, in order to fully determine the environmental benefits of various hemp-based products, thorough comparisons need to be made against the products they are designed to replace, including resource availability, growth, and harvesting as well as production processes, product lifespan, degradation, and overall recyclability. Methods such as life cycle assessment offer important insights in this regard, such as Mirabella et al.'s (2013) evaluation of bioplastic-based disposable diapers. What is more, efforts toward sustainable product development (and sustainable farming practices) face challenges associated with the organization of economic production and the objectives of capitalism (Lynch et al., 2013). As such, examinations of environmentally beneficial activities must also acknowledge the broader contexts and influences of the political economy, and the overarching goal of reducing the environment harms—and ecological disorganization more broadly—being caused (and perpetuated) by the "treadmill" of global capitalism (Lynch et al., 2013; Stretesky et al., 2013).

Hemp Regulations and Canada's *Cannabis Act*

To explore the criminalization of hemp's environmental benefits, it is helpful to first outline the increments of change for both hemp and marijuana legislation in Canada in recent years. After prohibiting cannabis for much of the twentieth century, in 1998 Canada began granting licenses to grow hemp under the Industrial Hemp Regulations (hereafter IHR). These regulations made it possible to grow, sell, transport, process, export, and import hemp as long as this was done according to the conditions laid out in the IHR (Baxter & Scheifele, 2000). These regulations outlined a range of requirements that needed to be met to legally grow hemp, including minimum acreage requirements; a minimum age for applicants (18 years); storing hemp in a restricted access or locked location; and keeping records, such as details regarding the import, sale, shipment, and testing of hemp (Government of Canada, 1998). Perhaps the most interesting regulation being the requirement to not grow hemp "within one kilometer of any school grounds or any other public place usually frequented by persons under the age of 18 years" (Government of Canada, 1998, pp. 17–18). These regulations reflect the legal climate at the time, which saw marijuana outlawed as a controlled substance. In the decades following the 1998 re-introduction of hemp in Canada, famers and producers have gained experience both growing hemp and navigating the regulations and licensing procedures.

The first decade of hemp production in Canada was inconsistent in terms of area under cultivation, ranging from as low as 1,312 hectares (3242 acres) to as high as 19,458 hectares (48,082 acres), largely explained by shifting values of other crops and complications with the U.S. market, leading to surpluses in some years (Brook et al., 2008; Laate, 2012). The Canadian Hemp Industry Review Project (CHIRP), published by the Ontario Hemp Alliance in 2009, offers additional insights—from the perspective of the industry itself—regarding the experiences and challenges of growing hemp in Canada during this first decade (Hansen-Trip & Schiefele, 2009). This report includes several recommendations for making the regulation of the industry more efficacious, such as reducing the minimum acreage requirements, and streamlining testing and licensing (Hansen-Trip & Schiefele, 2009). Additionally, requirements regarding growing hemp away from schools and storing hemp under lock and key are criticized as both impractical and contributing to the notion that hemp is dangerous (Hansen-Trip & Schiefele, 2009). As outlined in the CHIRP, the first decade of growing hemp provided indications that the IHR presented farmers with unique hurdles in adopting this new crop, though it is unclear as to the extent these regulations limited the growth of the industry overall.

In response to industry pressure—as well as recommendations from the Red Tape Reduction Commission, a federal government initiative launched to identify barriers and irritants to businesses in Canada (Government of Canada, 2012)—Health Canada reviewed the IHR and related policies in 2013. This review included a public consultation process with the aim of engaging "the hemp industry, agricultural associations, provincial governments and other affected stakeholders in discussions on a range of issues pertaining to the IHR" (Ianiro, 2013, p. 2059). Among the changes considered by Health Canada through this consultation process are reduced minimum acreage requirements (from 4 to 2 hectares), the elimination of redundant THC[1] testing, and lessening the restrictions regarding cultivation near schools and public places frequented by young persons (Health Canada, 2013).

In December 2013, at the end of Health Canada's consultation process about the IHR, the Canadian Hemp Trade Alliance (hereafter CHTA)—which is a national industry association that promotes hemp and represents various actors involved in Canada's hemp industry (Canadian Hemp Trade Alliance, 2021)—published a press release calling for further deregulation of hemp production, processing, and export (Canadian Hemp Trade Alliance, 2013). This press release includes statements regarding the need for amendments beyond what was being proposed by Health Canada in response to the regulatory review, including the need for industry management under Agriculture and Agri-Food Canada instead of Health Canada (CHTA, 2013). Such a change has been echoed by others in the industry, and would arguably help to diminish the lasting association between hemp and marijuana (Tourangeau, 2015).

The 2015 election of Prime Minister Justin Trudeau marks a critical turning point for the regulation of hemp in Canada. One of the campaign pledges for Trudeau's Liberal Party was the legalization and regulation of marijuana (CBC News, 2015, October 1), and after winning a majority government this pledge became a mandate to be accomplished through a federal-provincial-territorial process (Harris & Crawford, 2015, November 15). During the years-long process of legalizing marijuana, the hemp industry went through its own processes of change. On November 21, 2016, Health Canada issued a "Sect. 56 Class Exemption in Relation to the Industrial Hemp Regulations" (Health Canada, 2016), based on provisions laid out in subsection 56(1) of the *Controlled Drugs and Substances Act* that allows the Minister of Health to make exemptions to the Act when "necessary for a medical or scientific purpose or is otherwise in the public interest" (Government of Canada, 2020b). Issuing the Sect. 56 exemption was described as "an interim

[1] THC, or tetrahydracannabinol, is the compound in cannabis with intoxicating/psychoactive effects.

measure to simplify the license application process as the Government moves forward with its commitment to legalize, strictly regulate, and restrict access to marijuana" (Health Canada, 2016). This exemption provided a more simplified license application process and reduced regulatory requirements for hemp, including eliminating minimum acreage requirements and THC testing for grain and fiber cultivation (only requiring testing during seed production and development) (Health Canada, 2016). These changes addressed several of the hemp industry's ongoing concerns regarding the unnecessary and cumbersome aspects of the IHR (Hansen-Trip & Schiefele, 2009; Tourangeau, 2015).

On April 13, 2017, Bill C-45—titled *An Act respecting cannabis and to amend the Controlled Drugs and Substances Act, the Criminal Code and other Acts*, or simply the *Cannabis Act*—was introduced for the first time in Canada's Parliament (House of Commons, 2017). Enacted to legalize and regulate cannabis, the introduction of this Bill also included a set of objectives as stated in the summary:

> The objectives of the Act are to prevent young persons from accessing cannabis, to protect public health and public safety by establishing strict product safety and product quality requirements and to deter criminal activity by imposing serious criminal penalties for those operating outside the legal framework. The Act is also intended to reduce the burden on the criminal justice system in relation to cannabis (House of Commons, 2017).

This context regarding the intended scope and purposes of the *Cannabis Act* contributes to a potential reimagining of the hemp industry. The *Cannabis Act* was passed on June 21, 2018, and the IHR were subsumed under this new legislation (Parliament of Canada, 2018). Overall, the hemp industry has welcomed the change as an opportunity for further growth and investment, including using hemp to produce cannabidiol or "CBD" (CHTA, 2018), an increasingly popular health product. Cannabis contains hundreds of chemical compounds, including compounds called cannabinoids like THC and CBD, the latter of which is not intoxicating and may actually reduce some of the effects of THC

(Government of Canada, 2020a). The Canadian Health Food Association (CHFA) has also commented on the potential for natural health products derived from cannabis or hemp, such as CBD products (CHFA, 2021).

The 2018 legalization and regulation of cannabis has opened Canada's hemp industry to new pathways, including CBD products, though there remain concerns regarding how hemp is regulated. The CHTA and CHFA (2019) released a position paper offering a critique of how Canada's new cannabis laws approach CBD, arguing that:

> the current regulation of CBD, particularly when derived from industrial hemp, is not appropriate given the safety/risk profile of CBD, fails to position Canada and the Canadian industry to establish a global leadership position relating to CBD, and will permit the continuation of the illegal CBD market, at risk to Canadians and the legal cannabis industry. (CHTA & CHFA, 2019, p. 5)

The key issue highlighted by these two organizations is that the *Cannabis Act*, and the Cannabis Regulations, do not distinguish between THC and CBD, or between CBD derived from marijuana plants and CBD derived from hemp plants, even though the associated risks would make such distinctions worthwhile in terms of industry development around hemp-derived CBD products (CHTA & CHFA, 2019). The CHTA is also working toward changes internationally, coordinating with the European Industrial Hemp Alliance and other hemp associations to advocate a common position on the regulation of hemp (CHTA, 2020). These organizations (11 in total) published a position paper calling for "the need for clarification and a transparent debate on international law and regulations related to hemp," including considering it an agricultural product and making clear definitions for hemp varieties based on THC limits (Baňas et al., 2020, p. 1). Their main position is that misinterpretations of international law have resulted in market barriers for hemp, and the position paper includes a detailed explanation for why hemp is actually exempt from the scope of the Single Convention on Narcotic Drugs of 1961 as amended by the 1972 Protocol and the Convention on Psychotropic Substances of 1971 (Baňas et al., 2020). Moreover, the World Health Organization (WHO) has recently supported these (and related) positions, noting that cannabis "for industrial and horticultural purposes (commonly known as hemp) is specifically excluded from control by the 1961 Convention," and regarding CBD, a WHO committee recommended that

> a footnote be added to Schedule I of the 1961 Convention to read "Preparations containing predominantly cannabidiol and not more than 0.2 per cent of delta-9-tetrahydrocannabinol [THC] are not under international control." (UN Commission on Narcotic Drugs, 2019)

While the Commission on Narcotic Drugs recently decided to remove cannabis from Schedule IV of the Single Convention (keeping it only on Schedule I), which showcases trends toward seeing cannabis as offering medical benefits (United Nations, 2020, December 2), it is unknown if a footnote regarding cannabidiol will be considered in the future. However, the next decade will undoubtedly bring further debate over the regulation of cannabis (both hemp and marijuana) in Canada, and internationally. In the next section, the regulation of hemp is considered within the context of its potential as a sustainable and ecologically beneficial food and fiber source.

Criminalizing Environmentally Beneficial Activities

Green criminology offers a perspective for contemplating the spaces in which the environment is being harmed, with a focus on examining the role of associated legal and regulatory structures and systems. Before the perspective and sub-field of green criminology was firmly established, Halsey (1997) tackled the topic of criminalizing environmentally beneficial activities by considering the environmental harms that resulted from clear-felling old-growth forests for paper production while simultaneously prohibiting the production of a more sustainable alternative (hemp). On this point, Halsey (1997, p. 134) argues:

> that social inquirers concerned with explicating the phenomenon of environmental crime need to focus not so much on how industries can be made to capitulate to existing laws, but on how adhering to certain laws may actually facilitate the process of environmental ruin.

Of concern here, are the ways in which social, economic, and political relations and arrangements can work to facilitate pathways toward activities that are ecologically destructive and away from those that are ecologically beneficial—or at least benign (Halsey, 1997). This understanding of environmental crime/harm aligns with Lynch et al.'s (2013, p. 1005) position "that a green crime is a behaviour that produces unnecessary ecological harm—harms that can be avoided by organizing production in different ways than are currently practised". Within this view we can consider the unnecessary ecological harms that result from an adherence to laws, including laws that permit the clear-felling of old-growth forests and criminalize the production of hemp (see Halsey, 1997). In the words of Brisman (2011, p. 162), "green criminology needs to consider not just activities that hurt the environment and that are unregulated or underregulated, but also activities that are proscribed yet benefit the environment." Beyond activities strictly proscribed by law, we can also consider the over-regulation of environmentally beneficial activities in this redefining of environmental harms (Tourangeau, 2015). In the sections below, I contribute to scholarship on the criminalization of environmentally beneficial activities by outlining a typology that captures important distinctions beyond strict prohibition. Ideally, this typology will facilitate green criminologists seeking to explore the dampening effects that various socio-legal arrangements can have on transformations to more sustainable and ethical ways of living. Three types of arrangements can be imagined: (1) the prohibition of environmentally beneficial activities, (2) the over-regulation of environmentally beneficial activities, and (3) the absence of supportive policies for environmentally beneficial activities. A brief elaboration of each type is presented in turn.

The Prohibition of Environmentally Beneficial Activities

The first type is indeed the only type that can technically be considered "criminalizing" environmentally beneficial activities—it involves the explicit legal prohibition of activities that benefit or have the potential to benefit the environment, particularly in comparison to less sustainable alternatives. Brisman (2011, p. 162) explains how "junk poaching, recyclable rustling, street scavenging, dumpster diving, and other forms of trash picking" are criminalized (as well as marginalized and stigmatized) in various jurisdictions in the USA, even though their actions contribute to critically needed reductions in the production, consumption, disposal, and incineration of various products. Additionally, Brisman (2011) points to the ban against bee keeping in New York—which has since been lifted (Adler, 2010, April 3)—as another example of unnecessarily criminalizing an activity that benefits the environment, which in this case is the pollination of rooftop and community gardens and the production of local honey. Finally, laws that ban hemp cultivation also fit into this first category of prohibiting environmentally beneficial activities. This was the basis of Halsey's (1997) argument against the prohibition of hemp and the simultaneous (legal) clear-felling of old-growth trees in Australia to produce paper—though laws allowing the cultivation of hemp under license have now been introduced in Australia.

The focus here are the laws that prohibit people from engaging in certain activities. This includes the *Controlled Drugs and Substances Act*, which prior to the 1998 introduction of the IHR, prohibited people from growing hemp in Canada. However, to be considered environmentally harmful, and deemed a "green crime," there must also be a clear indication that the existence of this legislation results in the forestalling of actual or potential environmental benefits. As detailed above, there are direct environmental benefits attainable through the farming of hemp, as well as potential benefits from using hemp in exchange for less sustainable resources/products, for example, in the production of building materials. Whether it is the prohibition of hemp, dumpster diving, or bee keeping, the point is that unnecessary environmental harms are being produced. The presence of these harms, and indications that these harms could be avoided through alternative socio-legal arrangements—that is, "by organizing production in different ways than are currently practised" (Lynch et al., 2013, p. 1005)—reveals how we might consider such instances green crimes that require preventative action.

The Over-Regulation of Environmentally Beneficial Activities

The second type of criminalizing environmentally beneficial activities involves imposing regulations on permissible activities in a way that hampers the environmental benefits that might result from these activities. Starting in 1998, the IHR have outlined the rules for growing hemp in Canada, including who can grow it, where it can be grown, and how it must be grown, stored, and processed (Government of Canada, 1998). This effectively criminalizes the cultivation of hemp outside these requirements—including growing hemp without a license. These regulations arguably forestall the realization of this industry's potential environmental benefits, limiting industry growth and expansion in all directions, sustainable or otherwise (Tourangeau, 2015). Brisman (2011) also provides an example of this by discussing the over-regulation of pedicabs in New York. Pedicabs, also known as bike taxis and cycle rickshaws, are a human-powered form of hired transportation used all over the world, and their environmental benefits are evident, mainly the reduction in pollution and fossil fuel consumption used by other forms of transport. In New York, operating a pedicab is not illegal and it therefore does not belong in the first category described above. Instead, pedicab drivers face a unique constellation of regulations and restrictions, some of which are due to a lack of regulation—this includes pedicab drivers receiving tickets for traffic violations and 'disorderly conduct,' which may be given for various reasons, including parking or unloading passengers in the wrong areas (Brisman, 2011).

With the introduction of the *Cannabis Act* in Canada, it is now easier to grow hemp than any other time since 1998. Various regulations such as minimum acreage requirements, multi-stage THC testing, and growing away from school grounds have been eliminated under the new IHR (Government of Canada, 2018). Nevertheless, hemp cultivation is still controlled through licenses granted by Health Canada and rules set out in the IHR, now enabled by the *Cannabis Act*. Further, the industry's ongoing efforts to influence regulatory changes in Canada, and internationally, illustrate the continued interest in changing (or at least improving) how hemp is being governed. Thus, the expansion of Canada's hemp industry still faces hurdles in terms of the regulations farmers and producers must follow, as well as any lingering effects that result from hemp's continued legal entanglement with marijuana legislation. Until hemp is treated in the same way as buckwheat, flax, or any other crop in Canada, the (over-)regulation of this industry is arguably limiting its potential environmental benefits.

The focus here, in this second type of criminalizing environmentally beneficial activities, are the laws, regulations, and policies that control the way legal activities are conducted. Continuing the application of Lynch et al.'s (2013) definition, in order to be considered a green crime, the environmental harms being examined must be unnecessary, and avoidable through alternative means of organizing production. As a result, we can consider the over-regulation of hemp unnecessary by pointing to mounting evidence regarding the safety of hemp (Baňas et al., 2020; Brook et al., 2008), and review hemp as a potential replacement for a number of less sustainable products, including concrete, insulation, and various papers and textiles, all while improving soil conditions (and in some cases remediating soil). Overall, it is useful to consider the unnecessary over-regulation of environmentally beneficial activities as a form of criminalizing environmentally beneficial activities, and definable as green crimes that are harmful to the environment.

The Absence of Supportive Policies for Environmentally Beneficial Activities

This third type of criminalizing environmentally beneficial activities involves something quite distinct from the first two categories—instead of looking at the imposition of laws and regulations on activities that benefit the environment, we can consider the lack of support for these (actual or potential) benefits. Regarding the potential environmental benefits of Canada's hemp industry, perhaps lessening regulatory constraints is insufficient. As noted in previous work on Canada's hemp industry, considering hemp's unique image and history, perhaps "economic incentives (such as government subsidies) could be experimented with for their efficacy in stimulating industry growth in directions that benefit the environment" (Tourangeau, 2015, p. 545). Importantly, the Government of Canada has recently awarded the CHTA with $330,550 (CAD) in funding to generate new market opportunities, which will include developing standards for grading (and thereby demonstrating) the quality of hemp produced in Canada (Mentor Works Ltd., 2018). However, this funding is not specifically geared toward environmentally sustainable and beneficial initiatives.

The focus of this third and final type of criminalizing environmentally beneficial activities is the absence of government support for these activities. If green crimes are essentially behaviors that produce unnecessary and avoidable environmental harms (Lynch et al., 2013), then the failure to act in preventing these behaviors is a reasonable extension of this concept. Indeed, laws regarding omission—the failure to act—are common in circumstances such as the legal duty parents or guardians have for caring for their children. There are also a range of examples in terms of Canadian policies initiated for the express purpose of protecting, conserving, or otherwise benefiting the environment. Protecting species at risk on private farmland presents an important example, since voluntary approaches to stewardship are often used instead of mandatory laws and regulations (Olive, 2015; Olive & McCune, 2017). For example, best management practices on agricultural lands, like raising mower blades and managing riparian buffers (vegetated land near a river or stream), can reduce the risks faced by at-risk species, like Wood Turtles

(Sherren et al., 2020). Protecting various species at risk, such as the Piping Plover and Bobolink, through farmers' voluntary efforts can be supported by government through education and awareness campaigns, and incentives like funding (Brown, 2019). While motivating farmers to adopt conservation practices like wildlife stewardship is arguably more complex than simply providing financial incentives (see Sherren et al., 2020), the key point here is the potential for mitigating environmental harms via policies and programs that support environmentally beneficial activities.

Conclusion

Initiated by Brisman's (2011) discussion of the indiscriminate criminalization of dumpster diving and pedicabs, the criminalization of environmental benefits is an important development in green criminology.

In this chapter, Canada's hemp industry and the changes brought by the introduction of the *Cannabis Act* have provided an effective case study on the criminalization of environmental benefits. Over the last 25 years, Canada has moved from prohibiting both hemp and marijuana, to permitting the growth of hemp under strict conditions since 1998, and the loosening of these restrictions since the process of marijuana legalization was initiated in 2015. These changing laws, regulations, and associated socio-legal understandings have led to the development of a Canadian hemp industry that is deeply entangled with—and hampered by—the same governance mechanisms that enable its existence. Hemp cultivation in Canada continues to garner interest, and as of 2019 reached 37,435 hectares (92,504 acres) in cultivated area (Government of Canada, 2020c). This case study, viewed through definitions of environmental harms, or 'green crimes' (Halsey, 1997; Lynch et al., 2013; Tourangeau, 2015), informs an expanded understanding of how environmentally beneficial activities can be criminalized. Three types of criminalizing environmentally beneficial activities are presented in an effort to capture important nuances (see Table 8.1). The resulting typology showcases how environmentally beneficial activities can be

Table 8.1 Typology of the criminalization of environmentally beneficial activities

	Prohibition of environmentally beneficial activities	Over-regulation of environmentally beneficial activities	Absence of supportive policies for environmentally beneficial activities
Definition	Laws are in place that make it illegal for people to engage in specific activities that benefit, or have the potential to benefit, the environment	Laws, regulations, policies, and practices hamper engagement in legal activities that benefit, or have the potential to benefit, the environment	Engagement in legal activities that benefit, or have the potential to benefit, the environment is not facilitated by supportive policies
Focal point	Legislation prohibiting activities	Regulations governing activities	Policies promoting activities
Example	Laws against dumpster diving, street scavenging, and other activities that reduces wasteful production and consumption practices by using and repurposing discarded goods (Brisman, 2011)	Regulations hampering the development of Canada's hemp industry in environmentally beneficial directions, such as the production of sustainable building materials (Tourangeau, 2015)	On private farmland in Canada, species at risk are protected by adopting voluntary stewardship practices. These practices can sometimes be facilitated through government incentives and related policies and programs (Brown, 2019)

criminalized through laws that proscribe certain activities, through regulations that control the way certain activities are conducted, and through an absence of policies that support and encourage certain activities.

Green criminology provides a platform for connecting socio-legal systems, structures, and ideas to environmental issues. While some criminologists limit the scope of analysis to violations of existing laws (sometimes called the *legal-procedural approach*), this chapter is situated within green criminology approaches that explore environmental harms regardless of whether they are prohibited by law (sometimes called the *socio-legal approach*) (Brisman & South, 2020). Continuing on from earlier work on Canada's hemp industry and the re-defining of environmental harms (Tourangeau, 2015), the typology presented in this chapter is a small but significant step in broadening our understandings of what can be considered environmentally harmful, and thus subject to critical analysis within green criminology.

References

Adesina, I., Bhowmik, A., Sharma, H., & Shahbazi, A. (2020). A review on the current state of knowledge of growing conditions, agronomic soil health practices and utilities of Hemp in the United States. *Agriculture, 10*(4), 129.

Adler, M. (2010, April 3). Finally, New Yorkers Can Bee All They Can Bee. Retrieved from https://www.npr.org/templates/story/story.php?storyId=125389428

Awwad, E., Mabsout, M., Hamad, B., Farran, M. T., & Khatib, H. (2012). Studies on fiber-reinforced concrete using industrial Hemp fibers. *Construction and Building Materials, 35*, 710–717. https://doi.org/10.1016/j.conbuildmat.2012.04.119

Baňas, B., Beitzke, B., Haney, T., Kruse, D., Riboulet-Zemouli, K., Romanese, L., & Wilson, C. (2020). Common position of the industrial Hemp sector on the single convention and the international drug control system. Retrieved from http://eiha.org/wp-content/uploads/2020/09/Common-position-of-the-Industrial-Hemp-Sector.pdf

Baxter, W. J., & Scheifele, G. (2000). Growing industrial Hemp in Ontario. Retrieved from http://www.omafra.gov.on.ca/english/crops/facts/00-067.htm

Brisman, A. (2011). The indiscriminate criminalisation of environmentally beneficial activities. In R. White (Ed.), *Global environmental harm: Criminological perspectives* (pp. 161–192). Routledge.

Brisman, A., & South, N. (2020). The growth of a field: A short history of a 'green' criminology. In A. Brisman & N. South (Eds.), *Routledge international handbook of green criminology*. Abingdon, Oxon: Routledge.
Brook, G., Liljefors, K., Brook, D., & Stewart, A. (2008). National industrial hemp strategy. The AGRICOLA Group.
Brown, H. C. P. (2019). Exploring rural landowners' willingness to protect species at risk in Prince Edward Island. *The Canadian Geographer/le Géographe Canadien, 63*(2), 312–325.
Campos, I. (2012). *Home grown: Marijuana and the origins of Mexico's war on drugs*. University of North Carolina Press.
Canadian Health Food Association (CHFA). (2021). Our messages. Retrieved from https://chfa.ca/en/Regulatory/advocacy-platform
Canadian Hemp Trade Alliance (CHTA). (2013). Canada's hemp industry calls for deregulation [Press release].
Canadian Hemp Trade Alliance (CHTA). (2018). CHTA Presentation to the Senate Social Affairs, Science and Technology Committee. Retrieved from https://sencanada.ca/en/committees/SOCI/Briefs/42-1?oor_id=470882
Canadian Hemp Trade Alliance (CHTA). (2020). It is time to remove hemp from list of controlled substances globally [Media release].
Canadian Hemp Trade Alliance (CHTA). (2021). Who is CHTA. Retrieved from https://hemptrade.ca/content.aspx?page_id=22&club_id=950211&module_id=402348
Canadian Hemp Trade Alliance (CHTA) and Canadian Health Food Association (CHFA). (2019). *A call for smart regulation of CBD*. Retrieved from https://chfa.ca/en/Regulatory/cannabis-regulations/resources
CBC News. (2015 October 1). Trudeau pledges to work on pot legalization policy 'right away' if elected. *CBC News*. Retrieved from https://www.cbc.ca/news/politics/trudeau-pot-marijuana-legalization-timeline-1.3252088
Cherney, J. H., & Small, E. (2016). Industrial hemp in North America: Production, politics and potential. *Agronomy, 6*(4), 58.
da Silva Vieira, R., Canaveira, P., Da Simões, A., & Domingos, T. (2010). Industrial hemp or eucalyptus paper? *The International Journal of Life Cycle Assessment, 15*(4), 368–375.
Earleywine, M. (2002). *Understanding marijuana: A new look at the scientific evidence*. Oxford University Press.
Ehrensing, D. T. (1998). Feasibility of industrial hemp production in the United States Pacific Northwest. Retrieved from https://catalog.extension.oregonstate.edu/sites/catalog/files/project/pdf/sb681.pdf

Gibson, K. (2006). Hemp: A substance of hope. *Journal of Industrial Hemp, 10*(2), 75–83.

Government of Canada. (1998). Industrial Hemp Regulations (SOR/98-156). Justice Laws Website. Retrieved from https://laws-lois.justice.gc.ca/eng/regulations/sor-98-156/page-1.html

Government of Canada. (2012). Red tape reduction action plan. Retrieved from https://www.canada.ca/en/government/system/laws/developing-improving-federal-regulations/requirements-developing-managing-reviewing-regulations/red-tape-reduction-action-plan.html

Government of Canada. (2018). Industrial Hemp Regulations (SOR/2018-145). Justice Laws Website. Retrieved from https://laws-lois.justice.gc.ca/eng/regulations/SOR-2018-145/

Government of Canada. (2020a). Cannabidiol (CBD). Retrieved from https://www.canada.ca/en/health-canada/services/drugs-medication/cannabis/about/cannabidiol.html

Government of Canada. (2020b). Exemptions. Retrieved from https://www.canada.ca/en/health-canada/services/health-concerns/controlled-substances-precursor-chemicals/exemptions.html

Government of Canada. (2020c). Industrial hemp licensing statistics. Retrieved from https://www.canada.ca/en/health-canada/services/drugs-medication/cannabis/producing-selling-hemp/about-hemp-canada-hemp-industry/statistics-reports-fact-sheets-hemp.html#_2018

Halsey, M. (1997). The wood for the paper: Old-growth forest, hemp and environmental harm. *Australian & New Zealand Journal of Criminology, 30*(2), 121–148.

Hansen-Trip, N., & Schiefele, G. (2009). *Canadian Hemp Industry Review Project*. Ontario Hemp Alliance.

Harris, K., & Crawford, A. (2015 November 15). Trudeau mandates pot legalization, overhaul of Conservative justice reforms. *CBC News*. Retrieved from https://www.cbc.ca/news/politics/liberal-crime-justice-reform-1.3317891

Health Canada. (2013). *Consultation document on the review of the industrial hemp framework*. Retrieved from https://www.canada.ca/en/health-canada/services/health-concerns/consultations/review-industrial-hemp-framework/consultation-document.html

Health Canada. (2016). Notice to Industry.

House of Commons. (2017). Bill C-45 (First Reading). In *An Act respecting cannabis and to amend the Controlled Drugs and Substances Act, the Criminal Code and other Acts*: Parliament of Canada.

Ianiro, R. (2013). *Notice to interested parties — Review and potential amendments to the Industrial Hemp Regulations made under the Controlled Drugs and Substances Act*. Canada Gazette, Part I.

Kymäläinen, H.-R., & Sjöberg, A.-M. (2008). Flax and hemp fibres as raw materials for thermal insulations. *Building and Environment, 43*(7), 1261–1269. https://doi.org/10.1016/j.buildenv.2007.03.006

Laate, E. A. (2012). Industrial hemp production in Canada. Alberta Agriculture and Rural Development.

Lynch, M. J., Long, M. A., Barrett, K. L., & Stretesky, P. B. (2013). Is it a crime to produce ecological disorganization? Why green criminology and political economy matter in the analysis of global ecological harms. *British Journal of Criminology, 53*(6), 997–1016.

Mentor Works Ltd. (2018). Canadian Hemp Trade Alliance awarded $331k in funding for agriculture. Retrieved from https://www.mentorworks.ca/blog/government-funding/agririsk-agriculture-grants-canadian-hemp-success/

Mirabella, N., Castellani, V., & Sala, S. (2013). Life cycle assessment of bio-based products: A disposable diaper case study. *The International Journal of Life Cycle Assessment, 18*(5), 1036–1047.

Olive, A. (2015). Urban and Rural Attitudes Toward Endangered Species Conservation in the Canadian Prairies: Drawing Lessons From the American ESA. *Human Dimensions of Wildlife, 20*(3), 189–205. https://doi.org/10.1080/10871209.2015.1004207

Olive, A., & McCune, J. (2017). Wonder, ignorance, and resistance: Landowners and the stewardship of endangered species. *Journal of Rural Studies, 49*, 13–22.

Pappu, A., Pickering, K. L., & Thakur, V. K. (2019). Manufacturing and characterization of sustainable hybrid composites using sisal and hemp fibres as reinforcement of poly (lactic acid) via injection moulding. *Industrial Crops and Products, 137*, 260–269. https://doi.org/10.1016/j.indcrop.2019.05.040

Parliament of Canada. (2018). Bill C-45 (Royal Assent). In *An Act respecting cannabis and to amend the Controlled Drugs and Substances Act, the Criminal Code and other Acts*.

Ranalli, P., & Venturi, G. (2004). Hemp as a raw material for industrial applications. *Euphytica, 140*(1–2), 1–6.

Rheay, H. T., Omondi, E. C., & Brewer, C. E. (2020). Potential of hemp (Cannabis sativa L.) for paired phytoremediation and bioenergy production. *GCB Bioenergy*.

Roulac, J. W. (1995). *Industrial hemp: practical products-paper to fabric to cosmetics*: Hemptech.

Schumacher, A. G. D., Pequito, S., & Pazour, J. (2020). Industrial hemp fiber: A sustainable and economical alternative to cotton. *Journal of Cleaner Production*, 122180.

Sherren, K., Tourangeau, W., Lamarque, M., & Greenland-Smith, S. (2020). Exploring motivation crowding around farmer incentives for riparian management in Nova Scotia. *The Canadian Geographer/le Géographe Canadien, 64*(2), 250–265.

Smith-Heisters, S. (2008). Environmental costs of hemp prohibition in the United States. *Journal of Industrial Hemp, 13*(2), 157–170.

Stretesky, P. B., Long, M. A., & Lynch, M. J. (2013). *The treadmill of crime: Political economy and green criminology*: Routledge.

Tourangeau, W. (2015). Re-defining Environmental Harms: Green Criminology and the State of Canada's Hemp Industry. *Canadian Journal of Criminology and Criminal Justice, 57*(4), 528–554.

UN Commission on Narcotic Drugs. (2019). Questions and answers relating to WHO's recommendations on cannabis and cannabis-related substances. United Nations.

United Nations. (2020, December 2). UN commission reclassifies cannabis, yet still considered harmful. Retrieved from https://news.un.org/en/story/2020/12/1079132

van der Werf, H. (1994). *Crop physiology of fibre hemp (Cannabis sativa L.)*. Wageningen University & Research,

van der Werf, H. (2004). Life cycle analysis of field production of fibre hemp, the effect of production practices on environmental impacts. *Euphytica, 140*(1–2), 13–23.

9

Dirty Legislation for Dirty Work

Charles Louisson

Introduction

As humanity pursues a course toward what is fast becoming an inevitable planetary catastrophe, governments and nation-states across the world attempt to ratify within domestic law environmentally conscious initiatives in the hopes that the due processes and efficacy of legal systems might lead to some form of significant environmental change, thereby beginning the process of steering humanity away from the precipice of disaster. These looming interrelated environmental disasters include but are not limited to climate change, food scarcity, deforestation, and the pollution of critical water and air sources. At a glance, prioritizing the needs of a nation's environment through the implementation of domestic laws provides both a logical and promising start, however, eliminating adverse environmental phenomena on a scale needed to subvert the level

C. Louisson (✉)
Victoria University of Wellington, Wellington, New Zealand
e-mail: charles.louisson@vuw.ac.nz

J. Gacek and R. Jochelson (eds.), *Green Criminology and the Law*, Palgrave Studies in Green Criminology,
https://doi.org/10.1007/978-3-030-82412-9_9

of predicted environmental collapse involves more than convoluted legal engagement, and what is oftentimes confused enforcement.

This chapter shall examine the efficacy of New Zealand's overarching piece of environmental legislation, the Resource Management Act (RMA) 1991, specifically, within the context of water pollution. This chapter will elucidate how the purpose of the RMA, paying particular focus to its pollution regulations, is circumvented by legal mechanisms within the legislation itself. This chapter shall illustrate this conundrum through an examination of the ongoing pollution discharging from a legacy landfill onto Houghton Bay beach, located on Wellington's Southern coastline, New Zealand. I propose that South's "legislative balancing act" (2011, p. 161) can provide a possible explanation as to why such environmental legislation, like the RMA, falls short of enabling significant positive environmental change, in addition to its failure in bringing new levels of legislative and practical protection for environments included under its remit. The chapter will conclude that a departure from capitalist-orientated legislation and the creation of an independent body able to hold government institutions accountable for their lack of pro-environmental initiatives are both required to enact significant positive environmental change.

Theoretical Orientation

The argument espoused in this chapter adopts the worldview of Eco-Marxism (Foster et al., 2010). Eco-Marxism combines ecology with the anti-capitalistic doctrine found within the works of Marx and Engels. Attempting to reduce such a nuanced topic into a few sentences is bound to be clunky in its result but in very brief terms, Eco-Marxists consider the relationship between the world's dominating political economy (capitalism) and the environment to be unsustainable (Foster et al., 2010). It is the perceived infinite growth of exchange value offered by a capitalist mode of political economy and the finite and limited nature of the planet's environment and natural resources that creates such an unsustainable, antithetical relationship between these two forces (Foster et al., 2010; Lynch et al., 2019). As the source of all value begins as raw materials extracted from the natural environment (Foster et al., 2010). Environments can only sustain a given level of raw material subtraction, when too much raw material is extracted the environment's sustainability becomes compromised and it loses the ability to reproduce and recover from what has been taken (Foster et al., 2010; Lynch et al., 2019).

This exploitation wrought on the world's natural environments stems from the inherent unsustainability found within the capitalist modes of political economy and is the underlying critique at the core of the Eco-Marxist theoretical orientation. This is of utmost relevance to the research this chapter reports on as it suggests that landfills, their existence, operation, and purpose, are an essential tool of the capitalist mode of production servicing inflated consumer habits and indirectly, benefiting those who service our inflated consumption. This chapter argues, in part, that the ineffectiveness of environmental legislation, within the context explored here, can be partially explained through implementation of provisions within legislation that offer successful capital accumulators with a way to legitimize adverse environmental phenomena under a facade of protection. Provisions that in their operationalization, provide a "legal immunity'" to both those responsible for the adverse environmental phenomena and to institutions whose legal portfolio would include the payment and implementation of remedial efforts. This is part of the possible explanation and proposed line of argument generated through the adoption of the Eco-Marxist lens when considering a case of a legacy landfill.

The RMA's Legal Melange Explored

Before exploring the issues associated with the case study of the Houghton Bay (HB) legacy landfill, a discussion is warranted concerning the relevant piece of environmental legislation, the RMA 1991. The RMA is a comprehensive collation of different pieces of environmentally orientated statues that were previously located across fifty different Acts (Reeves, 2015; Ministry for the Environment or MftE, 2021). The RMA combined what was a scattered litany of existing environmental statutes under one overarching piece of legislation (Reeves, 2015; MftE,

2021). It should be stated that there still exists environmental legislation that sits outside of the boarders of the RMA which include but are not solely limited to the Fisheries Act 1996, the Forests Act 1949, the Health Act 1956, and the Hazardous Substances and New Organisms Act 1996 (Reeves, 2015; MftE, 2021).

The practical purpose or objective of the RMA is to ensure the sustainable management of New Zealand's natural resources, paying particular attention toward both the long-term and immediate effects human activities can incur on the natural environment (Reeves, 2015; MftE, 2021). This means that in addition to protecting the environment immediately in the present, the RMA looks to ensure the future sustainability of New Zealand's environment. "Sustainable management" is defined as "the use, development and protection of natural and physical resources in a way, or at a rate, which enables people and communities to provide for their social, economic, and cultural well-being and for their health and safety" (RMA, 1991, s. 5). The RMA sets out three specific goals that read as follows: (a) "sustaining the potential of natural and physical resources (excluding minerals) to meet the reasonably foreseeable needs of future generations; and (b), safeguarding the life-supporting capacity of air, water, soil and ecosystems; and (c), avoiding, remedying, or mitigating any adverse effects of activities on the environment" (RMA, 1991, s. 5).

The comprehensive detail contained within the Act means it retains the scope to include the many diverse aspects of NZ's environment from the ecosystems, lifeforms, physical environments with attention directed toward how human activities may impinge upon the environment's ability to sustain itself. Others have argued that the RMA is an example of limited government intervention under a neoliberal state of political economy that overly relies on the free market and its processes, leading to the continued internalization of environmental externalities encouraged in a neoliberal economy (Jackson & Dixon, 2007). Some consider this attempt to fuse the inherently antithetical concepts of neoliberalism and environmental sustainability under one piece of legislation as being fallacious and wrought with contradictions that culminate with environmentally conscience initiatives and innovations being circumvented and rescinded for short-term socioeconomic gain, thereby undercutting the

RMA's long-term goal of intergenerational environmental sustainability for New Zealand citizens (Grundy & Gleeson, 1996).

The aforementioned critique also speaks to the Eco-Marxist theoretical paradigm discussed earlier. In a society dominated by the market forces of neoliberal free market capitalism, including its environmental legislation, with the basis for exchange value generation beginning with the subtraction of raw materials from the earth's ecosystems, it follows that such an essential step of the profit generation process will be prioritized over other concerns, including environmental ones (Foster et al., 2010). The RMA may be wide in its scope and functions, yet the generation of capital and the protection of market forces will diminish its potential impact for significant environmental change (Foster et al., 2010). Perhaps the most glaring example of the prioritization of capital generation over environmental protection within the RMA comes from the resource consent process. This process is the result of the Act devolving power from central government to local territorial authorities that, in turn, are plagued by a bureaucratic emphasis on budget austerity resulting in insufficient policy implementation (Jackson & Dixon, 2007; The Environmental Defence Society, 2016).

The Local Government Acts of 1987 and 2002 (Local Government Act or LGA 1987, 2002) established the local government structure that is responsible for achieving the goals of the RMA 1991 (MftE, 2021). The LGA 1987, 2002 created 13 regional councils atop a two-tier local government system, with the second tier underneath comprising of territorial authorities (city and district councils) that operated within the jurisdiction of the larger regional councils (Jackson & Dixon, 2007; MftE, 2021). The RMA places the responsibility of enforcement, implementation, and regulation of its environmental objectives and purpose to both levels of local government (Jackson & Dixon, 2007; MftE, 2021). The LGA 1987 and 2002 delineated boundaries and local responsibilities within specific regions that would now be responsible for implementing and enforcing the environmental objectives, goals, and considerations as stipulated by the RMA 1991.

Each level of local government has different environmental responsibilities. The top tier is responsible for the management of land use to avoid natural hazards, coasts, air, water, soil conservation, preparing regional policy statements, transport planning, and the discharge of contaminates (Jackson & Dixon, 2007; MftE, 2021). The second-tier authorities, district and city councils, oversee more local-orientated demands of constituents that include responsibilities such as the formulation of district plans, contracting infrastructure work and maintenance to both private companies and public subsidiaries in addition to a myriad of other quality of life services at the local level (Jackson & Dixon, 2007). Regional authorities are required to produce a regional plan that must be consistent with the purpose, goals, and objectives stipulated in the RMA 1991 and sets out the specific actions that will help the region achieve these goals (Environment Foundation or EF, 2018).

District plans, like regional plans, describe how territorial authorities will achieve the national standards and policies contained within the RMA 1991 (EF, 2018). As these are territorial tier plans, they must be consistent with not only the provisions of the RMA 1991, but regional plans as well in order to maintain consistency across environmental initiatives from central government, to regional then to territorial (EF, 2018). The plans differ from authority to authority due to the different environments and interests present within each jurisdiction but typically include regulating the effects of land usage; activities on lakes and rivers; maintaining biological diversity and the management of contaminated land (EF, 2018). Territorial plans also stipulate the methods to be employed in order to achieve its environmental goals as stipulated by the RMA 1991 and regional plans and include monitory procedures, anticipated environmental outcomes, and the mechanisms required (EF, 2018).

Another responsibility of regional and territorial authorities is to process resource consents (MftE, 2021). Resource consents are a form of authorization for an activity that is deemed prohibited by either the RMA 1991, a regional or territorial plan, or an activity that is not identified as permitted (Jackson & Dixon, 2007; RMA, 1991). Section 87 subsections (a) through (e) of the RMA 1991 stipulate the five different types of resource consents available that each pertains how an activity may impact a type of environment (RMA, 1991, s. 87). These are land use consents; subdivision consents; costal consents; water consents, and finally a discharge consent (RMA, 1991, s. 87). All applications for consent must include an assessment of the environmental effects or (AEE) must be conducted to determine the potential impact of any environmental externalities the said activity might incur (Jackson & Dixon, 2007; RMA, 1991).

Yet this process is not without its pitfalls (Gleeson, 2000; Jackson & Dixon, 2007). Gleeson describes "the commodification of the consent approval process" (Gleeson, 2000, p. 115), which can be seen in the typical consent application trajectory: An applicant must obtain written approval from any persons "who may be adversely affected" (RMA, 1991, s. 94b) by their proposed activity. If an applicant obtains such written approval from all potentially affected persons, then a significant segment of the resource consent process is circumvented, specifically the time-intensive public hearings and the various opportunities for public submission (Gleeson, 2000; Jackson & Dixon, 2007). This has effectively encouraged the creation of a "consent approval market" where applicants can quite literally buy their way into obtaining resources consents faster while simultaneously eliminating the opportunity for wider public input (Gleeson, 2000; Jackson & Dixon, 2007).

However, it is the consent authority itself, either a regional council or territorial body, that compares the anticipated adverse environmental outcomes contained with an AEE, if there are any, against environmental baselines established by themselves (Jackson & Dixon, 2007; RMA, 1991). This provides consent authorities with total discretion and the opportunity to prioritize the completion of the development over any potentially adverse environmental impacts. Regional and territorial officials retaining full discretion over discerning whether environmental impacts being minor without further checks and balances provided by a third party provides those authorities with the power and opportunities to circumvent their environmental responsibilities (Jackson & Dixon, 2007; RMA, 1991).

When processing a resource consent, the regional or territorial authority shall determine whether the consent itself shall be made known to the public and to what extent (EF, 2018; RMA, 1991). Resource consents can be deemed as requiring full public notification, partial or limited notification, or no notification whatsoever, termed non-notification consents (Jackson & Dixon, 2007; RMA, 1991). Consents that are deemed non-notified are not presented to the public and therefore accrue zero public scrutiny or criticism, consents that are deemed limited notification require that only those who might be adversely impacted by anticipated outcomes be notified of the consent (RMA, 1991). In 2018, less the five percent of the resource consents granted across NZ fell into the category requiring full public notification and were therefore subject to public scrutiny, the rest were either completely non-notified or have partial notification (EF, 2018; Jackson & Dixon, 2007).

If a consent authority determines from that the environmental impacts of an activity shall be "minor" (RMA, 1991; s. 93, 1b), or in the situation where the effects are minor but the applicant has included written approval from those likely to be effected, then the resource consent can be deemed non-notified eliminating public scrutiny (Jackson & Dixon, 2007). Consent authorities also have the power under Sect. 94A of the RMA (1991), to disregard any potential adverse environmental effects that are the result of an activity stipulated in a regional or territorial plan (RMA, 1991, s. 94A). In other words, Sects. 94 and 94A provide local government authorities with an opportunity to permit adverse environmental effects, so long as the activity generating those effects has been stated in a regional or territorial plan, and if written consent has been obtained by those deemed to be likely effected, the opportunity for public criticism and scrutiny is removed (Jackson & Dixon, 2007).

This ability evidences South's "legislative balancing act" (2011), illustrating that the implementation of environmental law extends only as far as deemed convenient for economic and institutional considerations. When a region deems the development of infrastructure within a regional plan as essential for that region's economy, the environmental considerations are rescinded for that particular economic development and the ecological considerations accepted as another "cost of doing business." Local government authorities embody this conflict of principle, they are charged with enforcing and implementing ecological initiatives as per the RMA, but are also responsible for the economic development of their respective region and so environmental policy, and its implementation, are adopted so far as its economically and institutionally convenient to do so (South, 2011). Unfortunately, this institutional autonomy is created by the RMA itself, an act that vies to be environmentally conscience while providing opportunity for the circumvention of its core environmental principles.

These statutes contained within the RMA 1991 bequeath a massive amount of both discretion and power to local government managers and officials who are responsible for determining the outcomes of resource consents, a process that can also be kept away from the prying public eye that ultimately rescinds environmental sustainability and protection, as stipulated by the purpose and objectives of the RMA 1991, in favor of expediting the development use of environments for economic ends (Jackson & Dixon, 2007). In the case of non-notified consents, members of the public who become aware of such consents are only left with bringing a case before the environment court, but this requires a significant monetary and time investment, in addition to the high standards of proof that are practically unobtainable for laypeople without specialized training or expertise (Louisson, 2021; Scott, 2015). This is how environmentally conscious legislation can undermine its own legal purpose and objective through the fashion by which it is implemented. The chapter shall now consider the case of a legacy landfill in Houghton Bay, on Wellington's Southern coastline in illustration.

Houghton Bay

A landfill is a location that is used by a population within a geographical area to deposit their unwanted waste products. Modern landfills are typically constructed with various environmental safeguards, such as plastic liners that reduce seepage and the movement of harmful liquids produced by landfills, referred to as leachate, and vents to monitor the production of landfill gases such as hydrogen sulphide and methane, although these safeguards are not 100% full-proof and have been documented to fail over time (Renou et al., 2008). In New Zealand, the RMA 1991 contains legislation that requires landfills built after the commencement date of the Act to include those safeguards (RMA, 1991). A legacy landfill, however, is a landfill that's construction, operation, or decommission predates the commencement date of the RMA 1991 and as a result, are built with no environmental safeguards in place and are significantly more problematic for the surrounding environment than their more modern counterparts (Rotolo, 2017).

The HB landfill is a legacy landfill (Purchas, 1998). The landfill is situated at the base of a valley and was filled and operated in two sections, an upper and lower section. From this lower section, a row of houses separates the lower region of the old landfill from HB beach, an area of coastline that has been deemed a marine reserve. The lower section was filled first and at its greatest depth extends 18 m down from the surface while the upper sections extends to 36 m at its greatest dept (Purchas, 1998). Combined, the two sections contain over 1,462,500 cubic meters of waste that is stored underneath HB. The landfill was in operation between 1950 and 1971 and in its time serviced many different forms of household and industrial types of waste, including bitumen and gas-works materials. It should be noted, however, that there is still considerable debate as to the exact contents of the landfill (Purchas, 1998).

As the landfill was filled from the base of the valley upward, portions of each section were covered with varying depths of clay-heavy topsoil that was subsequently compacted with heavy machinery (Purchas, 1998). No other environmental safeguards have been implemented. This has led to the development of a significant leachate seepage issue from the HB landfill onto the Houghton Bay beach and into the sea that is part of a marine reserve (Jayaratne et al., 2015; Wellington Water & WCC, 2018; Purchas, 1998). Leachate is created when water percolates down through the layers of compacted waste and as it does various microbial, physical, and chemical processes transfer pollutants from the landfill and into the water (Renou et al., 2008). Once absorbed into the percolating water, the leachate then seeps down throughout the bottom of the landfill until it eventually encounters another portion of the neighboring environment. In the case of the HB landfill, leachate is partially captured by a network of pipes and is diverted into the stormwater system, the outflow for which is situated on HB beach at the very bottom of the valley.

There can be no argument that leachate generated from legacy landfills poses significant risks for humans, nonhumans, and physical environments alike (Lisk, 1991; Plotkin & Ram, 1984). Leachate is toxic for luminescent bacteria and zooplankton within marine environments both of which are essential components of the marine food chain (Lisk, 1991; Plotkin & Ram, 1984). Once the pollutants contained within leachate are absorbed into a creature that is unlucky enough to encounter it, many pollutants remain present within the organism and can travel up the food chain until eventually being consumed by humans (Lisk, 1991; Plotkin & Ram, 1984).

Leachate has been periodically discharging from the HB outfall and into the sea since in early 1980s (Jayaratne et al., 2015; Purchas, 1998). To date, there has been no remedial action on behalf of the WCC or the Greater Wellington Regional Council or (GWRC), despite various attempts made by local residents to spur the Wellington City Council (WCC) into addressing the problem. One of these attempts occurred in 2013, after locals banded together and formed the "Friends of HB Association." The Association privately funded scientific testing of the outfall contents in order to ascertain exactly what pollutants were present within the discharge (Louisson, 2021). The tests measured $42ugL^{-1}$ of lead present within the discharge, $30ugL^{-1}$ over the prescribed limit as stipulated by national standards, in addition to other substances including mercury, zinc, iron, and cadmium (Australian and New Zealand Environment Conservation Council or ANZECC, 2000; Corbishley & Vorster, 2020). It should be noted that according to the World Health Organization (WHO), there is currently no known level of lead exposure that does not precipitate harmful effects on the human body (WHO, 2019).

The Association submitted the findings to the WCC in the hopes that the results might be enough to prove the harmful potential of the outfall discharges of leachate and result in some form of practical action to address it (Louisson, 2021). However, much to the despair of the Association, WCC council officials dismissed the tests on two counts (Louisson, 2021). According to residents, the first grounds for the dismissal of the tests were claims that the tests had been carried out by people lacking the formal qualifications and specialist training that ultimately led to the tests being deemed as "inaccurate," this is despite the fact that a professional testing company was commissioned to produce the results (Louisson, 2021). Additionally, the WCC argued that the community-funded tests were "unnecessary" because the WCC conduct their own tests on the outfall and would use their own tests as the basis for any practical actions that could be taken to reduce the discharges (Louisson, 2021).

This dismissal of community-generated science within institutions and legal proceedings is a documented phenomenon within many green criminological studies (Fischer, 2000; Ottinger, 2009; Scott, 2015; Shriver et al., 2019). It has been argued that within legal forums and proceedings that oversee environmental disputes, there exists an unhealthy sycophantic devotion to the scientific quantitative forms of evidence over personal lived experiences, including the experiences of environmental victims (Scott, 2015). An interviewee living in proximity to the HB landfill reported that on occasion, the taps in her home will occasionally discharge fluid with a strong orange tinge, the same color as the leachate contamination within the area (Louisson, 2021). Unable to obtain scientific data ratifying the issue, her experiences of victimization are rescinded in favor of that devotion to quantitative forms of evidence. A similar situation arose within a tar sand mining operation in Canada where a lengthy observational data set created by someone living downwind of the mining operation was ruled by a Canadian judge to be "inadmissible and struck from the record" (Scott, 2015, p. 273). Within the HB context, the provisions in a resource consent obtained/held by WCC explains why scientific evidence could be refuted.

The RMA 1991 clear states under Sect. 15 the legislation surrounding the discharge of any form of contaminates into the environment (RMA, 1991, s. 15). Subsections (a) and (b) expressly prohibit the discharge of contaminates into any body of water be it marine or freshwater environments, in addition to a range of other discharge scenarios (RMA, 1991 S. 15). The RMA defines a "contaminate" as,

"any substance (including gasses, odorous compounds, liquids, solids and micro-organisms) or energy (excluding noise) or heat, that either by itself or in combination with the same, similar or other substances, energy or heat that, (a) when discharged into water, changes or is likely to change the physical, chemical or biological condition of the water or, when discharged onto or into land or into air, changes or is likely to change the physical, chemical or biological condition of the land or air onto or into which it is discharged" (RMA, 1991, s. 2).

The levels of contaminates detected by the tests commissioned by the Friends of HB Association should satisfy this definition and would therefore constitute a breach of the RMA Sect. 15 concerning discharges, giving those effected within HB an opportunity to use the judicial system as a means to instill practical change and attain compensation. All that would remain for HB residents to successfully bring a case against the WCC would be to prove that the leachate entering HB would fit the definition of "contaminates" within the interpretation section of the RMA. It would additionally be reasonable to assume that the periodic discharge of leachate across a public beach and into a portion of the coast designated a marine reserve, offering another layer of legal protection within the delineated zone, would be protected from such adverse activity (Department of Conservation, 2021). And yet a case has not been brought and the protection has not been forthcoming. The reason for why lies with the RMA's inclusion of the resource consent process. The WCC, the territorial authority responsible for the management of the contamination from the HB landfill holds a resource consent from the GWRC, that permits the discharge of "stormwater, and occasionally contaminated stormwater, into the Wellington Harbour and the coastal marine area on the southern coastline" (Wellington Water & WCC, 2018, pg. 3). This removes any fear of legal indictment under Sect. 15 of the RMA 1991 and also provides the consent holder (WCC) with a monopoly on the monitoring and testing of the pollution (Wellington Water & WCC, 2018), meaning they and they alone have the power to criticize and refute third-party testing like that conducted by Friends of HB Association.

Despite all the lofty pro-environmental initiatives, goals, and aims of the RMA 1991, the inclusion of the resource consent process in how it currently operates allows for local government institutions, like the WCC and GWRC, to legalize adverse environmental phenomenon thereby greatly reducing the possible assistance legal proceedings might be in aiding those who live in proximity and who stand the highest chance of being negatively impacted. I argue that the explanation for such institutional dismissal of experiences of environmental victimization lies in what is termed as "the legislative balancing act" (Du Rées, 2001, pg. 115) in addition to the inefficiencies of institutions dominated by a focus on resource austerity and management of adverse environmental phenomena rather than a commitment to significant practical change (South, 2011, 2014).

South (2014) when discussing implementation failure of environmental policy and regulation notes that: "politics and law enforcement frequently share a short-term horizon dictated by seeking the approval of the general public, superiors and peers and avoiding the uncomfortable" (South, 2014, p. 375). The "uncomfortable" is the reality that the forces of neoliberal market capitalism and ecological preservation are antithetical. As the Eco-Marxist paradigm illustrates, ecological destruction, in the form of raw material extraction, is an essential step for a successful capitalist economy to viably function (Foster et al., 2010). The RMA 1991 offers a façade to satisfy the environmental sensibilities of the lay public, all the while protecting business interests by offering those who would be financially penalized with an escape route in the provision of resource consents. A consent holder is immune from legal action taken against their role in precipitating adverse environmental phenomena and/or being made responsible for remedying it.

The "legislative balancing act" within the realm of environmental policy and implementation describes the way environmental criminal law is constructed as a compromise or set of compromises between ecological considerations and economic factors (Du Rées, 2001; South, 2011). This encapsulates the antithetical grating at the core of why environmental law and its implementation oftentimes struggle to hold those responsible for the generation of adverse environmental phenomena, like in the case of the HB legacy landfill. South (2011) argues that "serious ecological damage can be carried out with official license..." (South, 2011, p. 166), which bears true in the resource consent process of the RMA 1991. If the leachate discharges occurring at HB were taken away from the context of operating under a resource consent, then the situation of leachate containing high levels of toxic contaminants seeping out into a marine environment (a protected one no less) would easily satisfy a breach of Sect. 15 of the RMA. Yet said the situation has been legitimized with "official license" (South, 2011). In this respect, the resource consent process contained within the RMA 1991 offers nothing more than a means for those in possession of capital, and those within the structure of local government institutions, with a pathway to deem unfavorable environmental situations as legal when it is convenient for them to do so. While those humans and nonhumans living in proximity to such adverse scenarios, and the environment continue to unduly suffer.

Conclusion

The passing of environmental laws alone, and in their current state, are by no means sufficient in bridling the rampant decline of the earth's ecosystems and environments. As the case of HB shows, this insufficiency regarding the practical change precipitated by environmental law is stunted by the tightrope it is forced to walk, a "legislative balancing act" (Du Rées, 2001; South, 2011) between the inherently opposed forces of capitalistic profit generation and the ecosystems which much suffer as the initial step for this generation of profit to begin in earnest (Foster et al., 2010). The devolvement of a nation's environmental sustainability has set the burden of proof for environmental victims to an almost unobtainable level (Scott, 2015), while simultaneously devolving the responsibility to achieve these environmental goals to local government institutions wrought with budget austerity and fears of accountability, result in adverse environmental phenomena being legalized and managed rather than prohibited and accountability established. Truly effective environmental legislation would offer no allowances for the production of environmental externalities. The creation of an overseeing environmental body with the legal authority to hold those in charge of industry and local government institutions accountable for their role in either creating adverse environmental conditions, or stifling the implementation of practical change, would also act as a potential source of legal leverage for environmental victims providing a channel in which their experiences of environmental victimization will be heard and acted upon. This is a call for legislative reform, a reform that must decouple itself from the shackles of capitalistic orientation unlike the current legal environmental framework of NZ. If nothing more, the façade presented by legislation such as the RMA 1991, must be exposed for its falsehood.

References

Australian and New Zealand Environment Conservation Council (2000). *Australian and New Zealand Guidelines for Fresh and Marine Water Quality*.

Corbishley, G., & Vorster, J. (2020). *Houghton Vally's web*. [online] Houghton-valley.org.nz. Available at: http://houghtonvalley.org.nz/playing/Leachate/HB%20Leachate%20analysis%20report.pdf.

Department of Conservation (2021). *Taputeranga marine reserve*. [online] Doc.govt.nz. Available at: https://www.doc.govt.nz/globalassets/documents/conservation/marine-and-coastal/marine-protected-areas/taputeranga-marine-reserve-brochure.pdf.

Du Rées, H. (2001). Can criminal law protect the environment? *Journal of Scandinavian Studies in Criminology and Crime Prevention, 2*(2), 109–126.

Environment Foundation (2018). *Introduction • environment guide*. [online] Environmentguide.org.nz. Available at: http://www.environmentguide.org.nz/rma/.

Environmental Defence Society (2016). *Evaluating the environmental outcomes of the RMA*. [online] Auckland: Environmental Defence Society, pp.1–17. Available at: https://www.eds.org.nz/assets/Publications/Evaluating%20the%20Environmental%20Outcomes%20of%20the%20RMA%20Report%20Final.pdf?k=cdcb980c81.

Fischer, F. (2000). *Citizens, experts, and the environment*. Duke University Press Books.

Foster, J., Clark, B., & York, R. (2010). *The ecological rift* (1st ed.). NYU Press.

Gleeson, B. (2000). The politics of consent notification. In P. Memon & H. Perkins (Eds.), *Environmental planning and management in New Zealand* (1st ed., pp. 115–122). Dunmore Press.

Grundy, J. and Gleeson, J. (1996). Sustainable management and the market: the politics of planning reform in New Zealand. *Land Use Policy*, 13(3), 197–211. Available at: https://www.sciencedirect.com/science/article/pii/0264837796000014.

Jackson, T., & Dixon, J. (2007). The New Zealand resource management act: an exercise in delivering sustainable development through an ecological modernisation agenda. *Environment and planning B: planning and design, 34*(1), 107–120. Available at: https://journals.sagepub.com/doi/abs/10.1068/b32089.

Jayaratne, R., Williamson, B., Idris, I., Wood, N., Bhula, J. & Wilson, A., 2015. *Our capital beaches - effect of stormwater discharges.* Wellington: Water New Zealand Organisation.

Lisk, D. (1991). Environmental effects of landfills. *Science of the Total Environment, 100*, 415–468.

Local Government Act 1987.

Local Government Act 2002.

Louisson, C. (2021). *Seeping ugly*. Victoria University of Wellington.

Lynch, M., Long, M., & Stretesky, P. (2019). Connecting ecological decline and eco-justice. In M. Lynch, M. Long, & P. Stretesky (Eds.), *Green criminology and green theories of justice* (pp. 21–40). Palgrave.

Ministry for the Environment (2021). *About the resource management act 1991.* [online] Mfe.govt.nz. Available at: https://www.mfe.govt.nz/rma/about-rma.

Ottinger, G. (2009). Buckets of resistance: Standards and the effectiveness of citizen science. *Science, Technology, & Human Values, 35*(2), 244–270.

Plotkin, S., & Ram, N. (1984). Multiple bioassays to assess the toxicity of a sanitary landfill leachate. *Archives of Environmental Contamination and Toxicology, 13*(2), 197–206.

Purchas, C. (1998). *Landfills in the Wellington Region.* [online] Wellington: Wellington Regional Council, pp.2–4, 250–251. Available at: http://www.gw.govt.nz/assets/council-publications/Landfills-in-the-Wellington-Region.pdf.

Reeves, S. (2015). *Environmental law in New Zealand. 2nd, rev. ed*. 2nd ed. Alphen aan den Rijn: Kluwer Law International, pp.94–206, 443–453.

Renou, S., Givaudan, J., Poulain, S., Dirassouyan, F., & Moulin, P. (2008). Landfill leachate treatment: Review and opportunity. *Journal of Hazardous Materials, 150*(3), 468–493.

Resource Management Act 1991.

Rotolo, G. (2017). Historical pollution: in search of a legal definition. In: F. Centonze and S. Manacorda, (Eds.), *Historical Pollution*, 1st ed. [online] Cham: Springer, pp.57–91. Available at: https://doi.org/10.1007/978-3-319-56937-6.

Scott, D., 2015. We are the monitors now. *Social & Legal Studies*, [online] *25*(3), pp.261–287. Available at: https://doi.org/10.1177/096466391560 1166.

Shriver, T., Messer, C., Whittington, J., & Adams, A. (2019). Industrial pollution and acquiescence: Living with chronic remediation. *Environmental Politics, 29*(7), 1219–1238.

South, N. (2011). Environmental offending, regulation and 'the legislative balancing act'. In: J. Gorbet and A. Pascal (Eds.), *European Developments in Corporate Criminal Liability*, 1st ed. [online] New York: Routledge Taylor and Francis Group, pp. 161–174. Available at: https://www.routledge.com/European-Developments-in-Corporate-Criminal-Liability/Gobert-Pascal/p/book/9781138019874.

South, N. (2014). Green criminology, environmental crime prevention and the gaps between law, legitimacy and justice. *Journal of Criminal Science and Criminology, 64*(4), 373-381.

Wellington Water & WCC (2018). *Stormwater discharge consent annual report*. Wellington: Wellington Water, pp.1–3, 26–28.

World Health Organisation. (2019). *Lead poisoning and health*. [online] Who.int. Available at: https://www.who.int/news-room/fact-sheets/detail/lead-poisoning-and-health.

Part III

Retracing Legal Rights and Responsibilities

10

Palliative Animal Law: The War on Animal Cruelty

Justin Marceau

Professor of Law at the Sturm College of Law, the Brooks Institute Faculty Research Scholar of Animal Law and Policy, and an affiliated faculty member with the Institute for Human Animal Connections at the Graduate School of Social Work. A version of this chapter previously appeared in the Harvard Law Review Forum, 134 Harv. L. Rev. F. 25 (2021).

J. Marceau (✉)
Brooks Institute, University of Denver, Sturm College of Law, Denver, CO, USA
e-mail: jmarceau@law.du.edu

J. Gacek and R. Jochelson (eds.), *Green Criminology and the Law*, Palgrave Studies in Green Criminology,
https://doi.org/10.1007/978-3-030-82412-9_10

Introduction

In 2019 President Donald Trump signed into law the Preventing Animal Cruelty and Torture (PACT) Act.[1] Although every state already permitted felony animal cruelty liability, animal lawyers hailed the PACT Act as a "defining moment" for animal law because it allowed acts of animal cruelty to be charged as federal felonies.[2] In the wake of the enactment, one of the most influential animal protection organizations in the world revealed that it had been working to pass the legislation for decades,[3] and described the new felony law as one of the organization's "highest priorities,"[4] and "one of the largest victories for animals in a long time."[5] During the signing statement, President Trump was flanked by leaders of the animal protection movement, one of whom proclaimed that with "one stroke of the pen, the President has done more to protect animals and stop animal cruelty in America than anyone in history."[6] The President responded that this was "really a very nicely put statement."[7]

The circumstances surrounding the PACT Act—the efforts to obtain it, the celebration of it, and its effects—represent a microcosm of animal law efforts in the realm of carceral animal law more generally (see generally, Marceau, 2019). It is a high-profile palliative intervention that provides a sense of accomplishment without addressing any of the underlying causes of animal suffering. Politicians and advocates celebrate the

---

[1] Pub. L. No. 116–72, 133 Stat. 1151 (2019) (codified at 18 U.S.C. § 48).

[2] Press Release, Humane Soc'y of the U.S., Extreme Animal Cruelty Can Now Be Prosecuted as a Federal Crime (Nov. 25, 2019), https://www.humanesociety.org/news/extreme-animal-cruelty-can-now-be-prosecuted-federal-crime [https://perma.cc/9ZP9-E5G3].

[3] *Id.* ("For decades, a national anti-cruelty law was a dream for animal protectionists.").

[4] Kitty Block and Sara Amundson, *HSLF and HSUS Deliver Big Wins for Animals in 2019: Our Banner Year in the Nation's Capital*, A Humane World: Kitty Block's Blog (Dec. 13, 2019). https://blog.humanesociety.org/2019/12/hslf-and-hsus-deliver-big-wins-for-animals-in-2019-our-banner-year-in-the-nations-capital.html [https://perma.cc/L6N3-UA7Q].

[5] Patrick Eckerd, *Senate Unanimously Passes PACT Act Against Extreme Animal Cruelty*, Jurist (Nov. 7, 2019). https://www.jurist.org/news/2019/11/senate-unanimously-passes-pact-act-against-extreme-animal-cruelty [https://perma.cc/7ALP-9CVX].

[6] Remarks on Signing the Preventing Animal Cruelty and Torture Act, 2019 Daily Comp. Pres. Doc. 2 (Nov. 25, 2019). https://www.govinfo.gov/content/pkg/DCPD-201900823/pdf/DCPD-201900823.pdf [https://perma.cc/M9X3-Y65L].

[7] *Id.*

efforts as landmark victories, but in fact, as this chapter argues, the efforts tend to do more harm than good by reinforcing, and even exaggerating, the invisibility of most animal suffering in law.[8]

This chapter situates animal law's exaltation of vigorous prosecutions within the emerging body of academic scholarship examining so-called "progressive carceralism" (Gruber, 2018; Levin, 2019). Scholars of progressive carceralism have shown that criminal responses to social problems not only fail to achieve radical change, but worse, they ultimately impede it. Aya Gruber, for example, has methodically dismantled the pro-carceral narratives in the realm of interpersonal violence, and shown that rather than facilitate incremental social change, as is often assumed, these law reforms set feminist goals back.[9]

The PACT Act and other tough-on-crime measures are celebrated by many animal lawyers because they provide symbolic proof of the increasingly strong "public concern for animal welfare."[10] Adopting the mindset that social problems are solved through criminal law, animal law commentators assume that the absence of a sufficiently punitive response signals a lack of social standing for animals. Thus, as one group celebrated, "PACT makes a statement about American values" (Press Release, 2019).

Rather than catalyze change in American values, however, these war-on-crime approaches create a distracting sideshow that diverts public scrutiny away from matters of the most urgent concern. Carceral animal law consumes resources and scarce public attention. It is not a symbolic or incremental victory for animals—it is legal escapism. Put differently, this is not a chapter advocating that animal lawyers should prioritize the

---

[8] Some commentators would argue that even a focus on systemic forms of animal oppression ignores some of the greatest threats to species preservation. *See generally* Carter Dillard, *Fundamental Illegitimacy*, Willamette L. Rev. (forthcoming 2021) (on file with the Harvard Law School Library) (arguing that patriarchy-driven population growth has caused, and will continue to fundamentally cause, the majority of human and nonhuman suffering).

[9] Aya Gruber, *The Feminist War on Crime*, 92 Iowa L. Rev. 741, 801–20 (2007) (exploring feminism's reliance on carceral logic, specifically in the domestic violence context, and the patriarchal patterns such reliance reinforces); *see generally* Aya Gruber, The Feminist War on Crime (2020) [hereinafter Gruber, The Feminist War on Crime].

[10] Courtney G. Lee, *The PACT Act: A Step in the Right Direction on the Path to Animal Welfare*, Jurist (Dec. 1, 2019). https://www.jurist.org/commentary/2019/12/courtney-lee-pact-act [https://perma.cc/EY8W-UKUC].

rights and suffering of humans, as my critics will no doubt allege. Rather, the point is that the prioritization of felony laws amounts to a grand mirage. The promise of incremental progress in favor of general animal protection is a false one, not because incrementalism can never work, but because this is not an incremental gain for animals. Contrary to the conventional narrative, more prosecutions and longer sentences are not paving a path to animal rights.

The carceral animal lawyers imagine themselves as realists, proceeding incrementally on behalf of animals. This commentary challenges that framing by shining a spotlight on the text of the PACT Act, and by considering the on the ground work of lawyers and advocacy groups at the intersection of animal law and criminal law. Specifically, I will use two states, New York and Iowa, as case studies for showing how the criminalization impulse does more to hinder than to advance animal protection efforts in law. This chapter is not a blueprint for next steps, but a deliberate call for a reallocation of resources away from the carceral, and toward corporate or systemic accountability.

I. The Plain Language of the PACT Act

As a quick primer on how criminal law connects with animal law, it is worth examining the recently enacted and much-celebrated PACT Act. The centerpiece of the statute is the criminalization of conduct in which an animal is "purposely crushed, burned, drowned, suffocated, impaled, or otherwise subjected to serious bodily injury."[11] But the real story is the range of conduct that is exempted from the law's coverage, and the efficiency with which the law reaffirms social hierarchies through the use of criminal prosecutions.[12] Prioritizing the suffering of *very few* animals, by excluding others, this law creates and strengthens animal hierarchies;

[11] Preventing Animal Cruelty and Torture Act, Pub. L. No. 116–72, 133 Stat. 1151, 1552 (2019).

[12] *See generally* Donald Black, The Behavior of Law (1976). "If the offense was committed against someone of sufficiently high status," Professor Donald Black writes, a team of detectives might "be directed to work around the clock until a suspect is found and charged with the offense," but if the victim is "low status," the investigation will likely be minimal and soon abandoned. Donald Black, The Manners and Customs of the Police 14–16 (1980).

thus, the very reforms championed by animal lawyers may reinforce the painful irony at the core of animal law—that is, as a historical matter, the law of animals has been a vehicle for the protection of institutionalized animal abuse (Beirne, 1999, p. 129; see also Bryant, 2010, p. 62). Rather than serving as a gateway to greater protection for all species, legally entrenched hierarchies degrade the socio-legal status of animals as a group, and allow for the infliction of horrific animal suffering under the "mantle of complying with state and federal laws that purport to protect animals" (Bryant, 2010, p. 62; see also Satz, 2009, p. 79).

Among animal lawyers and commentators, the need for harsher sentences for animal cruelty is often justified in terms of an interest in proportionality (Bagaric et al., 2019). Because there is an interest in recognizing animal abuse as serious, it is argued that the penalties should be proportionately severe.[13] But this tidy mathematical notion of proportionality has always been a criminal law myth. In the realm of human victims, there is a large body of research documenting the fact that the most severe punishments are imposed on persons with low social status who harm a high-status victim (Kleinfeld, 2013, pp. 1151–1152). For example, black men who are convicted of killing white victims are considerably more likely to be sentenced to death, and to be executed (Baldus et al., 1990; Phillips & Marceau, 2020). These divergent results among human victims are the result of human biases that are baked into the system rather than explicitly mandated by statute. Generally speaking, scholars have approached disparities in the treatment of human victims as one of the indicia that the criminal justice system operates arbitrarily and unfairly.

Yet, when it comes to animal victims, the plain text of the PACT Act mandates a hierarchy that all but guarantees inequitable treatment and suffering among animals.[14] The law explicitly creates categories of exemptions for animals whose victimhood is often invisible to the law

---

[13] Animal Legal Def. Fund, Animal Legal Defense Fund Position Statement: Sentencing for Animal Cruelty Crimes 1–2. https://aldf.org/wp-content/uploads/2019/09/Position-Statement_Sentencing-2019.pdf [https://perma.cc/HN7U-HQ7J] (concluding that the criminal system "ranks crimes by their perceived severity, ascribing the harshest sentences" to the most reprehensible crimes).

[14] *See* Preventing Animal Cruelty and Torture Act, Pub. L. No. 116–72, 133 Stat. 1151, 1552 (2019) (codified at 18 U.S.C. § 48[d]).

and therefore beyond criminal opprobrium. Consider the list of conduct that is lawful even if it involves purposeful crushing, burning, drowning, suffocating, impaling, or otherwise subjecting an animal to serious bodily injury:

(A) a customary and normal veterinary, agricultural husbandry, or other animal management practice;
(B) the slaughter of animals for food;
(C) hunting, trapping, fishing, a sporting activity not otherwise prohibited by Federal law, predator control, or pest control;
(D) medical or scientific research;
(E) necessary to protect the life or property of a person.[15]

The breadth of these exemptions in a law heralded as one of the most important developments for animal law in decades is striking. Animals raised for food make up well over 90% of the domestic animals in this country, and yet the corporations operating slaughterhouses are arguably inoculated from prosecution unless a prosecutor can show beyond a reasonable doubt that the pain and suffering they might cause is not "customary and normal." Likewise, corporate dairies in the United States that confine up to 36,000 animals per facility for constant cycles of impregnation and milking are shielded from liability, as long as they can attest that their animal management or husbandry practices are customary among their competitors, and perhaps as long as they can find a veterinarian that will endorse the practice.[16] Moreover, it is not a violation of the statute to beat or drown to death a raccoon that is deemed a pest, or an opossum or stray cat that otherwise threatens one's flower garden.

---

[15] *Id.*

[16] The American Veterinary Medical Association approves, for example, the use of blunt force trauma to euthanize an animal. Am. Veterinary Med. Ass'n, AVMA Guidelines for the Euthanasia of Animals: 2020 Edition 100 (2020). https://www.avma.org/sites/default/files/2020-01/2020-Euthanasia-Final-1-17-20.pdf [https://perma.cc/8KCY-GXUY]. Moreover, drowning birds in foam is among the "preferred methods" for depopulating "confined poultry," and electrocution is a preferred method for depopulating pigs. Am. Veterinary Med. Ass'n, AVMA Guidelines for the Depopulation of Animals: 2019 Edition 53 (2019). https://www.avma.org/sites/default/files/resources/AVMA-Guidelines-for-the-Depopulation-of-Animals.pdf [https://perma.cc/9DA8-S2UM] [hereinafter AVMA Guidelines for the Depopulation of Animals].

In sum, when it comes to the much-heralded PACT Act, it is difficult to imagine a clearer way of perpetuating the existing hierarchies among animal victims. Suffering matters, and animal victimhood is recognized up until the point when it would become morally or commercially relevant to most Americans.[17] There is no evidence of a trickle-down theory of animal rights, and the creation of victim hierarchies in other realms has created lasting barriers to substantive progress (Gruber, 2020, p. 96).

II. Enforcement Practices in Criminal Animal Law: A Story of Two States

Some may read the description of the PACT Act above and wonder, "Isn't some animal protection better than no protection?" A dog and cat felony must be better than no felony. This is the myth of incrementalism through criminal law, which turns not on empirical data, but rather on assumptions about social progress occurring one felony enactment at a time. A focus on felonies and prosecutions is treated as imperfect progress, but progress nonetheless.

To challenge this narrative as overly sanguine, if not willfully blind, this section juxtaposes recent events in two different states. Lawyers make a spectacle out of the few (individual abusers), and in the process miss the forest (of systemic abuse) for a few rotten trees. Movement lawyers and organizations often overstate the benefits to animals of a war-on-crime approach, while simultaneously understating (or obfuscating) the role of grassroots activism and civil disobedience. The refusal to acknowledge

[17] Other federal statutes are similarly tailored to a predominantly Eurocentric approach to protecting animal suffering. For example, while federal law permits whales, primates, and elephants to be held in captivity and displayed for entertainment, the law criminalizes animal fighting, which is often associated with nonwhite cultures. Similarly, while the PACT Act permits cruel treatment and the killing of animals in the course of hunting or fishing, federal law prohibits the humane slaughter of dogs and cats for consumption. Dog and Cat Meat Trade Prohibition Act of 2018, H.R. 6720, 115th Cong. (2018); *see also* Marceau (2019, pp. 175–176).

the law-reform potential in activism, and the dogmatic faith in the power of felony (Ristroph, 2018),[18] are two sides of the same carceral coin.

A. New York: Focusing on Individuals as Bad Apples

Even relatively small acts of violence against animals by individuals can become international media sensations, particularly if the accused can be portrayed as a low-status offender because of poverty, race, or prior criminal record. The animal protection movement has mastered the art of fanning these flames of retribution, even when doing so also stokes narratives about racialized justice and inequality.[19]

Illustrative is the Andre Robinson case from New York.[20] Robinson was a young black man who in 2014 lured a stray cat and kicked it into the air near the housing project where he lived in Brooklyn.[21] The cat was not seriously injured; indeed, even before the cat was adopted out to a caring home, lawyers argued over whether there was any proof of injury at all. Moreover, no one seriously disputes that if Robinson had kicked a person and caused similar injuries, or even a couple of people, he probably would not have been charged with a crime.

Because of the involvement of animal lawyers and advocates, however, the case became an international media sensation. Not only were charges filed, but all parties agreed that the Robinson case was handled differently by prosecutors because of the intense and sustained involvement of animal protection groups and the pressure campaign they mounted.[22] Animal lawyers celebrated the fact that a petition calling for the

---

[18] *See generally* Alice Ristroph (2018) (arguing for the eradication of the category of "felon").

[19] Professor Gary Francione warns that the animal protection movement's obsession with favorable press coverage puts it at risk of becoming superficial and inattentive to the interests of most animals. *See* Gary Francione (1996) on pages.

[20] Stephanie Clifford, *He Kicked a Stray Cat, and Activists Growled*, N.Y. Times (Sept. 29, 2014). https://www.nytimes.com/2014/09/30/nyregion/animal-abuse-gains-traction-as-a-serious-crime-with-jail-more-often-the-result.html [https://perma.cc/T7WY-TF44].

[21] *Id.*

[22] *Id.* The *New York Times* story detailing the case noted that interviews with lawyers revealed a persistent trend favoring incarceration, and a number of successes in obtaining it. *Id.*

maximum punishment gathered more than 60,000 signatures,[23] and the media's attention focused on Robinson and the animal lawyers seem to be exactly the goal. It is a high-profile, sensationalized case of individualized violence against a beloved animal.

The Robinson case is not an anomaly. On their websites and in lectures, animal lawyers describe prosecutorial pressure campaigns and amicus briefs in support of longer sentences as ideal forms of grassroots activism. Animal lawyers fetishize policing and prosecution as unmitigated advancements.[24] But perhaps the most important detail about the Robinson case is just how differently it was handled as compared to cases of widespread animal violence. In stark contrast to the proactive efforts to pursue prosecutions in Robinson-like cases, many of the movement's lawyers have been surprisingly quiet when it comes to pressing for the prosecution of corporate animal abuse, even when the abuse seems to meet the statutory definition of cruelty. When it is not a broken window such as an attack on a single animal, but a broken system such as factory farms filled with abuse, the public outreach and prosecutorial pressure are considerably muted.

Consider, for example, that about one hundred miles north of the Brooklyn courthouse where Andre Robinson was prosecuted is the Hudson Valley Foie Gras facility, which unnaturally fattens the livers of hundreds of thousands of animals per year using a production process that experts across the world have avowed causes suffering.[25] Unlike

---

23 Animal Advocates, *Punish Andre Robinson, Man Accused of Kicking Stray Cat in Brooklyn, NY to Full Extent of the Law*, Care2 Petitions. https://www.thepetitionsite.com/554/529/298/punish-andre-robinson-man-accused-of-kicking-stray-cat-in-brooklyn-ny-to-full-extent-of-the-law/ [https://perma.cc/86PV-92EW].

24 Policing continues to be celebrated even as research shows that companies generally viewed as anathema to animal protection, like Chevron and Shell, are corporate sponsors and featured "partner[s]" of local police departments across the country. Gin Armstrong and Derek Seidman, *Fossil Fuel Industry Pollutes Black & Brown Communities While Propping Up Racist Policing*, Eyes on the Ties (July 27, 2020). https://news.littlesis.org/2020/07/27/fossil-fuel-industry-pollutes-black-brown-communities-while-propping-up-racist-policing/ [https://perma.cc/JKH9-2HKS].

25 *See* Humane Soc'y of the U.S., An HSUS Report: The Welfare of Animals in the Foie Gras Industry 1 (2012). http://www.humanesociety.org/assets/pdfs/farm/HSUS-Report-on-Foie-Gras-Bird-Welfare.pdf [https://perma.cc/7Q8G-NLBD] ("[S]ubstantial scientific evidence suggests that force-feeding... is detrimental to [the birds'] welfare."); *see also* Humane Soc'y of the

the Robinson case, which involved an animal victim with high social status and a human perpetrator who was perceived as low status, Hudson Valley Foie Gras is a well-established corporation making high-end food for the wealthy, its avian victims are not nearly as beloved, and yet there is no evidence that the movement has leveraged its celebrated relationships with prosecutors to force a corporate prosecution of these factory-farming practices. To put a finer point on the issue, if criminal prosecution is treated as valuable, and if animal lawyers can argue that horses have a freestanding right to sue in court for restitution,[26] or that an Orca has a claim under the Thirteenth Amendment,[27] surely such creativity could identify a colorable argument that the production of foie gras is a corporate crime.[28]

Corporate prosecutions are vanishingly rare, and the focus of carceral animal law has been on individual actors as opposed to systemic accountability. One might worry that in the criminal realm, the amount of focus and fury surrounding a case is inversely linked to the amount of animal suffering that actually occurred.

U.S., Scientists and Experts on Force-Feeding for Foie Gras Production and Duck and Goose Welfare 1. https://www.humanesociety.org/sites/default/files/docs/hsus-expert-synopsis-force-feeding-duck-and-goose-welfare.pdf [https://perma.cc/XQ6G-B3KH].

[26] Karin Brulliard, *Seeking Justice for Justice the Horse*, Wash. Post (Aug. 13, 2018). https://www.washingtonpost.com/news/national/wp/2018/08/13/feature/a-horse-was-neglected-by-its-owner-now-the-horse-is-suing/ [https://perma.cc/LUC9-G4YQ].

[27] Tilikum, Katina, Corky, Kasatka, and Ulises, Five Orcas, *ex rel.* PETA v. SeaWorld Parks & Ent., 842 F. Supp. 2d 1259 (S.D. Cal. 2012).

[28] N.Y. Agric. & Mkts. Law § 353 (McKinney 2005) (making it a crime to "cruelly beat[] or unjustifiably injure[], maim[], mutilate[], or kill[] any animal," and refusing to provide an explicit agricultural practices exemption); *see* People v. Voelker, 658 N.Y.S.2d 180, 183 (N.Y. Crim. Ct. 1997) ("Whether or not the People can prove that defendant 'unjustifiably' committed these acts is a matter best left to the trier of fact."). It does not seem radically far-fetched to believe that a jury might find that according to the "moral standards of the community," *id.*, the injuries caused by force-feeding a bird with a funnel multiple times per day could constitute unjustified injuring, maiming, mutilation, or torture.

B. Iowa: Disavow Civil Disobedience and Celebrate Expanding Felony Liability

Recent events in Iowa provide a second case study in the way that carceral animal law operates on the ground. The state of Iowa expanded the definition of animal cruelty offenses and increased the maximum penalty for the crime of animal cruelty, accomplishments that were celebrated by many in the movement as major advances for the status of animals under Iowa law. Within weeks of these legislative changes, Iowa also passed its third Ag-Gag law,[29] and it was the site of a groundbreaking undercover investigation at a factory farm. Juxtaposing the reaction of many animal lawyers to these contemporaneous events in the same state provides an insight into the way that law-and-order thinking is impacting efforts to advance animal status in law and policy.

Iowa has been home to some of the most strident efforts to sweep systemic animal abuse under the rug. The state was among the first to pass an Ag-Gag law criminalizing whistleblowing investigations in agricultural facilities, and following a federal injunction of the law, passed a second such law, which was also enjoined.[30] In June of 2020, Iowa's governor signed into law a third attempt to provide unique protection against investigations to agricultural facilities.[31] Around that time, activists engaged in civil disobedience by trespassing and placing hidden cameras in the largest pig farm in Iowa. The cameras captured footage of a "ventilation shutdown" to kill all of the pigs. The factory farm's management had decided that because of the COVID-19 downturn in pork sales, feeding their pigs was no longer profitable. To avoid further lost profits, management decided to kill all of the pigs by, as summarized

---

[29] Ag-Gag laws are "agriculture security legislation... that... restricts — or 'gags' — methods used to gather and disseminate information about the conditions" of animal agricultural production. Shaakirrah R. Sanders (2020, p. 1172) (documenting legislative history showing that the laws were a reaction to animal activists "running out to a news outlet," *id.* at 1175 [citation omitted]).

[30] Animal Legal Def. Fund v. Reynolds, 353 F. Supp. 3d 812, 816–17, 827 (S.D. Iowa 2019).

[31] S.F. 2413, 88th Gen. Assemb. (Iowa 2020). The newest Ag-Gag law is unquestionably less of a direct affront to free speech rights insofar as it targets certain trespasses for higher penalties, as opposed to criminalizing pure speech. But the legislative debate provides strong evidence that the motive for the law was similar.

by a Pulitzer Prize-winning journalist, "sealing off all airways to their barns and inserting steam into them, intensifying the heat and humidity inside and leaving them to die overnight."[32] According to the American Veterinary Medical Association Guidelines, which approve this method of killing, "[i]n realistic terms, death may result from any combination of excessive temperature, CO2, or toxic gases from slurry or manure below the barn."[33] In short, pigs were killed by the thousands in Iowa by essentially cooking them to death.

Confronted with such abject and incontestable cruelty, the same community of lawyers that urged charges against Andre Robinson, and commented favorably to journalists for the *New York Times* on the case, was, by comparison, quite restrained in their responses to these events in Iowa. Unlike cases involving a single, high-status animal victim, there has been no public statement demanding charges, no mailers urging constituents to reach out to their elected officials, and no grandstanding about the injustice of no criminal charges in this case. A mailer sent out by one organization in 2019 reminded supporters that it is important to tell their elected officials that, when it comes to animal cruelty, "the punishment... [should] fit[] the crime."[34] Cases like Andre Robinson's illustrate what the lawyers mean when they demand that the punishment fit the crime, and the silence in the face of revelations like those at the Iowa farm reveals the other side of the carceral animal law coin.[35]

The animal lawyers' complete silence about the need for a criminal response to the systemic animal abuse documented in the undercover investigation in Iowa might justify generalizations about the impacts of tough-on-crime thinking. One could extrapolate that the law-and-order

---

32 Glenn Greenwald, *Hidden Video and Whistleblower Reveal Gruesome Mass-Extermination Method for Iowa Pigs Amid Pandemic*, Intercept (May 29, 2020, 12:08 PM). https://theintercept.com/2020/05/29/pigs-factory-farms-ventilation-shutdown-coronavirus/ [https://perma.cc/9WFS-N7VU].

33 AVMA Guidelines for the Depopulation of Animals, *supra* note 24, at 45.

34 Petition from Animal Legal Def. Fund to Jared Polis, Governor of the State of Colorado (Summer 2019) (on file with the Harvard Law School Library) (petitioning the governor to support laws that "guarantee animal abusers are punished harshly").

35 The willingness of animal lawyers to prioritize incarceration cannot be fairly disputed. As one prominent group framed the agenda for years to come, "[our Criminal Justice P]rogram... inspired our famous bumper sticker: 'Abuse an Animal, Go to Jail!' And we mean it." Stephen Wells, *Letter from the Executive Director*, The Animals' Advoc., Summer 2006, at 1, 2.

culture among animal lawyers has conditioned them to believe that, as a policy matter, they should not pursue legal actions or public outreach based on video evidence obtained through civil disobedience or illegality. The law-and-order lawyers of the movement, it appears, want to create a clear demarcation between their work and that of activists on the ground who will risk jail time to expose animal suffering on a massive scale. Indeed, the animal lawyers rarely even suggest that the criminal defense of such activists, who are literally saving animal lives and documenting abuse, has a home in the realm of animal law. Prosecutions of individual abusers are treated as somehow directly serving the interests of animals, but the defense of a person who is engaged in activism that does in fact directly save animals is rejected. It is a policy of disavowing the "radical flank," and refusing to defend them or even rely on their work product and video footage, much less celebrate them as part of the law-reform effort (NeJaime, 2013, p. 898).[36]

Animal lawyers might respond that, while deplorable, the actions at the Iowa pig farm are not deserving of intervention because the cruelty exposed may not have been criminally prohibited. But even if the abuse in Iowa did not fit the definition of corporate criminality, again, it is telling that the movement did not leverage its connections or call upon its members to demand law reforms that would hold the corporation responsible for the abuse revealed in Iowa. A rigid belief in the need for adherence to existing law may be limiting social change, and causing movement lawyers to fail to imagine possibilities beyond the status quo. When courts decide cases recognizing the sentience of animals as a justification for a harsher criminal justice response, commentators declare that the practical value to the movement of such holdings "cannot be overstated" (Dunn & Rosengard, 2017, p. 456) and yet, when it comes to systemic suffering uncovered by "outlaw" activists,[37] the response of many animal lawyers is silence. The reason for this disconnect is the law-and-order orientation of the animal protection movement.

---

[36] (Noting that social movement research has shown that the "moderate movement factions benefit from their radical counterparts").

[37] *See* G. Alex Sinha, *Virtuous Law-Breaking*, Wash. U. Juris. Rev. (forthcoming) (manuscript at 17–24) (on file with the Harvard Law School Library).

Even more stunning than these failures, animal lawyers and advocates were actually working with legislators in Iowa on amendments to the Iowa cruelty code during this precise legislative session. During the 2020 legislative session, Iowa's legislature amended its criminal code to diminish the mens rea required for guilt, expand the scope of criminal liability, and increase the maximum sentence for certain animal offenses.[38] According to the sponsor of these amendments, the Iowa legislature acted in response to national ranking systems generated by animal lawyers that rank states based on their legal protections for animals.[39] The sponsor explained that "[w]hat we're trying to solve here is Iowa being one of the lowest-ranked states in regards to animal abuse."[40] This is proof positive that lawmakers consider the movement's rankings and input. But it turns out that this only compounds the problem.

The animal law ranking system rewards things like first-offense felonies and higher sentences, but it does not penalize exemptions for cruelty to farm animals or the apparent absence of corporate liability for video-captured abuse.[41] The ranking system allows a state like Iowa to be celebrated in 2020 as incrementally improving its protections for animals, when in fact nothing could be further from reality. Notably,

---

38 H.F. 737, 88th Gen. Assemb. (Iowa 2020).

39 *E.g.*, Animal Legal Def. Fund, Animal Protection: U.S. State Laws Rankings Report (2019). https://aldf.org/wp-content/uploads/2020/02/2019-Animal-Protection-US-State-Laws-Rankings-Report.pdf [https://perma.cc/M4RC-XPAD] [hereinafter Animal Legal Def. Fund, Rankings Report].

40 Stephen Gruber-Miller, *Iowa Senate Passes Bill Increasing Penalties for Animal Abuse, Neglect*, Des Moines Reg. (Mar. 4, 2020, 9:08 PM). https://www.desmoinesregister.com/story/news/politics/2020/03/04/iowa-senate-passes-bill-strengthening-penalties-animal-abuse-neglect-torture/4952238002 [https://perma.cc/9WA2-JWU8]; *see also Gov. Reynolds Signs Bill to Strengthen Iowa's Animal Cruelty Laws*, KCRG (June 30, 2020, 9:06 a.m.). https://www.kcrg.com/2020/06/30/gov-reynolds-signs-bill-to-strengthen-iowas-animal-cruelty-laws [https://perma.cc/8XDD-M24M].

41 Animal Legal Def. Fund, Rankings Report (2019) on pages 26, 33. The rankings report provides only a cursory summary of its methodology, so it is not possible to replicate the findings or assess how the categories of evaluation are weighted or compared. Notably, however, none of the recommendations for improving rankings include, for example, abandoning standard agricultural exemptions. By contrast, the list of suggested improvements suggests a common theme. The surest path to a higher ranking, as Iowa recognized, is more felonies and higher criminal penalties.

within weeks of the investigation in Iowa revealing pigs being overheated to death by the thousands and the state enacting a new Ag-Gag law, animal protection groups across the country took to the press to applaud Iowa for its "necessary" upgrades to the cruelty code.[42] At the very moment when the Iowa Select Farms abuse was making headlines, instead of bemoaning the absence of corporate accountability in the criminal law, the movement lawyers shifted the narrative to Iowa's successes by noting that their ranking system was relied on by the "legislative drafters, as well as advocates" in order to "ensure the bill addressed the state's biggest shortcomings" and was "as impactful as possible."[43] The animal movement deploys its pro-carceral agenda in ways that affirmatively distract attention away from systemic abuse.

To celebrate Iowa's animal protection efforts in the spring of 2020 was nothing short of public obfuscation. This was not a time of "impactful" change for the animals in Iowa—it was a year of horrific policymaking and absenteeism when it came to corporate accountability. Understanding how the lawyer-created rankings work, recognizing the community's triumphant celebration of the expanding criminal provisions for individuals, and examining the nonresponse of some lawyers to factory-farm abuse exposed by activists all underscore the extent to which the carceral focus distracts from and undermines the interests of animals. It is not a neutral or incrementally beneficial set of policy preferences; it is affirmatively harmful.

* * *

A tough-on-crime logic operates across large segments of the animal law world. Animal law commentators and practitioners overwhelmingly embrace criminal law as a salient example of the rising tide of animal law. The focus may be unduly limited now, they argue, but the benefits of the criminal law's narrow focus will trickle down and benefit all animals over time. By this logic, an expanded criminal code or a new mandatory

---

[42] Several animal law groups released statements celebrating the amendments to Iowa's code, and praising the increased penalty provisions. *See, e.g., Updating Iowa's Animal Protection Laws (Iowa)*, Animal Legal Def. Fund, https://aldf.org/project/updating-iowas-animal-protection-laws-iowa/ [https://perma.cc/5FVF-6DDY].

[43] *Id.*

minimum today is a foothold toward animal rights (perhaps on factory farms) tomorrow. But the logic of increased attention to crimes and penalties for individual animal abusers actually reinforces hierarchies and perpetuates larger-scale animal abuse and exploitation caused by corporations.[44] One need not focus on the damage to human communities from increased policing and prosecution to realize that criminal animal law is not a harmless sideshow.

More prosecution will never lead to greater animal rights. Longer sentences have not incrementally advanced the standing of animals in society. Like other palliative treatments, the carceral agenda provides pain relief for the humans disturbed by animal violence, but it masks rather than cures the structural violence involved in the ordinary commercial exploitation of animals. As societal concern for animal protection increases,[45] one should expect that the public will be hungry for this sort of palliative treatment; instead, I hope that animal lawyers will be up to the task of providing interventions aimed at a cure.

References

Bagaric, M., Kotzmann, J., & Wolf, G. (2019). A rational approach to sentencing offenders for animal cruelty: A normative and scientific analysis underpinning proportionate penalties for animal cruelty offenders. *South Carolina Law Review, 71,* 385–427.

Baldus, D. C., Woodworth, G., & Pulaski, C. A. (Eds.). (1990). *Equal justice and the death penalty: A legal and empirical analysis.* UPNE.

[44] *See* Alec Karakatsanis, *Why "Crime" Isn't the Question and Police Aren't the Answer*, Current Affs. (Aug. 10, 2020). https://www.currentaffairs.org/2020/08/why-crime-isnt-the-question-and-police-arent-the-answer [https://perma.cc/L8XW-T228] (explaining how a focus on individualized incidents of "crime" distracts from more systemic problems and reinforces social power structures already in place); *see also* Marceau (2019, p. 6) ("Cruelty prosecutions allow for a collective transference or displacement of guilt from mainstream society onto the 'other,' the socially deviant animal abuser.").

[45] *See* Rebecca Riffkin, *In U.S., More Say Animals Should Have Same Rights as People*, Gallup (May 18, 2015). https://news.gallup.com/poll/183275/say-animals-rights-people.aspx [https://perma.cc/2STM-WGCP].

Beirne, P. (1999). For a nonspeciesist criminology: Animal abuse as an object of study. *Criminology, 37*(1), 117–148.
Bryant, T. L. (2010). Denying animals childhood and its implications for animal-protective law reform. *Law, Culture and the Humanities, 6*(1), 56–74.
Black, D. (1976). *The behavior of law*. Academic Press.
Black, D. (1980). *The manners and customs of the police*. Academic Press.
Dunn, L., & Rosengard, D. B. (2017). Comment: A dog is not a stereo: The role of animal sentience in determining the scope of owner privacy interests under Oregon law. *Animal Law Review, 23*(2), 451–477.
Francione, G. (1996). *Rain without thunder: The ideology of the animal rights movement*. Temple University Press.
Gruber, A. (2007). The feminist war on crime. *Iowa Law. Review, 92,* 741–843.
Gruber, A. (2018). Equal protection under the Carceral state. *University of Colorado-Northwestern University Law Review, 112*(6), 1337–1384.
Gruber, A. (2020). *The feminist war on crime: The unexpected role of women's liberation in mass incarceration.* University of California Press.
Kleinfeld, J. (2013). A theory of criminal victimization. *Stanford Law Review, 65,* 1087–1152.
Levin, B. (2019). Mens rea reform and its discontents. *Journal of Criminal Law & Criminology, 109*(3), 491–558.
Marceau, J. (2019). *Beyond cages: Animal law and criminal punishment.* Cambridge University Press.
NeJaime, D. (2013). Constitutional change, courts, and social movements. *Michigan Law Revew, 111,* 877–902.
Phillips, S., & Marceau, J. (2020). Whom the state kills. *Harvard Civil Rights—Civil Liberties Law Review, 55,* 2–69.
Ristroph, A. (2018). Farewell to the felonry. *Harvard Civil Rights—Civil Liberties Law Review, 53,* 563–618.
Sanders, S. R. (2020). The corporate privacy proxy. *Cornell Law Review, 105,* 1171–1210.
Satz, A. B. (2009). Animals as vulnerable subjects: Beyond interest-convergence, hierarchy, and property. *Animal Law Review, 16,* 65–122.

11

Responsibility in End Time: Environmental Harm and the Role of Law in the Anthropocene

Pierre Cloutier de Repentigny

Introduction

The concept of the Anthropocene has garnered a lot of attention in scholarly debates over the last decade or so (Webster & Mai, 2020). According to the Anthropocene Working Group of the International Commission on Stratigraphy—the body tasked with determining the units (periods, epochs and age) of the geologic time scale—the Anthropocene denotes "the present geological time interval, in which many conditions and processes on Earth are profoundly altered by human impact. This impact has intensified significantly since the onset of industrialization, taking us out of the Earth System state typical of the Holocene Epoch that post-dates the last glaciation" (Subcommission on Quaternary Stratigraphy, n.d.). The Anthropocene is the first geological epoch that is the

P. Cloutier de Repentigny (✉)
Department of Law and Legal Studies, Carleton University,
Ottawa, Canada
e-mail: pierre.derepentigny@carleton.ca

J. Gacek and R. Jochelson (eds.), *Green Criminology and the Law*,
Palgrave Studies in Green Criminology,
https://doi.org/10.1007/978-3-030-82412-9_11

result of one of Earth's species, humans, rather than a strictly geological phenomenon (e.g. an ice age or a massive flood). It thus highlights the capacity of humans to fundamentally interfere with the biological, geological and chemical systems of our planet, and, consequently, emphasises the role of humankind in ecology (Crutzen & Stoermer, 2000; Steffen et al., 2007). The Anthropocene is intellectually appealing in part because it offers a unifying concept of anthropogenic environmental impacts, mostly harm, that is so often divided into various categories (e.g. climate change, water pollution, species extinction, etc.) (Keys et al., 2019). It is also the signifier of our failure to adequately deal with environmental harm (Grear, 2015; Steffen et al., 2015).

The meta-concept of the Anthropocene thus offers an interesting framework to question the way we have dealt with environmental harm through law. I argue that the nature of the harm environmental law is attempting to regulate with little success requires a different framework of responsibility than the one currently adopted by the law (Bosselmann, 2016; Cloutier de Repentigny, 2020). This chapter explores, using critical environmental law methodology (Philippopoulos-Mihalopoulos, 2017) and green criminology, the role of law regarding anthropocenic harm and responsibility. The first part critically conceptualises anthropocenic harm. Based on the anthropocenic understanding of environmental harm, the second part explores the concept of anthropocenic responsibility. Firstly, it looks at the meaning of responsibility in a systemic context based on the understanding that humans' geological agency is tied to the dominant system of production. Secondly, it further contextualises systemic responsibility based on the differentiated agency of humans regarding anthropocenic harm. The final part delves into the shortcomings of contemporary environmental law as a tool to address anthropocenic harm. Using marine biodiversity degradation in Canada as an example, it first highlights the disconnect between the methods of environmental law and the nature of and responsibility for anthropocenic harm. From that point, the chapter concludes on some observations about how to begin addressing these shortcomings.

Conceptualising Environmental Harm in the Anthropocene

The concept of harm describes a normative social judgement about behaviours that result in negative consequences (Lin, 2006). Environmental harm is thus a social wrong that must be redressed. While environmental law aims to address or minimise in some fashion environmental harm (Lin, 2006), its ontology of reprehensible harm is much more limited than the true extent of anthropogenic harm to the environment (M'Gonigle & Takeda, 2013, pp. 1059–1079; White & Heckenberg, 2014, pp. 9–10). The law is permissive of harmful activities through a series of mechanisms that allows for pollution, ecologically destructive or disturbing activities, the killing of wildlife, etc., in order to fuel economic growth (Lynch et al., 2020). What the law considers to be sufficiently harmful to be prohibited is but a small fraction of what most would consider environmental harm (Dybing, 2012, p. 274; see also Lynch et al., 2020; White, 2011; White & Heckenberg, 2014). Focussing on illegal harm would leave out of the concept of harm most activities that resulted in the Anthropocene (Steffen et al., 2015; White, 2011).

Typical conceptualisations of environmental harm include negative impacts on the environment that create "a setback to human interests that community norms have deemed to be significant" (Lin, 2006, p. 901), and activities that negatively impact sustainability—i.e. behaviour that threatens the ecological balance and socio-economic stability of a region or ecosystem (Mohamed Al-Damkhi et al., 2009). These conceptualisations reflect a more anthropocentric view of the environment—one that the law usually adopts—and thus leave out a significant portion of anthropogenic harm (Halsey, 2016, pp. 43–45). Environmental harm can also be viewed as any activities that harm the environment and wildlife (White, 2011, p. 20; White & Heckenberg, 2014). This more ecocentric and holistic definition is more in line with the human behaviour that led to the Anthropocene. Our new geological era was caused by the accumulation of all anthropogenic disturbances to the environment, not only by activities that have a negative impact on human life. Laws protecting endangered species or sensitive ecological areas are arguably following this conceptualisation (although some remain entrenched in anthropocentrism). Nonetheless, this conceptualisation is problematic as it lacks conceptual precision and would potentially include acts that are necessary for human life. Even those approaches that do try to build a more defined ecocentric approach tend to, for example, reproduce romantic, idealised or reified version of ecology (e.g. that it is beautiful, static and harmonious) or portray humans as a unified and universal subject (Halsey, 2016, pp. 45–50).

It is the all-encompassing nature of environmental harm that renders the concept unruly. Nearly all of human activities have an impact on our environment as we cannot live independently from the rest of the biosphere. In fact, the distinction between humanity and the so-called natural environment or the nature/culture divide is artificial (Philippopoulos-Mihalopoulos, 2017, p. 136). Nonetheless, the Anthropocene highlights that humans are not like any other species (Grear, 2015). Our relatively new status as geological agent means that we can and have in fact caused significant and dangerous disturbances within the biosphere. While not all impact should be qualified as harm as this would make our continued existence as a species ethically questionable, we do need to find a way to conceptualise anthropogenic harm that takes into account the complex and interconnected nature of the biosphere and our status as geological agent. This line of inquiry is important as understanding harm is the first step to addressing it and building an effective environmental legal regime.

Philippopoulos-Mihalopoulos (2017, pp. 137–142) suggests a new grammar for the environment: the continuum. This continuum builds on the epistemically fuzzy nature of the environment and is described as an *assemblage* of collectivities of objects, bodies, discourses and more (for the broader concept of assemblage, see Deleuze & Guattari, 1980). He states that

> the continuum I am suggesting here is acentral and multi-agentic, constituted of affective excess and of bodies melting into each other's contours. It is also a tilted, power-structured surface, on which bodies move, rest and position themselves, affecting the tilt while being affected by it.

> Stronger bodies affect the continuum in radical ways, making it tilt according to their positions ... (Philippopoulos-Mihalopoulos, 2017, p. 137)

This continuum is constantly ruptured—a continuity of ruptures—by various acts that cut or modify the various links between the objects or configuration of objects. Ruptures are not to be avoided; they are an integral part of the continuum as an ever-moving and changing object-concept. In terms of harm, the various anthropogenic acts that cause these ruptures (which are distinct to other ruptures that are linked to non-anthropogenic causes) become concerning when they threaten the viability of the continuum itself. In other words, environmental harm is the ruptures that amount to ecological disorganisation, that is, the disruption of relationships between different elements of the continuum resulting in threats to ecosystems or the biosphere as a whole (Stretesky et al., 2014, p. 22). To a certain extent, this conceptualisation of environmental harm could be interpreted as excluding certain individual acts that could amount to non-negligible injuries to one or a very small amount of people. Suffice to say, for the purpose of this chapter, that adopting a particular understanding of environmental harm—that is, harm to the environmental continuum—does not preclude the conceptualisation of other "harms" that need to be prohibited, prevented and/or limited. Multiple conceptualisations can coexist, especially given their interrelation. As such, we can differentiate the independent concept of injurious acts which might be reprehensible (e.g. a person suffering from injuries due to contact with a pollutants) from the role such acts may or may not play in ecological disorganisation.

The difficulty is that the individual acts leading to ecological disorganisation (including the vast majority of, if not all, environmental injuries) do not exist independently of one another. Like the environment itself, they form part of a harm-*assemblage*. Considering the individual actions and inactions independently ignores the ways they cumulate, compound, interconnect and otherwise interact with each other at multiple different levels, from your backyard to the entire biosphere. Therefore, even though the concept of environmental injuries and environmental harm can be distinguished, it is highly unlikely that the two can be separated in practice. Morton refers to these complex all-encompassing abstract yet material concepts as hyperobjects (Morton, 2010, pp. 130–135). Hyperobjects are.

> *viscous*, which means that they "stick" to beings that are involved with them. They are *nonlocal*; in other words, any "local manifestation" of a hyperobject is not directly the hyperobject. They involve profoundly different temporalities than the human-scale ones we are used to. [...] Hyperobjects occupy a high-dimensional phase space that results in their being invisible to humans for stretches of time. And they exhibit their effects *interobjectively*; that is, they can be detected in a space that consists of interrelationships between aesthetic properties of object. (Morton, 2013, p. 1)

Anthropocenic harm is viscous as it sticks to all humans as we are all involved, to different degrees of course, in the degradation of the biosphere or the harmful rupturing of the environmental continuum. It is nonlocal as the local manifestation—e.g. the construction of an open-pit mine—is but a manifestation of the larger issue of environmental degradation. It exists in a timescale equal to our own as a species; although its truly disastrous effects are relatively recent (Steffen et al., 2015).[1] Its most rupturing effects were also quasi-invisible to human consciousness for a long time,[2] and it continues to be relatively invisible to those with sufficient privileges (UNHCR, 2019). Finally, anthropocenic harm appears to us and has meaning when we look at its interobjective effects, or, in other words, when we focus not on the rupturing acts themselves, but rather on the effects of their interconnection, i.e. their interobjective spaces.[3]

[1] However, there are debates on when exactly the starting point of the Anthropocene or similar concepts should be: see e.g. issue 2 of volume 2 of the *Anthropocene Review*.

[2] Climate change offers an excellent example as the production of greenhouse gases that would result in climate change started with the industrial revolution, but it is only in the last few decades that climate change became a "visible" problem to most people; see Chakrabarty (2009).

[3] Interobjectivity can be understood more easily when referred to the more well-known concept of intersubjectivity. Intersubjectivity—the space where humans create meaning—is an anthropocentric segment, hence a subjective one, of interobjectivity, which act as a meta-space where we can create meaning related to the interconnection of objects; see Morton (2013, pp. 81–86).

Targeting the individual actions, in a piecemeal approach, as environmental law tends to do, does not address the hyperobject that is anthropocenic harm (Philippopoulos-Mihalopoulos, 2017, p. 144; see also Bugge, 2013, pp. 17–18; M'Gonigle & Ramsay, 2004, pp. 335–339). Even relative successes, like the dramatic reduction of ozone depleting substances since the adoption of the *Montreal Protocol on Substances that Deplete the Ozone Layer* in 1987 (Roberts, 2017), only slightly shift the harm-assemblage. Moreover, attempts to solve one issue, like using biofuels to limit greenhouse gases, may create additional or amplify existing problems (IUCN, 2014). Environmental law is ill-adapted to effectively address the hyperobject of anthropocenic harm to the environmental continuum. Significant changes will be needed to adapt environmental law to the reality of the Anthropocene, particularly the nature of anthropocenic harm.

A Framework of Responsibility for Anthropocenic Harm

Related to the issue of harm is the issue of responsibility. In other words, who is responsible for environmental harm? This question is both retroactive (i.e. who is responsible for causing the harm) and prospective (i.e. who is responsible for repairing the harm). Currently, dominant forms of environmental law, broadly speaking, tend to rely on an individualistic understanding of responsibility (e.g. criminal liability for a corporation violating a regulation prescribing a maximum amount of a certain substance a firm can discharge in waters, or civil liability for toxic substance leaking from the land of person A to the land of person B) (Lee, 2002; Saxe & James, 2019).[4] The state distributes the responsibility among individuals through various legal mechanisms, while public law offers a frame of responsibility for the state itself, which is often limited by various doctrines, procedures and other mechanisms, as well

[4] This is particularly true in Civil (Roman) Law systems and Common Law systems, but not necessarily so as, for e.g., Canada's environmental laws are based on both systems (depending on the province), but Indigenous peoples possess their own legal system based on a completely different understanding of responsibility: see Borrows (1997).

as by the state's competing interests (usually economic interests) (Elgie, 1993; Knox, 2020). Even within public law, the rights or interests of individuals (acting in their name or through legal bodies) take a predominant place as an impact on them is habitually needed to engage in legal proceedings (Stern, 2019). International law tends to create broader frames of responsibility (e.g. obligations *erga omnes*—towards the international community—or concept like common concern of humankind in the Convention on Biological Diversity), but still relies on an individual state responsibility framework limited by very similar concerns as with public law (ITLOS, 2011; Mayrand, 2018).

Overall, as M'Gonigle and Takeda (2013) aptly explain, environmental law is structured by its liberal paradigm which focussed, among other things, on individual freedoms (see also Mayrand, 2018). Individuals are free to pursue their economics interest through state guarantees such as contracts and private property. In return, the state imposes some restrictions on this freedom by making individuals responsible for the harm they cause, which help to maintain state legitimacy and correct market failures. Environmental law thus serves as a way to institutionalise a form of responsibility associated with the agency of individuals (be they natural or legal persons)—i.e. our ability to make conscious actions (Frith, 2014; Green, 1943)—which may result in environmental harm by associating a consequence with harm (Halsey, 2016, pp. 43–45; see also Brisman & South, 2019). Furthermore, since the 1980s, environmental regulations have moved away from the direct imposition of responsibility on individuals (e.g. criminal liability for killing an endangered species) and towards an economic model that further distances the state from environmental responsibility (M'Gonigle & Takeda, 2013, pp. 1068–1071). This neoliberal move relies on the internalisation of environmental cost in decision-making through free-market mechanisms (e.g. carbon caps and trades or eco-labelling) which is supposed to influence the decision-making of firms and consumers by reducing the cost of "green" products, increasing the cost of pollution and providing "green" signalling (i.e. identifying "eco-friendly" products) (Czarnezki & Fiedler, 2016). The state no longer directly limits people's freedom; it instead makes harm part of the cost of doing business and leaves individuals to decide for themselves how they should reduce harm and what harm is worthy of being reduced based on economic calculation and environmental information.

This legal liberal approach to environmental responsibility, even if we presume that it works as "advertised" (i.e. fully implemented and enforced), is simply incapable of dealing with the scope and nature of anthropocenic harm. Conceptualising agency and correlated actions on an individual level in an interconnected ecological world composed of an assemblage of objects that is continuously moving and ever changing simply dooms the approach from the start. Environmental law targets the actions of individuals in silos when such actions, taken independently, are but a drop in the ocean of anthropocenic harm. It creates a system of responsibility where the default stance is freedom and the law provides generally applicable exceptions to this freedom or tries to motivate individuals to exercise their freedom in a responsible way. Responsibility for individual harm—whether directly through regulation or indirectly through the market—hides the true scope of environmental harm; a form of harm that is not the result of a collection of independent individual actions. Furthermore, the increased focus on economic mechanisms diverts attention from the political responsibility associated with environmental harm (Wanner, 2015). Individual agency and responsibility are ill-suited for the Anthropocene and detract from broader systemic issues (Lynch et al., 2017, pp. 211–214). The era and concept of the Anthropocene has highlighted our geological agency and the law must take this fact and the extent of anthropocenic harm it implies seriously. In the words of Crutzen and Stoermer (2000, n.p.), the Anthropocene "emphasize[s] the central role of mankind in geology and ecology." This brings forth a "human species-responsibility" towards the current socio-ecological state of our planet rather than an individual one (Grear, 2015, p. 227). This responsibility towards our place in the ecological continuum and our role in fostering environmental harm must be fully taken into account by environmental law if it is to be the tool of environmental protection it claims to be. In other words, law needs to move towards embracing anthropocenic responsibility (Cloutier de Repentigny, 2020, pp. 182–184). This section first addresses the systemic aspect of anthropocenic responsibility. It then analyses how this systemic responsibility should be differentiated given the persistent inequalities within humanity, both in terms of differing roles in bringing forth the Anthropocene and of capacities to deal with the socio-ecological consequences of that era.

A Systemic Responsibility

Determining the level of responsibility and who should bear it depends on the level of abstraction applied (White & Heckenberg, 2014, p. 20). Since we are dealing with the geological scale, the level of abstraction is quite high. The difficulty here comes from the fact that ascribing intentionality—a crucial element of responsibility that links moral blameworthiness to agency and harm—to the whole of humanity does not seem feasible or even desirable (Smiley, 2017):

> Human exceptionalism must be managed in order to create the conditions for assuming responsibility, regardless of proof of causal link. There is no doubt that humans are only one participant in the environmental decline; yet, as the Anthropocene has taught us, they are *always* a participant, always situated within the ecological conditions of our planet. Strict liability for historical anthropocenic environmental degradation is consonant with assemblage-thinking, where all bodies are complicit with the degradation. (Philippopoulos-Mihalopoulos, 2017, p. 151)

Furthermore, as Takemura (Takemura, 2011, p. 223) states, "because the causality of environmental crime/harm is too complicated to be ascribed to only one cause–effect relation or one factor, it is necessary to introduce a nonlinear way of thinking in order to recognise this problem as a whole." Thus, traditional ways of thinking about responsibility, even collective responsibility, are not necessarily useful in determining the nature of anthropocenic responsibility.

Several green criminologists claim that global political economy is a better site to determine responsibility for environmental harm (Lynch et al., 2017, p. 245; White, 2011, pp. 15–16). This is particularly true when considering the deeply political nature of the Anthropocene concept (Harrington, 2016, p. 483). We are not simply dealing with facts (i.e. humans cause environmental destruction); we are also dealing with power (i.e. who sets the structural parameters of society, or who controls collective actions). At the abstract level of geological agency, the hegemonic ideology of capitalism acts as the starting point of anthropocenic responsibility given its status as one of the, if not *the*, main constitutive frameworks of society. Capitalist production is the main cause of contemporary anthropocenic harm as it is inherently environmentally destructive due to its need to exploit natural resources to feed its perpetual growth paradigm (also referred to as the treadmill of production) (Gould et al., 2016, pp. 7–13; Lynch & Stretesky, 2014, pp. 140–142; Lynch et al., 2013, 2017, pp. 15–17; Moore, 2016; Stretesky et al., 2014, pp. 20–21). The structure and ideology of capitalism contributes greatly to the hyperobject nature of anthropocenic harm. It is this overall system of exploitation (of nature and labour) that makes environmental harm so difficult to grasp and makes individual responsibility so inefficient at responding to what is in fact a systemic problem. It is important to note, however, that while capitalism serves as the main culprit given its omnipresence (even in non-capitalist society through the global market), other ideologies that depend on similar environmentally exploitative methods of production should also trigger anthropocenic responsibility (see White & Heckenberg, 2014, p. 65).

The theory of the treadmill of production indicates that responsibility lies specifically at the production level, where key decisions about the nature of social system–ecosystem relationships are made (Gould et al., 2016, pp. 20–22). Other decisions within the system (like consumption) are dependent on production and the decisions made by those who control production. Individual agency is thus severely limited by systemic political and economic factors. The potential place of individual responsibility is within the political realm (Gould et al., 2016, 23–24), that is, individuals as citizens and workers are responsible for demanding change within their capacity and limited agency rather than being responsible for their every action that might impact the environment. Therefore, those who control (directly, like a CEO of a large corporation or investors, or indirectly, like political office holders or those who influence indirectly capital flow and benefits from capitalism) bear the primary burden of anthropocenic responsibility. However, in the context of systemic responsibility, these people are not necessarily individually responsible. Their responsibility lies in their participation in creating and maintaining the exploitation system that threatens to disorganise the ecological continuum. Ultimately, anthropocenic responsibility must first and foremost deal with our system of endless economic growth if it is to tackle anthropocenic harm.

A Differentiated Responsibility

One of the critiques of the Anthropocene as a concept is its tendency to universalise, or Eurocentralise, narratives of human–nature relations (Davis & Todd, 2017; Simpson, 2020). While the systemic nature of anthropocenic responsibility already recognises that not all humans are equally responsible for environmental harm by linking the concept to capitalist production, further differentiation is needed to recognise the true extent of environmental injustices. A differentiated framework of responsibility is in line with the assemblage nature of both ecology and anthropocenic harm: not all relationships created within these assemblages are equal and thus responsibility depends both on where an object is in the assemblage and on its historical presence (Philippopoulos-Mihalopoulos, 2017, p. 151). Pollutions and other environmental harms affect poor people and racialised people in higher concentrations and with disproportionate impact, a fact compounded by inequalities between the global north and the global south (Lynch et al., 2017, pp. 189–190, 198–200; Nurse, 2020, pp. 574–575; South, 2011, pp. 236–237). This issue—often captured by the concept and movement of environmental justice—is not distinct from the systemic responsibility associated with capitalism; rather, it is an essential aspect of it as systemic racism and global socio-economic inequalities are essential ingredients for a thriving capitalist system (Lynch & Stretesky, 2014; p. 153; Gould et al., 2016, pp. 72–75).

At the global level, colonialism, imperialism, and North–South relations are also of central importance when thinking of anthropocenic responsibility. Again, there is a strong link to capitalism production as the global north has pillaged the resources of the global south to fuel its economic growth (Brisman & South, 2020; Gonzalez, 2015; White,

2011, p. 3). In return, the global south as long demanded that the north assume responsibility for environmental harm, which has led to a half-baked solution where "the North has only grudgingly accepted the principle of common, but differentiated, responsibility on the basis of its superior technical and financial resources while disavowing responsibility on the basis of its historic contributions to these crises" (Gonzalez, 2015, p. 409). Settler colonialism adds another layer to the issue as many Indigenous Peoples' land continues to be occupied by forces that have not only caused significant violence and environmental harm, but have also had profoundly negative impacts on ways of life build on mutually supportive relationships between humans and "nature" (Davis & Todd, 2017, pp. 770–771; Salih & Corry, 2021; Simpson, 2020, p. 65).

While the Anthropocene offers a common frame of understanding for the hyperobject of anthropocenic harm and assists with the extirpation of individual agency and responsibility out of our consciousness to replace it with a form of geological agency and responsibility, this level of generalisation should not erase the violence experienced by various segments of humanity; it should rather reinforce and expand the attention we give to specific injustices linked to the Anthropocene (Salih & Corry, 2021). Anthropocenic responsibility is thus based on two additional elements: (1) the burden of responsibility should be greater on states that have participated and benefited from colonisation, imperialism and continuing North–South inequities; and (2) groups who have suffered disproportionately from anthropocenic harm are entitled to restitution (which could take various forms depending on the situation, for example, giving sovereignty back to Indigenous Nations and/or ensuring that these groups have sufficient resources to adapt to the Anthropocene).

Anthropocenic responsibility goes beyond law and asks each of us to be conscious of our relationship with the biosphere and to start reimagining it. For some, this is life as usual, but for others, it will require considerable efforts (and a great deal will undoubtedly be reluctant). Law, however, allows for the formalisation of responsibility and to create a set of rules to implement it within society. Given how steeped law is within the liberal and capitalist paradigm, re-forming it into something that reflects anthropocenic responsibility and that is thus capable of dealing with anthropocenic harm will be arduous. It is clear, from the nature of the harm, that a systemic and differentiated approach is needed. Such an endeavour will not be easy, nor will it be a quick fix. But through strategic actions—actions that progressively destabilise current paradigm and institute new ways of being—we can start modifying the current legal structure to implement anthropocenic responsibility (Cloutier de Repentigny, 2020, pp. 192–193). What exactly this will look like is impossible to predict and will probably require experimentation. The next section offers some potential starting point in the context of Canadian marine life protection.

The Shortcomings of Environmental Law: The Case of Canadian Marine Life

Environmental law in Canada, as in many other states, is a complex network of statutes, regulations and administrative decision-making. Offering a comprehensive analysis of Canadian environmental law through the lens of anthropocenic responsibility is beyond the scope of this chapter. The purpose of this section is to offer a short example of environmental law's lacuna in light of anthropocenic harm and responsibility to concretise the limits of the current approach and to begin the exploration of what anthropocenic law could resemble. The example is based on laws that purport to protect marine life. While, as with many environmental issues, marine life protection is impacted by a myriad of legislation of specific (e.g. aquaculture regulations) or more general application (e.g. environmental assessment legislation) at the federal, provincial/territorial and municipal levels and by Indigenous laws, this section focuses on the three most relevant and directly applicable of pieces of legislation, all at the federal level[5]: the *Fisheries Act*,[6] the *Species at Risk Act* (*SARA*),[7] and the *Oceans Act*.[8]

The Sad State of Canadian Marine Protection Law

I first offer a general overview of the three acts in question. The purposes of the *Fisheries Act* are twofold: "(a) the proper management and control of fisheries; and (b) the conservation and protection of fish and fish habitat, including by preventing pollution" (*Fisheries Act*, s. 2.1). The Act has been traditionally viewed as primarily a resource exploitation statute (Campbell & Thomas, 2001), and the enduring and central role that commercial fisheries play within the Act and the department in charge of its implementation continues to lay credence to this characterisation (Castañeda et al., 2020; CESD, 2016; Government of Canada, 2012). It gives great discretion to the minister to issue various fish exploitation licences (including marine mammals, which the Act includes in the definition of fish), with some constraint imposed via general and specific regulations (*Fisheries Act*, s. 7). The minister can also issue fisheries management orders "to address a threat to the proper management and control of fisheries and the conservation and protection of fish" (*Fisheries Act*, s. 9). The *Fisheries Act* also includes provisions that prohibit individuals from damaging fish habitat and from depositing pollution in waters frequented by fish (s. 34–36). While these protections may appear broad, ministerial power and regulations exempt a great deal of harmful activities from the prohibitions, and instead permit these damaging activities if they comply with certain mitigation measures.

[5] While marine life or the marine environment is not an existing area of jurisdiction under the Canadian constitution, the federal Parliament is the level of government best equip, jurisdictional wise, to deal with the issue of marine life protection: *The Constitution Act, 1867*, 30 and 31 Vict, c 3, s 91(10), (12); *Reference Re: Offshore Mineral Rights*, [1967] SCR 792; *Reference re Newfoundland Continental Shelf*, [1984] 1 SCR 86; *Moore v Johnson*, [1982] 1 SCR 115; *Ward v Canada (Attorney General)*, 2002 SCC 17; *Northwest Falling Contractors Ltd v The Queen*, [1980] 2 SCR 292; *R v Crown Zellerbach Canada Ltd*, [1988] 1 SCR 401.

[6] RSC 1985, c F-14.

[7] SC 2002, c 29.

[8] SC 1996, c 31.

SARA offers protection to endangered species within Canada. The Act separates species between federal species and provincial ones. Only federal species benefit from the full protection of the Act.[9] These include aquatic species. *SARA* is a reactive legislation as protection is provided only when a species becomes at risk of extinction or extirpation and after it was recommended for listing by the Committee on the Status of Endangered Wildlife in Canada (COSEWIC) and listed as such by the Governor in Council (*SARA*, s. 14–31). If an aquatic species is listed, *SARA* prohibits the harming, killing, trade or possession of an individual from the species and prohibits damaging or destroying its residence (*SARA*, s. 32–33). The government must create recovery strategies and action plans aimed at removing the species from the list (i.e. to ensure it is no longer endangered) (*SARA*, s. 37–55). *SARA* also prohibits the destruction of aquatic species' critical habitat (identified through the recovery strategies) and allows the Governor in Council to make emergency orders to protect any listed species (*SARA*, s. 58, 80). The Act, however, allows for various ways to exempt activities from the statute's protection (*SARA*, s. 73–79).

Finally, the *Oceans Act* offers broader tools for ocean governance. The Act provides for two mechanisms relevant for the protection of marine life: establishing an ocean management strategy and creating marine protected areas (MPAs) (*Oceans Act*, s. 29, 35). The strategy must be based on the principles of sustainable development, integrated management and precaution (*Oceans Act*, s. 30). As part of the current strategy (DFO, 2002), the government has adopted in 2016 an Oceans Protection Plan (OPP) (Office of the Prime Minister, 2016). The plan provides for $1.5 billion over five years in coastal projections. It also indicates that the government will work with Indigenous communities and others to identify areas of high ecological sensitivity and of cultural, social and economic importance, and will strengthen pollution control, marine mammal protection and enforcement. The plan is a policy and thus

[9] Provincial species still benefit from the Act's provisions, like the establishment of a recovery plan, but their protection is primarily the responsibility of the provinces. The Act does allow for emergency protection if a listed species faces eminent threat or the full application of the Act if the minister believes the province is not effectively protecting the species: see *SARA*, s. 34, 35, 61, 80.

offers even greater discretion to the government. Lastly, while the powers of the Governor in Council are quite broad with regard to the establishment of MPAs, the Governor in Council has considerable discretion over what is covered in an MPA (both geographically and in terms of activities) (*Oceans Act*, s. 35).

One of the main issues of this legislative regime is shared by most environmental laws: it attempts to regulate and manage activities and species on an individual level and attempts to deal only with immediate and actualised harm on a local level. For example, the *Fisheries Act* creates limits of particular pollutants for individual facilities and evaluates the impact of individual activities on the marine environment.[10] There is no integrated and systemic plan that manages all fisheries activities and the various threats to marine life on various ecosystemic levels. The Ocean Strategy and the OPP may appear to play this role, but the scope of these instruments is very limited as they only deal with certain activities and does not provide for any mandatory planning and decision-making framework, relying instead on policy guidelines for what remain mostly discretionary decision-making. Generally, Fisheries and Oceans Canada has failed to implement an ecosystem approach to fisheries management and has tended to disregard what some have considered progressive policies (Baum & Fuller, 2016).[11]

Despite overexploitation being the biggest treat to marine life internationally and nationally (Regional Seas Office, 2010; Baum & Fuller, 2016), the *Fisheries Act* did not have, for the longest time, any measure trying to address overexploitation. Since the amendments of 2019, the Act now mandates that the minister needs to take measures to ensure the sustainability of stocks (*Fisheries Act*, s. 6.1, 6.2). The same amendments have also added general guidelines integrating environmental principles to be considered in the management of fisheries (*Fisheries Act*, s. 2.5). Despite what could appear has progress, both these provisions and the

---

[10] See e.g. *Pulp and Paper Effluent Regulations*, SOR/92-269; *Metal and Diamond Mining Effluent Regulations*, SOR/2002-222; *Aquaculture Activities Regulations*, SOR/2015-177.

[11] For e.g., the Wild Salmon Policy, which was regarded as a model for wild pacific salmon management, was adopted in 2005, but went largely unimplemented by 2021. While the government has adopted an implementation plan, it remains to be seen if the plan can have any success given the dire situation of pacific salmon species.

pollution prevention and habitat protection provisions of the Act give considerable discretion to the executive (Johnson, 2020). Additionally, the government has often failed to follow scientific advice regarding quotas and has had issues with the proper enforcement of existing rules (Baum & Fuller, 2016; Lee & Cloutier de Repentigny, 2019). Overall, the *Fisheries Act* attempts to deal with discreet parts of the assemblage of anthropocenic harm. Its failure to deal with the systemic causes of harm has unsurprisingly not resulted in much success (Baum & Fuller, 2016; Castañeda et al., 2020).

SARA may appear more promising at first view, but it contains several issues. Similar to the *Fisheries Act*, the protection offered by *SARA* can be circumvented by the executive in order to promote economic growth.[12] *SARA* protects against individual actions that harm endangered species, not systemic issues that result in the amorphous all-encompassing hyper-object that is anthropocenic harm. The Act does approach systemic issues a bit more through its strategies and plans, however, aside from implementation issues, these intervene only too late in the timeline of anthropocenic harm—i.e. they are created only when species have suffered considerable harm—and those plans do not have the strength to address all the needs of endangered species (e.g. not protecting the prey species of a predator species) (Brilliant, 2018; Favaro et al., 2014; McDevitt-Irwin et al, 2015). Furthermore, the government has often either refused to list commercial aquatic species that were recommended for listing by COSEWIC or has yet to respond to recommendations several years after they were made.[13]

The most promising aspect of the *Oceans Act* is its MPAs regime. While the number of MPAs has increased significantly over the last few years, it remains to be seen if the government will provide sufficient resources (human and financial) for the implementation of the MPAs (Hubert & Gray, 2020). Many MPAs do not include protection for

[12] See e.g. the approval of the trans mountain pipeline by the federal government despite the incredibly high risk the project poses for endangered populations of orca whales: *National Energy Board reconsideration of aspects of its OH-001-2014 Report as directed by Order in Council PC 2018-1177*, MH-052-2018 (February 2019); *Coldwater First Nation v Canada (Attorney General)*, 2020 FCA 34.

[13] See e.g. the bluefin tuna and several populations of the sockeye salmon: https://www.canada.ca/en/environment-climate-change/services/species-risk-public-registry.html.

commercial species and thus do not protect against overexploitation.[14] MPAs also apply only to limited geographical areas and thus have limited effectiveness against anthropocenic harm as it transcends geographical bounds. Given the Act's discretionary nature, the government's poor track records and the existing flaws within the protective scope of MPAs suggest that the regime is currently not well adapted to the numerous threats that marine life faces (Jessen, 2011; Office of the Auditor General of Canada, 2005, 2018). Without systematic and integrated planning of all activities impacting marine life, which current laws and policies do not do (or at least not effectively and holistically), the MPAs regime of the *Ocean Act* will likely have a limited impact on the protection of marine life.

Furthermore, the application of the regulatory regime also exemplifies the gross disproportionality of harm that Indigenous Nations in Canada suffer. Recent issues concerning Mi'kmaq lobster fisheries (a right technically protected by Canadian constitutional law) showed the unequal treatment of fisheries law as corporations seem to easily evade enforcement while modest Indigenous fisheries become a sustainability concern without evidence (Bailey, 2020; Ecology Action Centre, 2019). Moreover, the Trans Mountain pipeline was approved over the objection of many Indigenous Nations, including the Tsleil-Waututh Nation who has a culturally significant connection with the orcas threaten by the project and who provided the government with a holistic environmental assessment of the pipeline project (Lands & Resources Department, 2015). This approval happened despite the fact that the orca population in question enjoys the protection of *SARA* (Rehberg-Besler & Jefferies, 2019). Canadian environmental law ensures that settler corporations and governments benefit from the exploitation of natural resources, while excluding as much as possible Indigenous people who bear the brunt of the resulting anthropocenic harm.

Overall, the three pieces of legislation in Canada aimed at protecting marine life fail to address the systemic causes of anthropocenic harm. Rather than dealing with the up-stream causes of marine life decline—that is the free-market paradigm that feeds the treadmill of production

---

[14] See e.g. *St. Anns Bank Marine Protected Area Regulations*, SOR/2017-106.

and the colonial past and present of the state—it offers a myriad of relative restrictions on individual acts that damages marine life, with disproportionate negative effects on Indigenous communities. Responsibility is delegated to Individuals who are free to engage in destructive activities—many who may appear benign individually but create serious damage when considered in totality—within the limited restrictions imposed by the state to maintain the appearance that it is dealing with anthropocenic harm (M'Gonigle & Takeda, 2013; Wood et al., 2010).

What Anthropocenic Marine Law Could Be

What would Canadian marine protection law look like if it was to adopt anthropocenic responsibility? While it is beyond the scope of this chapter to propose a detailed solution, I offer a few general observations to beginning the process of thinking and discussing what anthropocenic law could be. First, the scope of legislation must be as broad and as holistic as possible instead of patching together various laws that discretely address different issues related to marine biodiversity.[15] A framework legislation, somewhere in-between our current understanding of constitution and regular statute, that encompasses all anthropogenic oceans activities could serve as the basis of a new regime. The framework statute would coordinate government and civic actions in the field, create mandatory standards based on ecosystem parameters and establish adaptable oceans use plans to structure subsequent legislative, administrative and civic actions. Such legislation should also provide for mechanisms aimed at assessing the need (in terms of human and social needs, not purely economic ones) for anthropogenic ocean activities and the capacity of relevant ecosystem to meet that need. It should also holistically, as opposed to a piecemeal approach, address land-based ocean pollutions by creating approval and assessment mechanisms based on need (both human and ecosystemic) for activities that result in that

[15] The federal government possesses sufficient jurisdiction to legislate in this domain, particularly given its broad criminal law power and its jurisdiction over marine issues: see note 5; *R v Hydro-Québec*, [1997] 3 SCR 213; *Groupe Maison Candiac Inc v Canada (Attorney General)*, 2020 FCA 88; Chalifour (2016). The latter article by Chalifour does not deal with marine issues, but it offers a great example of the breath of federal powers for environmental issues.

form of pollutions, while rejecting the mitigation model unless necessary (i.e. prevention over mitigation). Some issues that affect marine life, like climate change, would remain outside of the scope of the framework legislation. This is unsurprising as one statute cannot address the complexity of anthropocenic harm in and of itself. This highlights the need to have a network of complimentary and interconnected system of anthropocenic law. Furthermore, discrete legislation could be adopted under the framework to address more specific issues. For example, a more stringent version of *SARA* (i.e. one that would holistically address the needs of endangered species and that would not allow economic considerations to nullify protection) could exist to act as a safeguard since the unpredictable and complex nature of anthropocenic harm could lead to blind spots in the "regular" protection of marine species.

Second, anthropocenic law needs to move away from our current dominant destructive and exploitative relationship with the biosphere and ourselves. Moving forward, we must avoid reproducing the anthropocentric and hierarchical thinking that puts humans above other species and certain humans above others (Grear, 2015, p. 231). This is probably one of the most difficult tasks of the shift towards anthropocenic law given how engrained capitalism and associated mode of thinking are in society (Blühdorn, 2015). Nonetheless, given the anthropocenic responsibility of capitalist production, it is a necessary one. The law can, strategically and progressively, (1) divert resources and power away from capitalist production (e.g. by reducing and potentially eliminating the legal concept of private property as we know it); and (2) creating new ways to relate to the biosphere (inclusive of humans) (e.g. by trying to create reciprocal relationships that gives and takes rather than exploit). In the context of fisheries, for example, this would mean removing property interests in fish through fishing licences and moving away from an economic growth vision of fisheries. Instead, we could create a regime where fishing is structured by ecosystem boundaries and the food security/sovereignty needs of people. Those who fish should also be part of the system of care for marine biodiversity to create a reciprocal relationship and a proximity between the fishers and their environment.[16] This would act as anthropocenic *responsabilisation*; that is, the act of making people attuned to anthropocenic responsibility through a new, responsible system (Cloutier de Repentigny, 2020). Current fisheries regulations place the onus of responsibility on individual fishers or corporation through extractive licences (usually by allocating a geographically bound species quota and limiting fishing methods). In contrast, anthropocenic *responsabilisation* puts the onus on the state (or another entity that represents and is authorised to make decisions on behalf of a collective/community) to create a system of collective and reciprocal responsibility that is able to take into account our place in the environmental continuum and the nature of environmental harm. Thus, rather than determining how much fish can be extracted to meet the demands of the industry and divvying up this amount among individual actors who become responsible for their share, anthropocenic law would embed human actions in ecosystem and establish spaces where fishers can interact responsibly with fish and the environment they both share based on an understanding of our needs (rather than greed) and the needs of the ecosystems and species that inhabit it. In addition, for the transitions period between the old and the new, mechanisms to ensure that individual fishers are not penalised by the systemic changes to a production system that they did not control are necessary to implement anthropocenic responsibility. If we do not ensure the well-being of these people, we would be holding them individually responsible, which would go against the systemic nature of anthropocenic responsibility. It would further make fishers and other similarly situated workers very reluctant to embrace anthropocenic responsibility (Gould et al., 2016, p. 85).

Third, reparation and restitution is due to those who have disproportionally suffered from anthropocenic harm. This is not simply a question of compensation (although it could be part of it). It is a question of allowing these communities to rebuild what was lost, to resituate themselves within the ecological continuum in a way that dominant

16 This thinking is inspired by Indigenous relational ethics, specifically the work of Métis scholar Dr. Zoe Todd (https://fishphilosophy.org/), see e.g. Davis and Todd (2017); see also Todd (2014).

ideology had, until the implementation of anthropocenic responsibility, foreclosed. Restitution will take different forms depending on the needs of the community in question. Within our marine protection example, there is no doubt that coastal Indigenous people have suffered in various ways because of settler colonialism. Anthropocenic law in this context would leave it to each nation or community to adopt their own laws that reflect their own relationship with the marine environment. Even within a context of embedded settler colonialism, Indigenous people have demonstrated that they are far better caretakers of the biosphere (Schuster et al., 2019; Tran et al., 2020). Indigenous laws tend to already be built on principles that demonstrate a deep understanding of the responsibility we have towards "nature" (Borrows, 1997; Chang, 2013; Techera, 2012; Todd, 2014).[17] What settler law can do is ensure that Indigenous people have all the resources they need to implement their laws, and ensure that support can be offered when needed and in solidarity. In terms of marine "resources", this may mean that settlers will have little direct role in obtaining resources from the marine environment, unless allowed so under Indigenous law. Anthropocenic responsibility demands that the course we are on be reversed, which includes dealing with deep and complex impact of colonialism both on the biosphere and on Indigenous Peoples. As Davis and Todd (2017, p. 769) state: "[i]f we use the momentum that this concept [(the Anthropocene)] has gained to train our imaginations to the ways in which environmental destruction has gone hand in hand with colonialism, then we can begin to address our relations in a much wider context." Given the legal space that was taken by settler colonialism, giving back that space is part of this process and of anthropocenic responsibility.

[17] It should be noted that reparation is not linked to the conservation skills of a particular Indigenous nation or community. It is linked to historical oppression. Not every Indigenous person, nation or community is necessarily well-versed in what could be referred broadly as ecological stewardship or has a good conservation track record. The information on Indigenous conservation efforts and laws is provided to counter the argument that western laws are needed to protect the environment. They are not and, according to the evidence, they appear to be less effective (at least on average). Furthermore, this demonstrates how Indigenous laws already reflect many of the principles associated with anthropocenic responsibility and *responsabilisation.*

Conclusion

The emergence of the Anthropocene, both materially and linguistically, demonstrates that humanity, a certain aspect of it to be more precise, has emerged over the last centuries has the most destructive force of the biosphere. The concept is, in a way, the sign of the dominant strata of society's failure regarding the stewardship of our planet. It highlights the urgency to adapt to this reality and change our ways to avoid complete catastrophe. Law, as one of the primary tools of social regulation, clearly has a role to play in adapting society to the Anthropocene. However, this cannot happen without first coming to terms with environmental law's own inability to stem the flow of environmental harm that transformed humanity from just one of a multitude of species on this planet, to a geological agent. To address the socio-ecological crisis of the Anthropocene, environmental law must move away from a liberal framework of individual responsibility. Without such distancing, environmental law cannot hope to address the hyperobject—a viscous assemblage of causes, effects and bodies that is difficult to pinpoint in time and space—that is anthropocenic harm. A move towards anthropocenic responsibility—one based on a systemic and differentiated understanding of responsibility for anthropocenic harm—is needed to ensure the relative stability of the ecological continuum (in as much as something that is constantly moving can be stable).

The journey to anthropocenic law will not be easy, like the long unpaved country road that leads to the middle of a forest, but like that country road, this journey is well worth the destination. Much work needs to be done, from civic society mobilisation in our respective metaphorical backyards, to international actions to modify global regimes. A lot of it is already happening (for example, the resistance acts of water and land protectors and associated solidarity action against pipelines in Canada, and the granting of rights to natural features like rivers in different states) (see Cochrane, 2020; Cunningham, 2020; Fisher & Parsons, 2020; Jolly & Roshan Menon, 2021; Kestler-D'Amours, 2021), but more will be needed to rectify past errors and move away from capitalist and other modes of production that threatens the ecological continuum. Of these needed actions, considerable imagination will be needed, particularly from thinkers, be they academics or simply people hungry for change. Social scientists, particularly criminologists and jurists, can play a particularly important role in trying to think of a geologically responsible world, and, more specifically, of approaches, techniques and tactics to adapt law in ways that promotes anthropocenic *responsabilisation* and addresses past and continuous anthropocenic harm.

References

Bailey, M. (2020, October 20). Nova Scotia lobster dispute: Mi'kmaw fishery isn't a threat to conservation, say scientists. *The Conversation.* https://theconversation.com/nova-scotia-lobster-dispute-mikmaw-fishery-isnt-a-threat-to-conservation-say-scientists-148396.

Baum, J. K., & Fuller, S. D. (2016). *Canada's marine fisheries: Status.* University of Victoria & Oceana Canada.

Blühdorn, I. (2015). A much-needed renewal of environmentalism? Eco-politics in the anthropocene. In C. Hamilton, C. Bonneuil, & F. Gemenne (Eds.), *The anthropocene and the global environmental crisis: Rethinking modernity in a new epoch* (pp. 156–167). Routledge.

Borrows, J. (1997). Living between water and rocks: First nations, environmental planning and democracy. *University of Toronto Law Journal, 47*(4), 417–468.

Bosselmann, K. (2016). A normative approach to environmental governance: Sustainability at the apex of environmental law. In D. Fisher (Ed.), *Research handbook on fundamental concepts of environmental law* (pp. 22–49). Edward Elgar.

Brilliant, S. (2018). Is Canada protecting its marine species at risk? In International Ocean Institute Canada (Ed.), *The future of ocean governance and capacity development* (pp. 293–297). Brill Nijhoff.

Brisman, A., & South, N. (2019). Green criminology and environmental crimes and harms. *Sociological Compass, 13*, e12650.

Brisman, A., & South, N. (2020). Toward a green cultural criminology of the South. In A. Brisman & N. South (Eds.), *Routledge international handbook of green criminology* (2nd ed., pp. 624–637). Routledge.

Bugge, H. C. (2013). Twelve fundamental challenges in environmental law: An introduction to the concept of rule of law for nature. In C. Voigt (Ed.), *Rule of law for nature: New dimensions and ideas in environmental law* (pp. 3–26). Cambridge University Press.

Castañeda, R. A., Burliuk, C. M. M., Casselman, J. M., Cooke, S. J., Dunmall, K. M., Forbes, L. S., Hasler, C. T., Howland, K. L., Hutchings, J. A., Klein, G. M., Nguyen, V. M., Price, M. H. H., Reid, A. J., Reist, J. D., Reynolds, J. D., Van Nynatten, A., & Mandrak, N. E. (2020). A brief history of fisheries in Canada. *Fisheries, 45*(6), 306–318.

Chalifour, N. J. (2016). Canadian climate federalism: Parliament's Ample Constitutional Authority to legislate GHG emissions through regulations, a National Cap and Trade Program, or a National Carbon Tax. *National Journal of Constitutional Law, 36*, 331–407.

Campbell, M. L., & Thomas, V. G. (2001). Protection and conservation of marine mammals in Canada: A case for legislative reform. *Ocean and Coastal Law Journal, 7*(2), 221–258.

Commissioner of the Environment and Sustainable Development (CESD) (2016). *Reports of the commissioner of the environment and sustainable development to the Parliament of Canada: Report 2—Sustaining Canada's major fish stocks—Fisheries and Oceans Canada.* Office of the Auditor General.

Chakrabarty, D. (2009). The climate of history: Four theses. *Critical Inquiry, 35*(2), 197–222.

Chang, W. B. C. (2013). Indigenous values and the law of the sea. In J. M .Van Dyke et al. (Eds.), *Governing ocean resources: New challenges and emerging regimes* (pp. 427–445). Martinus Nijhoff.

Cloutier de Repentigny, P. (2020). To the anthropocene and beyond: The responsibility of law in decimating and protecting marine life. *Transnational Legal Theory, 11*(1/2), 180–203.

Cochrane, D. T. (2020, February 19). Wet'suwet'en blockades: No more business as usual in Canada. *The Conversation.* https://theconversation.com/wetsuweten-blockades-no-more-business-as-usual-in-canada-131961.

Crutzen, P. J., & Stoermer, E. (2000). The anthropocene. *IGBP, 41*, 17.

Cunningham, N. (2020, August 14). Canada's trans mountain pipeline inches forward, but opposition intensifies. *DeSmog*. https://www.desmogblog.com/2020/08/14/canada-trans-mountain-pipeline-tiny-house-warriors.

Czarnezki, J. L., & Fiedler, K. (2016). The neoliberal turn in environmental regulation. *Utah Law Review, 1*(1), 1–41.

Davis, H., & Todd, Z. (2017). On the importance of a date, or decolonizing the anthropocene. *ACME, 16*(4), 761–780.

Deleuze, G., & Guattari, F. (1980). *Milles Plateaux: Capitalisme et schizophrénie 2*. Éditions de Minuit.

DFO. (2002). *Canada's ocean strategy: Our oceans, our future*. https://waves-vagues.dfo-mpo.gc.ca/Library/264675.pdf.

Dybing, S. S. (2012). Environmental harm: Social causes and shifting legislative dynamics. In R. Ellefsen, R. Sollund, & G. Larsen (Eds.), *Eco-global crimes: Contemporary problems and future challenges* (pp. 273–294). Ashgate.

Ecology Action Centre. (2019, February). Clearwater's Illegal fishing brought to court. *Ecology Action Centre*. https://ecologyaction.ca/clearwater?fbclid=IwAR2IrzQiWz-gByZQYZ64ZobtZ-w6V_S6rDuS84x640x2wP-fsZDZJbBKCp4.

Elgie, S. (1993). Making bureaucracies accountable: Judicial review of environmental decisions. In S. A. Kennett (Ed.), *Law and process in environmental management* (pp. 196–216). Canadian Institute of Resource Law.

Favaro, B., Claar, D. C., Fox, C. H., Freshwater, C., Holden, J. J., Roberts, A., & UVic Research Derby. (2014). Trends in extinction risk for imperiled species in Canada. *PLoS One, 9*(11), e113118.

Fisher, K., & Parsons, M. (2020). River co-governance and co-management in Aotearoa New Zealand: Enabling indigenous ways of knowing and being. *Transnational Environmental Law, 9*(3), 455–467.

Frith, C. D. (2014). Action, agency and responsibility. *Neuropsychologia, 55*, 137–142.

Gonzalez, C. G. (2015). Bridging the north-south divide: International environmental law in the anthropocene. *Pace Environmental Law Review, 32*, 407–433.

Gould, K. A., Pellow, D. N., & Schnaiberg, A. (2016). *The treadmill of production: Injustice and unsustainability in the global economy*. Routledge.

Government of Canada. (2012). *Commission of inquiry into the decline of Sockeye Salmon in the Fraser River, the uncertain future of Fraser River Sockeye: Recommendations, summary, process, by The Honourable Bruce I Cohen,* (Vol. 3). Public Works and Government Services Canada.

Grear, A. (2015). Deconstructing anthropos: A critical reflection on "anthropocentric" law and anthropocene "humanity." *Law & Critique, 26*, 225–249.

Green, A. W. (1943). The concept of responsibility. *Journal of Criminal Law and Criminology, 33*(5), 392–394.

Halsey, M. (2016). *Deleuze and environmental damage: Violence of the text*. Routledge.

Harrington, C. (2016). The ends of the world: International relations and the anthropocene. *Millennium, 44*(3), 447–498.

Hubert, A., & Gray, S. (2020). Area-based marine protection in Canada. *Asia-Pacific Journal of Ocean Law & Policy, 5*, 142–168.

ITLOS. (2011, February 1). *Responsibilities and obligations of States sponsoring persons and entities with respect to activities in the Area (Request for Advisory Opinion submitted to the Seabed Disputes Chamber)*, Advisory Opinion, No. 17.

IUCN. (2014). *A global assessment of the environmental and social impacts caused by the production and use of biofuels*. IUCN.

Jessen, S. (2011). A review of Canada's implementation of the Oceans Act since 1997—From leader to follower? *Coastal Management, 39*(1), 20–56.

Johnson, J. (2020). Environmental protection under the Fisheries Act and Bill C-68: Progress or regress? *University of New Brunswick Law Journal, 70*, 104–127.

Jolly, S., & Roshan Menon, K. S. (2021). Of Ebbs and flows: Understanding the legal consequences of granting personhood to natural entities in India. *Transnational Environmental Law*. https://doi.org/10.1017/S2047102520000424.

Kestler-D'Amours, J. (2021, April 3). This river in Canada is now a 'legal person'. *Al Jazeera*. https://www.aljazeera.com/news/2021/4/3/this-river-in-canada-now-legal-person.

Keys, P.W., Galaz, V., Dyer, M., Matthews, N., Folke, C., Nyström, M., & Cornell, S. E. (2019). Anthropocene risk. *Nature Sustainability*, 1–7. https://doi.org/10.1038/s41893-019-0327-x.

Knox, J. H. (2020). Constructing the human right to a healthy environment. *Annual Review of Law and Social Science, 16*(24), 1.

Lands & Resources Department. (2015, May). *Assessment if the trans mountain pipeline and tanker expansion proposal*. Treaty, Lands & Resources Department, Tsleil-Waututh Nation.

Lee, A., & Cloutier de Repentigny, P. (2019). Farming at sea, a false solution to a real problem: Critical reflections on Canada's aquaculture regulations. *Ottawa Law Review, 50*(1), 29–63.

Lee, M. (2002). Tort, regulation and environmental liability. *Legal Studies, 22*(1), 33–52.

Lin, A. C. (2006). The unifying role of harm in environmental law. *Wisconsin Law Review, 3*, 898–985.

Lynch, M. J., & Stretesky, P. B. (2014). *Exploring green criminology: Toward a green criminological revolution*. Ashgate.

Lynch, M. J., Long, M. A., Barrett, K. A., & Stretesky, P. B. (2013). Is it a crime to produce ecological disorganization? Why green criminology and political economy matter in the analysis of global ecological harm. *British Journal of Criminology, 53*(6), 997–1016.

Lynch, M. J., Long, M. A., Stretesky, P. B., & Barrett, K. A. (2017). *Green criminology: Crime, justice, and the environment*. University of California Press.

Lynch, M. J., Stretesky, P. B., & Long, M. A. (2020). The treadmill of production and the treadmill of law: Propositions for analyzing law, ecological disorganization and crime. *Capitalism Nature Socialism, 31*(1), 107–122.

M'Gonigle, M., & Ramsay, P. (2004). Greening environmental law: From sectoral reform to systemic re-formation. *Journal of Environmental Law & Practice, 14*, 333–356.

M'Gonigle, M., & Takeda, L. (2013). The liberal limits of environmental law: A green legal critique. *Pace Environmental Law Review, 30*, 1005–1115.

Mayrand, H. (2018, September). Déconstruire et repenser les fondements du droit international de l'environnement. *Revue québécoise de droit international*, 35–59.

McDevitt-Irwin, J. M., Drake Fuller, S., Grant, C., & Baum, J. K. (2015). Missing the safety net: Evidence for inconsistent and insufficient management of at-risk marine fishes in Canada. *Canadian Journal of Fish & Aquatic Science, 72*(10), 1596–1608.

Mohamed Al-Damkhi, A., Mohamed Khuraibet, A., Ahmed Abdul-Wahab, S., & Abdul Hameed Al-Attar, F. (2009). Toward defining the concept of environmental crime on the basis of sustainability. *Environmental Practice, 11*(2), 115–124.

Moore, J. W. (2016). The rise of cheap nature. In J. W. Moore (Ed.), *Anthropocene or Capitalocene? Nature, history, and the crisis of capitalism* (pp. 78–115). PM Press.

Morton, T. (2010). *The ecological thought*. Harvard University Press.

Morton, T. (2013). *Hyperobjects: Philosophy and ecology after the end of the world*. University of Minnesota Press.

Nurse, A. (2020). Environmental justice and the rights of Indigenous peoples. In A. Brisman & N. South (Eds.), *Routledge international handbook of green criminology* (2nd ed., pp. 573–587). Routledge.

Office of the Auditor General of Canada. (2005). Report of the commissioner of the environment and sustainable development to the House of Commons: Chapter 1: Fisheries and Oceans Canada—Canada's Oceans Management Strategy. *OAG*. https://www.oag-bvg.gc.ca/internet/docs/c20050901ce.pdf.

Office of the Auditor General of Canada. (2018). Fall reports of the commissioner of the environment and sustainable development to the Parliament of Canada. *OAG*. https://www.oag-bvg.gc.ca/internet/English/parl_cesd_201810_02_e_43146.html.

Office of the Prime Minister. (2016). Canada's ocean protection plan. *Government of Canada*. https://tc.canada.ca/en/initiatives/oceans-protection-plan.

Philippopoulos-Mihalopoulos, A. (2017). Critical environmental law as method in the anthropocene. In A. Philippopoulos-Mihalopoulos & V. Brooks (Eds.), *Research methods in environmental law* (pp. 131–155). Edward Elgar.

Regional Seas Office. (2010). Global synthesis—A report from the regional seas conventions and action plans for the marine biodiversity assessment and outlook series. *UNEP*. https://wedocs.unep.org/handle/20.500.11822/8822.

Rehberg-Besler, N., & Jefferies, C. S. G. (2019). The case for a southern resident killer whale emergency protection order under Canada's species at risk act. *Journal of Environmental Law & Practice, 32*(2), 137–161.

Roberts, M. W. (2017). Finishing the job: The Montreal protocol moves to phase down hydrofluorocarbons. *Review of European, Comparative & International Environmental Law, 26*, 220–230.

Salih, R., & Corry, O. (2021). Displacing the anthropocene: Colonisation, extinction and the unruliness of nature in Palestine. *Environment and Planning E: Nature and Space*. https://doi.org/10.1177/2514848620982834.

Saxe, D., & James, M. (2019). Holding directors and officers liable for environmental problems: Sentencing and regulatory orders. In A. E. Ingelson (Ed.), *Environment in the courtroom* (pp. 325–337). Calgary University Press.

Schuster, R., Germain, R. R., Bennett, J. R., Reo, N. J., & Arcese, P. (2019). Vertebrate biodiversity on indigenous-managed lands in Australia, Brazil, and Canada equals that in protected areas. *Environmental Science and Policy, 101*, 1–6.

Simpson, M. (2020). The anthropocene as colonial discourse. *Environment and Planning d: Society and Space, 38*(1), 53–71.

Smiley, M. (2017, Summer). Collective responsibility. In E. N. Zalta (Ed.), *The Stanford encyclopedia of philosophy*. https://plato.stanford.edu/archives/sum2017/entries/collective-responsibility/.
South, N. (2011). The ecocidal tendencies of late modernity: Transnational crime, social exclusion, victims and rights. In R. White (Ed.), *Global environmental harm: Criminological perspectives* (pp. 228–247). Routledge.
Steffen, W., Broadgate, W., Deutsch, L., Gaffney, O., & Ludwig, C. (2015). The trajectory of the anthropocene: The great acceleration. *The Anthropocene Review, 2*(1), 81–97.
Steffen, W., Crutzen, P. J., & McNeil, J. R. (2007). The anthropocene: Are humans now overwhelming the great forces of nature? *Ambio, 36*(8), 614–621.
Stern, S. (2019). Standing for everyone: *Sierra Club v. Morton*, Justice Blackmun's dissent, and solving the problem of environmental standing. *Environmental Law Reporter, 49*(1), 10063–10086.
Stretesky, P. B., Long, M. A., & Lynch, M. J. (2014). *The Treadmill of crime: Political economy and green criminology*. Routledge.
Subcommission on Quaternary Stratigraphy. (n.d.). *Working group on the 'anthropocene'*. International Commission on Stratigraphy. http://quaternary.stratigraphy.org/working-groups/anthropocene/. Accessed 25 January 2020.
Takemura, T. (2011). The criticality of global environmental crime and the response of chaos criminology. In R. White (Ed.), *Global environmental harm: Criminological perspectives* (pp. 210–227). Routledge.
Techera, E. J. (2012). *Marine environmental governance: From international law to local practice*. Routledge.
Todd, Z. (2014). Fish pluralities: Human-animal relations and sites of engagement in Paulatuuq Arctic Canada. *Études/inuit/studies, 38*(1/2), 217.
Tran, T. C., Ban, N. C., & Bhattacharyya, J. (2020). A review of successes, challenges, and lessons from indigenous protected and conserved areas. *Biological Conservation, 241*, 108271.
UNHCR. (2019). *Climate change and poverty: Report of the Special Rapporteur on extreme poverty and human rights*. UNHRC, 41st Session, UN Doc A/HRC/41/39.
Wanner, T. (2015). The new 'passive revolution' of the green economy and growth discourse: Maintaining the 'sustainable development' of neoliberal capitalism. *New Political Economy, 20*(1), 21–41.
Webster, E., & Mai, L. (2020). Transnational environmental law in the anthropocene. *Transnational Legal Theory, 11*(1/2), 1–15.

White, R. (2011). *Transnational environmental crime: Toward an eco-global criminology*. Routledge.
White, R., & Heckenberg, D. (2014). *Green criminology: An introduction to the study of environmental harm*. Routledge.
Wood, S., Tanner, G., & Richardson, B. J. (2010). What ever happened to canadian environmental law? *Ecology Law Quarterly, 37*, 981–1040.

12

Te Awa Tupua: An Exemplary Environmental Law?

Sarah Monod de Froideville and Rebekah Bowling

Introduction

On 20 March 2017 the New Zealand (NZ) government passed the Te Awa Tupua (Whanganui River Claims Settlement) Act ("Te Awa Tupua"), giving the Whanganui river legal personhood, with all the duties, rights and liabilities of a human citizen (Hutchinson, 2014). Believed to be the first to award a river such a status, Te Awa Tupua has been celebrated by scholars worldwide as an exemplary piece of environmental legislation that promises to usher in a new global environmental ethics. A missing component among many of these assessments, however, is that Te Awa Tupua is also the outcome of the longest-running legal case in NZ's history, taken against the NZ government by Whanganui iwi (local Māori, collectively called Ngāti Hāu) for colonial grievances (Hutchinson, 2014). Among these was the government's assuming of river control and subsequent obstruction of Ngāti Hāu's access to the

S. M. de Froideville (✉) · R. Bowling
Victoria University of Wellington, Wellington, New Zealand

J. Gacek and R. Jochelson (eds.), *Green Criminology and the Law*, Palgrave Studies in Green Criminology,
https://doi.org/10.1007/978-3-030-82412-9_12

river. Nor does Te Awa Tupua recognise Ngāti Hāu and the river as intricately intertwined as whānau (family, kin) and restore traditional practices of kaitiakitanga (guardianship), as was guaranteed in the Treaty of Waitangi of 1840. When viewed from the standpoint of tangata whenua (people of the land), Te Awa Tupua represents a compromise on behalf of Ngāti Hāu in an agreement with the NZ government regarding the river's governance.

Thus far, few green criminologists have made mention of Te Awa Tupua, despite its potentially ground-breaking approach to advance the protection of the natural environment. This is surprising considering that the study of law and legal systems is central to green criminology. As Hall (2014) notes, the fact that environmental harm tends to stem from activities that are "lawful but awful" (Passas, 2005) means analysis of law (and its absence) is vital to understanding the nature of crimes against the planet and its inhabitants. It is also perplexing given the history of Ngāti Hāu's legal struggle to have the Whanganui river returned to them, and of Te Awa Tupua as a provision for enhanced environmental protection in redress for colonial harm. This chapter will remedy this absence. Specifically, it will explore a number of tensions embodied in Te Awa Tupua that arise from its dual functions. The argument the chapter will advance is that the case of Te Awa Tupua makes clear that further thinking is required in relation to how Western and indigenous worldviews might come together in approaches to environmental protection, and that there are important implications for green criminologists to consider with regard to the development of environmental law that is developed in response to grievances for colonial atrocities.

Green Criminology and the Law

If we understand law as a barometer of social tolerance (Durkheim, 1984), it is safe to say that harms against the environment have been (and are) exhaustingly tolerated in most Western societies. This is not to say that it will remain that way. Albert Cohen's (1974) "elasticity of evil" captures the way that law responds to changing social designations of deviant behaviour.

Green criminologists tend to be divided, however, on the value of law for environmental protection. For some, the law presents as the most powerful vehicle to advance the interests of ecosystems and non-human animals, and therefore the task of the green criminologist is to expedite the criminalisation of acts and omissions that compromise ecological and species wellbeing. To avoid alarming legislators, Williams (1996) argues environmental harm should be articulated as "injury", a term that criminal justice systems are familiar with and that political sensibilities will find palatable. Others, such as White (2018), are more positive about the human capacity for reimagining law, but at the same time acknowledge that many environmental laws are anthropocentric in their nature and either wholly or partially instrumental towards meeting human needs. White (2018) notes the Rio Declaration of 1992 that asserts to protect the environment for the increased wellbeing of a healthy planet lends to human beings. An earlier declaration in 1972 claimed the environment as a human resource, as can be seen in its title: "UN Declaration on the Human Environment". NZ's leading environmental statute, the Resource Management Act 1991 (RMA), also provides for the protection of the environment but only insofar as human interests are not compromised by doing so. The RMA promotes "sustainable management", which is defined as "managing the use, development, and protection of natural and physical resources in a way, or at a rate, which enables people and communities to provide for their social, economic, and cultural well-being and for their health and safety" (s5).

The fact that law in Western nations was designed to protect capitalist enterprise is the very reason Lynch and Stretesky (2014) have little faith that it can truly provide for the protection of the environment. Insofar as capitalist enterprise relies on the extraction of resources from the earth followed by the input of waste from the production process, practices creating a "metabolic rift" (Foster, 1999), means it is fundamentally at odds with environmental wellbeing. Lynch and Stretesky (2014) add that criminology's continued privileging of criminal law to define harm has rendered the discipline virtually meaningless (see also Hillyard & Tombs, 2007; Michalowski, 2016). They propose a radical revision of criminology from one tethered to a criminological perspective (that is, one based on understandings of crime as defined in criminal law) to one that adopts an environmental frame of reference. This revised criminology would broaden the scope of what can be considered criminal and who (and what) might be considered a victim. Issues include the propagation of agnosis in relation to historical pollution (see Louisson, 2021); victimisation of dairy cows by industrial agriculture; and misleading food labels that seduce consumers into purchasing unethical products. These are just three examples of harm to the planet and its inhabitants that cannot be captured by current criminal codes but would be by a revised and environmentally focused criminology.

Though necessary, a radical overhaul of criminological thought and practice is not yet within sight. Alternative avenues for seeking environmental justice within the systems that currently preside include restorative justice (Hall, 2014) and pre-emptive environmental legislation (Iorns, 2019; White & Heckenberg, 2014). Restorative justice would involve environmental offenders offering reparation to the entity or entities harmed by their activities, akin to a fine. Pre-emptive laws would calculate the greatest possible harm to the environment from an action and legislate accordingly.

The passing of Te Awa Tupua that granted legal personhood to the Whanganui river is said to offer a new way of thinking about how law can secure environmental protection. In the next section we outline the development of Te Awa Tupua and its underlying principles, and document the responses to it as a ground-breaking piece of environmental legislation. We then detail the history behind the law's development and its manifestation as an effort towards redress for harms suffered by Ngāti Hāu during the early colonial period and beyond. These harms stem from fundamental breaches of the Treaty of Waitangi 1840, considered to be NZ's founding document, on behalf of the NZ government.

Te Awa Tupua

The Whanganui river is nestled among the central plateau of NZ's North Island, and is the country's third longest river. Commencing at the foot of Ruapehu, one of three volcanos that stand at in the centre of the North Island, the river has been described as a "scenic wonder" that "twists like an eel … its currents loaded with flotsam and foam" on its journey to the sea 180 miles away (Warnes, 2019). The granting of legal personhood to the Whanganui River was an attempt to recognise its identification as living tūpuna (ancestors) through the closest Western legal equivalent, transforming the river from an object in law to a legal person who has the same rights and duties of a human citizen (Hutchison, 2014). According to O'Donnell and Talbot-Jones (2017), these legal rights are not synonymous with Westernised human rights, which include political and civil rights. What the Whanganui river is entitled to, however, is the right to sue and be sued in court, the right to enter and enforce legal contracts and the right to own property (Naffine, 2009; O'Donnell & Talbot-Jones, 2017).

Te Awa Tupua resulted from an eight-year development of an institutional framework which could incorporate values from te ao Māori (the Māori worldview) to work in tandem with pre-existing Westernised laws and social norms (Salmond, 2014). According to te ao Māori, geographical features such as rivers, mountains and trees are inhabited by spirits of past loved ones (tūpuna), and it is the responsibility of present-day Māori to act as guardians of their environmental ancestors, which will in turn protect the people (Iorns, 2019; Ruru, 2018). All iwi throughout NZ have geographical identity markers that are linked to large bodies of water, and accordingly, numerous rivers and lakes across the land are culturally important for their identity (Jackson, 1988; Ruru, 2018). This philosophy of an ancestral connection with nature signifies that Māori considers themselves to be *of* nature, rather than separate, above from or in proprietorship of, as exemplified in the Ngāti Hāu proverb "ko te awa te au, ko te au te awa – I am the river and the river is me" (Iorns, 2019; Morrison-Shaw & Buxeda, 2017, p. 30). Moreover, the rights of tangata whenua are seen as indivisible from the rights of the land, water and skies, which are all viewed holistically as part of the natural world, emphasising that the relationship Māori have with natural resources extends beyond physical interests to a deeper metaphysical connection (Johnston, 2018; Ruru, 2018). An intrinsic relationship between human beings and the land is seen across all indigenous cultures (Salmón, 2000), and was fundamental to the way of life among Western peoples too, prior to the arrival of industrial capitalism (Foster, 1999).

While Te Awa Tupua is an Act that sits at the national level and is backed up by legislative authority, it simultaneously emphasises the Māori custom of kaitiakitanga and provides for decentralised decision-making by enabling community participation to operationalise legal personhood (Kauffman & Martin, 2017; O'Donnell & Talbot-Jones, 2018). Accordingly, two guardians (as opposed to "elected officials") were appointed to speak on behalf of the river's spiritual and cultural rights—not solely its physical and ecological rights (Kauffman & Martin, 2017; O'Donnell & Talbot-Jones, 2018). This guardian body, named Te Pou Tupua, or the Human Face of the River, is to comprise of one Ngāti Hāu representative and one Crown representative, both being charged with protecting the river's interests as guided by a list of ecocentric values that view the river as "incapable of being owned as property in an absolute sense" (Hutchison, 2014, p. 179; Kauffman & Martin, 2017). Furthermore, a strategy group was established to develop, approve, review and monitor the implementation of Te Awa Tupua, as required by the statutory process for managing the Whanganui River catchment (O'Donnell & Talbot-Jones, 2018). This group, called Te Kōpuka nā Te Awa Tupua, consists of 17 stakeholder representatives with interests in the Whanganui River—including local and central government representatives, those from the recreation, conservation and tourism sectors, wild game interests and Genesis Energy Limited (O'Donnell & Talbot-Jones, 2018). In relation to Te Pou Tupua, the "collaborative, integrated watershed management body" of Te Kōpuka nā Te Awa Tupua are responsible for providing a forum to discuss issues regarding the river's health and wellbeing (Kauffman & Martin, 2017, p. 2). So, while Te Awa Tupua has legally deemed its own person, there is a myriad of voices tasked with speaking up for the welfare of this non-verbal entity. Te Awa Tupua also provided a settlement of $80 million for Ngāti Hāu, and contributed an additional $30 million fund to restore the river's health and wellbeing, as well as for litigation purposes (New Zealand Parliament, 2017, p. 1; Eckstein et al., 2019).

Having outlined the principles and provisions of Te Awa Tupua, we now turn to examine the responses to its passing.

Exemplary Environmental Legislation?

Few green criminologists have offered any analysis of Te Awa Tupua so far. Among those who have, White (2018) considers the Act an example of a law that recognises the intrinsic rights of nature, its mana (authority) and mauri (life force). In his view, then, Te Awa Tupua embodies principles of ecojustice. And Biard et al. (2020), writing about the Murray Basin water theft in the Australian context, see Te Awa Tupua as a development in *Earth Jurisprudence* (that holds that humans are but *one* part of an interconnected world, as opposed to being above or separate from it) that has significant potential for rethinking responses to issues of water-related crimes. Most of the relevant commentary for our argument in this chapter comes from outside of the discipline. Much of it, like that of White (2018) and Biard et al. (2020), is positive, however it is also amidst these assessments that we identify some tensions emerging from the attempt to provide for environmental protection while redressing colonial harm.

Hutchinson (2014) argues that the awarding of legal personhood marks a significant shift in how NZ society has come to value the environment, or at least an aspect of it. And, in one sense, Te Awa Tupua is a demonstration of law's amenability through its extension of "personhood" to include entities other than human beings. As Hutchinson (2014) points out, corporations have long been able to hold personhood status, reflecting the value that NZ, like other Western nations, places on in its neo-liberal free-market economy. Similarly, O'Donnell and Talbot-Jones (2018) argue that legal personhood offers a new pathway for managing freshwater bodies that could potentially transform approaches adopted in NZ and those beyond. For Iorns (2019), Te Awa Tupua could be the commencement of a reconceiving of the relationship that humans have with the environment. Like Biard et al. (2020) Iorns considers it an example of Earth Jurisprudence insofar as it recognises the responsibilities of others to act in the river's best interests (rather than "rights" belonging to the river), which in turn signifies that the right to live as best of a life as possible is indistinguishable between all of Earth's inhabitants (Iorns, 2019). O'Donnell and Talbot-Jones (2018) conceive of the "responsibility" ethos as a shift in the conception of property, from the river as a resource to be owned by human beings to the river that is a self-determining resource. Lynes (2017), too, considers Te Awa Tupua to have shifted the conception of property, loosening it from the sense of a bounded territorial space. She additionally imagines it as a model for incorporating Indigenous worldviews into Western paradigms, which could help states meet their Paris Agreement obligations to address climate change. Ruru (2018), alternatively, argues Te Awa Tupua consolidates for Māori that Treaty settlements hold the most potential for restoring their traditional roles as kaitiaki (guardians) of the environment, the recognition of tikanga Māori (Māori custom) and the intent of tangata whenua to care for the land.

Yet for all of Te Awa Tupua's positive aspects, the commentary around it also identifies a number of thorny issues. Hutchison (2014), for example, notes that corporations are the only other legal non-human entities commonly recognised by law to behold such rights and liabilities of a human citizen. Companies with a legal personhood status can enter into contracts, own property and sue and be sued in their own name (Hutchison, 2014). According to Naffine (2009), everything in the Western paradigm is either an owner of property or property itself, yet the personhood of a corporation ensures that it holds a *dual* status—meaning corporations are entities that can simultaneously own property, but are also property in a sense that they are owned by shareholders. Hutchison (2014) argues that this dual status can also be applied to Te Awa Tupua, whose guardians are able to hold property in its name. However, parts of the river that were privately owned prior to 2017 have remained so and these continue to be viewed as "property". The duality of Te Awa Tupua leads to the illogical situation where it legally owns the space in which the river's water occupies, however, its guardians are unable to veto the pre-existing ownership rights apparent in that space (Johnston, 2018).

The legislation states that the once Crown-owned riverbed will be owned by Te Awa Tupua itself (barring the pre-existing private property agreements) and that its appointed guardians have the authority to make decisions around the river's management, exclusion and access. However, this authority does not extend to the water or aquatic life of the river (O'Donnell & Talbot-Jones, 2018; Talbot-Jones & Bennet, 2019). This means that permission from the guardian body is first required before granting resource consent for projects in relation to the riverbed, but permission is not required regarding the use of water—creating ambiguity in terms of the *scope* of decision-making authority that Te Awa Tupua has and violating the te ao Māori view of the river as an "indivisible whole" (Biggs, 2017, p. 179; Macpherson & Clavijo Ospina, 2018; Talbot-Jones & Bennet, 2019).

What is more, the notion of Te Awa Tupua as an example of Earth Jurisprudence is undermined insofar as the efficacy of the enforcement of its legal rights is dependent on those who are connected to the river in recognising its rights, duties and responsibilities (Talbot-Jones & Bennet, 2019). That is, whether the Whanganui river will remain a legal person is based not on any inherent qualities of the river, but the government and Whanganui community to uphold their recognition of their duties to the river, which could possibly give rise to legal struggles down the track (Talbot-Jones & Bennet, 2019). Warnock (2012, p. 61) also argues that legal standing for environmental entities that can only be directly enforced by individuals directly connected to said entities raises the question of whether the necessary human intervention would really protect the "interests" of nature or those of its human stakeholders. Furthermore, Eckstein et al. (2019) note how different the recognition of a river as a legal person looks like in the political system in comparison to a human citizen, meaning that for Te Awa Tupua's rights to be upheld, new ways and legislative means of doing so must be created, in turn imposing unexpected costs and legal hassles to wider society. Granting of legal rights to nature can also potentially compromise the "moral authority and public confidence" in the justice system, and following, recognition of nature's rights may compel judges to increase their use of discretion when making decisions based on the potential consequences of their decrees (Eckstein et al., 2019).

Additionally, despite efforts to provide for the protection of the Whanganui river, legal personhood is a concept that sustains a legal and cultural understanding that humans are "categorically different" from non-human animals and nature (Hutchison, 2014, p. 180). Indeed, that legal "*person*hood" is what can offer the river protection demonstrates the Western propensity to position human beings above the natural world and its non-human inhabitants (Hutchinson, 2014). Furthermore, the fact that NZ's legal system, like most others, fails to recognise the rights of the environment as a whole, despite recognising the rights of abstract corporations, exemplifies the priority placed on profit-making above all else (Hutchison, 2014; Naffine, 2009).

There are, thus, a number of tensions inherent in Te Awa Tupua that challenge the notion that it is an exemplary piece of environmental legislation. These tensions are:

- That self-determined activity guided by the philosophy of te ao Māori and the interconnectedness of all living things is at odds with an anthropocentric, neoliberal capitalist context;
- That given the above relation, projecting the dawning of a new environmental ethos is premature (for example, Biard et al., 2020; Iorns, 2019);
- That similarly, it is superfluous to speak of Te Awa Tupua as an example of ecological justice (for example, White, 2018);
- That continuing to speak of the Whanganui river in abstract terms (i.e. as 'a river') undermines the endorsement of the indivisible connection between the river and its people (see Hutchinson, 2014);
- That additionally, claims that the law is an instance of an "Indigenous paradigm" for restoring environmental wellbeing are invalid when that paradigm would extend the awarded protections to all other environmental entities in the same jurisdiction.

We are mindful here that our commentary is specifically about Te Awa Tupua, and specifically in relation to te ao Māori. However, we contend that these tensions (and more) are likely to materialize in other attempts to combine Western and indigenous understandings of the environment in law. That said, there is another important (and specific) point to be made in our discussion, which is that Te Awa Tupua did not emerge from concern for the environment, but from a long campaign on behalf of Whanganui iwi Ngāti Hāu to have their grievances for harm suffered under colonisation redressed, including the restoration of their traditional role as kaitiaki (guardians) of the Whanganui river. We discuss the criticality of this origin for understanding Te Awa Tupua next.

Partial Redress for Colonial Harm?

In the signing of the Treaty of Waitangi (the Treaty) in 1840 the Crown naturalized the presence of British settlers in NZ and at the same time became legally obligated to respect the rights of Māori as tangata whenua to have authority over their own territories, exercise their own customs and protect their own treasures (Biggs, 2017). According to most critics, however, the Treaty was a ruse to make way for a comprehensive land grab (Wynyard, 2017). Indeed, across the following decades the Crown passed multiple statutes that criminalised Māori practices and traditions, in particular their actions to protect their territories from impending British control. Millions of hectares of land were illegally removed from Māori control in what has been described as a campaign of "primary accumulation" (Wynyard, 2017). Bodies of water that ran through the stolen lands were also assumed under the Crown. This included the Whanganui river.

Resistance to state control on behalf of Ngāti Hāu to harms enacted against the river goes back as far as the 1870s. The iwi's efforts to defend its claim as the rightful guardian can be seen in multiple petitions, Royal Commission reports, Waitangi Tribunal claims and court cases occurring between 1938 and 2010 (Hutchison, 2014; Iorns, 2019). It would be 150 years from the first petition, however, before an agreement could be reached between Ngāti Hāu and the NZ government regarding the river's "ownership" status. Moreover, as the Waitangi Tribunal Whanganui River Report (1999) report documented, each claim would draw a response from the state intent on reasserting its control.

In 1938 the Native Land Court, for example, following claims on behalf of Ngāti Hāu against the use of the river by a steamer company; the destruction of fish stock; the introduction of foreign species (specifically trout); and the taking of gravel from the riverbed, ruled that the iwi retained its interests in the river (Waitangi Tribunal, 1999). In 1949 the government appealed to the Supreme Court to overturn the ruling, which it did on the basis that the Coal Mines Amendment Act 1903 had vested ownership of the riverbed in the NZ government. In 1950, this decision was challenged by a royal commission that argued Ngāti Hāu nevertheless remained the customary holder of the riverbed. In order to put the matter to rest, in 1954 the NZ government passed special legislation that would allow it to seek a decision from the Court of Appeal. That court, in 1962, adopted from English law assumption that ownership of land adjacent to a river includes the section of riverbed from the water's edge to the river's centre, and subsequently ruled that Ngāti Hāu's interests in the Whanganui river had therefore been extinguished when land surrounding the river had passed into government hands (Waitangi Tribunal, 1999). Though this would not be the end of the matter, the claim-ruling-response pattern is indicative of the NZ government's exploiting of legislative processes with respect to the Whanganui river. The resulting state occupation of and damage to the river has not only been detrimental to the physical quality of the waterway, but has systemically degraded the river's cultural and spiritual relationship with Ngāti Hāu (Iorns, 2019; New Zealand Parliament, 2017).

Few commentators have expressly recognised Te Awa Tupua as part of a settlement for colonial harm or made a full assessment of it in light of settlement obligations. Lynes (2017), in fact, makes the curious assessment that Te Awa Tupua embodies "active reconciliation" with Ngāti Hāu on behalf of the NZ government. However, the awarding of legal personhood to the river does not restore Ngāti Hāu's role as sole kaitiaki that they petitioned for and were guaranteed as signees of the Treaty of Waitangi. As we outlined above, legal personhood is a Western legal concept that at the same time it recognises an indigenous jurisdiction limits the possibility of indigenous tradition to shape law to its full potential (see also Johnston, 2018). For O'Donnell and Macpherson (2019, p. 40) Te Awa Tupua is therefore best described as "an advanced collaborative governance approach". Insofar as it continues the denial of rangatiratanga (chieftanship) of tangata whenua in accordance with the Treaty and requires Māori to work within the constraints of a system which has historically minimised their ability to fulfil their kaitiakitanga obligations to marine and freshwater bodies (Mercier et al., 2011; Clappcott et al., 2018), Te Awa Tupua could also be seen as an example of "epistemic violence". Spivak (1995) described the construction of frameworks that legitimise practices of domination in neo-colonial settler societies as epistemic violence arising from the "entrenched beliefs in the superiority of Eurocentric epistemologies", in accordance with the marginalisation of the "subjugated knowledges" of Indigenous peoples (Cunneen & Rowe, 2015; Foucault, 1980, pp. 81–85). That many Waitangi tribunal settlements, including Te Awa Tupua, are inconsistent with the United Nations declaration on the Rights of Indigenous Peoples (Te Aho, 2017) supports this claim.

The discussion in this section cements our view that it is inappropriate to applaud the NZ government for passing a law that was drafted on the back of a century and a half of harm enacted in its name, the harm that the law's passage extends. Much like the river itself, the harm-grievance-settlement trajectory of relations between Ngāti Hāu and the government must be seen as an indivisible whole. We argue that a consideration of historical context is one of several implications that arise for green criminology with regard to environmental harm and the law, as discussed in the next section.

Implications for Green Criminology

The tensions that emerge from the passing of Te Awa Tupua illustrate why it is critical to pay close attention to the intricacies of laws that are said to adopt indigenous principles for ecological protection. At the outset, the passing of such laws needs to be contextualised and all caveats considered. The passing of Te Awa Tupua, for example, exposes the insidious violence of the NZ government in enacting various statutes to displace te ao Māori and deny Ngāti Hāu's claims, and in doing so it throws a spotlight on the role of law in operationalising state-corporate crimes against the environment in settler states. As Whyte (2017) argues, "settler colonialism is an 'environmental injustice'" (p. 165) insofar as the ecological bases of indigenous cultures are destroyed or altered by settler colonial tactics (such as law-making) and technologies (such as those in law enforcement).

Against this backdrop are questions about the efficacy of approaches to environmental planning that espouse "decolonising" principles. In the NZ context, the RMA requires that local authorities confer with Māori in accordance with Treaty principles when making decisions about the environment, yet the outcome of such consultation is rarely put into practice to its full intent. As discussed, it is the outcome of Waitangi Tribunal settlements that have proven most effective in restoring kaitiakitanga, in turn securing environmental protection. Ultimately, this outcome is a reflection of the entanglement of ecojustice and indigenous sovereignty (Hsiao, 2012) and, given so, it is an illustration of how important it is for green criminologists in settler states to critically reflect on "rights" approaches to environmental management that potentially reproduce colonial logics. Such paradigms eclipse the fact that indigenous peoples have been successfully "managing" the environment for millennia (O'Donnell, Poelina, Pelizzon, and Clark, 2020). Critics should also be mindful of accommodations for the respondent in environmental law that is drafted in redress for colonial harm, however benign they appear (Macpherson & Clavijo Ospina, 2018). Relatedly, it is premature to speak of the recognition of the intrinsic rights of environmental entities, such as rivers, when Te Awa Tupua, for example, has accorded rights to just one river, among a possible 1146 in NZ. Moreover, whether those rights will advance the wellbeing of the Whanganui river still remains to be seen.

Ultimately, the entanglement of colonization with environmental harm places an onus on green criminologists to advance indigenous epistemologies in environmental governance. To that end, Goyes' (2018) proposes a "southern green criminology" that draws together Western and indigenous understandings of environmental harm, facilitating the latter to influence—and even transform—the former. In the NZ context, including or adopting matauranga Māori (Māori epistemologies) in research designs would be aligned with practices of a southern green criminology, whereas both would exemplar the sort of revised criminology imagined by Lynch and Stretesky (2014).

Conclusion

The granting of legal personhood to Te Awa Tupua in 2017 embodies a struggle that spans a century and a half between Ngāti Hāu and the NZ government for the rights and protection of the Whanganui River (Biggs, 2017). While some have hailed this piece of environmental legislation innovative in recognising the rights of nature and integrating an indigenous worldview into Western legislation (i.e. White, 2018), Te Awa Tupua is thick with ambiguities, complexities and caveats, including an anthropocentric orientation in awarding personhood to an environmental entity; the separation of a whole river into parts; and, self-determination for the river alongside the retention of existing property interests in the riverbed. Moreover, Te Awa Tupua undermines the tino rangatiratanga of Ngāti Hāu as guaranteed by the Treaty of Waitangi of 1840. As a result, the indivisible river and iwi have been unable to be fully redressed of their grievances suffered under its protections. We conclude, therefore, that rather than an exemplary piece of environmental legislation, Te Awa Tupua is at best an imperfect merger of two opposing paradigms and at worst a spectacular failure to enact justice for colonial harms done. The awarded legal personhood to the Whanganui river enacts neither ecojustice nor colonial justice. That said, Te Awa Tupua may prove to be a catalyst in reimagining the relationships between human beings, non-human animals and the environment in societies that are currently dominated by Western anthropocentric paradigms. As always, assuming there are shifts in the content and structure of environmental law as these new relationships transform how societies conceive of themselves, questions of power will remain critical.

References

Biard, A., Walters, R., & White, R. (2020). Water Theft Maleficence in Australia. *International Journal for Crime, Justice and Social Democracy, 9*(3), 1–15.

Biggs, S. (2017). Rivers, Rights and Revolution: Learning from the Maori. In S. Biggs, B. K. Tom., & O. O. Lake (Eds.), *Rights of Nature and Mother Nature: Rights-Based Law for Systemic Change.* Movement Rights, 179–182.

Cohen, A. K. (1974). *Elasticity of Evil*. John Wiley and Sons.

Cunneen, C., & Rowe, S. (2015). Decolonizing Indigenous Victimization. In D. Wilson & S. Ross (Eds.), *Crime, Victims and Policy: International Contexts, Local Experiences* (pp. 10–26). Palgrave Macmillan.

Durkheim, E. (1984). *The Division of Labour in Society* (W. D. Halls, Trans.). MacMillan.

Eckstein, G., D'Andrea, A., Marshall, V., O'Donnell, E., Talbot-Jones, J., Curran, D., & O'Bryan, K. (2019). Conferring Legal Personality on the World's Rivers: A Brief Intellectual Assessment. *Water International, 44*(6–7), 804.829.

Foster, J. B. (1999). Marx's theory of metabolic rift: Classical foundations for environmental sociology. *American Journal of Sociology, 105*(2), 366–405.

Foucault, M. (1980). *Power/Knowledge: Selected Interviews and Other Writings 1972–1977* [Translated by C. Gordon]. In C. Gordon (Eds.). New York: Pantheon.

Goyes, D. R. (2018). Green Criminology as Decolonial Tool: A Stereoscope of Environmental Harm. In K. Carrington, R. Hogg, J. Scott, & M. Sozzo (Eds.), *The Palgrave Handbook of Criminology and the Global South* (pp. 323–346). Springer International Publishing.

Hall, M. (2014). Environmental Harm and Environmental Victims: Scoping Out a 'Green Victimology.' *International Review of Victimology, 20*(1), 129–143.

Hillyard, P., & Tombs, S. (2007). From 'crime' to social harm? *Crime, Law and Social Change, 48*(1–2), 9–25.

Hsiao, E. (2012). Whanganui River Agreement - Indigenous Rights and Rights of Nature. *Environmental Policy and Law, 42*, 371–375.

Hutchison, A. (2014). The Whanganui River as a Legal Person. *Alternative Law Journal, 39*(3), 179–182. https://doi.org/10.1177/1037969X1403900309.

Iorns, C. (2019). Legal Personality for the Environment in Aotearoa New Zealand. In E. Elgar (Eds.). *Human Rights and the Environment: Legality, Indivisibility, Dignity and Geography.* Northampton, MA: Edward Elgar Publishing.

Jackson, M. (1988). *The Māori and the Criminal Justice System - A New Perspective - He Whaipaanga Hou.* Wellington: Department of Justice.

Johnston, A. (2018). Murky Waters: The Recognition of Maori Rights and Interests in Freshwater. *Te Mata Koi: Auckland University Law Review, 24*, 39–65.

Kauffman, C. M., & Martin, P. L. (2017). *When Rivers Have Rights: Case Comparisons of New Zealand, Colombia and India.* [Conference Proceedings]. Retrieved from http://files.harmonywithnatureun.org/uploads/upload585.pdf

Louisson, C. A. (2021). *Seeping Ugly.* Masters Thesis. Victoria University of Wellington, New Zealand.

Lynch, M. J., & Stretesky, P. B. (2014). *Exploring Green Criminology: Toward a Green Criminological Revolution.* Ashgate Publishing, Ltd.

Lynes, L. S. (2017). *Climate Change Law and Colonialism: Legal Standing of Three Rivers and a Hypothetical Case of Bison Personhood in Canada.* Working Paper. Glasgow, UK: Centre for Environmental Law and Governance, University of Strathclyde.

Macpherson, E., & Ospina, F. C. (2018). The Pluralism of River Rights in Aotearoa New Zealand and Colombia. *Journal of Water Law, 25*, 283–290.

Mercier, R. O., Stevens, N., & Tia, A. (2011). Mātauranga Māori and the Data-Information-Knowledge– Wisdom Hierarchy: A Conversation on Interfacing Knowledge Systems. *Mai Journal, 1*, 103–116.

Michalowski, R. (2016). What is Crime? *Critical Criminology, 24*, 181–199.

Morrison-Shaw, V., & Buxeda, N. (2017). *Whanganui River and Legal Personhood. Lawtalk, 907*, 30–31.

Naffine, N. (2009). *Law's Meaning of Life: Philosophy, Religion, Darwin and the Legal Person.* Hart.

New Zealand Parliament. (2017). *Innovative Bill Protects Whanganui River with Legal Personhood.* Retrieved from https://www.parliament.nz/en/get-involved/features/innovative-bill-protects-whanganui-river-with-legal-personhood/#:~:text=In%20New%20Zealand%20law%2C%20a,it%20a%20deep%20spiritual%20connection.

O'Donnell, E., & Talbot-Jones, J. (2017). Legal Rights for Rivers: What Does This Actually Mean? *Australian Environment Review, 32*(6), 159–162.

O'Donnell, E., & Talbot-Jones, J. (2018). Creating Legal Rights for Rivers: Lessons from Australia, New Zealand and India. *Ecology and Society, 23*(1), 7.

O'Donnell, E., & Macpherson, E. (2019). Voice, power and legitimacy: The role of the legal person in river management in New Zealand, Chile and Australia. *Australasian Journal of Water Resources, 23*(1), 35–44.

O'Donnell, E., Poelina, A., Pelizzon, A., & Clark, C. (2020). Stop Burying the Lede: The Essential Role of Indigenous Law(s). *Creating Rights of Nature. Transnational Environmental Law, 9*(3), 403–427.

Passas, N. (2005). Lawful but Awful: 'Legal Corporate Crimes.' *Journal of Socio-Economics, 34*(6), 771–786.

Ruru, J. (2018). Listening to Papatūānuku: A Call to Reform Water Law. *Journal of the Royal Society of New Zealand, 48*(23), 215–224.

Salmond, A. (2014). Tears of Rangi: Water, Power and People in New Zealand. *Journal of Ethnographic Theory, 4*(3), 285–309.

Salmón, E. (2000). Kincentric Ecology: Indigenous Perceptions of the Human-Nature Relationship. *Ecological Applications, 10*(5), 1327–1332.
Spivak, C. G. (1995). Can the Subaltern Speak? In B. Ashcroft (Ed.), *The Post Colonial Studies Reader* (pp. 24–28). Routledge.
Talbot-Jones, J., & Bennet, J. (2019). Toward a Property Rights Theory of Legal Rights for Rivers. *Ecological Economics, 164*, 106352.
Te Aho, L. (2017). The 'False Generosity' of Treaty Settlements: Innovation and Contortion. In A. Erueti (Ed.), *International Indigenous Rights in Aotearoa New Zealand* (pp. 99–117). Victoria University Press.
Waitangi Tribunal. (1999). *The Whanganui River Report.* Waitangi Tribunal.
Warnes, K. (2019). *National Geographic - Maori River in New Zealand is a Legal Person.* Retrieved from https://www.nationalgeographic.com/culture/2019/04/maori-river-in-new-zealand-is-a-legal-person/.
Warnock, M. (2012). Should Trees Have Standing? *Journal of Human Rights and the Environment* 3(Special Issue):56–67. http://dx.doi.org/https://doi.org/10.4337/jhre.2012.02.03.
White, R. (2018). Green Victimology and Non-Human Victims. *International Review of Victimology, 24*(2), 239–255. https://doi.org/10.1177/0269758017745615.
White, R., & Heckenberg, D. (2014). *Green criminology: An Introduction to the Study of Environmental Harm.* Routledge.
Whyte, K. P. (2017). The Dakota Access Pipeline, Environmental Injustice, and U.S. Colonialism. *Red Ink: International Journal of Indigenous Literature, Arts, & Humanities, 19*(1), 154–169.
Williams, C. (1996). An Environmental Victimology. *Social Justice, 23*(4 (66)), 16–40.
Wynyard, M. (2017). Plunder in the promised land: Maori land alienation and the genesis of capitalism in Aotearoa New Zealand. In A. Bell, V. Elizabeth, T. McIntosh, & M. Wynyard (Eds.), *A Land of Milk and Honey? Making Sense of Aotearoa New Zealand* (pp. 13–25). Auckland University Press.

13

Mother Earth in Environmental Activism: Indigeneity, Maternal Thinking, and Animism in the Keystone Pipeline Debate

Rebecca Jaremko Bromwich

Introduction

Green criminological scholarship has often said little about the subject of gender. Yet, gender clearly impacts how environmental harms are felt. As Lynch notes, those identified as women are disproportionately affected by pollution-related crime and regulatory offences relative to those identified as men (Lynch, 2016). There is certainly good reason for scholarship to look more deeply at green criminology through the lens of gender. Lynch argues that we need to integrate feminist criminological views with green criminology in order to better understand how differently situated people are differentially affected by environmental crime (Lynch, 2016). As Walklate (1990) comments, women's material reality as generally economically and socially subordinate to men worldwide

R. J. Bromwich (✉)
Carleton University, Department of Law and Legal Studies, Ontario, Canada
e-mail: Rebecca.Bromwich@gowlingwlg.com

J. Gacek and R. Jochelson (eds.), *Green Criminology and the Law*, Palgrave Studies in Green Criminology,
https://doi.org/10.1007/978-3-030-82412-9_13

too often renders women disproportionately vulnerable to victimization resulting from the impacts of environmental crime. Certainly, as a gender, women experience different harms and different victimization from men in terms of when toxic pollutants are released into the environment. Further, of course, intersectionally, women who are differently situated in terms of geography, race, and socioeconomic status, among other factors, experience this differently from each other.

Advocacy relating to environmental harms is linked to violence against women advocacy generally particularly because green victimization is violent. While it is often not conceptualized as violent, victimization by green crime is violent because it causes a variety of physical harms, many of which are transformative (Jarrell et al., 2013). Lynch (2016) notes that there is a significant gap in the literature where the intersection of gender and green crime is considered. Also understudied are ways in which feminist activism and environmental activism intersect. This chapter seeks to contribute to filling those gaps.

If we seek gender equality and environmental protection as feminists, environmentalists, and activists should we use the term "Mother Earth"? This chapter engages this question, since certain feminist critics have seen the gendering of the earth as essentialist and drawing on problematic constructions of maternality. The thematic question this chapter seeks to address is one of great relevance for environmental advocates seeking to work simultaneously towards reducing levels of gender inequality. Sarah Milner-Barry (2015) and Sherri Ortner (1974) have contended that the discursive figure of Mother Nature reinforces the idea that both women and nature should be subjugated. They argue that value systems failing to value the natural environment as well as women are enmeshed and mutually supportive. Consequently, these value systems continue to reinforce imagery of Mother Nature and Mother Earth that serves to maintain the subjugation of women while legitimizing the exploitation and depletion of natural resources. This chapter asks whether it is unethical or unwise for those who seek gender equality to use the discursive figure of Mother Earth in environmental advocacy.

In this chapter, I critically explore the arguments against using the terms "Mother Earth" and "Mother Nature," with specific reference to their use in advocacy around the Keystone XL pipeline. The overarching question this chapter discusses is whether in environmental advocacy, the term "Mother Earth," as well as its undergirding construct of the earth as maternal, is sexist and should be abandoned. I employ critical discourse analysis of the conversations around the Keystone pipeline case to reveal the implications of using the figure of Mother Earth in environmental advocacy.

This chapter first uses critical discourse analysis to explore how the subjectivization of the earth as a mother through deployment of the discursive figure Mother Earth has been deployed in debates surrounding the Keystone XL pipeline. The chapter then reviews literature that critiques discursive configurations of the earth as maternal as well as considers the use of the Mother Earth construct in recent environmental advocacy and law reform. After situating the case study in this context, the chapter analyses the representation effected by this construction, and its uses by advocates, in the Keystone XL case to address the question of whether feminist environmentalists should use or spurn the term.

I argue that the deployment of the discursive constructs of Mother Earth in environmental activism references and strengthens symbolic and ideological content from Indigenous worldviews and exists outside Western, patriarchal, and capitalist assumptions about what a mother is. The strategic deployment of the Mother Earth figure may neither be entirely unproblematic nor without risks, but it carries great potential to subvert capitalist and patriarchal logics. As deployed in contemporary environmental advocacy, this figure is given meaning within Indigenous, animist logics and should neither be dismissed as necessarily essentialist or disavowed as inevitably contributing to the continued subjection of women.

The Study: Critical Discourse Analysis

This chapter analyses documents—advocacy, quasi-legal, and media—produced in North America about the Keystone XL pipeline between 2010 and 2018. The study was a qualitative critical discourse analysis conducted to ascertain how representations of the maternal and the Mother Earth construct have been deployed by advocates in the case of the Keystone XL pipeline. The configuration of the environment as a maternal subject in this event is used as a case study from which I explore the implications of using the maternal earth as a discursive construct for gender relations.

Critical discourse analysis is a methodological framework for conducting research into how discourses function as instruments of power and control. It looks at social structures and processes involved in text production and makes relationships of causality that are otherwise opaque clear and visible; critical discourse analysis highlights the links between texts and broader social and cultural power relations and discursive processes (Fairclough, 1995).

The dataset for the analysis was obtained via Google searches as well as the news database Factiva. Such search terms as "Keystone XL" "environment" "protest" "earth" and "Mother Earth" were variously used. A Google news using the search terms "Keystone XL" and "Mother Earth" yielded 2,750 unique documents. The top 100 articles from this Google search became the dataset used for this research. This study quantitatively and qualitatively analyses how a variety of texts from sites of discursive production in media and legal discourses represented, articulated, and caused Mother Earth to emerge as a figure. It then critically analyses what figures of Mother Earth emerge in the texts, what public narratives and politics those figures support, and to what extent each configuration of Mother Earth is consistent or inconsistent with the philosophical orientation of maternal thinking.

For this work, I built on the method I used, and specifically the subject matter I studied, in my book analysing discursive figures of mothers, girls, and inmates in the case of Ashley Smith, a young woman who died in a Canadian prison and whose death was ruled a homicide perpetrated by the criminal justice and correctional systems (Bromwich, 2015). The current study, like this prior work, inquires into what Lauren Berlant calls the "caseness" of figures of Mother Earth. The analysis involved asking what figures of Mother Earth are constructed in the Keystone XL case.

I work with the concept of "figuration" (de Laurentis, 2007), which is the process by which a representation is given a particular form: "A figure is the simultaneously material and semiotic product of certain [discursive] processes" (Castaneda, 2002, pp. 3–4). A figuration is "a specific configuration of knowledges, practices and power" (Castaneda, 2002, pp. 3–4). Accordingly, I qualitatively study media and legal texts to determine what figurations emerge in these cultural domains.

The term "maternal thinking" (Ruddick, 1995) is used in this chapter to refer to a particular strain of feminist theory developed in large part by philosopher Sara Ruddick and more recently expanded upon and clarified by leading Canadian motherhood scholar Andrea O'Reilly. As discussed by O'Reilly (2011), Sara Ruddick, Patricia Hill Collins, and Adrienne Rich have helped to develop feminist motherhood theory. Ruddick (1995) sees maternal thinking as a discipline analogous to the discourses of religion or science with particular dimensions as a practice. Although traditionally understood as women's work, maternal thinking is not essentially female. It is a philosophical orientation that cognitively and performatively involves a kind of caring labour that is engaged and physical and that involves "protection, nurturance and training … care and respect" (Ruddick, 1995, p. 62). Ruddick identifies the "maternal standpoint" as a way of looking at all children and other people as human.

For Ruddick, mothering is work, not an identity. She focuses on the performativity of maternal thinking and not on essential biological traits, thereby disaggregating maternalism from any particular embodied subject. She focuses not on static personal attributes but on themes characteristic of maternal thinking (Ruddick, 1995). Similarly, O'Reilly draws together Judith Butler's notions about the performativity of gender with Ruddick's maternal thinking to further advance a nonessentialist understanding of maternal activism. She writes that far from being essentially feminine, "motherhood is similarly performed by maternalist activists" (O'Reilly, 2011, p. 16). Maternal thinking is performed rather than biologically inhabited.

The Keystone Pipeline

The Keystone pipeline is an oil pipeline system linking Canada to the United States, which is related to, but not the same as, the Dakota Access pipeline. The Keystone Pipeline system runs from the Western Canadian sedimentary basin, starting in Alberta, to refineries in Illinois and Texas and also to oil tank farms and to an oil pipeline distribution centre in Cushing, Oklahoma (Keystone, 2012). This pipeline was first commissioned in 2010. At time of writing, in 2020, it is now owned solely by the TransCanada Corporation.

The pipeline became a controversial focus of public attention when a planned fourth phase, Keystone XL, attracted growing environmental protest. This phase of the project became, for many, a symbol not only in the battle over climate change and fossil fuels but also in the struggles of Indigenous peoples for self-determination. In 2015, the Keystone XL Pipeline was rejected by then President Barack Obama (Canadian Press, 2020). Environmental activists lauded this as a victory, but it was short lived. On 24 January 2017, newly elected President Donald Trump took action intended to permit the pipeline's completion by signing a presidential memorandum to that effect (Canadian Press, 2020). This decision, in turn, led to a new wave of Indigenous opposition.

Findings

This study confirms that configurations of the natural environment as a maternal subject were consistently dominant in the texts produced by activists opposing the development of the pipeline during the period studied. In short, discursive configuration of the earth as a mother in this case was powerful, emotionally resonant, and effective at galvanizing activism. Activists deployed a unitary, intersectional, and self-described Indigenous construct of Mother Earth, which remained consistent over time in the texts studied.

Although there were certainly some texts that referred to "the earth" rather than "Mother Earth" in advocacy, the dominant figuration of the natural environment in texts produced by activists in relation to the pipeline was as a mother, a female, and a maternal figure, which is not only anthropomorphic but also communitarian in nature. This was not an ad hoc synergy, nor was it a coincidence. In September 2011, opponents of the Keystone Pipeline approval signed reading "Mother Earth Accord" at the Rosebud Sioux Tribe Emergency Summit (IEN,

2011). This accord affirmed the Indigenous view "that the Earth is our true mother, our grandmother who gives birth to us and maintains all life," demanded a "moratorium on tar sands development," and rejected "the Presidential Permit for the Keystone XL Pipeline" by Obama (IEN, 2011).

In prior and subsequent texts, the use of the Mother Earth construct by Indigenous activists in opposition to the Keystone XL pipeline remained linked to indigeneity, which served not only to gender the earth but also to reference anticapitalist alternatives to viewing the environment as property. The construct fostered a sense of belonging, mutual accountability, and shared interests among the Indigenous activists as well as their allies.

In November 2015, when Obama announced that the Keystone Pipeline proposal would be rejected, the decision was widely hailed by activists as "a victory for Mother Earth" (IEN, 2011). Although it was only a temporary decision, as Trump reversed the decision in January 2017, as noted above, the discursive resonances and power of the figuration of the earth as a maternal subject remain evidently powerful.

Indeed, opposition to the Keystone XL pipeline, as revealed in this study, centred on the Mother Earth figure and the reciprocal relationship of caregiving, of Indigenous peoples as caretakers of her, and of her role as a caregiver of life. The Mother Earth figure used by Indigenous activists is not simply a construction of personhood or femininity but a way of speaking about belonging and leadership. It is matched on several occasions by advocates referring to Obama as "the great white father" (e.g., White Plume, 2011). Mother Earth is, thus, presented as a counterpart to, or refutation of the power of, the patriarchal authority of colonial power.

The texts studied consistently framed Indigenous peoples' opposition to the Keystone pipeline as caretaking for Mother Earth. For example, in an article in *The Guardian*, activist Dallas Goldtooth (2015) identifies the figure of Mother Earth with Indigenous conceptions of an animistic worldview in which humans are part of nature and not separate from it:

> As Indigenous peoples, as Oceti Sakowin, we were handed down the original teachings on how to live in balance with Mother Earth. We must see

> all aspects of life as related, to respect the feminine principle of creation and to maintain a sustainable relationship with the land. These tenets are antithetical to the extractive economy we are faced with today. The land, air, and water are commodified. Mother Earth is being drilled, fracked, clear-cut, and destroyed with such brutality. We are on the brink of climate catastrophe. In order to avoid drastic climate change, we need a moratorium on fossil fuel development and we need to invest in a zero carbon economy: our original teachings demand no less than this.

Advocates do not uniformly articulate the figure of Mother Earth. The articulations are nuanced and overwhelmingly intersectional; they link the maternality of the earth to the connection Indigenous peoples have with the environment. Consider this example: "The Earth is our Mother—she ain't going no place. In fact, Earth is an Indian mom; powerful, resilient, beautiful and will survive the very worst that the universe can give. Sure, she had it rough early on, but she's got that elasticity in her skin" (Ross, 2014).

Although the specific characteristics of the Mother Earth differ during the period studied, the configuration of the natural environment as a mother by advocates remains consistent. For instance, in 2017, after President Trump's approval of the Keystone XL pipeline, protests were unified around the Mother Earth figure and the role of Indigenous peoples in protecting here. A 2017 Declaration updating the 2011 Mother Earth Accord, which was signed by the Blackfoot Confederacy and Great Sioux Nation, opponents of the pipeline, says the following: "It is our turn to *use the voices that the colonizers understand* to say our mother the earth has withstood all that she should ever withstand on our behalf" (my emphasis, CBC News, 2017).

In 2017, a group calling itself the Treaty Alliance against the Tar Sands, which is composed of 150 First Nations across Canada and the United States, actively used the Mother Earth figure as a central, galvanizing concept in its environmental advocacy (Treaty Alliance, 2016). Their 2016 Treaty Alliance against Tar Sands Expansion begins with a preamble that references Mother Earth and the need to protect it.

Contextualizing the Study

Critical Perspectives from Feminist Theory

Different lines of thought in feminist theory take divergent views on the configuration of the earth as a mother. Some feminists uncritically accept a naturalized view of the earth as feminine and seek to recuperate the subordinated feminine. Conversely, those who take a more social constructivist view of the cultural content of femininity reject the claim that nature is inherently feminine and problematize the discursive configuration of the earth as a mother. In feminist theoretical writing, gender essentialists and social constructivists often articulate the Mother Earth figure in their advocacy and rhetoric for different reasons. Gender essentialists tend to assume a naturalized connection of woman to nature and assume certain attributes to women and to nature that are shared; they see a central goal of feminism to be the recuperation and celebration of the feminine. Conversely, social constructivist feminist thinkers, such as Sherry Ortner, problematize the naturalization of traits conceived as feminine. Ortner contends in her 1974 article "Is Female to Male as Nature Is to Culture" that the association of women with nature is problematic because of its association of women with something societies devalue: "Woman is being identified with—or, if you will, seems to be a symbol of—something that every culture devalues, something that every culture defines as being of a lower order of existence than itself. Now it seems that there is only one thing that would fit that description, and that is 'nature' in the most generalized sense" (Ortner, 1974, p. 74).

Although there is a diversity of thought that considers itself to be ecofeminist, some of it being antiessentialist, many of the ecofeminists of the ecofeminism movement popular from 1970s through to the 1990s celebrated an essentialized connection of the sacred feminine to the natural environment (Sturgeon, 1997). In general, ecofeminists link the oppression of women to the oppression of animals and the natural environment; they have historically built on theories that femininity is associated with connectedness and nature, whereas masculinity is more associated with atomism and rights (Gaard, 1993).

However, a social constructivist approach does not necessarily find problematic configurations that relate the earth to having a female gender or maternal subjectivity.

For instance, Greta Gaard contends that the configuration of the earth as a mother has potential positive and negative effects. She asserts that on the positive side, conceptualizing the earth as a family member inspires humans to honour and care for the natural environment.

However, recent social constructivist feminist writing often criticizes the essentialization of the feminine and problematizes its association with nature. Several contemporary feminist scholars have argued that in the context of a patriarchal society, using the term "Mother Earth" and similar figurations of the natural environment as female and maternal encourages humanity to exploit and denigrate the earth in the same ways women are exploited; it also assumes that the earth, as our mother, will always nurture us. Sarah Milner-Barry (2015), for example, has critiqued representations of the earth as a maternal figure: "Unfortunately, the idea that women and nature are inherently linked is a tacit acceptance of their mutual exploitation." In fairness, as Gaard (1993) discusses, ecofeminist theory generally shares the view that the linkage of women to nature in patriarchal discourses supports the oppression of women and the exploitation of nature. However, most ecofeminist thought is characterized by some level of naturalization of the association of nature with the feminine and some level of essentialization of what it is to be a woman.

Critics of the use of the Mother Earth figure in environmental advocacy are often concerned that environmentalism involving a close association of women with nature invokes and reinscribes a nostalgic conception of preindustrial life, which masks the ways in which women were oppressed within it. For example, Jennifer Bernstein (2017) asks, "What would an environmentalism that takes feminism seriously look like?" She further contends the following:

> The glorification of nature and farming and the romanticizing of the home, domestic life, and the woman at the center of it are ultimately nostalgias that cover up the brutality of rural life and drudgery of domestic labor in a perfume of freshly cut hay and caramelizing

> onions. While the new domestics advocating home brewing, fermenting kombucha, and churning butter are likely aware of their irony in an era of unprecedented technological progress, this nostalgia does little to further the goals of middle- and lower-class women in the developed world.

Susan Schrepfer and Douglas Cazaux Sackman (2010), too, are critical of the use of the Mother Earth construct in environmental advocacy. They showcase the link between "ecological imperialism and sexual subordination" (Schrepfer & Cazaux Sackman, 2010, p. 119)—the basis for the notion that both women and the earth are passive and ideal for domination (p. 119) They argue further that "metaphors used to describe nature as mother … reflect and reinforce social divisions … [and] relations of dominance between men, women, and nature" (p. 117).

These theorists argue that the association of nature with women and with maternal subjects, which has been used to ideologically justify the denigration of women, devalues nature. Milner-Barry (2015) argues that the configuration of the earth as a mother and the devaluation of tasks associated with maternality, such as birth giving and childrearing, supports both the subjugation of women and the degradation of the natural environment:

> The term "Mother Nature," then, although it arose from spiritually rich traditions, has come to represent the twinned exploitation of all that patriarchal society considers to be inferior to men. As such, both are expected to be perpetually available to them, and to be accepting and accommodating of their desires. As long as the reason for gendered oppression is rooted in women's apparent closeness to nature, this kind of rhetoric provides another reason to view both women and the Earth as existing on an unequal plane with men. (p. 35)

Indigenous Contexts and Legal Construct of "Mother Earth"

The Mother Earth figure features prominently in contemporary writing about environmental advocacy as articulated by Indigenous advocates and organizations. Furthermore, the Mother Earth figure has a nascent presence as a liminal being in international and some domestic law. In the last decade, Ecuador and Bolivia have constitutionally enshrined protections for Mother Earth, which is discussed below. Although ecofeminist writing has expressed concerns about the colonization of Indigenous worldviews by environmentalists (Gaard, 1993) through their use of the Mother Earth in activism, it is also important to note that Indigenous activists and communities frequently deploy the term "Mother Earth" themselves. The Mother Earth figure is also taking on a legal existence in a growing number of jurisdictions.

As a preliminary note, it is the subject of academic debate whether the Mother Earth figure, as a gendered and maternal personification of the natural environment, is a longstanding feature of North American Indigenous traditions. Some scholars have argued that it is not (Gill, 1987; Bierhorst, 1994); rather, they have contended that prior to contact with European settlers, Indigenous peoples in North America did not conceptualize the earth as female or maternal. Sam Gill traces the historical development of the Mother Earth figure in American Indigenous traditions to argue that a theological construct of Mother Earth is not originally or fully Indigenous to North America. However, others have argued that to consider Gill's study as a refutation of the authenticity of Mother Earth as an Indigenous construct or figure is to misapprehend the nature of oral histories. Oral histories are crafted to engage with the present and invoke traditions in dynamic ways; they are not simply artefacts of the past (von Gernet, 1996, p. 11).

For the purposes of this analysis, Gill's critique of historical authenticity is not relevant. This is not a history or genealogy of the representation of Mother Earth; instead, this research asks in what ways the discursive construct of Mother Earth exists in the advocacy articulated by Indigenous peoples in North America today. It also looks at contemporary advocacy by people who, while not identifying as Indigenous, also fight against the Keystone Pipeline and at more general environmental advocacy that is framed in terms of Mother Earth as a figure. The Mother Earth figure is identified in this advocacy as an Indigenous concept, and it is constructed within logics that are claimed as Indigenous.

The maternality of the earth in Indigenous worldviews is not precisely the same thing as legal personhood for the earth. It is a broader conception of connectedness: it is bigger and more intimate than personhood. In general, most Indigenous advocates distinguish maternal configuration of the earth from granting it legal personhood and prefer using a configuration of Mother Earth over a genderless personhood for nature. The configuration of the earth as a mother has legal dimensions in Indigenous advocacy. It references not just femininity but an animist conceptualization of the land that counters colonial concepts of property and property law, a sentiment that has also been articulated as the principle "that land for Native Americans is a 'sacred and inalienable mother,' while for the whites it is a 'commodity'" (Washburn, 1971, p. 143). The use of the "Mother Earth" construct in this logic is not simply a personification of the earth. It is grounded in Indigenous conceptions of the world as animistic: earth is not a mother in a human sense. Indeed, the Mother Earth figure is not an extension of personhood. As such, Indigenous configurations of Mother Earth do not represent the colonization of the natural world with an analog to human rights discourse; these representations are not simply making the world into a human being. As John Burrows (2008) discusses, Indigenous traditions in Canada work from a worldview in which the earth is not an inanimate piece of property but rather a living being. Further, Burrows sees the animate, and not proprietary, nature of the earth as a configuration that is legal and is part of Indigenous law. In Indigenous legal traditions, the earth has a status that is nonhuman and legal.

The legal reconstitution of the natural world from human property into a rights-bearing entity is being driven, in many contexts, by the personification of the earth not as a human generally but as a mother specifically. Recent shifts in environmental regulation in several jurisdictions have invoked and deployed the Mother Earth figure. The Universal Declaration on the Rights of Mother Earth was presented at the World People's Conference on Climate Change and the Rights of Mother Earth, at Cochabamba, Bolivia, on April 22, 2010. It commences with a configuration of Mother Earth as follows: "We are all part of Mother Earth, an indivisible, living community of interrelated and interdependent beings with a common destiny."

In this legal construction, Mother Earth is configured not as a human being, or not only as a human being, but as a community. The figure has the relational and gestational attributes characteristic of an expectant mother. This configuration uses the concept of motherhood to interrupt the logic of the construction of atomistic human rights. It is not an outgrowth of, or an analogy to, human rights.

The underlying logics behind constructions of Mother Earth are indeed different from the logics of capitalism. The Declaration goes on to say: "The capitalist system and all forms of depredation, exploitation, abuse and contamination have caused great destruction, degradation and disruption of Mother Earth, putting life as we know it today at risk through phenomena such as climate change." As noted above, Mother Earth is a figure around which nascent legal cultures are developing across jurisdictions, especially in Latin America. In Bolivia, the Framework Law of Mother Earth and Integral Development to Live Well was enacted in 2012, after the country adopted a new constitution in 2009, as part of a complete restructuring of the Bolivian legal system (Hindery, 2013). This law reform has been heavily influenced by a resurgent Indigenous Andean spiritual worldview, which places the environment and the earth deity known as the Pachamama at the centre of all life. In this worldview, as expressed in the Law of Mother Earth, humans are considered equal to, and linked with, all other entities and are not set apart from nature (Hindery, 2013). In Ecuador, the figure of Pachamama, an Inca maternal deity symbolic of earth's fecundity, was introduced into the country's constitution in 2008 as a figure around which the rights of nature "to exist, persist, maintain and regenerate its vital cycles" are constructed (Berros, 2015). In both the Bolivian and Ecuadorian instances, Mother Earth is characterized as a community of living things.

Analysis of the Keystone Case

The Mother Earth figure used by advocates opposing the Keystone XL pipeline clearly represents the animist configuration of the natural world found in Indigenous advocacy more generally. This is one case of a more general type, in which the Mother Earth figure grounded in animist worldviews that are self-identified as Indigenous is emergent as a legal persona or rights-bearing entity. As an entity, Mother Earth, as articulated in the Keystone XL case, has gendered content. However, its gender and maternality are given meaning through systems of logic that are identified as Indigenous. These systems of logic are not the same as those that have produced gender inequality in the Western, industrialized, and capitalist world. Thus, those with feminist agendas should embrace the use of the Mother Earth figure for its revolutionary potential to interrupt and subvert capitalist, consumerist, and colonial notions of value in intersectional ways.

This analysis suggests that rather than swearing off using the maternal subjectivization of the natural world, feminist environmental activists would be wiser to deploy it in animistic and anticapitalist theoretical and logical frameworks. Instead of articulating the Mother Earth figure on its own, it may be better to also describe the concepts this figure intends to convey directly. It might be preferable to talk expressly about maternal thinking, caregiving labour, the motherwork, of the earth, and our belonging to it, rather than assuming that content is inherently signified by the construct of Mother Earth. The deployment of the discursive figure of Mother Earth is also a means to appeal to what Ruddick (1995) has identified as "maternal thinking"—a different way to conceptualize the embodiment and interdependency of humans and the natural world. The animistic conception of the earth as a mother that is found in the Indigenous advocacy opposing the Keystone XL pipeline resembles maternal thinking in that they both invoke ideas of belonging and accountability through interconnectedness.

Ubiquitous and powerful in environmental advocacy, the Mother Earth figure is not simply a person. It exceeds personhood. It is not simply an anthropomorphization that acquires rights and attributes of those of a female human being. Rather, it is a relational description of the connection that people have to earth. The metaphor of motherhood, with its gestational and communitarian implications, speaks back against capitalism and atomism in effective ways. The configuration in advocacy and legal discourse of Mother Earth is powerful in challenging precisely what troubles Sheryl Hamilton (2009) in her book *Impersonations*: the modernist binaries between nature and culture, object and subject. Thus, the configuration of the earth as a mother is a powerful discursive technology.

The configuration of earth as Mother Earth can play upon the benefits of legal personhood while subverting the capitalist philosophy beneath it. It is useful to think of the Mother Earth figure not as a person but as a member of a broader category of what Hamilton classes "persona"—a "liminal being," an entity capable of bearing rights that is not restricted to a "particular physical form" (2009, p. 21). As Hamilton argues, it is around these liminal beings that important social questions are worked through.

Equally, as Hamilton notes, the production of social personae can have unintended results. Hamilton cautions that the use of the Mother Earth figure in environmental advocacy may undermine the significance of the environment when it intersects with capitalism (2009, p. 30). However, it may also have an opposite effect. If Mother Earth is important, may this potentially trouble the undermining and undervaluing of unpaid labour performed by mothers within capitalism? The use of the Mother Earth construct provides a legible, or at least semi-legible, discursive figure that can resonate with colonial ideas to some degree. It is proving to be a tenacious and powerful discursive technology in the battles against corporate and colonial power. Moreover, non-Indigenous advocates for better environmental stewardship have no right to discipline or police the language used by Indigenous ones.

Postcolonial feminist philosopher and literary theorist Gayatri Chakravorty Spivak (1990) first coined the term strategic essentialism, which is undertaken intentionally by activists and advocates when they provisionally accept essentialist foundations for certain categories of identity as a strategy for collective representation in order to pursue their political ends. Even if feminists are concerned about the possible consequences of using Mother Earth and other maternal figurations of the natural environment, the power of the figure, as evidenced in recent Latin American law reform, means that it should not be dismissed or ignored by advocates as a tool, but the question of colonial appropriation of Indigenous ideas (Gaard, 1993) does merit critical exploration if advocates consider using the figuration. However, this study of the deployment of the Mother Earth figure in the Keystone XL pipeline debate shows the governmental efficacy of discursive configuration of the earth as maternal. The strategic deployment of the maternal figures of earth has been effectively used in the Keystone XL Pipeline case in negotiating power and control over the natural world, and it can be predictably and effectively used on a continuing basis.

Conclusion

In short, the research presented in this chapter answers the question of whether environmental advocates who also seek gender equality should use the term "Mother Earth" with a resounding yes. This analysis does not dispute the social constructivist theoretical point that assigning a gender and role to the earth is not inevitable and is to some extent arbitrary. This critical discourse analysis of the debates surrounding the Keystone XL pipeline shows that the configuration of the earth as a maternal subject, while it may be problematic, is also more complicated than simply being about gender. Perhaps, most importantly, the Mother Earth figure as a representation in discourse is a powerful resource.

This chapter has performed a critical discourse analysis of the uses, impact, and symbolic content of the discursive Mother Earth figure as deployed in the case of the Keystone Pipeline. It has critically assessed to what extent Western assumptions about mothers and gender are reinscribed by the deployment of this figure in advocacy and has revealed that the use of the Mother Earth figure in this case invokes and draws on notions of belonging and indigeneity that extend beyond legal personhood and female gender. As deployed by advocates in the Keystone XL pipeline case, the Mother Earth figure does not draw on but rather interrupts and unsettles colonial, settler assumptions about gender and maternality. Thus, rather than reinscribing patriarchal, capitalist logics, the Mother Earth figure has revolutionary potential to fundamentally trouble them.

This study has shown that contemporary discursive constructs of the earth as maternal in environmental activism draw largely on animistic conceptions of the earth found in Indigenous traditions rather than purely on Western notions of male and female, which Ortner (1974) and Milner-Berry (2015) are concerned about. Thus, these configurations do not necessarily carry the same stigmatizing or subordinating cultural baggage. Indeed, Ortner and Milner-Berry's arguments, respectively, against use of the term "Mother Earth" in environmental advocacy and counter to deployments of maternal figures of the natural environment seem to be ethnocentric and colonial in their understandings of what mothers are and can be.

The symbolic content of the Mother Earth figure in the advocacy around the Keystone XL case is not delimited by Western notions of maternality in its expression. However, this discursive figure does carry the potential to be received by Western listeners in the problematic ways that Milner-Barry and Ortner contend. To avoid the devaluation of the earth or femininity that these feminist theorists warn against, it may be wise for advocates speaking from outside of Indigenous traditions to explicitly ground deployments of the Mother Earth figure in internationally referenced idea systems. In my view, on the basis of this study, Western feminist environmentalists should, when employing the term "Mother Earth," reference not only maternality but also the implicit notions of belonging, connectedness, and animism that are invoked in by the term when used by Indigenous activists. It is, ultimately, not the construction of the earth as feminine but the notion of maternality in referencing our rootedness and belonging to her that most clearly undermines the capitalist and patriarchal logics supporting exploitation. This understanding has implications for green criminologists and activists concerned with green crime also: gendering and personification of the earth should not be dismissed as a legitimate discursive tactic.

Words matter. The way we talk about people and the natural environment creates discourse that can drive legal forms. This deep theoretical dive into how certain framings of the environment and the maternal perpetuate underlying cultural logics is, in my view, the type of analysis people who, like me, work as legal practitioners, should undertake in lieu of casually deploying cultural ideas when we seek to drive legal change and effect legal action. Lawyers too often are not mindful enough about what representations we perpetuate and reify when we represent people and institutions.

References

Berlant, L.(2007).On the case.Critical Inquiry, 33(4), 663–672

Bernstein, S. (2017). Why environmentalism has a gender problem. *Communists* in situ. Retrieve from cominsitu.wordpress.com/2017/09/06/on-mother-earth-and-earth-mothers/. Accessed 25 May 2020.

Berros, M. V. (2015). The constitution of the republic of ecuador: pachamama has rights. *Environment & Society Portal*, no. 11, Arcadia, Rachel Carson Center for Environment and Society.

Bierhorst, J. (1994). *Way of the earth: Native America and the environment.* William Morrow.

Bromwich, R. (2015). *Looking for Ashley: Re-reading what the smith case reveals about the governance of girls, mothers and families in Canada.* Demeter Press.

Burrows, J. (2008). Living law on a living earth: Aboriginal religion, law, and the constitution. In Moon, R. (Ed.), *Law and religious pluralism in Canada*, UBC Press, 2008, pp. 161–191.

Canadian Press. (2017). A chronological history of controversial keystone XL pipeline project. *CBC News*, www.cbc.ca/news/politics/keystone-xl-pipeline-timeline-1.3950156. Accessed 25 May 2020.

Castaneda, C. (2002). *Figurations: Child, bodies, worlds.* Duke University Press.

CBC News. (2017). Indigenous leaders sign opposition to keystone XL in Calgary. *CBC News,* 17. May, www.cbc.ca/news/canada/calgary/transcanada-keystone-calgary-indigenous-1.4119301. Accessed 25 May 2020.

De Laurentis, T. (2007). *Figures of resistance: Essays in feminist theory.* University of Illinois Press.

Fairclough, N. (1995). *Critical discourse analysis: The critical study of language.* Longman.

Gaard, G. (Ed.) (1993). *Women, animals, nature.* Temple University Press.

Gill, S. (1987). *Mother earth: An American story.* University of Chicago Press.

Goldtooth, D. (2015). Keystone XL would destroy our native lands. This is why we fight. *The Guardian,* 9 Jan. 2015, www.theguardian.com/commentisfree/2015/jan/09/keystone-xl-would-destroy-native-lands-we-fight. Accessed 25 May 2020.

Hamilton, S. (2009). *Impersonations: Troubling the person in law and culture*. University of Toronto Press.

Hindery, D. (2013). *From Enron to Evo: Pipeline politics, global environmentalism, and indigenous rights in Bolivia*. University of Arizona Press.

IEN. (2011). Mother earth accord. Rosebud Sioux tribe emergency summit, *IEN*, 2011, www.ienearth.org/mother-earth-accord/. Accessed 25 May 2020.

Jarrell, M. L., Lynch, M. J., & Stretesky, P. B. (2013). Green criminology and green victimization. In B. Arrigo & H. Bersot (Eds.), *The Routledge handbook of international crime and justice studies* (pp. 423–444). Routledge.

Johnson, R. (2002). *Taxing choices: the intersection of class, gender, parenthood and the law*. University of British Columbia Press.

Keystone Pipeline System. (2012). TransCanada.

Lynch, M. (2016). Acknowledging female victims of green crimes: Environmental exposure of women to industrial pollutants. *Feminist Criminology, 13*(4), 404–427.

Milner-Barry, S. (2015). The term 'mother nature' reinforces the idea that both women and nature should be subjugated. *Space Stereotypes*, qz.com/562833/the-term-mother-nature-reinforces-the-idea-that-both-women-and-nature-should-be-subjugated/. Accessed 25 May 2020.

Ortner, S. B. (1974). Is female to male as nature is to culture? In M. Z. Rosaldo & L. Lamphere (Eds.), *Woman, culture, and society*, Stanford University Press, pp. 68–87.

O'Reilly, A. (2011). *The twenty-first century motherhood movement*. Demeter Press.

Ross, G. (2014). Keystone XL and protecting mother earth: A fight all native people should fight. *Indian Country Today*, April 22, 2014.

Ruddick, S. (1995). Maternal thinking: Toward a politics of peace. Beacon Press.

Schrepfer, S. R., & Cazaux Sackman, D. (2010). *A companion to American environmental history*. Wiley-Blackwell.

Spivak, G. (1990). *The post-colonial critic: Interviews, strategies, dialogues*. Routledge.

Sturgeon, N. (1997). *Ecofeminist natures: Race, gender, feminist theory and political action*. Routledge.

Treaty Alliance. (2016). Treaty alliance against Tar sands expansion. www.treatyalliance.org/wp-content/uploads/2016/12/TreatyandAdditionalInformation-20161216-OL.pdf. Accessed 25 May 2020.

Von Gernet, A. (1996). *Oral narratives and aboriginal pasts: An interdisciplinary. Review of the literature on oral traditions and oral histories.* Department of Indian and Northern Affairs, April 1996.

Walklate, S. (1990). Researching victims of crime: Critical victimology. *Social Justice, 17*(3), 25–42.

Washburn, W. E. (1971). *Red Man's Land—White Man's Law.* Scribner.

White Plume, D. (2011). Testimony at the public hearing on the 1600 Mile TransCanada. Pipeline. U.S. State Department, *YouTube,* Oct. 7 2011, www.youtube.com/watch?time_continue=228&v=wJc5XPQXSCY.

Part IV

Future Directions for Green Criminology and Law

14

Widening the Scope of "Earth" Jurisprudence and "Green" Criminology? Towards Preserving Extra-Terrestrial Heritage Sites on Celestial Bodies

Jack Lampkin and Tanya Wyatt

Introduction

The Earth is facing several environmental crises. Human-caused climate change is already resulting in extreme weather, wildfires and ice melting at alarming rates among other concerns. The planet is also facing the sixth mass extinction with the loss of species estimated to be 100 to 1000 times higher than at other points in history (Wilson, 2016). This, too, is human-caused—habitat destruction being the main reason, and overexploitation being the second (Intergovernmental Science-Policy Platform

J. Lampkin (✉)
Leeds Trinity University, Leeds, England
e-mail: J.Lampkin@leedstrinity.ac.uk

York St John University, York, England

T. Wyatt
Northumbria University, Newcastle, England

J. Gacek and R. Jochelson (eds.), *Green Criminology and the Law*, Palgrave Studies in Green Criminology,
https://doi.org/10.1007/978-3-030-82412-9_14

on Biodiversity and Ecosystem Services, 2019). Human-caused environmental degradation is, however, not confined to planet Earth. Outer space, too, is potentially facing a human-caused environmental crisis.

The environmental degradation of the outer space environment is multifaceted. First, there is the tremendous amount of debris and electronic equipment in Earth's orbit. According to Schildknecht (2007, p. 107):

> The inventory of space debris ranges from large objects like defunct satellites and rocket upper stages over mid-size fragments of explosions or collisions, down to small-sized particles like paint flakes and solid rocket motor slag or dust. This debris poses an increasing threat to operational spacecraft and manned missions.

Undoubtedly, the problem has further degenerated in the last decade, particularly with the increase of the private space industry and the rise of what Takemura (2019) calls *space capitalism*. Amazon alone will launch 3000 satellites by 2029 (O'Callaghan, 2020). This is in addition to the 4200 satellites likely to be in orbit from the company SpaceX in the near future (O'Callaghan, 2020). Satellites create debris when they collide with one another or when they no longer function and there is no plan to return them to Earth. Such debris pose dangers to further spacecraft and outer space missions (Schildknecht, 2007). The sheer number of satellites also is likely to irreversibly change the night sky, impacting upon stargazers on Earth (O'Callaghan, 2020).

Second, there is the proposed mining of asteroids and other celestial bodies (like the Moon) and/or their relocation (Loder, 2018). Natural resource extraction, for the materials and for profit, is the main driver behind mining. Relocation of asteroids is to make it easier to extract those natural resources by moving them closer (from the asteroid belt between Mars and Jupiter, to Earth's orbit) (Loder, 2018). Relocation could also support further space exploration by placing asteroids in strategic locations to assist travel to deeper in space (Loder, 2018). All of these off-Earth bodies carry with them information about the history of our planet and of the universe (Lewis, 2015). Some asteroids have been found to have bacteria that could help explain the origins of life (Cooper, 2011). Mining and relocation, then, have potential costs. Their damage could mean the loss of scientific information about the cosmos. The damage or movement could also have unknown consequences related to the movement of other celestial bodies and the Earth. Human knowledge of the interaction of objects in space and the effects that moving or destroying objects may have is limited. Such actions could have unintended consequences that humans are unable to repair.

Furthermore, the mining of the Moon, in particular, poses a threat to space heritage. It is this aspect that the chapter focuses on as an example of how a combined green criminological and Earth jurisprudential framework could prevent such destruction from taking place. We first outline, what space heritage is and why it is important. We then outline what a green criminological framework can contribute to the preservation of space heritage. This is followed by the potential contribution of Earth jurisprudence and the existing legislative framework that pertains to the Moon. We then demonstrate how the combined green criminology-Earth jurisprudence framework could be utilised as a mechanism for protecting extra-terrestrial environments, and extra-terrestrial heritage sites on celestial bodies.

What is Space Heritage and Why Is It Important?

While humankind have sent many vehicles and spaceships to explore the solar system, only twelve have walked on the surface of another celestial body (Doyle, 2017, p. 144). This first occurred in 1969 when Neil Armstrong and Buzz Aldrin spent just 2 h and 31 min walking on Earth's Moon, conducting scientific experiments and exploring the lunar surface (Compton, 1989, p. 145). Since, and indeed prior to, Apollo, many more rovers and scientific apparatus have successfully landed on the Moon to conduct experiments (Neal, 2009; Spennemann & Murphy, 2020, pp. 5–7), and other exo-locations, such as the Mars Rovers (Carr, 2007). These endeavours in outer space represent the first steps in human space exploration. Many would agree, and many have argued

(Fishman, 2020), that these are momentous achievements in the story of humankind that represent the unique nature and ability of humans as an intelligent species, curious with their surroundings both on- and off-Earth. Those within the budding field of space archaeology have already started to study "human material culture in space", recognising its importance as a form of cultural heritage (Gorman, 2019; Gorman & Walsh, 2020, p. 1).

The significance of missions into outer space for humankind raises important questions around the preservation of sites and the recognition of their cultural and historical significance to humankind. Space related heritage sites could be split into those that are terrestrial or extra-terrestrial. Terrestrial Heritage Sites (THS), for example, could include rocket launch sites and control centres where important missions were coordinated on Earth. Extra-terrestrial Heritage Sites (ETHS) would include those places where humans have either set foot or landed scientific equipment (as displayed in Table 14.1). For example, several of NASA's premises could be of importance to human space heritage on Earth. Similarly, the landing site of the Luna 2 probe (the first human-made object to reach and impact another celestial body—Earth's Moon in 1959) could be viewed as important to Russian culture and space

Table 14.1 Categorising space heritage sites

Terrestrial Heritage Sites	Extra-Terrestrial Heritage Sites	
Specific Locations, Premises, Rooms or Sites Premises at organisations that have been influential in conducting and coordinating culturally and historically significant missions into outer space (such as, for example, NASA and the Apollo missions).	**Crewed Landings and Exploration Sites** The U.S. successfully landed six Apollo missions on the Moon between 1969 and 1972, which has led to 12 people walking on the lunar surface (Doyle, 2017). SpaceX also have plans to send humans to Mars by 2026 (Duff, 2020).	**Un-Crewed Landings and Exploration Sites** Many un-crewed missions have landed (successfully and unsuccessfully) on the Moon. The first was the Russian Luna 2 probe that crash landed on the Moon in 1959 (Matthews & McMahon 2018, p. 4).

heritage (Matthews & McMahon, 2018). Further than this, ETHS's can be split into those that involved crewed missions, and those that involved un-crewed/equipment only missions:

We suggest that space heritage is more than a single nation's history. Like cultural and natural heritage in the Convention Concerning the Protection of the World Cultural and Natural Heritage that arose from the 1972 General Conference of the United Nations Educational, Scientific and Cultural Organisation (UNESCO), we would consider "the deterioration or disappearance of any item of the space heritage constitutes a harmful impoverishment of the heritage of all the nations of the world" (World Heritage Convention, 1972). Furthermore, like cultural and natural heritage sites, space heritage sites are under increasing threat from social and economic conditions and it is the responsibility of everyone to protect these sites of outstanding interest for all of humankind (World Heritage Convention, 1972).

The challenge with ETHS's is that they exist on locations far from Earth in the global commons where objects cannot be owned or appropriated—at least according to Article 2 of the influential 1967 Outer Space Treaty (OST), which will be discussed later. Exo-locations that are contenders for space conservation are not just restricted to Earth's Moon, but include other spaces that human objects have explored, such as asteroids, planets, Moons and meteoroids. Gorman (2017, p. e63, in Lampkin, 2020) suggests various contenders for exogeoconservation:

> The planets nearest us—the Moon, Mars, and Venus—are littered with landers, rovers, probes, and craters where spacecraft have crashed on the surface. Further afield, spacecraft orbit the Sun, Saturn, and Jupiter. Others are roaming out at the edges: the Pioneers, Voyagers, and New Horizons.

Despite such an array of space exploration missions, there is currently no international law pertaining to the conservation of extra-terrestrial heritage sites. We argue that both green criminology and Earth jurisprudence provide a way forward to developing such law.

Pushing the Boundaries of "Green" Criminology

Green criminology studies crimes and harms against the environment. While there are numerous works that could be applied in the context of outer space, perhaps the two most important are White's (2008) categorising of green crimes by colours—brown, green and white—and green criminology's focus on crimes of the powerful, particularly corporations and states. "White" green crimes are particularly relevant to outer space as White (2008) conceptualised them to include challenges to new technologies that could have unforeseen consequences. Although, he was referring to genetically modified organisms or other technological innovations, the analogy to introducing new technologies and to disrupting the outer space environment are valuable. Furthermore, green criminology tries to question the power of corporations and states in causing environmental degradation, particularly in the extractive industries like oil, gas and minerals (see Ruggiero & South, 2013 among others), which is clearly relevant to many of the activities being proposed for celestial bodies. The human-centred neoliberal drive for profit underpins the destruction of the environment and numerous green criminological studies provide evidence that current human-centred legislation is inextricably intertwined in this destruction (Lampkin, 2018; Stretesky et al., 2014).

Regarding outer space and celestial bodies specifically, green criminology has remained virtually silent on issues pertaining to environmental harms associated with the space industry (whether those be on Earth in the supply chain, or actually in, outer space). Takemura (2019) produced a pioneering article calling for an astro-green criminology where, as mentioned above, he questions the rise and implications of "space capitalism". Lampkin (2021) has expanded upon this call through attempting to "map the terrain" of astro-green criminology—offering the first definition of the term, and examining key issues for astro-green criminological attention (including space mining, orbital debris, space heritage conservation, the impact of rocket launching emissions pollutions, and the various future usages of outer space). This definition suggested that astro-green criminology is: the theoretical and practical study of space-related environmental harms and crimes that are facilitated by human actions. These harms can be Earth-based, atmospheric, or extraterrestrial and may create human victims, non-human victims, and ecological victims both on Earth and in outer space (Lampkin, 2021, p. 7).

The limited amount of studies indicates the need for green criminology to engage more frequently with outer space, particularly since, as briefly mentioned here, there are lessons to be learned from previous green criminological studies and that there is a significant threat to the outer space environment from governments and multinational corporations. This chapter suggests that taking green criminology's roots in concern with technology, as well as crimes of the powerful and combining with Earth jurisprudence, could prove fruitful in preserving space heritage and the outer space environment in general.

Pushing the Boundaries of "Earth" Jurisprudence

Earth jurisprudence is a radical approach to legal systems that seeks to remake them to be Earth-centred rather than human-centred. To do so, would require completely new laws not simply adjusting the existing ones or implementing more environmental legislation. The outer space environment provides the perfect opportunity to take such a radical approach. In sum, Earth jurisprudence contains these principles (Table 14.2):

Whereas several of the principles as articulated by Cullinan talk about the *Earth community*, the first principle sets out Earth jurisprudence in the context of the *universe*. Furthermore, Swimme and Berry (1994) in *The Universe Story*, and Berry (1999) in *The Great Work*, provide the foundation for Earth jurisprudence in a framework of the cosmos and that humans are interlinked to everything on the Earth and beyond. Swimme and Berry (1994, p. 1) go so far as to suggest that "we [humanity] are somehow failing in the fundamental role that we should be fulfilling—the role of enabling the Earth and the universe to reflect

Table 14.2 Principles of earth jurisprudence. Adapted from Cullinan (2011, p. 13). See also, Lampkin and Wyatt (2019, p. 504)

Principles of Earth Jurisprudence	Description
Principle One	"The universe is the primary law-giver, not human legal systems" (Cullinan, 2011, p. 13)
Principle Two	"The Earth community and all the beings that constitute it have fundamental 'rights', including the right to exist, to habitat or a place to be, and to participate in the evolution of the Earth community" (Cullinan, 2011, p. 13)
Principle Three	"The rights of each being are limited by the rights of other beings to the extent necessary to maintain the integrity, balance and health of the communities within which it exists" (Cullinan, 2011, p. 13)
Principle Four	"Human acts or laws that infringe these fundamental rights violate the fundamental relationships and principles that constitute the Earth community ('the Great Jurisprudence') and are consequently illegitimate and 'unlawful'" (Cullinan, 2011, p. 13)
Principle Five	"Humans must adapt their legal systems, political, economic and social systems to be consistent with the Great Jurisprudence and to guide humans to live in accordance with it, which means that human governance systems at all times take account of the interests of the whole Earth community and must: determine the lawfulness of human conduct by whether or not it strengthens or weakens the relationships that constitute the Earth community; maintain a dynamic balance between the rights of humans and those of other members of the Earth community on the basis of what is best for Earth as a whole; promote restorative justice (which focuses on restoring damaged relationships) rather than punishment (retribution); recognise all members of the Earth community as subjects before the law, with the right to the protection of the law and to an effective remedy for human acts that violate their fundamental rights" (Cullinan, 2011, p. 13)

on and to celebrate themselves, and the deep mysteries they bear within them..." .

Thus, while Cullinan (2011) and others have taken to calling the Great jurisprudence that Swimme and Berry, and Berry proposed, Earth jurisprudence, the underpinnings of this perspective on jurisprudence were in the science and workings of the cosmos. Loder (2018) in her research on asteroid mining has taken this beyond an Earth-only perspective. She notes that physics, as a fundamental principle of the cosmos, connects humans to outer space and celestial bodies (Loder, 2018). At the most fundamental level then, an Earth jurisprudence inherently encompasses the universe:

> because scientific knowledge now shows the connections between Earth and the universe in terms of origins, energy, and capacities for living systems, 'Earth' jurisprudence should likewise expand to include off-Earth bodies and processes as they become increasingly subject to human intervention. (Loder, 2018, p. 278)

As of yet, however, there is very little legislation regarding space in general let alone any that incorporates an Earth jurisprudence perspective.

The Space Law Vacuum: Why is There so Little Law Pertaining to Space Heritage Sites and the Ownership of Matter in Outer Space?

The main reason for the lack of law pertaining to ETHS's surrounds the location of outer space, and the lack of appropriation of such spaces. The Moon, for example, is not owned by any nation state and therefore is not subject to the confines of any domestic legal system. This does not mean that human-made laws do not impact activity on the Moon, or indeed other exo-locations. Some domestic laws exist that influence (however minorly) activity on the Moon. For example, in 2011, the U.S. passed the *Apollo Lunar Legacy Landing Act* that attempted to preserve the Apollo Landing Sites (Hertzfeld & Pace, 2013). However, domestic law is only binding on actors operating within that nation, and who are therefore subject to those laws. As Jakhu (2006, p. 108) explains, due to a lack of sufficiently and precisely developed international law to protect and enhance global public interest in outer space, some States have started adopting national laws and policies to promote their exclusive national benefits and are thereby jeopardizing the inclusive interest of the international community.

It is international laws that carry significance where outer space is concerned, and the most momentous comes from the Outer Space Treaty of 1967. This treaty has been so influential in the domain of space law, that it has been dubbed the "constitution of outer space" (Jakhu, 2006, p. 31). We will now explore it in more detail.

A treaty was defined in the 1969 Vienna Convention as "an international agreement concluded between States in written form and governed by international law" (Aust, 2013, p. 14). The OST was a seminal treaty that signified unified international collaboration in outer space matters during the cold war era, unanimously agreed and signed by the 28 nations of the United Nations Outer Space Committee (Dembling & Arons, 1967).[1] The OST concentrated on issues that were politically relevant at the time of its formation, confirming previous fears and uncertainties proceeding World War II regarding the possible appropriation and weaponisation of outer space and celestial bodies by nation states on Earth. Article 2 of the OST, for example, identifies that "outer space including the Moon and other celestial bodies, is not subject to national appropriation by claim of sovereignty, by means of use or occupation, or by any other means" (Garber, 2006).

However, the problem with the OST is that it is a non-binding international agreement. Therefore, a nation could sign such an agreement, but the principles are not subject to enforcement. Consequently, there is no formal penalty for breaking terms within the OST, despite the fact there may be political strains and repercussions from other signatories. This is explained by Gupta and Rathore (2019, p. 78) when discussing General Assembly Resolutions (GARs) from which the OST was derived.

[1] The OST has now been signed by over 100 nations (Sivolella, 2019).

Although GARs formed the basis of space law principles, they are non-binding under international law. Non-binding denotes the fact that resolutions cannot be enforced against any state even if the state is party to the resolutions, and at times, resolutions are indefinite and unreliable.

The lack of international law and punishment pertaining to outer space leaves celestial bodies vulnerable to exploitation by nation states or powerful corporations. This is a clear example of how traditional criminal and international law could fail to protect the environment off-Earth in the very near future.

Several scholars have suggested that the OST is out-dated and no longer capable of protecting outer space environments resulting in contemporary space problems, such as the accumulation of space junk in low Earth orbit (Englehart, 2008; Muñoz-Patchen, 2018). Others have called for additional international laws or independent expert panels to provide advice and judgement on "specific matters related to outer space" which would subsequently give extensive and "pervasive value and impact on the further development of international space law" (Jakhu, 2006, p. 109). For instance, when discussing orbital space debris, Aydin (2019, p. 36) points to the "ambiguity in international treaties" that leads to their goals not being met. The fact treaties have decided that there is no ownership for defunct space debris eradicates responsibility for its removal. As such, "interested parties have proposed the adoption of voluntary 'rules of the road' to guide behaviours in space as an alternative to the long and delicate process of creating a legally binding treaty" (Aydin, 2019, p. 36). Despite such suggestions, the OST (drafted over 50 years ago) remains the most significant international law pertaining to outer space.

The OST is not, however, the only treaty to consider matters related to outer space. Others exist to address specific space issues, such as the 1971 "Convention on the International Liability for Damage Caused by Space Objects… and the (1976) Convention on Registration of Objects Launched into Outer Space" (Muñoz-Patchen, 2018, p. 243). Relating specifically to the concept of space conservation, Article 7 of the 1979 Moon Treaty suggests that "in exploring and using the Moon, States Parties shall take measures to prevent the disruption of the existing balance of its environment, whether by introducing adverse changes in that environment, by its harmful contamination through the introduction of extra-environmental matter or otherwise" (Larsen, 2006, p. 301).

The 1979 Moon Treaty, then, provides an apt example of the failure of such international law to protect extra-terrestrial environments. While Article 6 suggests that the lunar environment can be used for scientific exploration including the right for States Parties to collect and remove samples of minerals and other substances, Article 11 declares that "neither the surface nor the subsurface of the Moon, nor any part thereof or natural resources in place, shall become property of any State… national organization… or of any natural person" (De Gouyon Matignon, 2019, p. 1). This clear reference to protecting natural resources on the Moon has stood the test of time due to the logistical and financial difficulties associated with mining in outer space. However, several companies have emerged in recent years intent on mining lunar resources, such as "Planetary Resources, Inc., Deep Space Industries, Shackleton Energy and Moon Express" (Takemura, 2019, p. 8) which are in clear contravention of Article 11 of the 1979 Moon Treaty. Due to the restrictive nature of the Moon Treaty regarding private property rights, it has been described as "dead letter law" reflected by the fact only 18 countries have signed the treaty (compared to over 100 for the OST), none of which are "space-facing" nations (Sivolella, 2019, pp. 175–176). Therefore, Sivolella (2019) argues that the lack of signatories means the Moon Treaty, as a form of international law, is often disregarded through lack of political weight.

Despite the advancement of lunar mining in contravention of the 1979 Moon Treaty, law may still be a fruitful avenue for protecting celestial environments. The concept of Earth jurisprudence, combined with green criminology, presents a useful theoretical framework for thinking about the protection of natural environments within the wider cosmos.

Earth Jurisprudence and Green Criminology as a Solution to Protecting ETHS's

As indicated above, Earth jurisprudence is perhaps too narrow a term to describe a legal perspective that considers the whole universe. As a result, other scholars have proposed alternative titles that identify the extension of the perspective of law outside of planet Earth. *Space Jurisprudence*, for example, has been applied to legal issues in outer space (Loder, 2018). The long-established notion of *General*, or *Universal* jurisprudence, refers to "ends of law as are common to all systems, and... between systems" (Taylor, 1909, p. 247) which could easily be applied to natural bodies and systems occurring off-Earth.

Despite its narrow title, the perspective of Earth jurisprudence is still incredibly useful for considering off-Earth environmental issues. This is because Earth jurisprudence recognises the importance of everything in the cosmos originating from the same foundation. When discussing the concept of relational responsibility (one of Berry's founding principles), Koons (2011, p. 47) suggests that "each particle has been related to every other particle in the universe" since the beginning (the Big Bang). This is important when thinking about the application of Earth jurisprudence beyond planet Earth because it suggests that:

> everything in the universe is deemed to be related and, consequently, the moral worth of all particles is the same (regardless of humanity, sentience, thoughts, feelings, and meaningful constructions). The ontological reality of everything is the same, because all matter shares the identical basic standard of being created following the big bang. (Lampkin, 2020, p. 33)

This links heavily to points made by Berry (2006, p. 109) and Greene (2011, p. 126) who—when discussing whether nature has rights—suggest that such rights are derived from, and determined by, existence. In essence, because nature exists, an Earth jurisprudence proposes that it has rights and therefore should be respected, considered, and protected in (and from) human endeavours that may impact upon it. Ultimately, "rights originate where existence originates. That which determines existence, determines rights" (Berry, 2006, p. 149). This notion can be applied to off-Earth locales too. The mere fact the planet Mars exists in our solar system gives it intrinsic value (under Earth jurisprudence) because it exists as a result of the Big Bang, the same event that created matter on planet Earth. As a result, Earth jurisprudence could evidently be used to underpin the legal mechanism to protect ETHS's (and indeed extra-terrestrial locations, generally) from future anthropogenic harm. But how could such sites potentially be exposed to such harm? We will use the Apollo 11 lunar landing site as an example.

In 1969, Apollo 11 successfully landed in the Sea of Tranquillity, located in the North East of the Moon's near side (facing the Earth). This represented the first time humans had travelled from Earth, to another celestial body, and set foot on its surface. The Moon is roughly one sixth the size of planet Earth,[2] meaning there is less "lunar land" available to explore. As a result, other human missions could potentially contaminate the site of the Apollo 11 mission. As of September 2019, Spennemann and Murphy (2020, pp. 5–7) record that 89 anthropogenic events have impacted the Moon via landings and crash landings. These include landers, rovers, impactors, orbiters and sample return missions from several different countries since the USSR's seminal Lunar 2 mission that landed on the Moon in September of 1959 (Spennemann & Murphy, 2020). Many more missions are planned for the future, which could have a detrimental impact upon historically significant sites on the lunar surface. Currently there is nothing in place to protect such sites from a legal perspective, due to the location of the Moon, and its independent status.

Utilising the concept of Earth Jurisprudence, and perhaps recognising this via new universe-centred international law, could help to protect significant ETHS's on the Moon. The very existence of the Moon, under Earth jurisprudence, would guarantee its protection, as it would constitute part of Berry's interconnected cosmology.

The lessons from green criminology are that current legislative frameworks that govern new technologies and the extractive industries fail to protect both the environment and heritage. We mentioned White's

[2] At approximately 37,936,694.79 km2 (NASA, no date), the Moon's surface area is very slightly smaller than the continent of Asia.

(2008) analysis of "white" green crimes from new technologies as posing harm and then just one study by Ruggiero and South (2013) of the many that document corporate interests are prioritised over the environment. Green criminology studies like this evidence the need for an Earth or universe jurisprudence that departs from anthropocentric legal traditions to truly recognise humans' place in the cosmos and restrict our destructive behaviour.

Problems Surrounding the Implementation of Earth Jurisprudence in the Protection of ETHS's

Despite the prospective usefulness of Earth jurisprudence as a mechanism for protecting ETHS's, several obstacles exist in implementing such an approach in practice. Firstly, Earth jurisprudence still suffers from the same flaws as international law in that (in practice), it is essentially abstract, informal and imperatively, non-binding. The premise of Earth jurisprudence is that it represents a form of natural law (Greene, 2011), beyond that created by humans. The philosophical underpinning of Earth jurisprudence suggests that the natural laws of the universe exist and human interactions with the natural world should be such that they do not impact the ability of such natural systems and processes to continue to flourish.

Despite the existence of Earth jurisprudence as a perspective, humans have clearly had a significant impact upon the Earth's natural systems through deforestation, ocean acidification, global warming, and through various pollutions that disturb or extinguish life on Earth (White, 2020). There is, therefore, no reason to suggest that the same will not happen in outer space, on other celestial bodies. In fact, the lack of a human presence, and the hidden existence of exo-environmental harm out of view of most humans, may make it easier to conduct environmentally destructive practices in other areas of the universe—creating a *dark figure* of exo-environmental harm. While this may seem abstract and subjective, such behaviour may occur in the near future. As mentioned, in recent years, several companies have become interested in the possibility of mining extra-terrestrial environments, such as the Moon, Mars, asteroids and meteoroids (Sivolella, 2019; Takemura, 2019). Such practices could severely degrade space environments that have remained untouched for billions of years.

This is not to say that pursuing Earth jurisprudence is a futile endeavour. There are several success stories where the principles of Earth jurisprudence have been successfully implemented into legal systems in different parts of the world (Lampkin, 2020). The most notable and frequently cited examples include the legal personhood prescribed to the Whanganui River in New Zealand in 2011 (Hsiao, 2012), the rights of Pacha Mama (Mother Earth) inscribed into the Ecuadorian constitution in 2008 (Espinosa, 2019), and the rights of nature enacted in Bolivian legislation in 2012 (Calzadilla & Kotzé, 2018). Despite these high-profile examples, environmental harms (such as deforestation) are still prevalent in these areas, particularly in South America, suggesting that legal systems still fail to prevent environmental harm, even when Earth jurisprudence is promoted and enshrined in law. Therefore, it is reasonable to suggest that the promotion of Earth jurisprudential principles to guard activities in the global commons will not result in the absolute prevention of destructive human activity in such areas. However, scientific and human interest in celestial bodies may be enough to force states and companies to refrain from engaging in harmful behaviours as they are unappropriated areas outside of a countries' national jurisdiction. Therefore, enshrining principles of Earth jurisprudence into outer space law (domestic, international, or otherwise) could provide more certainty around what humans can and cannot do in outer space in the best interests of such environments.

Jakhu (2006, 109) provides a potential solution to this problem through advocating for an independent expert tribunal to judge on matters pertaining to outer space law: an independent international space law tribunal or panel—which may be designated as the International Commission of Space Jurists, or ICSJ—should be established with the mandate to express its opinions on specific matters referred to it by any national or international public or private entity. The proposed tribunal could be created on the same model as the "International Commission of Jurists" or any other similar international independent panel of legal experts. The opinions of such a tribunal would be available for use by the States members of the Legal Subcommittee of the COPUOS and thus will have extensive persuasive value and impact on the further development of international space law.

While Jakhu (2006) does not specifically identify who classifies as a legal expert, the inclusion of Earth jurisprudence scholars and astro-green criminologists into such a panel could result in the implementation of such concepts into international legal mechanisms concerning the formulation of international space law.

Conclusion

The purpose of this chapter was two-fold. Firstly, we have demonstrated why Green criminologists and Earth jurisprudence scholars should widen their horizons to include issues relating to environmental degradation in outer space. Originally, both disciplines have confined their arguments to issues on planet Earth alone and have failed to consider extra-terrestrial environments. Secondly, a further aim of this chapter was to demonstrate how the principles of Earth jurisprudence could be utilised as a mechanism for protecting extra-terrestrial environments, and extra-terrestrial heritage sites on celestial bodies and how green criminology evidences the need for such protections.

Ultimately, there is no human-made law that protects extra-terrestrial locales from anthropogenic destruction. We suggested that principles of Earth jurisprudence could be utilised, through the implementation of international law designed with Earth jurisprudence principles at the heart—to protect celestial bodies—and important human interactions with them (such as the quintessential Apollo 11 lunar landing mission). Additionally, green criminological research highlights the importance of challenging corporate behaviour and keeping an eye on new technologies that could prove harmful. Such universe-centred international law would be beneficial not just for extra-terrestrial environments, but also for the countries that wish to preserve culturally and historically significant exo-sites. As Hertzfeld and Pace (2013, p. 1049) propose, "all… nations… have much to gain and little or nothing to lose from a multinational agreement based on mutual respect and mutual protection of each other's historical sites and equipment".

As human and corporate interest in space exploration continue to increase and more missions send humans and spacecraft to explore celestial bodies in the solar system, so to the chances increase of destruction to such environments, and contamination of ETHS's. While the influential OST of 1967 did much to unite nations in collaborating in space activities in the politically turbulent Cold War Era, it did not set out to preserve space environments or ETHS's specifically. An international exo-environmental law embedding principles of Earth jurisprudence would go some way to addressing this absence, and thus protecting such places. To take from Loder (2018, p. 317) "it is time to expand our ethical framework, not leaving Earth behind, but preventing humanity from transporting planetary damage throughout the universe."

References

Aust, A. (2013). *Modern Treaty Law and Practice* (3rd ed.). Cambridge, UK: Cambridge University Press.

Aydin, L. (2019). *Geopolitics of Outer Space: Global Security and Development*. Westphalia Press.

Berry, T. (1999). *The Great Work: Our Way Into the Future*. Three Rivers Press.

Berry, T. (2006). *Evening Thoughts: Reflecting on Earth as a Sacred Community*. Sierra Club Books.

Calzadilla, P. V., & Kotzé, L. J. (2018). Living in Harmony with Nature? A Critical Appraisal of the Rights of Mother Earth in Bolivia. *Transnational Environmental Law, 7*(3), 397–424.

Carr, M. H. (2007). *The Surface of Mars*. Cambridge University Press.

Compton, W. D. (1989). *Where No Man Has Gone Before: A History of Apollo Lunar Exploration Missions*. The NASA History Series.

Cooper, C. (2011). *NASA Scientist: Evidence of Alien Life on Meteorite, CBS News*. Available at: http://www.cbsnews.com/news/nasa-scientist-evidence-of-alien-life-on-meteorite. Accessed 11 Jan 2021.

Cullinan, C. (2011). "A History of Wild Law." In: Burdon, P. (Ed), *Exploring Wild Law: The Philosophy of Earth Jurisprudence*. Mile End: Wakefield Press.

De Gouyon Matignon, L. (2019). *The 1979 Moon Agreement*. [Online]. Available at: https://www.spacelegalissues.com/the-1979-moon-agreement/. Accessed 12 Jan 2021.

Dembling, P. G., & Arons, D. M. (1967). The Evolution of the Outer Space Treaty. *Journal of Air Law and Commerce, 33*, 419–456.

Doyle, P. (2017). The Apollo Missions and Moon Rocks, 1969–1972. *Geology Today, 33*(4), 142–147.

Englehart, A. B. (2008). Common Ground in the Sky: Extending the 1967 Outer Space Treaty to Reconcile US and Chinese Security Interests. *Washington International Law Journal, 17*(1), 133–156.

Espinosa, C. (2019). Interpretive Infinities: The Constitutionalization of Rights of Nature, Pacha Mama, in Ecuador. *Journal of Environmental Policy & Planning, 21*(5), 608–622.

Fishman, C. (2020). *One Giant Leap: The Impossible Mission That Flew Us to the Moon*. Simon & Schuster Paperbacks.

Garber, S.J. (2006). *Outer Space Treaty of 1967*. Produced for: NASA. [Online]. Available at: https://history.nasa.gov/1967treaty.html. Accessed 31 Dec 2020.

Gorman, A., & Walsh, J.S.P. (2020). "Archaeology in a Vacuum: Obstacles to and Solutions for Developing a Real Space Archaeology." In: Barnard, H. and Boytner, R. (Eds.), *Archaeology Out-of-the-Box*. Los Angeles: Cotsen Institute of Archaeology Press.

Gorman, A. (2019). *Dr Space Junk vs the Universe: Archaeology and the Future*. The MIT Press.

Gorman, A. (2017). Comet Quest. *Anthropology News, 58*(1), e63–e70.

Greene, H.F. (2011). "Cosmology and Earth Jurisprudence." In Burdon, P.D. (Ed.), *Exploring Wild Law: The Philosophy of Earth Jurisprudence*. Mile End, Australia: Wakefield Press.

Gupta, B. & Rathore, E. (2019). United Nations General Assembly Resolutions in the Formation of the Outer Space Treaty of 1967. *Astropolitics: The International Journal of Space Politics & Policy*, 17(2), 77–88.

Hertzfeld, H. R., & Pace, S. N. (2013). Space Law: International Cooperation on Human Lunar Heritage. *Science, 342*, 1049–1050.

Hsiao, E. C. (2012). Whanganui River Agreement. *Environmental Policy and Law, 42*(6), 371–375.
Intergovernmental Science-Policy Platform on Biodiversity and Ecosystem Services. (2019). *IPBES Global Assessment Summary for Policymakers*. Available at: https://www.ipbes.net/sites/default/files/downloads/summary_for_policymakers_ipbes_global_assessment.pdf. Accessed 7 May 2019.
Jakhu, R. (2006). Legal Issues Relating to the Global Public Interest in Outer Space. *Journal of Space Law, 32*, 31–110.
Lampkin, J.A. (2021). Mapping the Terrain of an Astro-Green Criminology: A Case for Extending the Green Criminological Lens Outside of Planet Earth. *Astropolitics: The International Journal of Space Politics & Policy*, 18(3), accepted/ in press.
Lampkin, J. A. (2020). *Uniting Green Criminology and Earth Jurisprudence*. Routledge.
Lampkin, J. A., & Wyatt, T. (2019). Utilising Principles of Earth Jurisprudence to Prevent Environmental Harm: Applying a Case Study of Unconventional Hydraulic Fracturing for Shale Gas in the United Kingdom. *Critical Criminology, 28*, 1–16.
Lampkin, J. A. (2018). *Will Unconventional, Horizontal, Hydraulic Fracturing for Shale Gas Production Purposes Create Environmental Harm in the United Kingdom?* PhD Thesis. University of Lincoln. [Online]. Available at: http://eprints.lincoln.ac.uk/id/eprint/35711/1/Jack%20Lampkin%20PhD%20Thesis.pdf. Accessed 12 Jan 2021.
Larsen, P. B. (2006). Application of the Precautionary Principle to the Moon. *Journal of Air Law and Commerce, 71*(2), 295–306.
Lewis, J. (2015). *Asteroid Mining 101: Wealth for the New Space Economy*. Moffett, CA: Deep Space Industries.
Loder, R. E. (2018). Asteroid Mining: Ecological Jurisprudence Beyond Earth. *Virginia Environmental Law Journal, 36*(3), 275–317.
Matthews, J. J., & McMahon, S. (2018). Exogeoconservation: Protecting Geological Heritage on Celestial Bodies. *Acta Astronautica, 149*, 55–60.
Muñoz-Patchen, C. (2018). 'Regulating the Space Commons: Treating Space Debris as Abandoned Property in Violation of the Outer Space Treaty. *Chicago Journal of International Law, 19*, 233–259.
National Aeronautics and Space Administration (no date) *Earth's Moon*. [Online]. Available at: https://solarsystem.nasa.gov/moons/earths-moon/by-the-numbers/. Accessed 4 Jan 2021.
Neal, C. R. (2009). The Moon 35 Years After Apollo: What's Left to Learn? *Geochemistry, 69*(1), 3–43.

O'Callaghan, J. (2020). *Amazon is going to add 3,000 more satellites into Earth's orbit - and people are not happy.* Forbes. Available at: https://www.forbes.com/sites/jonathanocallaghan/2020/07/31/amazon-is-going-to-add-3000-more-satellites-into-earths-orbit--and-people-are-not-happy/. Accessed 11 Jan 2021.

Ruggiero, V., & South, N. (2013). Toxic State-Corporate Crimes, Neo-Liberalism and Green Criminology: The Hazards and Legacies of the Oil, Chemical and Mineral Industries. *International Journal for Crime, Justice and Social Democracy, 2*(2), 12–26.

Schildknecht, T. (2007). Optical Surveys for Space Debris. *The Astronomy and Astrophysics Review, 14*(1), 41–111.

Sivolella, D. (2019). *Space Mining and Manufacturing: Off-World Resources and Revolutionary Engineering Techniques*. Springer Praxis Publishing.

Spennemann, D.H.R., & Murphy, G. (2020). *Returning to the Moon: Heritage Issues Raised by the Google Lunar X Prize.* [Online]. Available at: https://researchoutput.csu.edu.au/en/publications/returning-to-the-moon-heritage-issues-raised-by-the-google-lunar-Prize.pdf. Accessed 15 Dec 2020.

Stretesky, P. B., Long, M. A., & Lynch, M. J. (2014). *The Treadmill of Crime: Political Economy and Green Criminology*. Routledge.

Swimme, B., & Berry, T. (1994). *The Universe Story: From the Primordial Flaring Forth to the Ecozoic Era – A Celebration of the Unfolding of the Cosmos.* United States: Harper Collins.

Takemura, N. (2019). Astro-Green Criminology: A New Perspective Against Space Capitalism Outer Space Mining may make the Same Mistakes in Space as we have on Earth. *Toin University of Yokohama Research Bulletin, 40*, 7–17.

Taylor, H. (1909). The Science of Jurisprudence. *Harvard Law Review, 22*(4), 241–249.

White, R. (2020). *Climate Change Criminology*. Bristol University Press.

White, R. (2008). *Crimes Against Nature: Environmental Criminology and Ecological Justice*. Cullompton, UK: Willan.

Wilson, E. O. (2016). *Half Earth: Our Planet's Fight for Life*. Liveright Publishing.

World Heritage Convention. (1972). *Convention Concerning the Protection of the World Cultural and Natural Heritage*. Available at: https://whc.unesco.org/?cid=175. Accessed 13 Jan 2021.

15

Red, White and Green: White Paper Assimilation Strategies in an Era of Environmental Crisis

Shawn Singh

Introduction

The Canadian federal government has fallen short of its reconciliatory objectives with Indigenous peoples[1] and of preventing anthropogenic climate change. In recognizing these issues, the Government of Canada implemented several policy initiatives to realign the industrial production and consumption, as well as to grow Indigenous participation in capitalist production as a means of approaching a form of self-government. The *Pan Canadian Framework on Clean Growth and Climate Change* (PCF) introduced a suite of measures to encourage consumers to

[1] I recognize the definitional distinctions between 'Indigenous' and 'Aboriginal', and use the terms as appropriately warranted within their given contexts.

S. Singh (✉)
University of Manitoba, Winnipeg, MB, Canada
e-mail: umsin248@myumanitoba.ca

J. Gacek and R. Jochelson (eds.), *Green Criminology and the Law*, Palgrave Studies in Green Criminology,
https://doi.org/10.1007/978-3-030-82412-9_15

reduce emissions of atmospherically harmful greenhouse gas (GHG) by putting a price on the carbon consumed in the production process (Environment and Climate Change Canada [ECCC], 2016a). The collected capital will be invested in the development of more sustainable consumption practices for the future. (ECCC, 2016a). As part of this policy agenda, the state targets Indigenous communities as leaders who hold the potential to implement more sustainable methods of energy production and becoming Canada's environmental stewards.

Although international environmental science organizations like the Intergovernmental Panel on Climate Change (IPCC) call for much stronger state intervention in natural resource consumption and the production of energy and derivative products, the PCF instead acts to modify existing production systems to limit the *growth* of non-renewable resource consumption by encouraging an increased use of renewable energy sources like solar and wind power (IPCC, 2013, 2018). In other words, the PCF maintains our current structures of natural resource consumption but provides new ways of opening untapped land bases to support the state's growth objectives related to the capitalist treadmill of production (Buttel, 2004; ECCC, 2016a; Schnaiberg et al., 2004). While global governments and industrial proponents herald the PCF as a meaningful approach to addressing our unsustainable consumption practices, other advocates are critical of the substantive effect of these policies in terms of meeting the dire recommendations of environmental scientists (Climate Analytics & new Climate Institute, 2020; Bein, 2020). They highlight that Canada's GHG reduction targets are woefully insufficient to limit the extent of global warming to the necessary 1.5 degrees above pre-industrial emission levels (Council of the European Union, 2015; Parker, 2017).

The imperative nature of climate change and the inadequacy of policies like the PCF raise several questions about the Canadian state's ability to achieve sustainability in natural resource extraction in ways that further its reconciliatory objectives with Indigenous peoples. Stakeholders note the PCF's insufficiency in terms of meeting its environmental objectives, but discussion of its effects towards opening Indigenous spaces for economic production is notably absent. The purpose of this chapter is to address this gap in the literature by offering a critical analysis of the federal government's dispersive approach to opening Indigenous territories for capitalist production to further its perennial objectives of achieving economic growth at the expense of environmental sustainability. To articulate the impact of these policies on the historical interests of Indigenous communities, I consider the environmental agenda of the Canadian state through the lens of neoliberal settler-colonialism to identify its striking consistency with past approaches of dislocating colonized populations and reclaiming power bases that are still within settler state control or influence. As a traditional state strategy that continues in contemporary governance, I review the Canadian settler state's modern approaches to erasing its obligations to Indigenous peoples—first by proposing the elimination of *Indian Act*, the jurisprudential interpretations of s.35 of the *Constitution* Act, 1982 (Borrows, 2019; *Constitution* Act, 1982), and the First Nations Land Management Agreements (FNLMAs) and associated incentive programs.

Treadmill of Production

To open the discussion, I first consider how the theoretical treadmill of production and its endless consumption of resources generate energy, resources, and capital at the direct expense of local environments.

Allan Schnaiberg, Kenneth Gould and David Pellow (Schnaiberg, 1980; Schnaiberg et al., 2004) articulate how the prevalent systems that operationalize the destruction of environments to transform its natural resources into commodities and capital as the theory of the treadmill of production. Systematic additions or withdrawals to natural systems are considered as a biophysical variable, which holds potential to deplete ecosystems of their ability to support life. Schnaiberg et al. posit the growing level of investable capital and shifts in its distribution led to increased demand for commodity production, which subsequently increased demand for natural resources. Investment of capital from Western stakeholders allowed for rapid development of new technology, which progressively replaced manual labour with processes that rely on energy and chemical consumption. Reducing labour costs means higher profit margins, which incentivizes structural managerial practices that minimize labour expenses to increase investment in better productive machinery. In essence, the treadmill theory recognizes that structures of capital investment and the generation of profits inherently encourages higher demand for natural resources in order to support the desired quotient of social welfare. As the hunger for generative production increases, conditions for the environment and for workers deteriorate in direct proportion. While that is the case, the rationalization of achieving adequate profit levels to keep people working and generating enough product to meet projected consumption needs continues to persuade decision-makers that the treadmill must be accelerated to sustain our current ways of life (Foster, 1992, 1999, 2000, 2002).

The treadmill of production also articulates the growth of the economic and political power held by capitalist stakeholders, such as investors, managers and political actors. Schnaiberg et al. explain that governmental decision-makers are continuously induced to support the acceleration of production to make jobs, attract support from investor-managerial groups and maintain the quality of life that was established as a consequence of wartime prosperity. During this period, exponential environmental degradation took place in order to fuel ongoing economic expansions. Contemporary concerns regarding the pace of energy consumption and the saturation of pollution were ignored in favour of driving economic expansion. Instead, the effects of consuming and generating pollution at this rate was not adequately researched and the management of waste was downloaded to public environmental spaces like the air, land and water that we all continue to share.

While pollution is generally concentrated in public spaces, the effects of direct environmental degradation became progressively allocated to spaces inhabited by workers and others without the power to be elsewhere. The elite and white-collar workers have the means to occupy upstream spaces that were unaffected by the harms exacted by treadmill consumption practices. Some middle-class workers could also avoid exposure to environmental harm because their skills maintain systems that encourage profit growth. Alternatively, frontline workers were encouraged to live downstream or in close proximity to sources of pollution by the combined effect of their lower earning potential and the reduced property costs in marginal spaces.

Schnaiberg et al. note the separation of corporate and governmental executives from the sources of environmental harm likely influence their decision-making in terms of extracting natural resources and destroying local ecosystems. They explain that, at the time the treadmill theory was introduced, decision-makers were dedicated to accelerating the pace of production as a response to declining productivity rates that emerged in the post-war period. Schnaiberg et al. identify a discursive shift at that time, which demanded higher productivity levels from workers. At the same time, such discourses also revealed the economic, social and political motivations that encouraged Western states to relocate global production processes to maintain their customary profit expectations.

To achieve the long-term maintenance of profit growth, executive leaders relocated sites of production from Western nations and into the Global South. Michael Lynch and Paul Stretesky (2018) indicate how working conditions in southern nations allow managers to reduce the cost of labour beyond Western minimum wage thresholds and underdeveloped institutional oversight allowed for virtually unlimited access to environmental resources. Workers were often not unionized and regional leaders were eager to access the commodified wealth that proliferated in the Western world. Relocation to southern jurisdictions allowed for rapid deployment and acceleration of treadmill operations, but the structural distribution of its benefits reflected the stratified social structures that emerged in the global north. Southern prosperity amounted to marginal improvements in domestic living conditions, exponential depletion of environmental resources, and drastic increases in ecological contamination. As Lynch and Stretesky contend, southern locals continue to resist capitalistic mentalities, which often results in social conflict and state efforts to eradicate such resistance.

In similar logic to relocating the harms of production to southern nations, decision-makers acted to transfer environmental harms to previously inaccessible domestic spaces, such as lands held by Indigenous peoples. While decisions were being made to export treadmill operations to southern nations, action was also being taken to move domestic harms away from metropolitan regions and into remote areas with marginalized people that could become workers. As nations built on a history of settler colonial expansion across the territories traditionally inhabited by Indigenous peoples by unilateral fiat, policies were introduced to open these spaces for productive consumption. The Canadian approach to operationalizing these objectives was articulated in the Trudeau federal Liberal government's White Paper of 1969, but could not be unilaterally imposed because of historical obligations undertaken by the Crown in the Royal Proclamation of 1763. Because Indigenous peoples benefit from a special relationship with the federal Crown, new strategies were deployed to manufacture its consensual elimination by Indigenous leaders. The objectives, factors and outcomes that compose Canada's settler-colonial history are complex. To adequately articulate the connection of this history to the treadmill of production and contemporary attempts to open Indigenous jurisdictions for capitalization, we now turn to consider the concept of settler colonialism and the theory of neoliberalism.

Settler Colonial Canada

What is now known as "Canada" was first settled by British colonizers under the authority of the Royal Proclamation 1763, but the document explicitly recognized Aboriginal title over all North American lands until ceded to the Crown by way of treaty. The Crown was the only entity that could purchase lands from First Nations, who could then allocate the space to settlers. Although the document defined processes for dealing with land claims, John Borrows (1997) explains that the Royal Proclamation was crafted unilaterally by British colonists without Aboriginal input. By establishing the guidelines for British dominion over North American lands in this way, it laid the groundwork for the Crown's monopoly over lands historically inhabited by Indigenous peoples.

Despite these legalistic guarantees, European dominion over North America continued with the intention of assuming complete control over the jurisdiction. Bonita Lawrence (2003) explains that several Canadian policies were introduced to remove Indigenous impediments to the expansion of colonial operations. The hallmark legislation of the Canadian state's Indigenous management policy is the Indian Act (1985), which continues to operationalize the federal state's highly invasive and paternalistic approach to Indigenous relations. The *Act* codified Canada's unilateral authority over every aspect of Indigenous life, such as defining Indian status, decision-making processes of Indian bands, the allocation of reserved lands, and even the permissibility of Indigenous cultural traditions (s.141). The *Indian Act* allowed the state to make all Aboriginal peoples legal wards of the state. From the start, Aboriginal peoples resisted their legalistic oppression by advocating for meaningful participation in defining their rights in law and against the criminalization of their cultural practices. Rather than meet their requests, the state amended the *Indian Act* to outlaw the hiring of lawyers and legal counsel by Indians. While their voices remained unheard, communities maintained resistance by continuing to practise their culture in underground locales. In response, these colonial policies were expanded to the extent that virtually any gathering of Indigenous peoples amounted to an offence worthy of imprisonment. The effects of settler-colonial criminalization continue today in Canadian criminal justice systems, where Indigenous peoples are disproportionately represented in virtually every aspect of criminal justice (AJI, 2001).

The *Indian Act* authorized the state's draconian efforts to eliminate all aspects of Indigeneity in Canada until the post-war period. As Western executives committed to the *United Nations' Universal Declaration of Human Rights*, federal decision-makers amended the *Indian Act* in 1951 to remove its most oppressive provisions. The Royal Commission of Aboriginal Peoples described these changes as a return to the original *Indian Act* of 1876 (RCAP, 1996). In essence, the international equality movement encouraged the federal government to recast the legal identity of First Nations from incapable wards of the state into populations that can be saved through assimilation into the socio-economic ethos of the broader nation.

The assimilation practices of the time culminated with the state's declared intent to abolish the *Indian Act* and progressively eliminate the Department of Indian Affairs. Prime Minister Pierre Trudeau proposed

"The White Paper", which called for the end of Crown's special legal relationship with Aboriginal peoples (Canada, Department of Indian and Northern Affairs, 1969). The government's expressed intention was to achieve equality for all Canadians by eliminating "Indian" as a distinct legal status. In other words, *Indian Act* policies were considered discriminatory because it created legal processes that could only be accessed by Aboriginal peoples. By removing their special status, the White Paper argued that Indigenous peoples would be free to redevelop their cultures on the same legal, social and economic grounds as other Canadians. Rather than creating pathways to include Indigenous perspectives in the development of governance and policy, Sally Weaver (1981) highlights the White Paper's latent objective of converting reserve lands into private property that could be sold by community leaders that were elected using *Indian Act* processes. Transforming territorial rights into property rights could allow communities to become economic participants and the state was ready to provide limited funding support to help them assimilate into the economic order. In other words, White Paper policies would allow the state to enter protected Indigenous spaces while maintaining limits on their ability to hold settlers accountable by law.

The White Paper policy agenda was informed by the research of Harry Hawthorn (1967), who investigated the socio-economic condition of Indigenous peoples in Canada. Hawthorn concluded that Aboriginal peoples were Canada's most marginalized populations. He attributed their circumstances to historical state failures which left Indigenous peoples unprepared as economic participants. Hawthorn recommended the implementation of Aboriginal-specific programming and resources to allow Indigenous communities to choose their own lifestyles, whether within reserve communities or elsewhere. He encouraged the removal of all forced assimilation programs, especially residential schools. Based on these recommendations, Jean Chrétien, Minister of Indian and Northern Affairs Canada (INAC) in Pierre Trudeau's government, engaged a national consultation program with local First Nations communities, at home and in Ottawa. Indigenous leaders expressed united concerns about the status of Aboriginal and treaty rights, the processes and contents of title to land, the legal recognition of a right to self-determination and ongoing access to education and health care systems. While these concerns were expressed, Minister Chrétien ignored them outright.

The White Paper's sweeping failure to recognize the historical grievances between Indigenous peoples and the state immediately galvanized First Nations into political action. In essence, White Paper policies were received by Indigenous peoples as the culmination of Canada's genocidal desire to assimilate Indigenous peoples into mainstream society. Harold Cardinal (1999), Cree leader of the Indian Association of Alberta, described White Paper policies as "a thinly disguised programme of extermination through assimilation" that he viewed as a form of cultural genocide. Cardinal (1970) rejected the White Paper on behalf of The Indian Association of Alberta in *Citizens Plus*, which became popularly known as the "Red Paper". Cardinal's position was quickly adopted as the Indigenous response to the state's proposal. Prior to Cardinal's rejection of the White Paper, other Aboriginal leaders like Rose Charlie, Philip Paul and Don Moses brought Western First Nations to develop their own rejection of White Paper policies in a document known as the "Brown Paper". The socio-political momentum of the united Indigenous peoples of Canada could not be ignored. The mobilization of Canadian Indigenous communities signalled the beginning of a political revolution in terms of Aboriginal rights and entitlement recognition through jurisprudential interpretation of s.35 of the *Constitution* Act, 1982. Constitutional recognition of Aboriginal rights was a monumental achievement in terms of protecting Indigenous entitlements in Canada, but closer analysis of juridical interpretations of s.35 reveals the ongoing erosion of these rights through Canada's courts. To articulate the neoliberal shift in recognizing Indigenous rights and entitlements, I now consider the constitutionalization of Aboriginal rights under s.35, as well as its jurisprudential interpretation by the Supreme Court of Canada (SCC).

Affirmation and Erosion of Aboriginal Rights

The socio-political momentum of the Indigenous movement in Canada played an important role in recognizing and affirming Aboriginal rights as part of patriating the Constitution from British Parliament. Patriation was achieved through the UK's *Canada* Act, 1982 and was subsequently confirmed with the passage of the *Constitution* Act, 1982 in Canada, which includes the *Charter of Rights and Freedoms* in Part I, recognition and affirmation of existing aboriginal and treaty rights in Part II, and several other substantive parts. Separation of Aboriginal rights from Part I ensured that federal governments could not override them in the same fashion as *Charter* rights.

The powerful political capacity that Indigenous leaders accrued in response to the White Paper allowed for a strong Indigenous presence during these negotiations. Michael Asch (1984) explains that Aboriginal rights were not included in initial drafts, but Indigenous demonstrations and campaigns persuaded lawmakers to constitutionally recognize Aboriginal rights. Indigenous peoples were suspicious of the Trudeau government as a result of the White Paper and believed that repatriation was just another avenue of completing the assimilationist vision of the Canadian settler state. Advocates like the *Constitution Express* worked diligently over two years to persuade international and domestic audiences before the Canadian government agreed to include s.35 in the repatriated constitution and accept some of their proposed amendments.

Section 35 recognizes and affirms that Aboriginal rights existed prior to the *Constitution* Act, 1982, but does not create these rights or establishes their contents. Rather, legal validation of Aboriginal title activates the legal recognition of the community's cultural, social, economic and political rights. These entitlements can include the right to land, to make use of land resources for sustenance, to practice culture and to establish land use agreements (Asch, 1984; Foster, 1999; McHugh, 2016). The content of s.35 came to be defined under SCC jurisprudence in *R v Calder*.[2] In this hallmark case, the SCC recognized that Aboriginal title to land existed, but remained split on the issue of whether Aboriginal title

[2] [1973] SCR 313, 34 DLR (3d) 145.

continued to exist once a treaty or land use agreement was struck. The perennial existence of Aboriginal rights was confirmed in *R v Guerin*, where Aboriginal title was declared a *sui generis* right.[3] Further, recognition of these rights imposed a fiduciary duty on the federal Crown to protect the space in question to ensure that entitlements can be met for current and future generations. Dickson J confirmed that the Crown's obligations regarding Aboriginal title could only be alienated with consensual surrender of these rights to the Crown, as *per* ss. 37–41 of the *Indian Act*.[4] Surrender can also be affected by way of treaty or land claim agreement, which extinguishes the Crown's fiduciary relationship with titleholders. While that is the case, the federal Crown remains bound to honour newly agreed terms with the relevant party.

These brightlines were followed by SCC decisions that prescribed criteria that can allow Indigenous communities to establish a bonafide claim to Aboriginal title, as well as criteria that government could meet to justify state infringements on established Aboriginal entitlements. Previous decisions told us that recognition of Aboriginal title and its associated rights requires the claimant to sufficiently demonstrate their historic and traditional relationship to the disputed lands using evidence that is recognized by settler institutions. In order to meet this expectation, the SCC provided several criteria that would sufficiently demonstrate a valid entitlement claim in *R v Van der Peet*.[5] In that case, the accused was charged for selling salmon that was caught under an Indian food-fishing licence. While the Stó:lō peoples were entitled to fish for sustenance and to engage in complex trade and barter relations with other First Nations, the majority held that general trade in salmon did not fall under s.35 protection. In reaching their conclusion, the court outlined ten criteria that must be met before a practice can benefit from constitution protection under s.35. Writing critically of this decision, Russell Barsh and James Henderson (1997) contend the *Van der Peet* test can allow the Crown to extinguish Aboriginal rights in the same moment they are recognized by the courts.

[3] [1984] 2 SCR 335, [1984] SCJ No 45.

[4] *Ibid* at paras 94–95.

[5] [1996] 2 SCR 507, 137 D.L.R. (4th) 289.

In contrast to the burden imposed on Indigenous peoples to legally recognize their rights, SCC jurisprudence also established a three-part test that can justify state infringements on spaces subject to recognized Aboriginal entitlements. In *R v Sparrow*, Dickson CJC and La Forest J quashed the claimant's conviction and ordered a new trial.[6] While doing so, their judgement established a series of criteria that, if sufficiently met by government, would legally authorize the state's encroachment on recognized Aboriginal rights under the common law. The claimant was charged under s.61(1) of the *Fisheries Act* for fishing with a drift net that was longer than the permissible length under his Indian food fishing licence. Dickson CJC provided three contextual inquiries that can justify a *prima facie* infringement on s.35(1) rights, such as those claimed by Sparrow. If state-imposed limits are reasonable, do not cause undue hardship or deny the claimant of their preferred method of exercising their right, the court may validate the state's limits despite its implications on recognized rights. If the Indigenous claimant meets these criteria, the burden shifts to the state to demonstrate the legitimacy of its legislative objective, such as improving natural resource management in the area of dispute. State objectives are then balanced against the Crown's fiduciary obligations to the claimant community. In Sparrow's case, the majority found that his right to fish for sustenance fell within the scope of his recognized rights, meaning that his charges were groundless. Even though the court ruled that Sparrow was fishing within the scope of his rights, he was forced to undergo a new trial before being exonerated for his "offence".

While enshrining Aboriginal rights into Canada's constitutional framework holds positive potential in terms of reconciling the state's settler-colonial history, the jurisprudence of the SCC shows us that the objectives of the state continue to move forward under the authority of the common law. Indigenous peoples came together to effectively resist the White Paper's blatant elimination strategies, but the state simply repositioned its approach to Indigenous management into the narrow focus of Canada's courts. To describe modern state strategies of using rights to impose responsibilities on their holders before their contents

---

[6] [1990] 1 SCR 1075, 70 DLR (4th) 385.

can be activated, we now turn to the theory of neoliberalism, which welcomes the recognition of marginal groups in exchange for their demonstrated acceptance of the dominant social, economic and political orders.

Neoliberal Approaches to Rights: Recognition

The Canadian settler-colonial state reasserted sovereignty over the territories of Indigenous peoples with the patriation of its constitution and created legal processes to maintain its dislocation of their communities, reclaim desirable land bases and eradicate their ways of life. State policies sought to separate, manage and eliminate Indigenous culture by reconstructing their rights under law. After recognizing Aboriginal rights in the *Constitution* Act, 1982, the federal state lost the ability to extinguish entitlements that were not relinquished under treaty or land use agreement. P. G. McHugh (2016) clarifies that, while constitutional codification is positive for Aboriginal claimants, elevating their claims into the realm of constitutional law allowed judges to create new pathways to consider the activation and contents of s.35. The SCC used constitutional ethics to create a body of common law principles that are applied when s.35 is involved. In essence, the SCC developed a framework where constitutional rights only activate when the claimant demonstrates the necessary criteria to justify the activation of the rights in context of the case. At the same time, the state can also meet defined criteria to justify policies that encroach on the constitutionally protected rights of relevant parties. In other words, SCC jurisprudence can allow the state to legally enact policies that are contrary to Canadian constitutional rights by virtue of a principled approach based on context.

The practice of using rights to impose responsibilities on groups aspiring for enfranchisement is known as neoliberalism. In the context of settler colonialism, Elizabeth Strakosch (2015) explains that settlers make use of the law to replace colonized peoples on their land and to justify their decisions to do so. Political actors employ discourses of inclusion to draw colonized populations into the state order and contrast their "capability" against state-defined "euro-normative" criteria to determine their level of right-recognition. Neoliberal decision-makers govern through polarities of compliance—freedoms are recognized when target groups align with euro-centric definitions, meaning their rights will be upheld by the rule of law. Alternatively, totalitarian regimes are assigned to those that reject the dominant social order. The substitution of Indigenous ways of life with majoritarian mentalities is gradually naturalized using a dispersive governmental approach, where fragmented policy applications work in tandem to create conditions where the state can justify the relocation of Indigenous peoples away from desirable social spaces and into those considered averse by majority populations. In this framework, colonized populations are encouraged to assimilate because no alternatives are available to meet community necessities, like protecting their territory.

If integration is not statistically successful, the state can push colonized groups to the edges of the acceptability matrix, meaning they are subject to near-authoritarian regimes that define many aspects of their daily lives. Under neoliberal frameworks, those identified for state intervention are viewed as takers that decrease productivity and risk becoming a perpetual burden on state resources or a barrier to achieving state objectives overall. Coercive measures are reapplied by the state to crush non-compliant behaviour by restricting access to certain social spaces or state resources. To avoid these presumptions, the individual must maintain self-reliance, consistently pay their dues and ultimately remain unidentified by state actors (Strakosch, 2015, pp. 25–28).

To encourage marginalized populations to work towards state acceptability, "exceptionalist" programs are deployed to instill pro-social behaviours. Strakosch explains that desired state resources are held hostage in these programs to encourage target populations to participate in activities like joining the labour market, generating capital and opening spaces for enterprise. Programs are established for a limited time in order to encourage assimilation before they close. Failure to adopt target behaviours within the defined period allows state actors to end the incentive program, declare the target population as "incapable", and relegate participants to totalitarian regimes where their rights do not apply.

From a settler-colonial perspective, Strakosch suggests exceptionalist programs require the consensual surrender of the Crown's fiduciary duty to the titleholding community to access much-needed state resources. After a community engages the state's acceptability matrix, they forfeit their fiduciary relationship with the Crown and it cannot be restored to its original status. Rather, failure to assimilate into euro-centric neoliberal ideals allows the settler state to concentrate its authority over the claimant and reassert its authoritative dominance. The colonized are expected to conform to neoliberal state ethics before accessing program resources and continue to be disciplined into compliance through their ability to attract investment capital. Strakosch highlights how discourses of risk, statistical deviance and national insecurity are deployed to operationalize the status of the colonized as a failed enterprise, which can justify their criminalization as "unable participants in the market." New forms of provisional citizenship emerge, where benefits in the traditional context must be earned in relation to the latent hierarchies of rights-access that are reassessed each day (Strakosch, 2015, pp. 27–32).

Considering the battle to constitutionally recognize Aboriginal rights in Canada and under the common law, Strakosch's theory aptly characterizes the legal pathways that act to justify the state's progressive encroachment into Indigenous jurisdictions. Section 35 embodies the existence of Aboriginal rights, which can be affirmed and enforced if the *Calder* and *Guerin* criteria are met. Before issuing benchmarks that could validate claims to Aboriginal title, the SCC created common law processes that could allow the state to justify policies that minimize Indigenous authority over entitled lands, such as matters of natural resource management, allocation of lands and opening spaces for economic production. In addition, the SCC's rulings in *Sparrow* and *Van der Peet* provided several criteria that must be met before a bonafide claim to Aboriginal rights can be acknowledged and enforced. Rights cannot be recognized unless the defined criteria are sufficiently demonstrated in court. Even if those entitlements are acknowledged, the state may enact policies that infringe on those rights unless the claimant can demonstrate "undue hardship" in relation to the policy's effect. In other words, the state retains the opportunity to justify infringements on terms that have been imposed unilaterally by settler decision-makers.

The sum effect of these measures appears to achieve the objectives of the White Paper through fragmented means. As the settler state progressively erodes the spaces protected under s.35 and its interpretation in court, statutory mechanisms have also been put in place to encourage claimants to forfeit their rights in exchange for access to capital investment, community revitalization and pathways to greater community autonomy. To describe the modern state approach in this regard, I now turn to consider FNLMAs, the PCF and INRPs.

Modern Enclosure of Indigenous Rights in Canada

In contrast to the 1960s approach, modern assimilation methods apply discourses of reconciliation to "break away" from Canada's colonial history, but state objectives remain the same. Prime Minister Justin Trudeau expressed an intention to renew the Crown-Indigenous relationship in ways that are based on respect, cooperation, partnership and recognition of Indigenous rights (Prime Minister of Canada, 2018). This intention was codified in the *Indigenous Rights, Recognition and Implementation Framework* (IRRIF) (CIRNA, 2018a, 2018b). The IRRIF was followed by several policies that reorient the settler-state's institutional management apparatus regarding its relationship with Indigenous peoples. For example, INAC service functions were separated from "Crown-Indigenous Relations," a Ministerial working group was struck to "decolonize" Canada's laws, and a series of principles were codified regarding the Crown's future relations with Indigenous populations. The titles of these initiatives appear positive, but the substantive effects of these changes are not clear.

Hayden King and Shiri Pasternak (2018) caution against taking these platitudes at face value. Writing critically, King and Pasternak conclude that the IRRIF operationalizes a renewed suppression of Indigenous capacities to achieve self-determination. Like the White Paper, Prime Minister Trudeau developed the IRRIF after "national consultations" between the Minister of Crown-Indigenous Relations and Northern Affairs (CIRNA) and Indigenous peoples across the country. Rather than establishing pathways to substantive autonomy from the Canadian state, the IRRIF pushes Indigenous communities into a narrower model of achievable self-government that retains elements of *Indian Act* policies. King and Pasternak assert that the Crown's modern approach to Indigeneity is simply a return to discredited approaches that were already taken in Canada's settler-colonial past.

King and Pasternak found that the state's principled approach to its relationship with Indigenous peoples retains historical emphases on the supremacy of Canada's constitutional framework while significantly restricting available avenues for Indigenous self-determination. The only substantive changes that were found in the IRRIF related to adopting new inclusivity terminology into policy. As part of meeting IRRIF commitments, Bill C-69 entered into force and overhauled the environmental assessment process to separate Indigenous consultations from broader resource development approvals.[7] The National Energy Board (NEB) was separated into the Canadian Energy Regulator[8] (CER) and Impact Assessments Agency of Canada (IAAC).[9] Contrary to the Crown's inclusivity discourses, the purpose of separating the NEB is to minimize barriers to resource development projects and the effect of community consultations on achieving the state's economic objectives (Ha-Redeye, 2020). The new process completely fails to consider whether an affected Indigenous community provides meaningful and informed consent to resource extraction decisions on their territorial lands. The IAAC assumes federal responsibility for carrying out and enforcing environmental impact assessments and consultations with affected stakeholders, such as Indigenous communities.[10] The *Impact Assessment Act* also serves to concentrate executive powers to the IAAC and shorten assessment timeline expectations from 450 to 300 days. Alternatively, the CER is empowered to direct Indigenous governing

[7] *National Energy Board Act*, RSC, 1985, c N-7; *Forest Ethics Advocacy Assn v National Energy Board (2014)*, 2014 CarswellNat 4233.

[8] *Canadian Energy Regulator Act*, SC 2019, c 28 [*CERA*].

[9] *Impact Assessment Act*, SC 2019, c 28 [*IAA*].

[10] *Ibid.*, ss 1, 12.

bodies, governments, or any other holder of resource assets to enforce its directives in respect of the asset in question.[11]

King and Pasternak characterize the IRRIF as a modified reification of the settler-colonial status quo. Rather than moving towards a meaningful "nation-to-nation" relationship, these discourses veil the Crown's real intent of eroding Indigenous jurisdiction outright. In terms of policy, the IRRIF acts to entrench reserve-based administrative models of governance that reflect municipal structures. Instead of improving methods of service delivery, transparency or accountability, the IRRIF imposes a new fiscal relationship that links ten-year funding grants to performance metrics that are related to economic capacity building. Land entitlements that fall outside of *the Indian Act's* reserve designation are no longer linked to state financial support, meaning that Indigenous communities must generate own-source-revenues (OSRs) by extracting natural resources for sale from within their traditional territories (AANDC, 2015; CIRNA, 2017). King et al. note this approach is premised on training Indigenous peoples to integrate into the market economy by forfeiting their special relationship with the federal Crown in order to begin exploiting their territorial environments.

A key component of generating OSRs depends on the extraction of natural resources from lands imbued with Aboriginal title or rights. While these frameworks were implemented by Justin Trudeau's government, they build on the Harper government's *Economic Action Plan* (EAP). Anna Stanley (2016, pp. 2423–2428) highlights the role of the EAP in reconfiguring Canada's resource regulation framework to minimize Indigenous consultation requirements and expand financial business incentive regimes to aggressively promote natural resource extraction in Canada. The EAP elicited strong opposition from Indigenous communities, but its policies remain in place. Rather than address these concerns, EAP programs were allocated a broader budget in 2018. In essence, policies like the IRRIF build on the incentives created under the EAP to establish a tandem enclosure of existing Indigenous land rights and simultaneous creation of exceptionalist programs to

[11] *Ibid.*, ss 10, 93–94.

encourage the opening of Indigenous environmental spaces for capitalistic exploitation. The settler state has carefully developed policy to enclose Indigenous territories and to ensure their participation in capital production is the only way to support their communities. While incentive programs have been put in place for investor-managers and for Indigenous communities, First Nations are expected to relinquish their historical relationship with the federal Crown before their lands can be accessed for capital generation. The following section describes the First Nations Land Management Agreement program, which operationalizes these requirements and applies limited exceptionalist programs to socialize participants into pro-state economics.

Neoliberalizing Treadmill 3.0 in Canada

The first step that an entitled Aboriginal community must undertake to participate in the management of their lands is to enter a FNLMA with the federal Crown. Doing so creates new obligations between the parties and releases the Crown from its fiduciary duty to the Indigenous claimant. Shaylene Jobin and Emily Riddle (2019) describe FNLMAs as a contemporary erosion of *Indian Act* protections that facilitates the applicant's economic independence by setting the expectation that Indigenous communities will support their own members by increasing economic activity on Indigenous lands. To this end, FNLMA holders become solely liable for environmental harms that are discovered after the FNLMA Land Code takes effect, where the liability previously fell to the Crown by virtue of their stewardship under the *Indian Act*. This is a drastic shift, in that Indigenous communities exclusively dealt with the federal Crown, who remained duty bound to uphold their best interests.

FNLMAs do not consider the impact of opening lands for business in terms of traditional Indigenous legal systems and culture. Programs like FNLMAs alienate Indigenous peoples by actualizing on the logics of settler colonialism. By assuming outright ownership of Indigenous lands at the behest of the Crown, Indigenous peoples are opening themselves to the latent governance regimes of the global capitalist marketplace. Doing so also closes avenues of legislative recourse that were available under the *Indian Act*. The powers allocated under the FNLMA program are attractive because they offer greater authority over Indigenous affairs to local communities, but this authority carries a cost of developing local environments to fuel capitalistic production. Despite these concerns, Jobin & Riddle note that FNLMAs do not force communities to cede Aboriginal title or to relinquish control over their lands. Rather, they found FNLMAs to be considered a "test" before the community can assume full governmental responsibility. Jobin and Riddle suggest the broader approach to modern Crown-Indigenous relations mirrors the challenges that arose in the 1960s, where First nations were forced to defend the *Indian Act* in order to protect their rights from state erosion. While leaders like Harold Cardinal rejected the Crown's proposals at that time, it appears that the same modalities are being mobilized in the modern era. Jobin and Riddle expect FNLMAs will continue to be the primary vehicle to push a diminished form of self-governance on Indigenous communities while responsibilizing them for their own economic prosperity and associated environmental harms.

The FNLMA program clearly lays the groundwork for opening Indigenous jurisdictions for capitalistic production. In line with Canada's settler-colonial history, the federal state constructed a series of conditions where Indigenous peoples cannot access community revitalization resources outside of the *Indian Act*. While this legislation is a living artefact of Canada's colonial history, it also acts as the protective authority that prevents the capitalistic expropriation of Indigenous spaces. Although strong social resistance from Indigenous leaders prevented the Canadian state's manifest efforts to eliminate its special relationship with Aboriginal peoples in the past, modern approaches compartmentalize aspects of the *Indian Act* into programs that must be accepted by Indigenous communities. Failure to do so may result in state infringements that progressively reclaim territorial spaces under SCC jurisprudence. While the state is actively removing alternatives to relinquishing the Crown's fiduciary relationship with Indigenous peoples, exceptionalist programs have also been implemented to encourage them to do so willingly.

In contrast to the patently colonial governmental approach of Stephen Harper's federal Conservative government, Justin Trudeau's federal

Liberal government utilized inclusivity discourses to encourage Indigenous populations to adopt capitalistic mentalities as part of its efforts to assimilate them into the state ethos. Strakosch contends neoliberal executives deploy exceptionalist programs to incentivize the shift of marginalized populations into accepting dominant economic mentalities and the greater influence of international flows of investable capital. In line with this theory, the Canadian settler-colonial state rolled out a series of programs to attract Indigenous leaders that want community autonomy and prosperity. FNLMAs allow them to exploit their territorial environments in order to access international capital investments, facilitate business enterprise on reserve and become masters of their own destiny, at least within the constitutional supremacy of the Canadian settler state.

FNLMAs are the primary vehicle for achieving the responsibilization of Indigenous communities and allows them to access to other exceptionalist programs that work together to entice their pro-social economic participation. For example, the federal PCF contains such programs to encourage Aboriginal participation in the green transition. The PCF designates Indigenous peoples as leaders in the transition to a low-carbon economy. Indigenous peoples are framed as key players in adopting and innovating new technologies that can defeat the threat of near-certain climatic catastrophe (ECCC, 2016b, pp. 37–44, 47). As partners with industry and government, the settler-state claims that Indigenous peoples hold the potential that is necessary to develop the science and evidence to advance clean growth and address climate change (ECCC, 2016a, p. 26). In a similar approach, the Crown also implemented the Indigenous Natural Resource Partnership program, which intends to grow Indigenous capitalization of business opportunities, facilitation of capital access, and to support community engagement related to oil and gas infrastructure projects. NRCan expressed an intent to partner Indigenous businesspeople with economic leaders in energy governance to develop new industrial best practices and to work with communities to encourage outright ownership of traditional and clean energy projects (NRCan, 2018, pp. 27–33, 46–50; NRCan, 2020).

Considering the settler-state's exceptionalist programs together, the PCF clearly creates conditions where the treadmill of production can enter Indigenous communities to generate renewable energy and extract natural resources. FNLMA holders can access PCF and INRP programs to begin transforming territorial environments into capital. In doing so, they assume full responsibility from the federal Crown for any environmental harms that take place. Further, global capitalists and governmental executives are free to negotiate with FNLMA holders directly. By placing self-governance powers beyond the scope of currently held Indigenous rights, the Crown is working to manufacture Indigenous consent to the expropriation of Indigenous lands under FNLMAs to accelerate of the treadmill of production once more. Since the post-war era began, expanded access to natural resources continues to drive economic growth in Canada in ways never thought possible. Globalization carried beneficial effects in terms of economic growth for some time, but accessible environments have been continuously depleted to support accelerated treadmill operations and resources are running out. Lynch and Stretesky (2018) explain how post-war capitalists exported treadmill operations out of domestic economies and into southern locales. While regulatory limits on treadmill processes have yet to reach their northern potential, southern executives and workers have come to understand the harmful scope of these practices. The marginal benefits that were exchanged for the effluence of Western economies has been further restricted in a new era of international trade agreements, stronger labour protections and a global concern for the long-term effects of climate change.

To maintain dominant social expectations, the Canadian settler state must find new spaces to fuel treadmill operations that also cannot resist. Indigenous social spaces are a suitable target because their natural resources remain untapped, their peoples have yet to achieve a fulsome recognition of self-determination and Canada's settler-colonial history has interrupted the sustainability of Indigenous ways of life. In other words, the federal Crown can absolve its immediate economic issues by opening these jurisdictions for business and postpone the need to meaningfully evaluate the consumption practices that continue unabated since the wartime era. FNLMAs lay the foundation for the operationalization of these objectives. The Canadian state also stands to benefit from the transition of Indigenous spaces into spaces that are economically viable. Policies like the EAP create financial incentives that can attract international investment capital to jumpstart economic production in Indigenous territories. IRRIF policies and its adherents were implemented to minimize bureaucratic impediments to environmental assessment and Indigenous consultation processes. In sum, the policy agenda of the settler-colonial state has successfully removed legislative barriers that protected Indigenous territories from the tyranny of local majorities to allow treadmill capitalism to complete its historical objective of assimilating Indigenous peoples into the state economic order.

Returning to Strakosch's theory of neoliberal settler-colonialism, these policies also hold the potential to allow the Crown to declare FNLMA holders as market failures for insufficiently meeting state environmental management expectations. Once limited exceptionalist programs expire, I argue FNLMA metrics can be used to rationalize the state's wholesale reclamation of Indigenous land bases. Perennial acceleration of the treadmill of production has resulted in a global climate crisis. Countries around the world recognize the imperative nature of reducing carbon emissions, limiting natural resource extraction and shifting to stronger reliance on sustainable energy sources. While that is the case, capitalistic production continues to grow to support the endless generation of profit. Considering these challenges and Canada's international obligations to meet carbon reduction targets (ECCC, 2016a; UN Framework Convention on Climate Change, 2021), it is possible that climate change may become the penultimate reason to justify the settler-state's termination of its special relationship with Indigenous peoples by declaring them incapable of managing their own affairs in a time of global crisis.

The trajectory of the policies of the Canadian settler-state and their neoliberal potential can be aptly described using Lynch and Stretesky's (2003) theory of environmental racism (ER). ER advocates fight for egalitarian environmental decisions, proportionate distribution of environmental harms, and elimination of harmful production processes, which are often allocated to the spaces inhabited by communities of colour. (Lynch & Stretesky, 2003, pp. 217, 223–224). In Canada,

ER movements fight for the legal recognition of Indigenous environmental stewardship, with particular focus on their traditional lands and territories. Connecting this discourse with the broader historical and contemporary policy agendas of the Canadian state, it is clear that executive decisions to translocate the consumptive practices of the treadmill of production has followed a seemingly racialized pathway. Historical decisions and modern action to move treadmill operations into the global south expose Indigenous territories for exploitation (Lynch & Stretesky, 2003). As global economics continue to shift during a time of global climate crisis, it appears that settler nation-states are taking steps to access the last environmental spaces that have yet to be transformed into profits or reclaim lands from deviants. While these observations are dire, there is hope that the environmental practices that are undertaken by Indigenous communities can sufficiently protect their lands and their traditional ways of life.

Conclusion

The current Trudeau federal government is making use of the global climate crisis to further its colonial objectives of assimilating Indigenous peoples into the capitalistic economic ethos and to open their territorial environments to the treadmill of production. The federal Crown recognized issues related to environmental sustainability, supporting economic growth and including Indigenous peoples in the state's acceptability matrix. The Canadian way of life is not sustainable and has resulted in irreparable harm to environments around the world. While that is the case, governmental and capitalistic executives remain committed to growing profits by accelerating the treadmill of production, whether that is in the global south or previously locked domestic spaces held by Indigenous peoples. Treadmill operations achieved acceptable levels of profit growth for many years, but southern leaders have come to understand the deleterious effects of allowing environmental degradation to take place in their jurisdictions. In response, the federal Crown is taking steps to open Indigenous territories in order to relocate the treadmill of production and maintain their profit expectations.

Conservative federal governments created incentive programs to attract capital investment and business enterprise; Liberal federal governments deployed discourses of inclusion and incentive programs to encourage Indigenous peoples to adopt pro-treadmill mentalities. Overall, the Canadian settler-colonial state has progressively operationalized its long-standing objectives of eliminating Indigenous jurisdiction over their lands, ending their special relationship with the federal state and downloading responsibility for their colonial oppression to individual communities. While these dispersive measures are new, Indigenous scholars highlight the striking consistency of the federal state's approach with the priorities declared in the 1969 White paper. In essence, the strategy of locating the harms of capitalistic production aligns with Lynch and Stretesky's focus on environmental racism. Regardless of where treadmill operations end up, it is clear that the Canadian settler-state is committed to eradicating Indigenous claims to autonomy and self-government. While these observations are dire, there is hope that the environmental practices that are undertaken by Indigenous communities can sufficiently protect their lands and their traditional ways of life. Failure to do so may amount to the forceful reclamation of Indigenous territories by the Crown, in the name of preventing the cataclysmic effects of irreversible climate change.

References

Aboriginal Affairs and Northern Development Canada. (2015). *Canada's fiscal approach for self-government arrangements*. https://www.aadnc-aandc.gc.ca/DAM/DAM-INTER-HQ-LDC/STAGING/texte-text/canadaS-fiscal_approach_1438090806392_eng.pdf.

Aboriginal Justice Inquiry. (2001). *Report chapter 4—Aboriginal over-representation*. http://www.ajic.mb.ca/volumel/chapter4.html.

Asch, M. (1984). *Home and native land: Aboriginal rights and the Canadian constitution*. Methuen.

Barsh, R. L. & Henderson, J. Y. (1997). The Supreme court's Van der Peet triology: Native imperialism and ropes of sand. *McGill Law Journal, 42,* 998.

Bein, S. (2020, December 7). *Global climate: Five years later, the Paris agreement is not aging well*. https://www.theglobeandmail.com/canada/article-globe-climate-five-years-later-the-paris-agreement-is-not-aging-well/.

Borrows, J. (1997). Wampum at Niagara: The royal proclamation, Canadian legal history, and self-government. In *Aboriginal and treaty rights in Canada: Essays on law, equality, and respect for difference* (pp. 155–172). University of British Columbia Press.

Borrows, J. (2019). Humility: Entanglement, Aboriginal title and private property. In *Law's indigenous ethic* (pp. 114–140). University of Toronto Press.

Buttel, F. (2004). The treadmill of production: An appreciation, assessment, and agenda for research. *Organization & Environment, 17*(3), 296–316.

Canada, Department of Indian and Northern Affairs. (1969). *Statement of the Government of Canada on Indian policy*. https://www.aadnc-aandc.gc.ca/DAM/DAM-INTER-HQ/STAGING/texte-text/cp1969_1100100010190_eng.pdf.

Canadian Energy Regulator Act, SC 2019, c 28. (2019).

Cardinal, H. (1999). *The unjust society*. Douglas & McIntyre.

Climate Analytics & New Climate Institute. (2020). *Canada: Country summary and assessment*. https://climateactiontracker.org/countries/canada/.

Constitution Act, 1982, RSC 1985, App II, No 44, Sched B, Pt II, ss 35–35.1. (1867).

Council of the European Union (2015). *Preparations for the 21th session of COP 21 to the UNFCCC—Council conclusions*. https://www.consilium.europa.eu/en/press/press-releases/2015/09/18/counclusions-un-climate-change-conference-paris-2015/.

Crown-Indigenous Relations and Northern Affairs Canada. (2017). *Own-source revenue for self-governing groups*. http://www.rcaanc-cirnac.gc.ca/eng/1354117773784/1539869378991.

Crown-Indigenous Relations and Northern Affairs Canada (CIRNA). (2018a). *Recognition and implementation of indigenous rights framework: Engagement guide*. http://www.publications.gc.ca/site/eng/9.851603/publication.html.

Crown-Indigenous Relations and Northern Affairs Canada (CIRNA). (2018b). *A recognition and implementation of indigenous rights framework*. https://www.rcaanc-cirnac.gc.ca/eng/1536350959665/1539959903708#chp4.

Environment and Climate Change Canada (ECCC). (2016a). *Pan-Canadian framework on clean growth and climate change.* http://publications.gc.ca/site/eng/9.828774/publication.html.

Environment and Climate Change Canada. (ECCC). (2016b). *Federal actions for a clean growth economy: Delivering on the Pan-Canadian framework on clean growth and climate change.* https://www.canada.ca/content/dam/themes/environment/documents/weather1/20170119-en.pdf.

Forest Ethics Advocacy Assn v National Energy Board, 2014 CarswellNat 4233. (2014).

Foster, H. (1999). Canada: 'Indian administration' from the royal proclamation of 1763 to constitutionally entrenched Aboriginal rights. In P. Havemann, (Ed.), *Indigenous peoples' rights in Australia, Canada, and New Zealand* (pp. 351–377). Oxford University Press.

Foster, J. B. (1992). The absolute general law of environmental degradation under capitalism. *Capitalism, Nature and Socialism, 3*(1), 77–81.

Foster, J. B. (1999). Marx's theory of metabolic rift: Classical foundations for environmental sociology. *American Journal of Sociology, 105*(1), 366–405.

Foster, J. B. (2000) *Marx's ecology: Materialism and nature*. Monthly Review Press.

Foster, J. B. (2002). *Ecology against capitalism.* Monthly Review Press.

Hawthorn, H. B. (1967). *A survey of the contemporary Indians of Canada: Economic, political, educational needs and policies.* https://www.aadnc-aandc.gc.ca/DAM/DAM-INTER-HQ/STAGING/texte-text/ai-arp-ls-pubs-sci3_1326997109567_eng.pdf.

Ha-Redeye, O. (2020). Duty to consult is not a veto. *SLAW*. http://www.slaw.ca/2020/02/09/duty-to-consult-is-not-a-veto/.

Impact Assessment Act, SC 2019, c 28. (2019).

Indian Act, RSC 1985, c I-5. (1985).

Indian Association of Alberta. (1970). *Citizens plus ("The red paper").* Indian Association of Alberta: See Cardinal, H. (1999). The Unjust Society. Douglas & McIntyre.

Intergovernmental Panel on Climate Change. (2013). *IPPC fact sheet: What is the IPCC?* https://www.ipcc.ch/site/assets/uploads/2018/02/FS_what_ipcc.pdf.

Intergovernmental Panel on Climate Change. (2018). *Special report: Global warming of 1.5C—Summary for policy-makers*. https://www.ipcc.ch/sr15/chapter/spm/.

Jobin, S., & Riddle, E. (2019). *The rise of the first nations land management regime in Canada: A critical analysis*. https://yellowheadinstitute.org/wp-content/uploads/2019/09/fnlma-report.pdf.

King, H., & Pasternak, S. (2018). *Executive summary: Canada's emerging indigenous rights framework: A critical analysis*. https://yellowheadinstitute.org/wp-content/uploads/2018/06/executive-summary-rights-framework-yi-final.pdf.

Lawrence, B. (2003). Gender, race, and the regulation of native identity in Canada and the United States: An overview. *Hypatia, 18*(2), 3–31.

Lynch, M. J., & Stretesky, P. B. (2003). The meaning of Green: Contrasting criminological perspectives. *Theoretical Criminology, 7*(2), 217–238.

Lynch, M. J., & Stretesky, P. B. (2018). Green criminology and native peoples: The treadmill of production and the killing of indigenous environmental activists. *Theoretical Criminology, 22*(3), 318–341.

McHugh, P. G. (2016). A common law biography of section 35. In P. Macklem & D. Sanderson (Eds.), *From recognition to reconciliation: Essays on the constitutional entrenchment of Aboriginal and treaty rights* (pp. 145–151). University of Toronto Press.

National Energy Board Act, RSC, 1985, c N-7. (1985).

Natural Resources Canada. (2018). *Generation energy council report: Canada's energy transition*. https://www.nrcan.gc.ca/sites/www.nrcan.gc.ca/files/energy/CoucilReport_july4_EN_Web.pdf.

Natural Resources Canada. (2020). *Indigenous Natural Resource Partnership Program*. https://www.newswire.ca/news-releases/government-of-canada-extends-funding-to-increase-indigenous-participation-in-oil-and-gas-infrastructure-development-889192468.html.

Parker, K. (2017). Assessing the European Union's global climate change leadership: From Copenhagen to the Paris agreement. *Journal of European Integration: Political Leadership in the EU, 39*(2), 241.

Prime Minister of Canada. (2018). *Government of Canada to create recognition and implementation of rights framework*. https://pm.gc.ca/en/news/news-releases/2018/02/14/government-canada-create-recognition-and-implementation-rights.

Royal Commission on Aboriginal Peoples. (1996). *Report of the royal commission on Aboriginal peoples: Looking forward, looking back* (Vol. 1). The Royal Commission on Aboriginal Peoples. https://www.bac-lac.gc.ca/eng/discover/aboriginal-heritage/royal-commission-aboriginal-peoples/Pages/final-report.aspx.

R v Calder, [1973] SCR 313, 34 DLR (3d) 145. (1973).

R v Guerin, [1984] 2 SCR 335, [1984] SCJ No 45. (1984).
R v Sparrow, [1990] 1 SCR 1075, 70 DLR (4th) 385. (1990).
R v Van der Peet, [1996] 2 SCR 507, 137 DLR (4th) 289. (1996).
Schnaiberg A. (1980). *Environment: From surplus to scarcity*. Oxford University Press.
Schnaiberg, A., Gould, K., & Pellow, D. (2004). Interrogating the treadmill of production: Everything you want to know about the treadmill but were afraid to ask. *Organization & Environment, 17*(3), 296–316.
Stanley, A. (2016). Resilient settler colonialism: "Responsible resource development", "flow-through" financing and the risk management of indigenous sovereignty in Canada. *Environment and Planning, 48*(12), 2422–2442.
Strakosch, E. (2015). *Neoliberal indigenous policy: Settler colonialism and the "post-welfare" state*. Palgrave Macmillan.
Union of British Columbia Indian Chiefs. (1970). *A declaration of indian rights: The B.C. Indian position paper*. UBCIC.
United Nations Framework Convention on Climate Change. (2021). *Cooperation with IPCC*. https://unfccc.int/topics/science/workstreams/cooperation-with-the-ipcc.
Weaver, S. M. (1981). *Making Canadian Indian policy: The hidden agenda 1968–1970*. University of Toronto Press.

16

Restorative Justice Conferencing: A Vehicle for Repairing Harm Emanating from Lawful but Awful Activity

Mark Hamilton

Introduction

One of the defining features of green criminology is its focus on environmental harm emanating from not only illegal activity (the 'unlawful'; White & Heckenberg, 2014, p. 3) and wrongful activity (e.g. tortious activity) but also legal activity, such as under a licence (so-called licence to pollute), permit or consent (the 'lawful but awful'; Passas, 2005; see also, White & Heckenberg, 2014, p. 3). Much of this legal activity is carried out by corporations and the state through its various entities. This dichotomy of harm is depicted in Fig. 16.1.

This focus acknowledges that environmental harm is caused by a multitude of activities and actors, both legal and illegal. Hence, illegal

M. Hamilton (✉)
Faculty of Law, University of New South Wales, Sydney, NSW, Australia
e-mail: mark.hamilton@unsw.edu.au

J. Gacek and R. Jochelson (eds.), *Green Criminology and the Law*, Palgrave Studies in Green Criminology,
https://doi.org/10.1007/978-3-030-82412-9_16

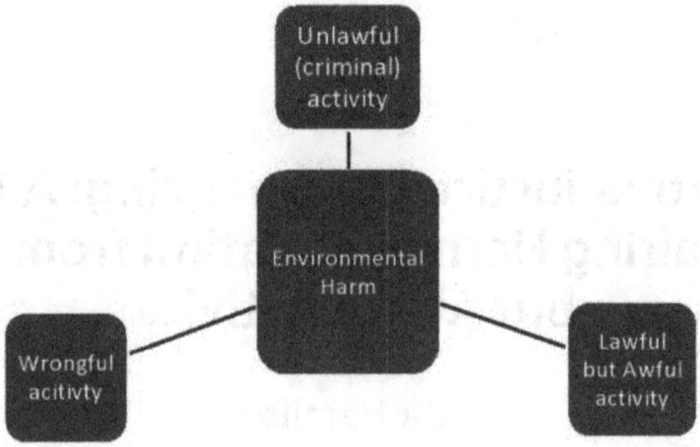

Fig. 16.1 Dichotomy of harm

dumping of pollution into a river and legal coal-fired electricity production, for example, both lead to environmental harm despite the fact that one activity is illegal and the other legal.

The fact that some activity that harms the environment is permitted under licence, permit or consent is an acknowledgment that for society to progress economically, technologically, and socially, some compromising of the environment is necessary. As Skinnider (2013, p. 3) highlights, '[t]he reality of our age is that much of the economy is based on the exploitation of natural resources'. Indeed, the referring to nature as a resource is anthropocentric, which views humans as the centre of the universe and therefore the most important, with nature being a resource to be exploited. Environmental regulation, therefore, is a balancing of economics and a healthy environment (an 'ecological-economic trade-off'; Lampkin & Wyatt, 2019), with the level of pollution permissible set by governments at levels acceptable to business and the public (Wolf & Stanley, 2011, pp. 5–6).

The victims of environmental harm (emanating from both legal and illegal activities) are a concern of green criminology and there are increasing calls to consider environmental victims, including questioning directed 'as to their needs and expectations of a criminal justice (or other) system' (Hall, 2012, p. 13; an observation echoed in 2014a, p. 104; see also, 2013, 2016).

One practice that has evolved to better accommodate the needs of victims within the criminal justice system is restorative justice. Notwithstanding the fact that green criminology has intra-disciplinary theoretical engagement (which sees micro or individual level, and macro or group level, criminological theories used to explain environmental crime) and extra-disciplinary theoretical engagement (that is, green criminology engagement with theories and ideas outside criminology) (Brisman, 2014, pp. 24–28), it has been slow to engage with the theory and practice of restorative justice. Where there has been engagement it has been through the ad-hoc use of restorative justice conferencing to deal with the harm arising from illegal activity. Given the fact that legal activity also harms the environment, resulting in environmental victims, this chapter will explore the applicability of restorative justice conferencing in repairing the harm arising from legal activity.

Restorative Justice: Definition, Conceptualisation and Functions

While there is 'debate ensuing over exactly what it is and what it involves and, indeed, what it isn't' (Hamilton, 2015, p. 164), one widely accepted definition of restorative justice is as 'a process whereby all of the parties with a stake in a particular offence come together to resolve collectively how to deal with the aftermath of the offence and its implications for the future' (Marshall, 1996, p. 37). There are at least three ways of conceptualising restorative justice. Firstly, as a social movement, with the goal being 'to transform the way contemporary societies view and respond to crime and related forms of troublesome behaviour... [through the use of] community-based reparative justice and moralizing social control' (Johnstone & Van Ness, 2011, p. 5; see also Sherman & Strang, 2012).

A second way to conceptualise restorative justice is as an intention, a reparative conception of justice which is concerned with outcome, where reparative sanctions can be ordered outside of a restorative justice encounter and administered by criminal justice professionals (Johnstone & Van Ness, 2011, p. 14). This is viewed as a maximalist model of restorative justice which posits that 'every action that is primarily oriented toward doing justice by repairing the harm that has been caused by crime' is restorative (Bazemore & Walgrave, 1999, p. 48).

A third way of conceptualising restorative justice is as a process, in which the encounter between stakeholders to crime or conflict are central—'victims, offenders and other 'stakeholders' in a criminal case should be allowed to encounter one another outside highly formal, professional-dominated settings such as the courtroom' (Johnstone & Van Ness, 2011, p. 9). When discussing restorative justice in this chapter, it is as a process/encounter conceptualisation as reflected in the Marshall (1996) definition just outlined.

The various principles (Zehr, 2015a, p. 43), values (Braithwaite, 2000, pp. 185–186), signposts (Zehr, 2015a, p. 51), accounts (Braithwaite, 1999), and guiding questions (Zehr, 2015a, p. 49) which have been used to characterise the essence of restorative justice can be distilled into three central tenets, which I set out in Hamilton (2019b, pp. 29–36; 2021, pp. 88–92). The first central tenet is that *crime is a violation of people and relationships*, which builds on the assumption 'that humans are profoundly relational. There is a fundamental human need to be in good relationship with others' because 'humans are communal' (Pranis, 2011, p. 64); 'we are all interconnected' and therefore it is people and relationships which are violated by crime (Zehr, 2015a, p. 29; 2015b, pp. 183–184). In terms of green criminology and the fact that victims of environmental offending can be non-human (the environment and its various components), crime also represents a violation of the relationship between people and their environment.

Building on this notion of humans as relational, *responses to crime should be inclusive*. 'Interrelationships imply mutual obligations and responsibilities' (Zehr, 2015a, p. 29), with restorative justice seeking to include all those 'stakeholders' whose relationship have been affected by the offending, even those relationships which have been created by the offending. Thus, '[r]estorative justice expands the circle of stakeholders – those with a stake or standing in the event or case – beyond just the government and the offending party to include those who have been directly victimized as well as community members' (Zehr, 2015a, p. 21). In terms of environmental offending, it is the non-human victims which should also be included in the response to crime, albeit it may have to be through human guardians as representatives.

If humans are relational, requiring an inclusive response to crime, then those *responses to crime should heal and put things right*. The centrality of healing and putting right (Zehr, 2015a, p. 16; 2015b, p. 198) flows from the understanding that '[i]nterrelationships imply mutual obligations and responsibilities' (Zehr, 2015a, p. 29); '[c]rime creates a debt to make right…' (Zehr, 2015b, p. 200). Therefore, those who cause harm 'have a responsibility to repair the harm, making things right as much as possible, both concretely and symbolically' (Zehr, 2015a, p. 33). Restorative justice provides 'the opportunity and encouragement for those who have caused harm to do right by those they have harmed' (Zehr, 2015a, p. 38), and the harm that needs to be repaired extends beyond humans to include non-humans, such as the environment. Notwithstanding the fact that these three central tenets of restorative justice have their genesis in the response to crime, they are relevant to harm caused by legal activity because such activity, just like crime, results in harm and therefore environmental victims.

The practice of restorative justice conferencing reveals its value in fulfilling four functions, or alternatively four elements of a resolution device, to deal with the harm occasioned by offending, which I conceptualise as communication, education, resolution, and reintegration (Hamilton, 2019b, pp. 36–39; 2021, pp. 92–94). Each of the functions build upon each other and therefore are symbiotic, and necessary to repair the harm that emanated from offending. Restorative justice, at its simplest, is a dialectic exchange between stakeholders to an incident (be that characterised as offending or wrongdoing). That is, communication is central and therefore one of the functions that restorative justice can fulfil. For example, victims can talk about the effect that the crime/conflict has had on them and their loved ones, i.e., 'how they have been violated and what they feel' (Hamilton, 2008, p. 271). Victims will get the opportunity to ask pertinent questions of the offender (Hamilton, 2015, p. 175) and describe the impact that the offending has had. Their personal and professional situations can be described by offenders as way of explaining the offending rather than as an excuse for it. In terms of environmental harm, it is obvious that not all victims can represent themselves at conferencing; a koala, for example, does not speak with a human tongue. That should not be seen as a barrier to non-human participation at conferencing, because such participation can be achieved through human guardians as representatives of non-human victims.

The communication that restorative justice facilitates can fulfil an educative function, which is the second function thereof. That is, victims can learn about the circumstances of the offending and how and why it came about, be that by accident, negligence or some deliberate action. The offender, through conferencing, will get to learn of the effect that the incident has had on victims (including the environment and its constituent parts) and experience first-hand the pain and hurt experienced by the victims.

Talking about the incident (communication function) which can result in learning (education function) will hopefully lead to resolution, being the third function of restorative justice. That is, repair of the 'physical, material, psychological or emotional' harm that crime or conflict causes (Hamilton, 2019b, p. 37). Resolution can come in different forms, such as material or symbolic reparation, which 'can be pivotal to recovery because it achieves four things: it can help repair damage, vindicate the innocent, locate responsibility and restore equilibrium' (Sharpe, 2011, p. 28). Material reparation may come in the form of covering the cost of treatment for a victim or the returning of stolen property to a victim. Symbolic reparation may come in the form of apology which may help a victim with their recovery and the moving on with their life; apology being an indicator of vindication. While apology, and its reciprocal forgiveness, are very powerful they should not be the result of coercion and only offered genuinely:

> [A]n apology may be a double-edged sword. A genuine apology may, but not necessarily so, foster forgiveness. But a non-genuine apology, for instance given out of a sense of obligation or because of the belief that it is part of the process, may lead to re-victimisation and breakdown in the whole restorative justice process. Hence, a restorative justice conference should focus on fostering a constructive dialogue between offender and victim rather than on some preconceived notion that apology and/or forgiveness is necessary to its success. (Hamilton, 2014, p. 361)

'Forgiveness is a personal thing' (Hamilton, 2017, p. 14) and therefore 'it is wrong to ask victims to forgive and very wrong to expect it of them. Forgiveness is a gift victims can give. We destroy its power as a gift by making it a duty' (Braithwaite, 2002a, p. 15; see also, Zehr, 2015a, pp. 13–14). Restorative justice conferencing is an ideal forum in which to assess the genuineness of apology and forgiveness, 'because tone and body language are interpretative tools' (Hamilton, 2017, p. 7).

Reintegration is the fourth function that restorative justice can fulfil and is concerned with the acceptance of the offender or wrongdoer back into society post offending or wrongdoing. Such reintegration 'is bound up with the offender's willingness to listen, learn and repair the harm caused...' (Hamilton, 2019b, p. 38). Reintegration is about resisting the temptation to ostracise, treat as a pariah, and relegate to the scrap heap of society, those who have offended or committed wrong. Rather, it is adopting the view that offenders and wrongdoers are good people who have done bad things rather than bad people per se, and there is a link here to Braithwaite's (1989) notions of stigmatising and reintegrative shaming. The concept of reintegration is strained somewhat when talking about lawful activity because the person or entity which has harmed the environment has done so under the veneer of legality. They in truth are not blameworthy in the sense of an offender and therefore it can be questioned whether they need to be reintegrated back into society. However, as will be seen when we explore the use of restorative justice conferencing for lawful harmful activity, the conferencing can be a forum through which the harmer can solidify their social licence to operate, which is loosely a form of reintegration.

It is the operation of these four functions which underpins the success of restorative justice conferencing in resolving the harm arising from offending, through exploring the harm, expressing hurt, exploration of ways to repair the harm and the reintegration of the offender back into society, whilst at the same time holding the offender accountable for their offending. It is these functions which will underpin any success of restorative justice conferencing following environmental crime, to which this chapter now turns, and potentially for the harm occasioned through legal activities which harm the environment, to which this chapter will turn shortly.

Utilising restorative justice for both illegal and legal environmental harm sees a traversing of the criminal-regulatory dichotomy. Whilst criminal proceedings are still backward looking and focussed on retribution, deterrence and denouncement, and regulatory action predominately forward looking, focussed on compliance, the inclusion of conferencing makes these processes more participatory through the inclusion of relevant stakeholders. Within that context, conferencing debunks the traditional view of humans as the primary victims of environmental harm by extending participation to the environment itself, albeit through human guardians as representatives.

Restorative Justice and Unlawful Activity or Wrongdoing

In an environmental offending context, restorative justice conferencing may be embedded as part of the sentencing of environmental offending (so-called 'back-end model' of conferencing; for an overview, see Al-Alosi & Hamilton, 2019). Examples of the back-end model of conferencing are *Williams*[1] (for an overview, see Hamilton, 2008; McDonald, 2008), *Clarence Valley Council*[2] (for an overview, see Ashton & Etherington, 2018; Hamilton, 2019a; Smith, 2019), and *Interflow*[3] (for an overview, see Sugrue, 2015; Fowler, 2016). Restorative justice conferencing can also be used as an alternative to prosecution (so-called 'front-end model' of conferencing), as in the schemes administered by Environment Canterbury, New Zealand (Alternative Environmental Justice; for an overview, see Environment Canterbury Regional Council Resource Management Act Monitoring and Compliance Section, 2012;

[1] *Garrett v Williams* (2007) 151 LGERA 92. This case is from New South Wales (Australia) and is in the context of cultural heritage offending, through the destruction of Aboriginal objects and an Aboriginal place.

[2] *Chief Executive, Office of Environment and Heritage v Clarence Valley Council* (2018) 236 LGERA 291. This case is from New South Wales (Australia) and is in the context of cultural heritage offending, through the lopping of an Aboriginal scar tree.

[3] *Canterbury Regional Council v Interflow (NZ) Limited* [2015] NZDC 3323. This is a New Zealand water pollution case.

McLachlan, 2014) and British Columbia, Canada (Community Justice Forums; for an overview, see Environment and Climate Change Canada, 2011; Market Wire, 2011; Proctor, 2016; Pynn, 2016). Restorative justice conferencing has been used to derive enforceable undertakings in a case of air pollution, emanating from a landfill, to circumvent the need for prosecution (*Hallam Road*; for an overview, see Victoria Environment Protection Authority, 2012); an enforceable undertaking being 'a binding agreement to undertake tasks to settle an alleged contravention of the law and remedy the harm caused to the environment and the community' (Victoria Government, 2012, p. 1).

There are occasions when a prosecutorial authority (that is the government agency or department empowered to undertake the prosecution of environmental offending) commences civil enforcement proceedings rather than commence a criminal prosecution. This could be in circumstances where 'an environmental incident is ongoing and there is a need to restrain the incident and stop any further environmental damage', and because of 'the wider range of orders available in civil enforcement proceedings compared to criminal prosecution', and 'the lower burden of proof in civil enforcement proceedings compared to criminal prosecution' (Hamilton, 2016, p. 494). An example, relating to the clearing of native vegetation, in which civil enforcement proceedings were commenced in lieu of criminal prosecution is *Lani*.[4] The utility of a restorative justice conference in a criminal prosecution could likewise extend to civil enforcement proceeding and I have proffered such use elsewhere, using *Lani* as a case study (Hamilton, 2016).

An offender's motivation to attend restorative justice conferencing may well be to heal the harm occasioned to the environment, individuals, communities, and relationships and put things right (central tenet 3), which arises from the fact that crime is a violation of people and relationships (central tenet 1). As restorative justice is inclusive (central tenet 2), it is important that victims, offenders and stakeholders participate in conferencing. There is debate as to the appropriate stakeholders to attend conferencing, i.e. those other than the offender and victim. In New Zealand, when conferencing is used in the sentencing process (that is,

---

[4] *Great Lakes Council v Lani* (2007) 158 LGERA 1.

when a court is sentencing an offender), the prosecutorial authority and offender's lawyers have attended conferencing. However, their presence in New South Wales, Australia, was excluded in *Williams* (and inferably, *Clarence Valley Council*). Even if legal representatives were permitted to attend conferencing, it would not be in the traditional sense but rather as an advisor:

> In no nation does it seem appropriate for defendants to have a right for their lawyers to represent them during a restorative justice process. Part of the point of restorative justice is to transcend the adversarial legalism, to empower stakeholders [(participants)] to speak in their own voice rather than through legal mouthpieces who might have an interest in polarizing a conflict. (Braithwaite, 2002b, p. 566)

A range of people were interviewed in preparation for the conference in *Williams*. These included 'representatives of the New South Wales Attorney-General's Department (including persons concerned with crime prevention, Aboriginal community justice and Aboriginal programs)' (*Williams*, [56]). These representatives could be considered stakeholders for the purpose of a restorative justice conference. Stakeholders could change depending on the specific case and therefore no definitive list is possible. However, notions of inclusivity and utility should guide the selection of stakeholders for participation in conferencing.

To ensure that a conference provides the opportunity to achieve its purposes, selection criteria have been advised. Such participant suitability criteria are also used to ensure that the chances of a victim being re-victimised in a conference are minimised or eliminated. UNODC (2006, 2020) suggests that an offender accept responsibility for their or its offending before being deemed suitable to participate in conferencing. Al-Alosi and myself (2019) suggest that contrition and remorse can demonstrate an offender's acceptance of responsibility for offending. According to Preston (2007, pp. 153–154), contrition and remorse can be evidenced by action to rectify harm, voluntary reporting of the offence, action to redress causes of the offence, and genuine regret and future plans to avoid repetition of such offences.

Given that restorative justice has transformative potential, Al-Alosi and myself (2021) suggest that provided an offender does not deny responsibility for offending, they should be permitted to attend conferencing. This is because an offender may not have insight into their offending pre-conference, and as a result may not readily accept responsibility at that stage. Conferencing however provides the forum in which an offender can have a 'light bulb' moment through which the gravity of the harm caused by their offending can be realised.

The notions of unlawful activity and wrongdoing imply an attribution of blameworthiness. That is, the offender or those engaging in wrongdoing are to be held accountable for the harm caused because they can be attributed the blame for that crime or wrongdoing. Hence, the reason that the offender or wrongdoer participates in conferencing, in order to heal and put things right, is because they are to blame in a criminal or civil sense for the harm caused. That is, they have something to be contrite or remorseful about. In sum, the obligations arising from the central tenets of restorative justice arise because of the blameworthiness of the offender or wrongdoer.

Restorative Justice and Lawful but Awful Activity

The same blameworthiness that can be attributed to those undertaking unlawful or wrongful activity that harms the environment cannot be attributed to those who have a licence, permit or consent to undertake activities which are indeed lawful yet awful. This is because the harm is licenced, permitted or subject to consent. Hence, that individual or corporation has nothing to be contrite or remorseful about. Given this observation, it will be argued that restorative justice conferencing has utility for lawful but awful activity causing environmental harm but in a different way to unlawful activity or wrongdoing.

Wilson (2016, pp. 252, 256–258) explores four restorative justice principles which she believes can be utilised 'throughout the application, assessment, approval and implementation process for major projects in New South Wales [Australia], to enhance public participation and improve environmental outcomes'. Those principles are constructive dialogue, knowledge sharing, allocation of benefits to local or Indigenous communities, and focus on future harm. Constructive dialogue is the opportunity for stakeholders to put their views forward and to have those views listened to, along with the proffering of helpful or constructive comments. Knowledge sharing is between those stakeholders affected by an activity and 'can include knowledge about a particular environment or area, local or Indigenous knowledge, or knowledge about the business concerns or operations of a person or corporation who wishes to carry out an activity' (Wilson, 2016, p. 257). Allocation of benefits to local or Indigenous communities is concerned with allocating benefits of an activity or project to stakeholders 'before a project or activity has been carried out, as a way of strengthening the relationship between the parties involved' (Wilson, 2016, p. 257). The last restorative justice principle is about focussing on preventing future harm that may arise from an activity or project.

There are a few assumptions underpinning this so-called 'proactive restorative justice'. It is proactive in that it is deployed before any environmental harm occurs as a means of preventing such harm. This can be compared with reactionary restorative justice deployed following offending or wrongdoing. Proactive restorative justice is utilised in relation to potential harm occasioned by lawful but awful activities, in the case of major projects. Major projects could include coal mines, wind farms, dams, logging, forest clearing, polluting industries, etc. Proactive restorative justice is inclusive, as Wilson posits it as a vehicle for enhancing public participation. Such inclusivity aligns with the second central tenet of restorative justice outlined earlier, that is, responses to crime or conflict should be inclusive. While Wilson (2016, p. 256) 'advocates a "maximalist" view of restorative justice…' she does not preclude the use of conferencing.

While I do not conceive a forum, such as conferencing, as being the appropriate forum for official decision-making pertaining to the granting of a licence, permit or consent, a proactive restorative justice conference would serve a useful communicative function relating to such licence, permit or consent (as embedded in Wilson's [2016] principles of constructive dialogue and knowledge sharing). Such a conference could be pre or post approval. If held post approval, it is recommended that the conference be held before operations actually begin because otherwise the community will think that its participation is an afterthought and/or tokenistic.

The conference could be a means of delineating the expected harms to emanate from the activity or project and the safeguards that will be implemented to minimise the environmental harm. Members of the community may not understand reports accompanying an application for a licence, permit or consent to undertake an activity or project which will cause environmental harm; such reports setting out the extent of environmental harm. Statements of environmental effects and environmental impact statements, for example, often include technical language and data which is directed to the approval authority (the authority whose role it is to determine whether an activity or project should be approved) and therefore may be beyond the grasp of ordinary citizens. Therefore, having the environmental impacts of an activity or project explained in accessible language at a conference would be beneficial for the community.

At this pre or post approval proactive restorative justice conference, the proponent could outline the necessity for environmental harm. That is, why environmental harm is unavoidable and what mitigation/elimination strategies the proponent has put in place and commitments to continue exploring ways to eliminate or mitigate environmental harm. Community members may be able to express their views relating to the proposed environmental harm and proffer any suggestions they may have regarding the elimination or mitigation of the proposed environmental harm to flow from the activity or project (knowledge sharing). This is particularly important in the context of non-humans which may be impacted by the activity or project and may otherwise not have had any input into the activity or project.

The proactive restorative justice conference could serve as the forum in which any benefits to the local community deriving from the activity or project could be discussed. For example, mining operations may provide for employment opportunities for the local community (for example, see *Williams* where the possibility of future Indigenous employment at the offending mine was discussed at conferencing). A wind farm may provide the local community with discounted or free electricity. Other activities or projects may provide public infrastructure such as roads, schools or hospitals, or donations thereto. While such benefits would be 'a way of strengthening the relationship between the parties involved', they should 'not be allocated arbitrarily…' with it being important 'that the parties discuss the type of benefits which the community actually wants' (Wilson, 2016, p. 257). Equally, community benefits should not be a bribe or pay-off to garner support for environmentally damaging activities or projects.

The effectiveness of the communication displayed through a proactive restorative justice conference and the allocation of benefits to the local community hosting the environmentally harmful activity or project link to the concept of a social licence to operate. Indeed, a major motivation for an applicant for, or holder of, a licence, permit or consent to undertake an environmentally harmful activity or project in attending conferencing is the desire to establish or strengthen a social licence to operate within the local community. A social licence to operate 'describes how much community support a project, company or industry has in a region' (Luke, 2018, p.n.p.). It is metaphoric (Bice, 2014; Parsons & Moffat, 2014) in the sense that it 'is intangible and unwritten; it is not the type of formal 'licence' that can be granted by civil, political, or legal authorities' (Hurst et al., 2020, p. 1; see also, Baumber, 2018: Franks & Cohen, 2012; Parsons & Moffat, 2014). Hence, a social licence to operate is something that is not applied for through formal avenues but rather is granted by the community and must be 'earned then continually renegotiated' (Hall, 2014b, p. 220). Equally, it does not exist for perpetuity, as it 'may be revoked at any stage of the project lifecycle based on changes in perceptions, and reflective of the relationships between a company and its external stakeholders…' (Mercer-Mapstone et al., 2017, p. 347, emphasis omitted), and therefore requires work to maintain. The loss of a social licence to operate 'can lead to serious delays and costs for organizations, reduced market access, boycotts or protests, community anger, increased regulations, loss of reputation, and, in extreme instances, the failure of a project, organization and/or industry' (Hurst et al., 2020, p. 1; see also Dare et al., 2014). A social licence to operate has been explored with regards to the following lawful but awful activities—wind farms (Hall, 2014b), mining (Mercer-Mapstone et al., 2018), energy (Shaffer et al., 2017), aquaculture (Baines & Edwards, 2018), forestry (Edwards et al., 2016), agriculture (Greiner, 2014), and pulp and paper manufacturing (Gunningham et al., 2004).

Central to garnering community support, central to social licence to operate, is dialogue which underpin five positive influences on, and determinants of, a social licence to operate. Those being transparency, engagement/constructive relationships, trust, procedural fairness, and understanding (see for example, Moffat & Zhang, 2014; Mercer-Mapstone et al., 2017; Luke, 2018). As will be argued, these determinants are embedded not only in a proactive restorative justice conference, but in conferencing held during the lifespan of an activity or project and following environmental offending if the environmental harm occasioned moves from being lawful to being unlawful.

Transparency involves 'not only being *seen* to be doing the right thing...[but] actually doing the right thing' (Luke, 2018, p.n.p., emphasis original). Hence, transparency is about complying with the law but also about being transparent to the community including when it comes to environmental harm. Transparency can be enhanced through proponents of activities or projects 'working in partnership with communities and actively engaging them in the process from the very start' (Luke, 2018, p.n.p.). A proactive restorative justice conference, either pre or post licence, permit or consent approval, is an ideal forum in which such partnerships can be established and solidified, and through which transparency achieved.

Constructive relationships are built on engagement, and are an important positive influence on, and determinant of, a social licence to operate. Effective dialogue is key with relationships built through dialogue being perceived as 'of higher quality than those relationships built through other forms of engagement...' (Mercer-Mapstone et al., 2017, p. 350). One of Wilson's (2016) restorative justice principles is constructive dialogue which is central to proactive restorative justice conferencing. Hence, dialogue which underpins engagement which in turn is central to constructive relationships, being a positive influence on, and determinant of, a social licence to operate can be achieved through a proactive restorative justice conference. This is because such conferencing is inclusive and allows all stakeholders to express their voice without being dominated.

Trust is an important influence/determinant of social licence to operate. '[B]uilding trust with local communities was crucial for mining companies to obtain and maintain a social licence to operate' (Moffat & Zhang, 2014, p. 61). Trust is built 'most successfully…through informal dialogue processes such as at the face-to-face, community, and site-specific level…' (Mercer-Mapstone et al., 2017, p. 350). A proactive restorative justice conference can provide the forum to build trust between the local community and the proponent for, or holder of, a licence, permit or consent for an activity or project which has harmful consequences for the environment.

Another important influence/determinant of social licence to operate is procedural fairness (Mercer-Mapstone et al., 2017), which includes the extent to which people in the community have opportunities to participate in the decisions of the company, the extent to which the company listens to and respects community members opinions, and whether the company is prepared to change its practices in response to community sentiment. Participation, listening, respect and willingness to change are either a feature of proactive restorative justice conferencing or could be explored at such conferencing.

Finally, understanding is an important influence/determinant of social licence to operate, characterised as a 'mutual process of reaching a shared understanding … [and] was seen to be important in problem solving, preventing conflict, and working towards solutions that were meaningful and mutually beneficial' (Mercer-Mapstone et al., 2017, p. 351). The dialogue central to proactive restorative justice conferencing can aid in the desired shared understanding.

Some consideration needs to be given as to whether the consent authority should be permitted to attend the pre-operations restorative justice conference, which as stated previously could be pre or post approval. I maintain the position that conferencing is not a suitable forum for official decision-making, but would there be some utility in the consent authority attending conferencing? Community sentiment towards a project will often flow into the official decision-making process relating to permits, licences and consents through 'objections' and such objections will be considered in the approval process. The community support or otherwise of an activity or project may be more readily apparent at a conference than through the objections process. This may support the inclusion of the consent authority at conferencing held at the pre-operations stage. However, issues of fairness to the applicant to undertake an activity or project must be considered because not all applicants will engage in the voluntary conferencing process. Even if the conferencing was not used as the forum for official decision-making, the desired position, a consent authority in attendance may be swayed by any community objection to the activity or project expressed at conferencing and therefore not able to bring an impartial mind to the approval process. Similarly, if a consent authority attended the conference and proffered suggestions as to how to mitigate/eliminate environmental harm emanating from the project, the community may feel that the consent authority is minded to approve the activity or project even if the conference was held pre-approval.

These observations may be sufficient to suggest that the consent authority should not attend a pre-operations restorative justice conference, especially if it is also pre-approval. However, further research is needed in this regard, and can draw on the experience of conferencing following environmental offending. This is so, even if the context is different. The prosecutorial authority attends conferencing when used as a diversion from, and alternative to, prosecution. Further, in New Zealand when conferencing is used as part of the sentencing process (back-end model), Environment Canterbury generally attends in an advisory or technical capacity. Contrastingly, in New South Wales, Australia, the prosecutorial authority was excluded from attending the conference in *Williams* (and inferably, *Clarence Valley Council*).

The role of restorative justice does not finish once a licence, permit or consent for a lawful but awful activity has been granted and the necessity for, and extent of, proposed environmental harm explored with the local community at a proactive restorative justice conference. A restorative justice conference could be held with relevant stakeholders, including members of the local community, once operations have commenced and lawful but awful environmental harm starts to manifest. The purpose of conferencing during the operations phase is maintenance. That is, the maintenance of everything achieved during the proactive restorative justice conference which was held before operations commenced: dialogue, relationships and social licence to operate. While an individual may support, or at least not oppose, an activity or project pre-commencement, such support may wane once environmental harm starts to manifest. A conference at this stage can reinforce the benefits of the activity or project to the community, reinforce the fact that environmental harm is unavoidable but has been mitigated to all possible extent, and importantly reinforce the fact that compliance is being maintained with the licence, permit or consent which authorises the environmental harm. As mentioned earlier, dialogue is central to a social licence to operate with dialogue during a restorative justice conference held during the operations of an activity or project being a natural extension of the dialogue established during proactive restorative justice conferencing.

One final role of restorative justice conferencing for approved activities or projects is when the environmental harm emanates from activity beyond the scope of approval. That is, activity which is beyond the scope of a licence, permit or consent. Hence, those situations where lawful but awful activity becomes unlawful activity. For example, mining activity permitted to hold 10 megalitres of dam tailings breaches its licence by holding 12 megalitres of dam tailings, leading to collapse of that dam resulting in pollution; forest activity permitting the clearing of 10 ha of forest, breaches its consent by clearing 12 ha of forest, resulting in the killing of wildlife and destruction of wildlife habitat; and, a wind farm causing noise pollution by breaching its permit to cause no more than X decibels of noise. Such environmental harm is not lawful because it is beyond the confines of the approved licence, permit or consent. The proponents of those activities or projects are blameworthy and have something to be contrite and remorseful about. A restorative justice conference can explore that contrition and remorse, the community member's views of environmental harm and ways in which to repair the harm that has been occasioned.

In summary, while restorative justice conferencing has been utilised following environmental offending, it has not been used to deal with the environmental harm that emanates from lawful but awful activity. That is activity that is subject to licence, permit or consent. Drawing upon, and expanding, the notion of proactive restorative justice (Wilson, 2016), conferencing involving licence/permit/consent holders, affected individuals, local community, and other relevant stakeholders can be utilised across the lifespan of lawful but awful activity which negatively impacts the environment, as depicted in Fig. 16.2.

The figure depicts various stages at which restorative justice can be used, with each of those uses of restorative justice having a different purpose. The scenario in Fig. 16.2 depicts an activity or operation which is lawful but in which some unlawful (offending) behaviour arises. Such a scenario is useful for demonstrating the different ways that restorative justice can be used for both lawful and unlawful activity. Yet, this scenario may not be typical. Not all lawful but awful activities will descend into offending activity. Equally, not all offending activity will derive from activity in breach of an approved license, permit or consent. Indeed, offending can be carried out by operators who do not have any licence, permit or consent relating to their activities. The following applications of restorative justice are depicted in Fig. 16.2:

1. At the application, assessment, approval and implementation stage (proactive restorative justice), as a means of delineating the expected environmental harm and explaining why such environmental harms are unavoidable, as a forum to explore some of the benefits to bestow on the local community through the activity or project, and, to establish a social licence to operate;
2. During the operations stage when environmental harm is lawfully caused by the activity (maintenance restorative justice), as a means

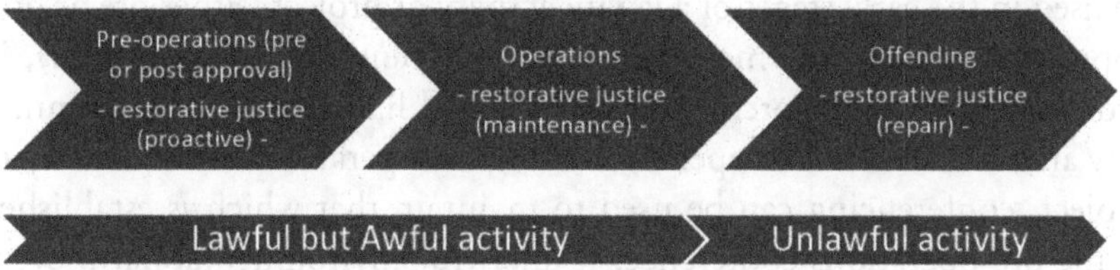

Fig. 16.2 Use of restorative justice for environmental harm

of maintaining and reinforcing that which was established during the proactive restorative justice conference: dialogue, relationships and social licence to operate; and
3. If the environmental harm moves from lawful to unlawful (such as in breach of licence, permit or consent), then following that environmental harm (repair restorative justice). The purpose of this conference is the repair of the harm arising from the offending. That is, repair to the environment, relationships, offender's reputation, and social licence to operate. The conferencing is an opportunity for an offender to express contrition and remorse, learn something about the impact of the offending, allowing victims to express their disappointment and hurt brought about by the offending, as a forum to derive effective ways in which to address the harm caused by the offending, and thereby reintegrate the offender back into society.

While restorative justice conferencing has been utilised for unlawful activity, such as water pollution (*Interflow*) and Aboriginal cultural heritage offending (*Williams* and *Clarence Valley Council*), and suggested for civil enforcement proceedings brought in lieu of criminal prosecution (*Lani*), there is a dearth of research and application to environmental harm emanating from lawful but awful activity. Given this book's focus on green criminology and harm, the fact that green criminology is concerned with environmental harm emanating from both legal and illegal activity, and the fact that both forms of activity result in environmental victims, it is fitting that this chapter explored the potential for the use of restorative justice conferencing for lawful but awful activity. Such conferencing can be used for lawful but awful activity but the role is different than when used for environmental offending. Conferencing can be used in the early stages of a lawful activity or project, either pre or post approval (arguably the most beneficial intervention is pre-approval), in order to explore the potential environmental harm, benefits to community and social licence to operate. During the operations of the activity or project, conferencing can be used to maintain that which is established in the pre-operations conference. If unlawful environmental harm eventuates from the operations of the activity or project then conferencing can be used in its more traditional way to repair the harm the offending has occasioned. Obviously, environmental harm is an important issue, regardless of whether that harm is caused through lawful or unlawful activity, and indeed is a central concern of green criminology. Restorative justice conferencing provides the vehicle through which such environmental harm can be discussed, mitigated, repaired, and eliminated, and through which victims can be given a voice.

References

Al-Alosi, H., & Hamilton, M. (2019). The Ingredients of success for effective restorative justice conferencing in an environmental offending context. *University of New South Wales Law Journal, 42*(4), 1460–1488.

Al-Alosi., & Hamilton, M. (2021). The potential of restorative justice in achieving acceptance of responsibility in the context of environmental crimes. *University of New South Wales Law Journal*, *44*(2), 487-512.

Ashton, S., & Etherington, S. (2018). Chief executive, office of environment and heritage V clarence valley council. *Newcastle Law Review, 13*, 86–91.

Baines, J., & Edwards, P. (2018). The role of relationships in achieving and maintaining a social licence in the new zealand aquaculture sector. *Aquaculture, 485*, 140–146.

Baumber, A. (2018). Energy cropping and social licence: What's trust got to do with it? *Biomass and Bioenergy, 108*, 25–34.

Bazemore, G., & Walgrave, L. (1999). Restorative juvenile justice: In search of fundamentals and an outline for systemic reform. In G. Bazemore & L. Walgrave (Eds.), *Restorative juvenile justice: Repairing the harm of youth crime* (pp. 45–74). Criminal Justice Press.

Bice, S. (2014). What gives you a social licence? An exploration of the social licence to operate in the Australian mining industry. *Resources, 3*(1), 62–80.

Braithwaite, J. (1989). *Crime, shame and reintegration.* Cambridge University Press.

Braithwaite, J. (1999). Restorative justice: Assessing optimistic and pessimistic accounts. *Crime and Justice, 25*, 1–127.

Braithwaite, J. (2000). Restorative justice and social justice. *Saskatchewan Law Review, 63*(1), 185–194.

Braithwaite, J. (2002a). *Restorative justice and responsive regulation.* Oxford University Press.

Braithwaite, J. (2002b). Setting standards for restorative justice. *British Journal of Criminology, 42*(3), 563–577.

Brisman, A. (2014). Of theory and meaning in Green criminology. *International Journal for Crime, Justice and Social Democracy, 3*(2), 21–34.

Canterbury Regional Council v Interflow (NZ) Limited. (2015). NZDC 3323.

Chief Executive, Office of Environment and Heritage v Clarence Valley Council. (2018). 236 LGERA 291.

Dare, M., Schirmer, J., & Vanclay, F. (2014). Community engagement and social licence to operate. *Impact Assessment and Project Appraisal, 32*(3), 188–197.

Edwards, P., Lacey, J., Wyatt, S., & Williams, K. J. H. (2016). Social licence to operate and forestry—an introduction. *Forestry: An International Journal of Forest Research, 89*(5), 473–476.

Environment and Climate Change Canada. (2011, May 13). *Tech Metals Ltd. agrees to pay $100,000 to evironmental damages fund for recent cemical spills.* (Online). https://ec.gc.ca/alef-ewe/default.asp?lang=En&n=8F711F37-1&news=B50A65F5-9475-479C-8E66-95E130777EA3. Accessed 15 April 2020.

Environment Canterbury Regional Council Resource Management Act Monitoring and Compliance Section. (2012). *Guidelines for implementing Alternative Environmental Justice.*

Fowler, C. (2016). *Environmental prosecution and restorative justice.* Adderley Head.

Franks, D. M., & Cohen, T. (2012). Social licence in design: Constructive technology assessment within a mineral research and development institution. *Technological Forecasting and Social Change, 79*(7), 1229–1240.

Garrett v Williams. (2007). 151 LGERA 92.

Great Lakes Council v Lani. (2007). 158 LGERA 1.

Greiner, R. (2014). Environmental duty of care: From ethical principle towards a code of practice for the Grazing Industry in Queensland (Australia). *Journal of Agricultural and Environmental Ethics, 27*(4), 527–547.

Gunningham, N., Kagan, R. A., & Thornton, D. (2004). Social license and environmental protection: Why businesses go beyond compliance. *Law & Social Enquiry, 29*(2), 3007–3341.

Hall, M. (2012). Environmental harm: The missing victims? *Criminal Justice Matters, 90*(1), 12–13.

Hall, M. (2013). Victims of environmental harms and their role in national and international justice. In R. Walters, D. S. Westerhuis., & T. Wyatt (Eds.), *Emerging issues in green criminology: Exploring power, justice and harm* (pp. 218–241). Palgrave Macmillan.

Hall, M. (2014a). Victims of environmental crime: Routes for recognition, restitution and redress. In T. Spapens, R. White., & M. Kluin (Eds.), *Environmental crime and its victims: Perspectives within green criminology* (pp. 103–118). Ashgate.

Hall, M. (2016). Criminal redress in cases of environmental victimization: A defence. *International Review of Victimology, 23*(2), 203–223.

Hall, N. L. (2014b). Can the "social licence to operate" concept enhance engagement and increase acceptance of renewable energy? A case study of wind farms in Australia. *Social Epistemology, 28*(3–4), 219–238.

Hamilton, M. (2008). Restorative justice intervention in an environmental law context: Garrett v Williams, Prosecutions under the Resource Management Act 1991 (NZ), and Beyond. *Environmental and Planning Law Journal, 25*(4), 263–271.

Hamilton, M. (2014). Restorative justice intervention in an aboriginal cultural heritage protection context: Conspicuous absences? *Environmental and Planning Law Journal, 31*(5), 352–367.

Hamilton, M. (2015). Restorative justice intervention in a planning law context: Is the "amber light" approach to merit determination restorative? *Environmental and Planning Law Journal, 32*(2), 164–177.

Hamilton, M. (2016). Restorative justice intervention in an environmental and planning law context: applicability to civil enforcement proceedings. *Environmental and Planning Law Journal, 33*(5), 487–501.

Hamilton, M. (2017). Restorative justice conferencing in an environmental protection law context: Apology and corporate offending. *Internet Journal of Restorative Justice, 5 Year Celebration Special Issue*, ISSN (online): 2056–2985.

Hamilton, M. (2019a). Restorative justice intervention in an aboriginal cultural heritage protection context: Chief executive, office of environment and heritage V clarence valley council. *Environmental and Planning Law Journal, 36*(3), 197–211.

Hamilton, M. (2019b). *Restorative justice conferencing in response to pollution offending: A vehicle for the achievement of justice as meaningful involvement.* Ph.D. Dissertation, UNSW.

Hamilton, M. (2021). *Environmental crime and restorative justice: Justice as meaningful involvement*. Palgrave Macmillan.

Hurst, B., Johnston, K. A., & Lane, A, B. (2020). Engaging for a social licence to operate (SLO). *Public Relations Review, 46*, 101931 (online).

Johnstone, G., & Van Ness, D. W. (2011). The meaning of restorative justice. In G. Johnstone & D. W. Van Ness (Eds.), *Handbook of Restorative Justice* (pp. 5–23). Routledge.

Lampkin, J., & Wyatt, T. (2019). Utilising principles of earth jurisprudence to prevent environmental harm: Applying a case study of unconventional hydraulic fracturing for shale gas in the United Kingdom. *Critical Criminology*. https://doi.org/10.1007/s10612-018-9426-7.

Luke, H. (2018). Not getting a social licence to operate can be a costly mistake, as coal seam gas firms have found. *The Conversation.*

Market Wire. (2011, May 12). Teck metals reaches agreement at community justice forum. *Yahoo! News*. (Online). https://www.yahoo.com/news/Teck-Metals-Reaches-Agreement-iw-3396199480.html. Accessed 15 April 2020.

Marshall, T. F. (1996). The evolution of restorative justice in Britain. *European Journal on Criminal Policy and Research, 4*(4), 21–43.

McDonald, J. M. (2008). Restorative justice process in case law. *Alternative Law Journal, 33*(1), 41–44.

McLachlan, M. (2014). Environmental justice in Canterbury. *Public Sector, 37*(4), 22–23.

Mercer-Mapstone, L., Rifkin, W., Louis, W., & Moffat, K. (2017). Meaningful dialogue outcomes contribute to laying a foundation for social licence to operate. *Resources Policy, 53*, 347–355.

Mercer-Mapstone, L., Rifkin, W., Louis, W., & Moffat, K. (2018). Company-community dialogue builds relationships, fairness, and trust leading to social acceptance of Australian mining developments. *Journal of Cleaner Production, 184*, 671–677.

Moffat, K., & Zhang, A. (2014). The paths to social licence to operate: An integrative model explaining community acceptance of mining. *Resources Policy, 39*, 61–70.

Parsons, R., & Moffat, K. (2014). Constructing the meaning of social licence. *Social Epistemology, 28*(3–4), 340–363.

Passas, N. (2005). Lawful but awful: 'Legal corporate crimes. *Journal of Socio-Economics, 34*(6), 771–786.

Pranis, K. (2011). Restorative values. In G. Johnstone & D. W. Van Ness (Eds.), *Handbook of restorative justice* (pp. 59–74). Routledge.

Preston, B. J. (2007). Principled sentencing for environmental offences—part 2: sentencing considerations and options. *Criminal Law Journal, 31*(3), 142–164.

Proctor, J. (2016, March 3). Punishing polluters: Can restorative justice work? *CBC News*. (Online). https://www.cbc.ca/news/canada/british-columbia/climate-talks-pollution-restorative-justice-1.3473076. Accessed 15 April 2020.

Pynn, L. (2016, June 20). Restorative justice can be more powerful than criminal justice system: B.C. Conservation Officer. *Vancouver Sun*. (Online). https://vancouversun.com/news/local-news/restorative-justice-can-be-more-powerful-than-criminal-justice-system-b-c-conservation-officer. Accessed 15 April 2020.

Shaffer, A., Zilliox, S., & Smith, J. (2017). Memoranda of understanding and the social licence to operate in Colorado's unconventional energy industry: A study of citizen complaints. *Journal of Energy & Natural Resources Law, 35*(1), 69–85.

Sharpe, S. (2011). The idea of reparation. In G. Johnstone & D. W. Van Ness (Eds.), *Handbook of restorative justice* (pp. 24–40). Routledge.

Sherman, L. W., & Strang, H. (2012). Restorative justice as evidence-based sentencing. In J. Petersilia & K. R. Reitz (Eds.), *The Oxford handbook of sentencing and corrections* (pp. 215–246). Oxford University Press.

Skinnider, E. (2013). *Effect, issues and challenges for victims of crimes that have a significant impact on the environment*. Vancouver: International Centre for Criminal Law Reform and Criminal Justice Policy.

Smith, D. (2019). Case note: Chief executive, office of environment and heritage v clarence valley council. *Australian Environment Review, 34*(1), 16–18.

Sugrue, V. (2015). What happens when values are put to work? A reflection in one outcome from a restorative justice conference in the Criminal Division of the District Court: Environment warranted judge jurisdiction. *Resource Management Journal*, 19–22.

United Nations Office on Drugs and Crime (UNODC). (2006). *Handbook on restorative justice programmes*. Criminal Justice Handbook Series.

United Nations Office on Drugs and Crime (UNODC). (2020). *Handbook on restorative justice programmes*. Criminal Justice Handbook Series.

Victoria Environment Protection Authority. (2012), *Hallam Road Landfill* (Publication 1503).

Victoria Government, 'Enforceable Undertakings Guidelines.' (2012, May 1). (*Gazette*, No S 142).

White, R., & Heckenberg, D. (2014). *Green criminology: An introduction to the study of environmental harm*. Routledge.

Wilson, C. (2016). Proactive restorative justice: A set of principles for enhancing public participation. *Environmental and Planning Law Journal, 33*(3), 252–263.
Wolf, S., & Stanley, N. (2011). *Wolf and Stanley on environmental law*. Routledge.
Zehr, H. (2015a). *The little book of restorative justice*. Good Books.
Zehr, H. (2015b). *Changing lenses: Restorative justice for our times*. Herald Press.

17

Green Criminology and an International Law Against Ecocide: Using Strict Liability and Superior Responsibility to Prevent State and Corporate Denial of Environmental Harms

Olivia Hasler

Introduction

A central topic for critical green criminology includes corporate criminality and the socio-legal dynamics that determine what is officially labelled as a crime. Activities involving the environment (from illegal waste disposal to environmental protests) done by corporations, states, activists and private citizens are labelled as either 'legal' or 'illegal' based on the legislation and politics of a jurisdiction. Bricknell (2010, p. 4) articulates a contradiction in legal conceptions of environmental harm:

> Of note is the consistent use of the preface 'illegal' in the listed activities constituting environmental crime, a preface not regularly employed when describing other categories of crime. This reflects the fact that some component or level of these activities is still condoned and that it only

O. Hasler (✉)
University of Tasmania, Hobart, TAS, Australia

J. Gacek and R. Jochelson (eds.), *Green Criminology and the Law*, Palgrave Studies in Green Criminology,
https://doi.org/10.1007/978-3-030-82412-9_17

> becomes illegal once a set boundary has been passed. The tipping point of illegality contrasts environmental crimes with other established criminal offences.

The 'wrongdoing' studied within green criminology is thus initially informed by legal conceptions and constructions of crime and harm and later moves to a broader view of environmental harm (White & Heckenberg, 2014). The notion of 'eco-crime', according to Walters (2010, p. 180) is useful for both 'existing legal definitions of environmental crime, as well as sociological analyses of those environmental harms not necessarily specified by law'. When eco-crime is contextualised within notions of harm we can observe a broadening of the gaze beyond legal terrains to include discourses on risk, rights and regulation. As a result, eco-crime extends existing definitions of environmental crime to include licensed or lawful acts of ecological degradation committed by states and corporations.

The destruction of the environment in ways that adversely affect humans, non-human species and ecosystems can be conceptualised as a specific type of crime: ecocide. 'Ecocide' describes an attempt to criminalise human activities that diminish the well-being and health of ecosystems and species within these. Where this occurs because of human agency, then it is purported that a crime of international significance has occurred (Higgins, 2010).

Critical criminology is also concerned with the ways in which crimes (or harms) are framed and denied. Sykes and Matza's (1957) seminal work with juvenile delinquents has since been applied to state denial of atrocities and corporate denial of environmental harms. Ecocide—and a legally enforceable crime of ecocide—could ensure the state and corporate actors that engage or allow ecocidal harms to occur are found liable.

This chapter discusses a proposed possible *Ecocide Act*, as authored by UK lawyer Polly Higgins in 2010 to constitute the 5th International Crime Against Peace. The chapter will demonstrate how such international law against ecocide would bring accountability to those in positions of power who make decisions regarding the use of natural resources and the environment through the inclusion of clauses on superior responsibility and strict liability.

Ecocide: A History

The term 'ecocide' emerged during the time of the Vietnam War. Historically during wartime, 'the other side' is accused of committing atrocities that violate the principle of *jus in bello* or justice in war. Citizens and activists who opposed the Vietnam War were faced with the same question: namely, how to convey to others that the war—and the environmental catastrophes resulting from the herbicidal warfare program (i.e. the use of Agent Orange in Operation Ranch Hand)—was, or should be, illegal (Zierler, 2011). To challenge American intervention in Vietnam required an articulation of particular actions as uniquely illegal and that could thereby also be used in tackling the legitimacy of the war as a whole.

Accordingly, a group of American scientists coined the term 'ecocide'. At the 1970 Conference on War and National Responsibility in Washington, Professor Arthur W. Galston proposed a new international agreement to ban ecocide (Gauger et al., 2012). Ecocide, he argued, presented one of the many varieties of the idea that aspects of the Vietnam War violated international law. The scientists' critique was one of a kind in two ways: first, the accusation was made against their own government—not the 'other side'; and second, this particular movement against ecocide was foundational in the later establishment of US national policy that renounced the use of herbicides in future wars (Zierler, 2011).

The term 'ecocide' became more popular during the opening speech of the 1972 United Nation's Stockholm Conference on the Human Environment, when the prime minister of Sweden at the time, Olaf Palme, explicitly referred to the Vietnam War as an instance of ecocide (Gauger et al., 2012). The Stockholm Conference was the first international meeting that focused on environmental issues, including transboundary pollution (Gauger et al., 2012). It 'highlighted the fact that pollution does not recognise political or geographical boundaries, but affects territories, countries, regions, and people beyond its point of origin' (Gauger et al., 2012, p. 5). Although the conference did not include the term in any of its official documents (Malhotra, 2017), it was an important milestone in environmental governance as the Conference established the UN's Environmental Programme (UNEP).

Although ecocide was not yet legally defined, scholars at this time were debating what would constitute the crime. The element of intent to commit destruction of ecosystems was particularly important. Professor Richard A. Falk (1973), an expert on international law of war crimes, wrote, 'man has consciously and unconsciously inflicted irreparable damage to the environment in times of war and peace'. Dr. Arthur H. Westing, a biologist, stated that 'intent may not only be impossible to establish without admission but, I believe, it is essentially irrelevant' (Westing, 1974).

The increased debate around the concept of ecocide along with an increase in environmental awareness during the 1970s led to a pressure on governments to address the issue (Gauger et al., 2012; Higgins et al., 2013). The UN led an inquiry into how the 1948 Convention on Genocide could be improved, including criminalising ecocide alongside genocide (Mehta & Merz, 2015). The International Law Commission (ILC) considered adding an environmental crime to the Draft Code of Crimes against Peace and Security of Mankind ('the Code'), which later became the Rome Statute—the foundation for the International Criminal Court (Malhotra, 2017). The ILC included in Article 26 of the Code that 'an individual who wilfully causes or orders the causing of widespread, long-term and severe damage to the natural environment shall, on conviction thereof, be sentenced...' (Gauger et al., 2012, p. 9). The governments of Australia, Belgium, Austria and Uruguay, however, openly criticised the use of word 'wilfully', which presupposes intent. These governments argued that ecocide during peacetime is often a crime without intent as it occurs as a by-product of industrial and other activity and successfully led the ILC to remove Article 26 from the Code (Gauger et al., 2012).

The version of the Code adopted by the ILC mentions the intentional creation of 'widespread, long-term and severe damage to the natural environment' during a war under Article 8 of the Rome Statute (UN General Assembly, 1998):

> Intentionally launching an attack in the knowledge that such attack will cause incidental loss of life or injury to civilians or damage to civilian

> objects or widespread, long-term and severe damage to the natural environment which would be clearly excessive in relation to the concrete and direct overall military advantage anticipated.

As it stands, the Rome Statute's Article 8 is the only stipulation in international criminal law that can hold a person responsible for environmental destruction. However, Article 8 limits the crime to wartime and situations of intentional damage; conditions of applicability that are difficult to meet (Freeland, 2015).

A 2016 Cambodian case involving land grabbing and forced evictions, however, led to the widening of the ICC mandate. The Office of the Prosecutor announced that it will 'give particular consideration to prosecuting Rome Statute crimes that are committed by means of, or that result in, inter alia, the destruction of the environment, the illegal exploitation of natural resources or the illegal dispossession of land' (Vidal & Bowcott, 2016). Considering a case involving environmental destruction during peacetime suggests a shift within the ICC to recognise violence committed against nature (Lay, 2016). Global Diligence LLP, a London-based human rights law firm stated this decision will allow the ICC to consider environmental crimes and that company executives or politicians could now be held responsible under international law for illegal land deals (Arsenault, 2016).

Nevertheless, the International Criminal Court statement did not expand Article 8 to include environmental crimes during 'peace-time' nor did it address the issues surrounding intent. While the ICC has limited power in enforcement, especially for states such as the USA that are not signatories to the Rome Statute, the ICC's statement nonetheless has the potential to shift corporate culture. The prospect of imprisonment under criminal law changes the relationship with the precautionary principle; the prospect of an international criminal court hearing may well affect corporate behaviour (Lay, 2016). The ICC's statement appears to be a step forward for an expanded international law against ecocide. In addition to the Code, The ILC also drafted international articles on state responsibility, adopting a provision linking state responsibility and damage to the environment in 1976. This provision, Article 19 of the International Crimes and International Delict, states:

> [A]n international crime may result, inter alia, from: (d) a serious breach of an international obligation of essential importance for the safeguarding and preservation of the human environment, such as those prohibiting massive pollution of the atmosphere or of the seas.' (Gauger et al., 2012).

Another draft article prepared by the ILC dealt with international liability for transboundary harm 'carried out in the territory or otherwise under the jurisdiction or control of a State'; injurious consequences arising out of acts not prohibited by international law (Gauger et al., 2012, p. 11). A provision of this article defines environmental damage as an international crime: 'a serious breach of an international obligation of essential importance for the safeguarding and preservation of the human environment, such as those prohibiting massive pollution of the atmosphere or of the seas' (Yearbook of the ILC 1980, Vol. II, Part 2, p. 32, as cited in Gauger et al., 2012, p. 12). However, state liability for transboundary harm was later reviewed and changed to refer to damage done to the environment by events such as 'the pollution of the air, sea or rivers, consequences of nuclear pollution, or oil spills' (Gauger et al., 2012, p. 13).

The Crime of Ecocide

Ecocide as a criminal offence can be conceptualised by distinguishing between perspectives that privilege humans and human well-being in its definitions of harm with those that include the non-human in its conceptualisations. Generally speaking, doing wrong and harming others is anthropocentrically framed and its basic considerations stem from and reflect the human rights paradigm (MacCarrick, 2016). Ecocide in this sense complements the existing approach of the Rome Statute that deals with crimes against humanity and crimes against peace. Protection of human rights is paramount and this includes protections pertaining to one's living environment. Thus, the demise of environmental amenity and security is considered a derogation of the duty to protect and enhance human rights, including the right to ecosystem services upon which human populations rely (MacCarrick, 2016).

Other conceptions of the crime of ecocide, however, see it as premised on the idea of 'Earth stewardship'. Ecocide in this instance is closely aligned with the concept of ecocentrism that views the environment as having value for its own sake, apart from any instrumental or utilitarian value to humans (see, for example Berry, 1999; Higgins, 2018). Ecocentrism views non-human animals, plants and rivers as rights holders and/or as objects warranting a duty of care on the part of humans (Fisher, 2010; Schlosberg, 2007). The decision by the New Zealand Parliament to grant the Whanganui River and the Te Urewera mountain ecosystem rights as legal persons is the most recent in 'the fastest growing legal movement of the twenty-first century' to grant non-human entities legal rights (Takacs, 2021, p. 1). In this context, establishing the crime of ecocide is motivated by the need to respond to a singularly important trend: the rapid degradation of the existing planetary environment. Fundamentally, this degradation stems from the systemic extraction and contamination of finite natural resources.

While no one and nothing can escape the violent impact of the transgressions presently impinging upon the biosphere, ecocide does not affect everyone and everything equally. Violence to the environment, for example, begets further violence within human communities. Diminished human security stems from the bio-physical and socio-economic consequences of various sources of threat and damage to the environment, including climate change (South, 2012). Shortages of food, water and non-renewable energy sources can trigger criminal activities involving organised criminal networks, transnational corporations, and governments at varying political levels (White, 2014).

Neither is ecocide socially (or ecologically and species) neutral. There are winners and losers in the contestations over natural resources. It is the poor, the marginalised, the dispossessed and the vulnerable that bear the brunt of environmental destruction (White & Hasler, 2019). For example, Indigenous peoples reliant upon clean water and arable lands for their livelihoods suffer greatly when large industrial projects—such as the Alberta Tar Sands project in Canada—impact their forests, rivers and soils (Short, 2016). Children are more likely than adults to be seriously affected by air pollution and water contamination stemming from activities that harm the environment (Stephens, 1996).

Yet it is the rich, the corporate, the elite and the powerful who stand to gain most from the demolition of formally sustainable ecosystems. In pursuit of the ownership and exploitation of natural resources state and corporation actors have worked with each other worked to break laws, bend rules and undermine participatory decision-making processes. Sometimes this takes the form of direct state-corporate collusion; in other instances, it involves manoeuvring by government officials or company executives to evade the normal operating rules of planning, development, and environmental impact assessment (Hasler, 2019). The appropriation of resources in specific bio-social locations has led to a proliferation of ownership contests (e.g. disputed islands involving China, Vietnam, the Philippines, and Japan; re-drawing of boundaries in the Arctic among border states such as Russia, Canada, Norway and the United States) (Brisman, 2013). The violence of war lurks behind the efforts of powerful interest groups to control natural resources. Those who are central in causing the problem are also those least likely (at least initially) to suffer the consequences of their actions. Yet, a consequence of the actions and omissions of the few is that violence and crime will pervade the lives of the less powerful and vulnerable people of the world (White & Hasler, 2019). For the perpetrators of the harm, however, justice is rarely applied nor the crimes officially recognised as 'crimes'.

The Ecocide Act

In April 2010, Polly Higgins, a Scottish advocate and leading expert in ecocide, submitted a draft law of ecocide to the United Nations Law Commission (Higgins, 2010). The draft Ecocide Act 2010 proposed Ecocide as the 5th International Crime Against Peace, with 'Ecocide' defined as:

> The extensive loss or damage or destruction of ecosystem(s) of a given territory, whether by human agency or by other causes, to such an extent that: (1) peaceful enjoyment by the inhabitants of has been or will be severely diminished; and or (2) peaceful enjoyment by the inhabitants of another territory has been severely diminished. (Higgins, 2012, p. 159)

This definition contains several concepts that require further explanation. The Prohibition of Military or any other Hostile Use of Environmental Modification Techniques (ENMOD), an international treaty which aims to prohibit the use of environmental modification techniques defines 'widespread', 'long-lasting' and 'severe' in the context of environmental damage: 'Widespread' involves an area of several hundred kilometres; 'long-lasting' encompasses a season or period of a couple of months; and 'severe' involves 'grave disorder or maltreatment to economic and natural resources, human life, and other resources (Gauger et al., 2012, p. 9). 'Peaceful enjoyment', a legal term that originates from civil law, is defined as 'a covenant that promises that the grantee or tenant of an estate in real property will be able to possess the premises in peace, without disturbance by hostile claimants'. Peaceful enjoyment in light of Higgins' (2010) definition of ecocide means 'peace, health and cultural integrity'. Higgins (2010) defines 'territory(ies)' as 'one or more of the following habitats, unrestricted by State or jurisdictional boundaries: (i) terrestrial, (ii) fresh-water, marine or high seas, (iii) atmosphere, (iv) other natural habitats' and understands 'inhabitants' to include humans; animals, fish, birds or insects; plant species; and other living organisms.

Ecocide can be understood as a crime against peace due to the potential consequences that arise from the damage to, destruction of or loss of these territory(ies) and ecosystem(s). This includes 'the loss of life, injury to life and severe diminution of enjoyment of life to human and non-human beings; the heightened risk of conflict arising from impact upon human and non-human life which has occurred as a result of the above; adverse impact upon future generations and their ability to survive; the diminution of health and well-being of inhabitants of a given territory and those who live further afield; and/or the loss of cultural heritage or life' (Higgins, 2012, p. 157).

A central aim of establishing the crime of Ecocide is to prevent war; loss and injury to life; dangerous industrial activity; pollution to all beings; and loss of traditional cultures, hunting grounds and food (Higgins, 2012). The Law of Ecocide would create an international and transboundary duty of care; one that imposes an obligation and pre-emptive legal duty of care upon all 'persons of superior responsibility' to prevent the risk of damage to or loss of any ecosystems.

States have a responsibility for ensuring the safety and well-being of its citizens. This duty suggests that states have a responsibility to exercise extreme caution before embarking on any project which is likely to have the possibility of adverse effects upon the ecosystems concerned (Hasler, 2020). The failure by states to prevent (or take responsibility for) dangerous industrial activities thus becomes the failure of the state to ensure the welfare of the people and the planet. Collusion with corporations that engage in dangerous industrial activities plays a significant role in a states' failure to prevent environmentally harmful projects (Hasler, 2019).

State-Corporate Denial of Harms

One of the issues in addressing crimes of the powerful, i.e. crimes involving state actors, corporate actors, or the collusion of both state and corporate actors, is the denial of the harmful actions by the perpetrators. The ways in which states and corporations cover up harmful and criminal acts and how they defer responsibility for these acts has been an increasingly important topic for investigation, in light of the recent 'post-truth' and 'fake news' digital age (Hasler, 2019).

In their study of juvenile delinquents, Sykes and Matza (1957) developed a classification of five methods actors employ to justify their morally questionable or illegal activities. These "techniques of neutralisation" can be understood as rhetorical devices used to deny or neutralise harm before the act in order to make delinquency possible and/or after the act, in order to shield the perpetrator from blame. Sykes and Matza's analytical framework contains five types of denial. The focus of this chapter will be on two of the five, denial of responsibility (i.e. 'the offender had no control over the action') and denial of injury (i.e. 'despite the action occurring, it did not cause any harm').

This framework has also been used to examine the denials of public and political atrocities committed by states (Cohen, 1993, 2001; Whyte, 2016), linking characteristics of individual denial to organisational denial. Developing the concept of techniques of neutralisation to the illegitimate activities of a corporation began in the 1980s and 1990s (see e.g. Box, 1983; Benson, 1985; Coleman, 1987; Braithwaite & Fisse, 1990). This body of research acknowledged that theories of individual action can also be applied to corporate action because corporations, too, can act, have intentions and commit crimes. Later, the organising framework of Sykes and Matza and Cohen was applied to corporate wrongdoing (Fooks et al., 2012; Heath, 2008; Piquero et al., 2005; Rosoff et al., 1998; Vieraitis et al., 2012).

'Corporate personhood' shields a corporation's owners and investors from the corporation itself, and establishes limited liability—key in denial of harm—for corporate officials. Tombs and Whyte (2015, p. 84) describe how limited liability encourages risky business:

> Investors can only lose the value of capital that they invested in the first place, so that, if the company incurs losses higher than the value of the sum invested, then the owners or shareholders bear no responsibility for this loss.

When a crime, or egregious harm is committed, everyone working within the corporation can, to some extent, point their finger to shift the blame to someone else. The person who carried out the action can defer blame to the person who made the decision; the person who made the decision can blame the people who assessed the action, and so on (Heath, 2008).

In rare instances when there is a prosecution, this blame-shifting results in workers at the bottom being penalised while those at the top are able to keep their positions (and reputations) (Diamantis, 2016; Tombs & Whyte, 2015). A corporation will also often cite the competitiveness of the marketplace as a reason for engaging in a harmful act. In order to 'survive' the marketplace, the action becomes a 'necessity', demonstrating a blend of denial of responsibility and a denial of injury with a defence of necessity.

Large-scale resource extraction projects require the cooperation of both corporation and government in order to proceed, so state officials are also heard making this argument as well (see Hasler, 2019 on the Australian Government's arguments for the Carmichael Coal Mine, for example). Since corporate personhood diminishes the potential personal risks involved in engaging in harmful behaviour for its owners or shareholders, the potential benefits to the corporation that can arise from those harmful activities are increased. The corporation's benefits are eventually distributed among its shareholders, which translates to a potential for increased personal gain through risky behaviour. This transfer of risks and benefits grants a unique legal loophole for the owners or shareholders of a corporation: Although they are able to make decisions on behalf of their corporation, they cannot be held responsible for the effects of those corporate decisions. Limited liability allows for the corporation, rather than an individual or individuals, to be subject to criminal prosecutions. The 'corporation person' can 'absorb the punishment, normally in the form of a fine, while its directors and senior managers are relatively rarely exposed to sanction' (Tombs & Whyte, 2015, p. 98). Responsibility is therefore evaded—legally—through the corporate structure.

Superior Responsibility

Denial of responsibility has been a script that persons in position of power use to present the harm as a 'bi-product of following orders'. As discussed above, the corporate structure is well suited for the denial of responsibility due to corporate personhood and the corporate veil. Therefore, in order to address the denial of responsibility for grave environmental destruction signed off by persons in power, ecocide legislation would have to contain a clause that establishes responsibility to persons of power within their respective organisations or territories.

The legal concept of 'superior responsibility' presents a direct counter to the denial of responsibility defence that states and corporations use to rid themselves of responsibility for environmentally harmful activities. Superior responsibility is also referred to as 'command responsibility' or the 'Yamashita' or 'Medina' standard, the legal doctrine of hierarchical accountability for war crimes (Isenberg, 2013). This legal concept has been established by The Hague Conventions of 1899 and 1907; and applied by the United States Supreme Court for atrocities committed by troops under the command of Japanese General Yamashita during

WWII as well as atrocities committed by troops under the command of U.S. Army Captain Medina in the My Lai Massacre during the Vietnam War (Hendin, 2003). At its core, the legal concept of superior responsibility refers to a superior's duty to supervise subordinates and grants liability for the supervisor's failure to do so (Bantekas, 1999). In most cases, the 'reasonable person standard' is considered when determining whether a subordinate committed a wrongful act by following orders (Tobia, 2018). The reasonable person standard is meant to objectively determine whether a defendant is liable for negligently causing harm For example, a jury might be asked to evaluate whether the defendant acted with 'reasonable care' or the care of a reasonable person (Dietrich & Field, 2017; Tobia, 2018).

Applying the principle of superior responsibility to legislation against ecocide would mean that 185 all Heads of State, Ministers, CEOs, directors and any other person who has rights over a given territory, regardless of knowledge or intent, would have a clear responsibility for any activity or offence that can be attributed to them as a consequence of their authority. Superior responsibility also extends to any person in a position of superior responsibility within any company or corporation (Bantekas, 1999). This would codify the reasonable person standard in a way that is uniform for every case by attaching an unconditional duty of care to the most powerful. Higgins' model law of ecocide, for example, places responsibility for offenses committed by members of staff on those with a position of superior responsibility: '[A] superior is responsible for offences committed by staff under his effective authority, as a result of his failure to take all necessary measures within his power to prevent or repress their commission or to submit the matter to the competent authorities for investigation' (Higgins, 2018). Accordingly, those persons with superior responsibility are liable to prosecution if a member of staff under their authority commits an offense that leads to the commission of the crime of Ecocide.

This principle emphasises the importance of prevention and precaution. Someone who holds a position of superior responsibility must ensure all necessary measures within their power to prevent or stop any activities that lead to the commission of the crime of Ecocide. Otherwise, this person will be held strictly liable under the act, regardless of whether they have any knowledge of the activities that lead to the commission of the crime. The principle of superior responsibility thus provides a legal counter to the denial of responsibility that has often been cited by politicians or members of corporations after large-scale destruction of the environment has been committed by their company or jurisdiction. The principle of superior responsibility would ensure that natural persons cannot hide behind nonnatural persons such as corporations and are instead held accountable for the ecocidal actions made at a corporate or government level (Higgins, 2010), effectively lifting the corporate veil. In addition, the principle of superior responsibility could extend to third parties. Agencies that lobby on behalf of persons with superior responsibility are 'regarded as aiding, abetting, counselling or procuring the commission of the offence' of ecocide (Higgins, 2018).

Strict Liability

The image of state representatives on public television and other media outlets rejecting climate change and other environmental harms has culminated in the 'Post-Truth Era', when statements that correspond with an individual's agenda are presented as fact while opposing statements are dismissed as propaganda or lies (Hasler, 2020). This agenda of misinformation, blurring the lines between fact and fiction, weakens climate science's position as unbiased and legitimate. When the individual doing the denying is in a position of power, the effects of a large-scale industrial project like the opening of a new coal mine for example—which are potentially ecocidal in their effects on the environment—become a politicised debate. Ecocide legislation must provide a solution to this problem (i.e. that indisputable harms are able to be denied). Higgins's conceptualisation of a crime of ecocide suggests that for the purposes of that definition, 'the Paris Agreement of 4 November 2016 shall be considered to be established premise for prior knowledge by State, corporate or any other entity's senior person, or any other person of superior responsibility' (Higgins, 2018).

Using the Paris Agreement as a premise for knowledge by persons of superior responsibility strengthens the Ecocide Act's notion of strict liability. Strict liability is liability for harm set upon a defendant without the need to prove either negligence or fault as long (as it can be proven that it was the defendant caused the harm). The legal concept of strict liability, which imputes liability to a person regardless of their culpability, is able to remove the mental element of the offense and hold a company (the corporate person) liable for its crimes. The mens rea usually required for prosecution of environmental harms is troublesome, as it requires a level of intent in committing the harm as part of a grander scheme against a specific group; yet 'many environmental harms happen as singular events and stem from economic motivations, such as attempting to avoid regulations to maximise profits' (Durney, 2018, p. 417).

The Australian Law Reform Commission has argued that strict liability overcomes 'a knowledge of law problem and may be appropriate to ensure the integrity of a financial or corporate regulatory regime' (ALRC, 2018). Legal recognition—through ecocide legislation such as Higgins' *Ecocide Act*—that knowingly emitting greenhouse gases is an act of ecocide allows for the prevention and punishment for such damages.

While no legal mechanism currently exists to hold a person, state or corporation accountable for greenhouse gas emissions, the Paris Agreement was an ideological step forward. 184 parties have ratified the Paris Agreement, which aimed 'to strengthen the global response to the threat of climate change by keeping a global temperature rise this century well below 2 degrees Celsius 188 above pre-industrial levels and to pursue efforts to limit the temperature increase even further to 1.5 degrees Celsius' (UN, 2018). As a signatory to the treaty, states publicly agree to strengthen their efforts against global warming and report their 'nationally determined contributions' of greenhouse gas emissions every five years (UN, 2018). By signing the Paris Agreement, the states also accept fundamental theories of global warming, such as the role humans have on increasing the Earth's temperature through consumption of fossil fuels.

However, despite signing the Agreement, government actors have supported corporate bids to build new coal mines (e.g. the Carmichael Coal Mine in Queensland—see Hasler, 2019); are continuing deforestation in key ecosystems such as the Amazon Rainforest; and allowing other environmentally destructive practices such as large-scale commercial fishing to go on as usual. These actions are contradictory, but by denying that these actions are injurious and due to the 'soft-law' nature of the Paris Agreement and the lack of a crime of ecocide under International Criminal Law, these contradictions are legal.

One particular example lies in the 'net emissions argument' presented by the Australian Government in arguing for the approval of what would be one of the largest coal mines in the world if built—the Carmichael Coal Mine in Queensland. In short, Australia's Environment Minister argued in the Federal Court of Brisbane that in order to prove that emissions from the Carmichael Project would result in higher global greenhouse gas levels, it must be proven that the emissions from the mine would not be offset by carbon-reducing initiatives elsewhere in the world (Hasler, 2019). This argument—denying the injury of the mine— was sufficient for the challenge to the mine by an environmental organisation to be thrown out. The 'net emissions' argument would not be able to be used if an ecocide law of strict liability existed. An Ecocide Act, if passed at an international level, would point to the signing of the Paris Agreement—as well as the contents of the document which acknowledge the 'injury' caused by greenhouse gas emissions—to support the claim that the government in question has committed ecocide.

By using the Paris Agreement (or any future international agreement on climate change) as 'proof of knowledge' of the need and the duty to reduce carbon emissions, ecocide legislation could effectively counter the net emissions argument. The Paris Agreement mandates states to reduce their GHGs. The Minister's justification for opening the mine on the basis that GHG-reducing initiatives will be taken up elsewhere is illogical, as Australia had also signed to reduce their emissions. The environmental harm that state and corporate officials have denied in order to justify their positions of support for the Carmichael Project are the same as those acknowledged (as real, problematic, and in need of managing) by Australian state by signing the Paris Agreement. In other words, through ecocide legislation, Australia's simultaneous signature and commitment to the Paris Agreement while approving the Carmichael Project would implicate these persons with superior responsibility as guilty of ecocide.

Conclusion

The destruction of the world's ecosystems presents one of the greatest risks to humanity as natural resources become more scarce; as climate change disrupts global weather patterns; and as pollution threatens food chains and ecosystems in water, on land, and in air. Creating a legally enforceable crime of ecocide that complements currently existing international offences such as crimes against humanity would make it possible to prosecute offending states and corporations around the world. The draft *Ecocide Act*, put forward by Higgins in 2010 contains two important legal clauses that would regulate state responsibility against ecocide: strict liability and superior responsibility.

Strict liability attributes liability to a person regardless of their culpability and would remove the mental element of the offense and hold a company (the corporate person) liable for the crime of ecocide. The Paris Agreement presents premise for prior knowledge by state or corporation, or person of superior responsibility. Encoding the concept of superior responsibility into Ecocide law would eliminate the ability for state or corporate actors to deny responsibility for their crimes and incentivise prevention and precaution of environmental harms.

An international law against ecocide, if modelled on Higgins' Ecocide Act could close two major legal loopholes in state and corporate criminality. However, the environmental rights movement, of which the movement for an international law against Ecocide stems, is motivated by a vision of progressive social reform yet relies on what some environmentalists consider regressive social policy (see Carmichael, 1995; Kiss & Shelton, 2007; Marceau, 2019). One of the problems with a focus on criminalising and punishing certain types of environmental harms is that it allows for the continuation of many more institutionalised forms of violence. A recent example of this can be found in the Tasmanian Government's sanctioning the destruction of old growth forests through the state-owned forestry enterprise Sustainable Timber Tasmania (Powell & Powell, 2020); as well as the general production and slaughter or animals for food. More critically, relying on punitive measures as a strategy for addressing environmental harms committed by state and corporate actors may be counterproductive for the larger aims of the concept of ecocentrism that views the environment as having value for its own sake, apart from any instrumental or utilitarian value to humans, which aims to end the exploitation of all beings, non-human and human alike. In establishing an international law against ecocide, caution must be taken not to perpetuate the inequalities of current criminal justice systems that see racial and ethnic minorities policed, arrested, prosecuted and incarcerated in greater numbers than white westerners.

This article discussed two important legal clauses that would regulate state and corporate responsibility against ecocide, but does not suggest that there aren't others. On the contrary, for an Ecocide Act to be successful in achieving the goals presented above, strict liability and superior responsibility are only the beginning.

References

(ALRC) Australian Law Reform Commission. (2018). *Strict and absolute liability*. Retrieved from https://www.alrc.gov.au/publications/laws-impose-strict-or-absolute-liability. Accessed 12 Aug 2019.

Arsenault, C. (2016). International court to prosecute environmental crimes in major shift. *Reuters*. https://www.reuters.com/article/us-global-landrights-icc/international-court-to-prosecute-environmental-crimes-in-major-shift-idUSKCN11L2F9. Accessed 2 Apr 2018.

Bakan, J. (2004). *The corporation: The pathological pursuit of profit and power*. Free Press.

Bantekas, I. (1999). The contemporary law of superior responsibility. *The American Journal of International Law, 93*(3), 573–595.

Bensen, M. L. (1985). Denying the guilty mind: Accounting for involvement in a white-collar crime. *Criminology, 23*(4), 583–607.

Berry, T. (1999). *The great work: Our way into the future*. Harmony/Bell Tower.

Box, S. (1983). *Power, crime and mystification*. Tavistock.

Braithwaite, J., & Fisse, B. (1990). On the plausibility of corporate crime theory. *Advances in Criminological Theory, 2*, 15–38.

Bricknell, S. (2010). *Environmental crime in Australia*. Research and public policy series No. 109. Australian Institute of Criminology. https://aic.gov.au/publications/rpp/rpp109.

Brisman, A. (2013). The violence of silence: Some reflections on access to information, public participation in decision-making, and access to justice in matters concerning the environment. *Crime, Law and Social Change, 59*(3), 291–303.

Carmichael, K. (1995). Strict liability for environmental violations: A need for judicial restraint. *Indiana Law Journal, 71*(3), 730–752.

Cohen, S. (1993). Human rights and crimes of the state: The culture of Denial. *The Australian and New Zealand Journal of Criminology, 26*(2), 97–115.

Cohen, S. (2001). *States of Denial: Knowing about atrocities and suffering*. Polity Press.

Cohen, S. (2011). *Folk devils and moral panics: The creation of the mods and rockers*. Routledge.

Coleman, J. W. (1987). Toward an integrated theory of white-collar crime. *American Journal of Sociology, 93*(2), 406–439.

Diamantis, M. E. (2016). Corporate criminal minds. *Notre Dame Law Review, 91*(5), 2049–2068. Accessed 22 Mar 2021.

Dietrich, J. & Field, I. (2017). 'The Reasonable Tort Victim': contributory negligence, standard of care and the 'Equivalence Theory'. *Melbourne University Law Review, 41*(2), 602. http://classic.austlii.edu.au/au/journals/MelbULawRw/2017/34.html. Accessed 12 Aug 2019.

Durney, J. (2018). Crafting a standard: Environmental crimes as crimes against humanity under the international criminal court. *Hastings Environmental Law Journal, 24*(2), 413–430. Accessed 22 Mar 2021.

Falk, R. A. (1973). Environmental warfare and ecocide—Facts, appraisal, and proposals (T. Marek Ed.). *Bulletin of Peace Proposals, 4*(1), 80–96.

Fisher, D. (2010). Jurisprudential challenges to the protection of the natural environment. In M. Maloney & P. Burdon (Eds.), *Wild law—In practice*. Routledge.

Fooks, G., Gilmore, A., Collin, J., Holden, C., & Lee, K. (2012). The limits of corporate social responsibility: Techniques of neutralization, stakeholder management, and political CSR. *Journal of Business Ethics, 112*, 283.

Freeland, S. (2015). *Addressing the intentional destruction of the environment during warfare under the Rome statute of the International Criminal Court*. Intersentia.

Gauger, A., Rabatel-Fernel, M. P., Kulbicki, L., Short, D., & Higgins, P. (2012). *Ecocide is the missing 5th crime against peace*. University of London.

Hasler, O. (2019). State-corporate crime and ecocide: A critical study of the Carmichael Coal Mine. Ph.D. thesis, University of Tasmania.

Hasler, O. (2020). Mining as ecocide: The Case of Adani and the Carmichael mine in Australia. In Y. Zabyelina & D. van Uhm (Eds.), *Illegal mining: organized crime, corruption, and ecocide in a resource-scarce world* (pp. 497–529). Springer.

Heath, J. (2008). Business ethics and moral motivation: A criminological perspective. *Journal of Business Ethics, 83*, 595–614.

Hendin, S.E. (2003). Command Responsibility and Superior Orders in the Twentieth Century—A Century of Evolution. *Murdoch University Electronic Journal, 10*(1), 2.

Higgins, P. (2010). *Eradicating ecocide: Laws and governance to stop the destruction of the planet*. Shepheard-Walwyn Publishers Ltd.

Higgins, P. (2012). *Earth is our business: Changing the rules of the game.* Shepheard-Walwyn Publishers Ltd.

Higgins, P. (2018). 'Ecocide Crime', eradicating ecocide. https://eradicatingecocide.com/the-law/the-model-law/. Accessed 20 Mar 2019.

Higgins, P., Short, D., & South, N. (2013). Protecting the planet: A proposal for a law of ecocide. *Crime Law and Social Change, 59*(3), 251–266.

Isenberg, D. (2013, 13 January). Lawbreakers at war: How responsible are they? *TIME*.

Kiss, A. & Shelton, D. L. (2007). Strict liability in international environmental law. In T. M. Ndiaye & R. Wolfrum (Eds.), *Law of the sea, environmental law, and settlement of disputes: Liber Amicorum Judge Thomas A. Mansah* (pp. 1130–1151). Brill Academic Publishers, GWU Legal Studies.

Lay, B. (2016). International ecocide law could criminalise Reef destruction. *Eureka Street, 26*(19), 62–66.

MacCarrick, G. (2016). *Amicus curiae to the International Monsanto Tribunal on the question of Ecocide*. International Monsanto Tribunal. Retrieved October, 2016, from www.monsanto-tribunal.org.

Malhotra, S. (2017). The international crime that could have been but never was: An English school perspective on the ecocide law. *Amsterdam Law Forum, 9*(3), 49–70.

Marceau, J. (2019). *Beyond cages: Animal law and criminal punishment*. Cambridge University Press.

Mehta, S., & Merz, P. (2015). Ecocide—A new crime against peace? *Environmental Law Review, 17*(1), 3–7.

Piquero, N. L., Tibbetts, S. G., & Blankenship, M. B. (2005). Examining the role of differential association and techniques of neutralization in explaining corporate crime. *Deviant Behavior, 26*(2), 159–188.

Powell, M. & Powell, S. (2020). Sustainable Timber Tasmania to half logging in 19 coupes during court case with Bob Brown Foundation. *The Examiner*. https://www.examiner.com.au/story/6953161/government-prepared-to-fight-as-tasmanian-logging-halted/. Accessed 22 Mar 2021.

Rosoff, S. M., Pontell, H. N., & Tillman, R. (1998). *Profit without honor: White-collar crime and the looting of America*. Prentice Hall.

Schlosberg, D. (2007). *Defining environmental justice: Theories, movements, and nature*. Oxford.

Short, D. (2016). *Redefining genocide: Settler colonialism, social death and ecocide*. Zed Books.

South, N. (2012). Climate change, environmental (in)security, conflict and crime. In S. Farrall, D. French, & T. Ahmed (Eds.), *Climate change: Legal and criminological implications* (pp. 97–112). Hart.

Stephens, S. (1996). Reflections on environmental justice: Children as victims and actors. *Social Justice, 23*(4), 62–86.

Sykes, G. M., & Matza, D. (1957). Techniques of neutralization: A theory of delinquency. *American Sociological Review, 22*(6), 664–670.

Takacs, D. (2021). We are the river. *University of Illinois Law Review, 2021*(2), 545–606.

Tobia, K. P. (2018). How people judge what is reasonable. *Alabama Law Review, 70*(2), 295–359.

Tombs, S., & Whyte, D. (2015). *The corporate criminal: Why corporations must be abolished*. Routledge.

(UN) United Nations. (2018). What is the Paris Agreement? United Nations Framework Convention on Climate Change. https://unfccc.int/process-and-meetings/the-paris-agreement/what-is-the-paris-agreement. Accessed 7 Feb 2019.

UN General Assembly. (1998). *Rome Statute of the International Criminal Court (last amended 2010)*. https://www.refworld.org/docid/3ae6b3a84.html. Accessed 22 Mar 2019.

Vidal, J. & Bowcott, O. (2016). ICC widens remit to include environmental destruction cases. *The Guardian*. https://www.theguardian.com/global/2016/sep/15/hague-court-widens-remit-to-include-environmental-destruction-cases. Accessed 4 April 2018.

Vieraitis, L. M., Piquero, N. L., Piquero, A. R., Tibbetts, S. G., & Blankenship, M. (2012). Do women and men differ in their neutralizations of corporate crime? *Criminal Justice Review, 37*(4), 478–493.

Walters, R. (2010). Eco crime. In J. Muncie, D. Talbot, & R. Walters (Eds.), *Crime: Local and global* (pp. 174–208). Willan.

Westing, A. H. (1974). Proscription of ecocide. *Science and Public Affairs, 30*(1), 24–27.
White, R. (2014). Environmental insecurity and fortress mentality. *International Affairs, 90*(4), 835–851.
White, R., & Hasler, O. (2019). Ecocide: Violence against the planet. In W. S. DeKeseredy, C. M. Rennison, & A. K. Hall-Sanchez (Eds.), *The Routledge international handbook of violence studies* (pp. 309–320). Routledge.
White, R., & Heckenberg, D. (2014). *Green criminology: An introduction to the study of environmental harm.* Routledge.
Whyte, D. (2016). It's common sense, stupid! Corporate crime and techniques of neutralization in the automobile industry. *Crime Law and Social Change, 66*(2), 165–181.
Zierler, D. (2011). *The invention of ecocide: Agent orange, Vietnam, and the scientists who changed the way we think about the environment*. University of Georgia Press.

Index

J. Gacek and R. Jochelson (eds.), *Green Criminology and the Law*, Palgrave Studies in Green Criminology,
https://doi.org/10.1007/978-3-030-82412-9